A Framework for the Good

# A Framework
## *for the* Good

Kevin Kinghorn

*University of Notre Dame Press*
*Notre Dame, Indiana*

University of Notre Dame Press
Notre Dame, Indiana 46556
www.undpress.nd.edu

Copyright © 2016 by the University of Notre Dame

All Rights Reserved

Published in the United States of America

*Library of Congress Cataloging-in-Publication Data*

Names: Kinghorn, Kevin Paul, 1967– author.
Title: A framework for the good / Kevin Kinghorn.
Description: Notre Dame : University of Notre Dame Press, 2016. | Includes bibliographical references and index.
Identifiers: LCCN 2015047536 (print) | LCCN 2015048839 (ebook) | ISBN 9780268033309 (pbk. : alk. paper) | ISBN 0268033307 (pbk.) | ISBN 9780268084653 (epub) | ISBN 9780268084646 ( pdf) | ISBN 0268084645 (pdf)
Subjects: LCSH: Good and evil. | Good and evil—Religious aspects—Christianity.
Classification: LCC BJ1401 .K56 2016 (print) | LCC BJ1401 (ebook) | DDC 170—dc23
LC record available at http://lccn.loc.gov/2015047536

∞ *This paper meets the requirements of ANSI/NISO Z39.48-1992
(Permanence of Paper).*

For Anna Keren

CONTENTS

Acknowledgments ix

Introduction 1

*Part One*
Placing the Good within an Ethical Framework

ONE   The Meaning of *Good*   11

*1.1 Our Pro-attitude toward the Good*   11
*1.2 Flourishing and the Good*   14
*1.3 Instrumental Goodness*   18
*1.4 Noninstrumental Goodness*   26
*1.5 The Morally Good*   31
*1.6 Closing Moore's Open Question*   38
*1.7 The Place of Semantic Analysis*   46

TWO   The Nature of the Good   57

*2.1 Hedonism*   58
*2.2 The Inadequate Alternative of Desire Satisfaction*   74
*2.3 L. W. Sumner*   78
*2.4 Nozick's Experience Machine*   83
*2.5 The Badness of Death*   89
*2.6 Is Schadenfreude a Special Problem?*   105

THREE   Motivations, the Good, and the Right   114
    *3.1 Sticking to Humean Guns*   114
    *3.2 The Source of Normative Force*   119
    *3.3 The Concepts "Right" and "Wrong"*   138
    *3.4 Moral Facts and the Place of Objectivity*   149

*Part Two*
## A Christian Framework for Choosing the Good Life

FOUR   Others and the Good   167
    *4.1 Perfectionism*   168
    *4.2 The Mental Experience of "Connecting"*   177
    *4.3 Are Relationships the Key to Our Well-Being?*   182
    *4.4 Making Others' Interests Our Own*   189
    *4.5 Divine Coordination*   195
    *4.6 Establishing Relationships*   203

FIVE   God, the Good, and Our Choices   212
    *5.1 The Place of Self-Interested Desires*   212
    *5.2 Can We Desire Relationships?*   218
    *5.3 Self-Directed Reasons for Benevolence*   222
    *5.4 God's Invitation to Pursue the Good*   229
    *5.5 Freedom in Choosing the Good*   239
    *5.6 The Final Dichotomy of Benevolent and Self-Interested Ends*   247

SIX   Feeling Our Way toward the Good   258
    *6.1 The Positive Feeling Tones of Benevolence*   258
    *6.2 "Morally Significant" Decisions*   272
    *6.3 Feeling Tones as Our Indication of the Good*   283
    *6.4 Some Theological Connections*   295

Notes   302
Works Cited   335
Index   343

## ACKNOWLEDGMENTS

In acknowledging helpful influences on my work, I will always feel the need to mention two individuals whose personal investments in me have greatly shaped the course of my academic life. Richard Swinburne took me on as a DPhil student, a decision for which I will always be thankful. Working under his guidance was a cherished opportunity. And his writings continue to be resources to which I turn again and again.

Jerry Walls introduced me to the subject of philosophy of religion some twenty-five years ago. His ongoing support and encouragement have been enormous through the years. Without necessarily trying to do so, he has taught me many lessons about friendship and about how to nurture students. I do not see how I would possibly have become a philosopher if I had not crossed paths with Jerry.

My parents, Ken and Hilda, probably imagined that their days of helping me improve my writing would have ended when I stopped bringing homework home from school. These many years later, they're still helping; and I remain grateful to them for this, among other things.

My wife, Barbara, has given me a variety of insights into what is good—the kinds of insights possible only when one is around another person every day. I've now written a book about goodness; she continues to live it out.

Our son, Joseph, has been a most welcome presence during the latter stages of this project. Joseph, you've given me examples of the joys that come within relationships of benevolence, just as I was trying to write on the subject. Thank you.

To our daughter, Anna Keren, you've more than lived up to the promise we believe we were given that you would be, in a word, good. Most of the early ideas for this book were formed as we took daily walks around University Parks. This book is dedicated to you.

# Introduction

The broad goals of this book are twofold. First, the book offers an analysis of the "good": the meaning of the term; the nature of goodness; and why we are motivated to pursue it. Setting this analysis within a larger ethical framework, the book also proposes a way of understanding the relationship between the good and the right. My discussion of these issues takes place in Part I of this book. I engage there with historic (and controversial) issues in moral philosophy, offering my own conclusions on such subjects as noninstrumental value and normativity.

Building on these more formal discussions of the nature of the good and our motivation to pursue it, I move in Part II to offer a substantive account of what the good life consists in—as well as how we can achieve it. This account is a decidedly Christian one, charting God's relationship to the good and to the right. While I note experiences from everyday life that, I believe, serve as cues pointing to the Christian affirmation that we are created in the image of a Trinitarian God, arguing this point is not a primary goal. Rather, I assume an orthodox, Christian understanding of God as the one who created humans in such a way that our ultimate flourishing is achieved only as our relationships mirror the loving, self-giving relationships within the Trinity. Jesus is recorded in John

10:10 as saying that he came to give us "life." I want to propose an ethical framework for understanding that claim. Accordingly, Part II offers a way of understanding substantive questions about how we can achieve a good life.

Even while my ultimate concerns in Part II of this book can be described as theological, my main interlocutors throughout the book remain philosophers within the analytic tradition. For the reader whose interests are primarily theological, I would emphasize that we often gain invaluable clarity on theological matters by drawing from the penetrating ways in which moral philosophers have framed discussions on such topics as intrinsic value, normativity, action explanation, and semantic analyses of moral concepts. For the reader whose interests are primarily philosophical, I would commend Part II as an important area of exploration. Christian theism offers a very interesting, as well as historically significant, context in which to find answers to some otherwise intractable difficulties in moral philosophy. And the resources it provides can, in my experience, prove both intellectually and existentially rewarding.

I find that my fellow Christian moral philosophers are often keen to explore whether there could be an "objective basis" for morality if there were in fact no God.[1] I will not be addressing this question, though I hope that by the end of the book it will be clear why I find the question so ambiguous. I *do* want to insist that, in a theistic, ethical framework, there are certain facts about how we should live that are not dependent on anyone's point of view. However, I distance myself from the attempt to find this objective element in discussions about the rightness and wrongness of actions. As will become clear in chapter 3, I do not believe it makes conceptual sense to suggest that some action could be "objectively wrong." This conclusion is certainly one reason I have for privileging the place of the good (and not of the right) in the ethical framework I propose.

I realize that I have many allies—from Aristotle through Aquinas—in privileging the place of the good and in exploring facts about human nature that help us identify conditions for a good life. I even share with this tradition in moral philosophy the conclusion that conceptual links exist between goodness and *life*. And given that facts exist about how living things do and do not flourish, the door is seemingly opened for me simply to follow this tradition in making objective (i.e., perspective-independent) claims about how we should live.

However, I find problems both with the methodology and with some of the common conclusions associated with the Aristotelian tradition. If I assert that some action or thing is good, I am in some sense commending it. So, while I agree that an important conceptual link exists between goodness and life, I also note the pro-attitude we often (usually? always?) have toward the things we judge to be good. Writers in the Aristotelian tradition seem to me not to offer a clear and adequate explanation for this pro-attitude.

I think the problem is partly a methodological one. Before tackling the *nature* of the good (e.g., linking it with the life functions of a living thing), we must first be clear about the *meaning* of *good*. What concept is denoted by this term? And how do we humans come to understand this concept, so that we have a pro-attitude toward the things we view as good? I do not find these questions adequately answered even by the more recent moral philosophers in the Aristotelian tradition who are cognizant of G. E. Moore's emphasis on the distinction between the meaning and the nature of the good.

Aristotelians will no doubt view my methodological point as uninteresting, given their strong tendency to eschew a Humean account of action explanation. And admittedly, our pro-attitude toward things we judge to be good is fairly inconsequential *if*, as someone like Philippa Foot insists, there is a "natural normativity" associated with the life functions of living things.[2] However, I find this manoeuver—as well, more generally, as the appeal to "there being reason" to perform some action—unpromising as an explanation of human *motivation*. Having abandoned a metaphysic assumed by Aquinas that humans (and other things) "tend toward" particular ends, I think we must follow David Hume in explaining human motivation in terms of human psychology—specifically, human desires.

I have stated that one of my aims in Part II is to identify facts—not dependent on any human's perspective—of how we ought to live. Given my support for a Humean theory of motivation, it might be thought that I will be hard pressed to meet this goal. My situation will only appear worse when I now acknowledge that the range of intrinsic values for which I allow is very narrow. I believe that the only states of affairs of intrinsic value are pleasurable mental states.[3] Anything else will be, at most, instrumentally valuable.

So the theological challenge I set myself is to offer an ethical framework that is recognizably orthodox Christian. I wish to offer a way of understanding the choices God invites people to make—choices that secure the kinds of relationships with God and others through which all people's ultimate flourishing is alone found. Yet in offering this theistic, ethical framework I will not follow philosophers such as Robert Adams and Jerry Walls and David Baggett in appealing to "objective" standards of right and wrong.[4] And in offering a framework privileging the good, I will not seek to argue against what seem to me the correct, broad conclusions of classical hedonists like Henry Sidgwick on intrinsic value or the desire-centered theory of motivation of Hume.

Here is a summary of the chapters ahead. In chapter 1 I argue that "good" is not a primitive concept. Instead, we understand the concepts "good" and "bad" by referencing our appreciation of the difference between our experiences of flourishing versus failing to flourish. This appreciation *is* primitive; and we draw upon it whenever we make assignments of goodness, or value. I defend the view that *good* means something along the lines of "answering to someone's interests" (though there can be derivative and deviant uses of the term). I then argue that "*moral* goodness" is a fuzzy-edged concept and that there is no nonarbitrary way to demarcate it from other forms of goodness.

My analysis of the concept "good" ends up a reductive, naturalistic one. I consider Moore's "open question" argument against naturalism. I note that, if the arguments of chapter 1 are correct, then one currently popular response to Moore—espousing synthetic naturalism—is not available to us. However, the kind of conceptual reductionism I offer readily overcomes Moore's objection to naturalism. I end the chapter by noting that, while a semantic analysis of *good* does not settle the issue of the *nature* of goodness, it nonetheless provides prima facie evidence as to where we should look for our answer.

Having discussed the meaning of *good*, I turn in chapter 2 to the question of what things *are* good. I focus on the much-debated question of that in which goodness, or final value, consists. I appeal to our intuitions in support of welfarism: the view that something can be good only if it is good *for* someone. I then argue that the only things that (noninstrumentally) make someone's life go better for her are her mental states.

I argue that mental statism can withstand objections commonly thought to arise from Nozick's experience machine; the badness of death; and the (im)plausibility of thinking that the pleasures of schadenfreude can rightly be called good. Throughout chapter 2, I work to compare and contrast my own position on noninstrumental value with similar welfarist and mental statist positions held by such philosophers as Griffin, Kraut, Sumner, Feldman, and Bradley.

Chapter 3 introduces the question of why people are motivated to pursue goals (including the goals people identify as good). I introduce the discussion by explaining why I find the currently popular focus on *reasons* an unpromising methodology for explaining motivation. I side with Hume in insisting that only desires move, or impel, us to act whenever we act intentionally. And I defend this uncompromising Humean position from the objection that I cannot account for the motivational force of moral *beliefs*.

Noting how we often feel that we *should* act in certain ways, even if we have desires to act otherwise, I offer an account of the source of normative force, or pressure. I focus on the phenomenology of feeling that one "should" or "ought" to do something; and I link this phenomenology with the negative feeling tone of a frustrated desire. After discussing the conditions under which this negative aspect of a desire comes to be felt as normative force, I turn to the meaning and nature of "wrongness" and "rightness." I note their contrasts to "goodness" and "badness," including the way they are conceptually linked to a cluster of further concepts involving guilt, blameworthiness, and punishment. I advance the idea, drawing from J. S. Mill's general comments, that "wrongness" is always linked to social sanction—that is, to the intent of some person(s) to sanction those who perform some action. I note how wrongness involves a violation of one's own *obligations* and of another individual's *rights* (that is, what another individual *owns*). However, I contend that nothing grounds these concepts beyond the intent of some person(s) to sanction those who interfere with this other individual having the final say on some matter. I then defend this account of wrongness from the objection that wrongness surely refers to something more objective. I resist the conclusion that wrongness even *can* be objective in the sense the critic wants, though I do explain why—despite its social root—the concept "wrong" has commonly come to mean for people something objective along the lines of "not to be done, period." I also note that, though there is no scope for true objectivity in matters of rightness and wrongness, there *is* wide scope for objectivity in matters of goodness and badness (i.e., on the question of what *does* make people's lives go well for them).

In Part II I construct a theistic framework for identifying facts both about all human flourishing and about the decisions we must make to attain this flourishing. I begin chapter 4 by noting the perfectionist element within my theistic framework. Building on the mental statist conclusions of chapter 2, I then look at the substantive question of *which* mental states ensure our welfare in the long run. Consonant with the Christian affirmation that we are created in the image of a relational God, I suggest that there is a common feeling tone—one of "connecting" with others—to many of our experiences. As my way of spelling out the theological claim that our well-being ultimately hinges on our relationships with God and others, I suggest that this experience of connecting is both necessary and sufficient for our ultimate flourishing as humans.

I turn in the latter half of chapter 4 to explore how we can establish and maintain the "ideal relationships" within which we can connect with others in such a way that our ultimate flourishing is realized. I identify as pivotal the mutual goal within a relationship of making the other person's interests one's own. After exploring the coordinating role that God must inevitably play if ideal relationships are to be established, I conclude the chapter with an overview of how *any* interpersonal relationship is established.

Having emphasized in chapter 4 the key role that benevolent commitments play in establishing ideal relationships, I begin chapter 5 by discussing the scope for self-interested pursuits within such a commitment. I then defend my advocacy of benevolence against the objections: that we can desire *relationships* (in addition to desiring the other person's welfare); and that my position emphasizing "mere benevolence" ignores the importance in friendships of desiring that *we* be the ones who help our friends to flourish (as opposed to desiring merely *that* our friends flourish).

Continuing to draw from discussions of earlier chapters, I go on to spell out an understanding of the Christian claim that God invites us into the ongoing life of the Trinity, which is the life that is good for us. I discuss the ways in which God communicates to us, prompting us toward the type of benevolent commitments that mark ideal relationships (as exemplified within the Trinity and within the community of the redeemed in heaven). I emphasize that God prompts us toward these commitments primarily by ensuring that we have various attractions to others and desires that their lives go well for them. I also note that God has given us strong desires for our own flourishing. Through our feeling the pulls of these contrasting sets of desires (toward benevolence and toward self-interest), scope for moral freedom is ensured. I defend the importance of the divine gift of freedom by showing how our acting as an ultimate cause allows for a particular kind of relationship with God and with others. I conclude the chapter by explaining why both benevolent and self-interested patterns of behavior are such that we will end up decisively committed to one or the other.

In chapter 6 I explore further the nature of those decisions that move us either toward or away from the life of ultimate flourishing that Christianity describes. I review my earlier conclusions that motivations—whether for benevolent or for self-interested pursuits—consist of desires with a common phenomenology. I defend my emphasis on desire from the objections that moral decisions involve seeing an act *as a kind* of act and that I have no way of distinguishing good motivations from bad motivations.

I then provide ways to distinguish "morally significant" decisions—that is, decisions that lead us further toward a fixed commitment either to benevolence or to self-interest—from decisions that do not have this significance. In further analyzing the decision whether to pursue benevolence or self-interest, I note that the attraction we feel toward benevolence involves different feeling tones than does the attraction we feel toward self-interested pursuits. Accordingly, the decision whether to pursue benevolence or self-interest can be analyzed in terms of the particular kinds of feeling tones to which we choose, qua free agents, to add our efforts. I respond to the objection that the feeling tones associated with a desire are simply not "weighty" enough to ground the moral significance of our decisions—especially those with eternal significance. I conclude by connecting my ethical framework to theological doctrines such as heaven, hell, and the nature of sin, noting some significant advantages of spelling out these doctrines within the framework I have outlined.

Once again, my aim in Part II will not be to argue for the truth of Christian theism (though I believe that the indispensable role loving relationships clearly play in our well-being hints at an explanation that we are created in the image of a Trinitarian God). Rather, my theological goal is one of clarity: to spell out a way of understanding the claim that God makes available a good life for us humans, as well as the claim that God invites us to make decisions through which we can come to live this good life. For my fellow Christian theists who do not agree with every philosophical conclusion in Part I, I hope that Part I will nevertheless prompt us to reflect seriously on where we should and should not seek to defend objectivity within discussions of morality. Important issues surrounding the relationship between the good and the right must be disentangled if we are to have anything to offer the serious moral philosopher. For those moral philosophers whose interests lie primarily with the material of Part I, I again also commend the substantive material in Part II as a resource for resolving some of the lingering questions raised in Part I about what makes our lives go well for us.

*Part One*

# Placing the Good within an Ethical Framework

CHAPTER ONE

# The Meaning of *Good*

## 1.1 Our Pro-attitude toward the Good

One of the primary concerns of moral philosophers for the past two and a half millennia has been to provide an analysis of the "good." Philosophers have been right to have this concern. No construction of a framework for ethics can get off the ground without an understanding of the good. And if one's aim is to make a comparative study of competing ethical frameworks, one will need to understand how proponents of each framework understand the nature of the good (i.e., which things in our world *are* good) and perhaps also the meaning of *good* (i.e., what we are doing when we call something "good").

Our everyday conversations bear out W. D. Ross's observation that "there is a wide diversity of senses in which the word [*good*] is used" (1930, 65). We make references to a good knife, a good steak, a good painting, a good mother, a good set of lungs, and many other things we call good. Many philosophers have looked for a commonality within these uses. Is there, as Aristotle asked, "the same account of good" that will "turn up in all" uses of the term, "just as the same account of whiteness turns up in snow and in chalk?" (1999, 1096b).

Aristotle for one did not think that there is such a single idea corresponding to every use of the term *good*. He remarked that "honor, prudence, and pleasure have different and dissimilar accounts, precisely insofar as they are goods" (1999, 1096b). Aristotle is certainly correct that, for example, prudence and pleasure each can have full rein only at the expense of the other. When we praise an action as prudentially good, we typically acknowledge that there were alternative actions that afforded more pleasure (at least, more immediate pleasure). Yet, from the fact that there are single actions that cannot be good both from prudential considerations and from considerations of pleasure, does Aristotle's conclusion follow that "the good is not something common corresponding to a single Idea" (1999, 1096b)?

In looking for commonality among our uses of the term *good*, we can begin by considering the etymology of *good* and its cognate sisters. Ross observes that the original connotation of the word *good* seems to be one of "indefinite commendation" (1930, 66).[1] Perhaps the more complete observation would be that the original use of the term soon *gave rise to* the connotation of indefinite commendation. Alasdair MacIntyre, in his *Short History of Ethics*, comments that the term stems from a particular usage within early Greek society, which placed heavy emphasis on one's performance of one's socially allotted function. More specifically, "The word ἀγαθός, ancestor of our *good*, is originally a predicate specifically attached to the role of a Homeric nobleman" (1998, 6). MacIntyre notes that ἀγαθός was a commendatory word; but this was simply because it was *interchangeable* with the words (e.g., for "brave," "skilful," "successful in war and peace") that characterized the qualities of the Homeric ideal:

> Aγαθός is not like our word *good* in many of its Homeric contexts, for it is not used to say that it is "good" to be kingly, courageous, and clever—that is, it is not used to commend these qualities in a man, as our word *good* might be used by a contemporary admirer of the Homeric ideal. . . . In our ordinary English use of *good*, "good, but not kingly, courageous, or cunning" makes perfectly good sense; but in Homer, "ἀγαθός, but not kingly, courageous, or clever" would not even be a morally eccentric form of judgment, but as it stands simply an unintelligible contradiction. (1998, 6)

The gap between evaluation and description would soon appear, however. MacIntyre goes on to tell that, once societal roles and expectations changed, the conceptual link was lost between ἀγαθός and the particular qualities of the Homeric ideal. Conflicting opinions naturally emerged as to when one should make the evaluation that someone is ἀγαθός, or good.

Given these differing opinions, and given that the term *good* remained evaluative, the term obviously could not remain conceptually linked to any narrow, descriptive set of attributes. It seems easy to imagine at this point how the accepted meaning of *good* came to be something along the lines of general commendation. So I think we can safely allow with Ross that there exists a long and ongoing history of *good* carrying the connotation of general commendation.

Setting aside for a moment the question of whether, in today's usage, the term *good always* expresses some kind of commendation, we can at least note that it typically does so. And this points up a phenomenon that needs explaining. Commending something seems to involve a pro-attitude toward that which is commended. People who agree that a knife is good will (in standard cases, at least) have a pro-attitude toward the knife. But what explains the phenomenon that each person should have this same kind of attitude toward the knife?

To see more clearly what it is that needs explaining, consider the way in which words can describe various objects or events. We can attribute or predicate the word *sharp* to a knife, or the word *juicy* to a steak, or the word *colorful* to a painting.[2] But such descriptions do not necessarily mean that I will have a pro-attitude toward these objects. I may view sharp knives as too dangerous to have around the house, juicy steaks as not sufficiently cooked, and colorful paintings as not subtle enough to be enjoyed on repeated viewings. However, when I describe a knife or steak or painting as "good," this commendation *does* (at least typically) carry with it a pro-attitude toward the object I describe.[3] And anyone else who describes the object as "good" also (typically) has this pro-attitude toward the object.

It is fairly straightforward to explain the shared attitude of people who refer to an object as "heart-rending" or "funny" or "sickening." We humans seem capable of experiencing similar feelings of poignant sadness, of amusement at an unexpected event, and of a churning in the stomach. Anyone who experiences these feelings can become a competent user of the terms *heart-rending*, *funny*, and *sickening*. Given that people typically have a pro-attitude toward that which they describe as good, the term *good* seemingly must be connected in some way with people's positive mental experiences. Cognitivists and noncognitivists may debate whether, in calling something good (at least, morally good), we are *merely* giving expression to our own emotions or attitudes. But even cognitivists will need to acknowledge that we have a pro-attitude toward those objects we believe to have the property of goodness. And this suggests that in recognizing an object's goodness we are referencing in some way some internal, positive feeling or experience of ours. So how are we to characterize this positive feeling or experience, which is common to all of us and which allows us each to be a competent user of the term *good*?

## 1.2 Flourishing and the Good

From an early age, humans experience a wide variety of both positive and negative feelings. We know what it feels like to be hungry, and we know what it feels like to have our stomachs full. We know what it is to be in pain and to be physically comfortable. We know what it is to feel alone and to feel connected to others. We become familiar with things like fear, guilt, and depression—and with the opposite feelings of safety, pride, and joy. There is a commonality to all these experiences. They are experiences of our lives either being enhanced or being damaged.

The term *experience* can be understood in two senses; and it is important to clarify the sense in which I will be using it in this discussion. We commonly use the term *experience* to describe some activity or event in which we participate. So, for instance, we might talk about our experience of visiting Paris or riding a horse or having a shoulder massage. As we engage in these activities, there is another sense in which we "experience" them. Certain mental states—which we might describe as having particular *feeling tones*—arise: for example, we feel a sense of wonder when seeing Paris, or a sense of exhilaration when riding a horse, or a certain sense of pleasure stemming from the stimulation of nerve endings by the masseur.[4] An experience in the first sense (of participation in an activity) may give rise to quite different feeling tones that we associate with mental experiences. For instance, a shoulder massage from a spouse may lead to feelings of relaxation, while a massage from a kidnapper will elicit feelings we associate with fear and panic. In pointing to our experiences of flourishing, I mean to focus on the second sense of a mental experience with certain feeling tones.

In the next chapter I will examine in more detail the nature of those mental states on which our well-being depends. But for now the point is that there is a commonality of feeling to those times when our lives are unambiguously going well. And, although there may be borderline cases, we can distinguish these feelings from the alternate feelings associated with those occasions when our lives are not going well in some respect. In offering an analysis of pleasure and pain, James Mill commented that "some sensations, probably the greater number, are what we call indifferent. They are not considered as either painful, or pleasurable. There are sensations, however, and of frequent recurrence, some of which are painful, some pleasurable. The difference is, that which is felt. A man knows it, by feeling it; and that is the whole account of the phenomenon" (1869, 2:184).[5] Whatever problems may exist with linking the simple notions of pleasure and pain to human well-being, Mill is correct in that experiences of flourishing (to use my language) are not analyzable in terms of further, more basic concepts. Rather, experiencing one's own life as flourishing is a basic, or primitive, concept we have as sentient beings.

Philosophers often use the term *flourishing* when speaking of the thriving of human life in its widest sense. I am indeed interested in this wide sense, which is perhaps sometimes referred to as fullness of life. *Flourishing* seems as good a word as any. It is difficult, without using terms like *good* or *better*, to say more here about the notion of flourishing. But to do so would be circular, for the term *good* is what we are trying to understand by appealing to our experiences of flourishing. I hope, though, that the phenomenology of our shared experiences is such that my description of life-enhancing and life-damaging experiences will be clear.

People of course may disagree about *which* experiences ultimately do promote human flourishing. Parents, for example, may disagree about whether the short-term discomfort of corporal punishment will lead to the greater, long-term well-being of their child. Also, individuals will find that a single experience at a given time sometimes contains elements that detract from, as well as elements that promote, the same general aspect of human flourishing. Strenuous exercise, for example, can produce both immediate physical discomfort and an immediate sensation of physical exhilaration. But these issues involve the potential difficulties in identifying which actions really do promote our overall flourishing. Certainly, we have a good grasp of the respective phenomenologies associated with those times when we clearly do and when we clearly do not flourish.

It is this phenomenology of flourishing that allows us to become competent users of the term *good*. Although some philosophers have viewed the good as a basic, unanalyzable concept, the proposal here is that this concept *can* be analyzed further. We understand the distinction between the concepts "good" and "bad" by relating it to our contrasting experiences of flourishing and failing to flourish.

The pro-attitude we naturally have toward our own flourishing explains why we will (typically) have a pro-attitude toward those things we view as good.[6] We saw earlier that my description of a knife as sharp does not necessarily denote a pro-attitude toward the knife. This is because I may not see a sharp knife as promoting my own flourishing. However, when I describe a knife as good I *do* (typically) view the knife as promoting, in some instrumental way, my flourishing.

Also, I may describe a knife as good—with an accompanying pro-attitude toward the knife—because I view it as promoting the flourishing of *someone else* about whom I care. Against the psychological egoist, it seems obvious that we do view some things as good irrespective of whether they promote our own personal flourishing. For example, a person may regard it as good that governments throughout Africa provide future generations of children free, high-quality educations—even if she can think of no way that she personally would benefit from such future programs.

All the same, it remains true that we understand the term *good* by means of our epistemically prior understanding of our own flourishing.[7] In the previous example of high-quality education for children, someone who sees this as a good thing may reflect on her own positive experiences within a solid educational system. If she is herself without a quality education, then she may reflect on what others have told her about *their* positive educational experiences, relating their descriptions to similar, positive experiences of her own. If such testimonies are also unavailable, then she may use her imagination as to the benefits that surely come from a high-quality education, again relating these imagined benefits to things in her own life that have enhanced her own flourishing. The general point is that, unless she relates the education of underprivileged children to *some* aspect of her own flourishing, she will have no understanding of why anyone might commend as *good*—rather than merely describe without evaluation—the education of children.

What has happened in our example is that the natural pro-attitude the person has toward her own flourishing has been extended toward the flourishing of others. We might say that she has made their interests her own. In chapter 3 I will examine in some detail this notion of making someone else's interests one's own. For now, it is sufficient just to note that our pro-attitudes toward those objects and events that promote flourishing can arise as we consider others' flourishing as well as our own. While it is true that we must reference some aspect of our own experiences of flourishing in order to understand *that* a particular object or event will promote someone's flourishing, the "someone" whose flourishing elicits our pro-attitude need not necessarily be ourselves. The "someone" can be others about whom we care.

In saying that we identify an object as good only by referencing some aspect of our own flourishing, I do not mean to suggest that this process need always involve conscious and reflective inferences. Sometimes our reactions to objects and events are immediate and noninferential: "knee-jerk reactions," we sometimes call them. Such reactions may amount to the immediate physical or emotional responses we have when we see an object or hear of an event. For example, the beauty of a sunset might suddenly strike me, eliciting a feeling of wonder (and of course a pro-attitude toward what I see); or the description of an unsanitary cooking method might induce physical nausea (and a negative attitude toward this food preparation procedure). In these cases, it is not as though I consciously reflect on the facts that exposure to beauty helps one to flourish and that unhygienic food tends to undermine one's flourishing. Rather, it is simply the respective feelings of wonder and revulsion that lead me to the immediate reactions that the sunset is good and that the food preparation procedure is bad.[8] Still, experiences of wonder and revulsion are feelings that fall under the phenomenological umbrellas of, respectively, flourishing and failing to flourish. We react to what we see (e.g., a sunset) and hear (e.g., a story about unsanitary cooking) by describing the object or state of affairs in question as "good" or "bad." *Which* of these two evaluations we offer is determined by the qualities of the mental experiences we have as we see the object or hear about the state of affairs. And so, whether or not we are consciously reflecting on our mental experiences of flourishing, it remains the case that our appreciation that something can be "good" or "bad" relies on our prior appreciation of the difference between flourishing and failing to flourish.

## 1.3  Instrumental Goodness

One objection to analyzing "good" in terms of our experiences of flourishing will insist that an appeal to flourishing simply does not cover every kind of goodness we attribute to things. While the examples I have given thus far may lend themselves to plausible analyses in terms of flourishing, so this objection might go, there are other examples where such an analysis is *not* plausible. To see the kinds of examples to which the critic might appeal, we can begin by noting two broad categories of goodness: instrumental goodness and noninstrumental goodness. Aristotle's distinction of these types of goodness is as follows: "Goods pursued and liked in their own right are spoken of as one species of good, whereas those that in some way tend to produce or preserve these goods, or to prevent their contraries, are spoken of as goods because of these and in a different way. Clearly, then, goods are spoken of in two ways, and some are goods in their own right, and others goods because of these" (1999, 1096b). An object or event is instrumentally good if it serves as a means of realizing some further good. Noninstrumental goodness involves those things that are good as ends in themselves: so-called *final goods*. In objecting to the link I have made between our understanding of the concept "good" and our reflections on our experiences of flourishing, the critic may point to purported examples in which judgments of instrumental and/or noninstrumental goodness are made at times with absolutely no reference to the idea of flourishing. In this section I shall address judgments about instrumental goodness, before turning in the next section to judgments of noninstrumental goodness.

J. L. Mackie observes that, in cases where we speak of the instrumental goodness of an object, the term *good* is often synonymous with *efficient*—as when we speak of a "good knife." In such cases, the word *good* serves, as R. M. Hare put it, as a "functional word" (1991, §6.4, 100). For, in explaining the meaning of, say, a "good" knife, we will need to say what function the knife serves as people use it. Yet Mackie also notes that *good* is sometimes used in contexts in which it is *not* synonymous with *efficient*—as when we speak of a good sunset. The challenge, then, is to arrive at a general meaning of *good* that would apply in *all* contexts and that would explain why *good* is sometimes synonymous with *efficient*. Mackie's own conclusion is that *good* should be defined in terms of "satisfying requirements of the kind in question" (1977, 55f.). Thus, for Mackie, any use of the term *good* assumes, either explicitly or implicitly, certain requirements or standards. To use one of Mackie's examples, the statement "'Billie Jean King [was] very good' will mean that she [was] a good tennis player if it occurs in the context of talk about tennis or if it is primarily as a tennis player that the speaker and hearer are interested in Billie Jean King" (1977, 53).

Mackie's account of the meaning of *good* provides the following challenge to the idea that we understand "goodness" in terms of our own flourishing. If the requirements or standards that provide the context for the evaluation of an object's goodness have nothing to do with my own well-being, then how can my personal experiences of flourishing be at all relevant to my judgment of whether that object is good?

One way of trying to meet this objection would be to question the premise that we can think of an object as good even if we in no way mean to personally commend it and in no way have a pro-attitude toward it. Mackie insists, though, that the scenario represented in this premise *is* indeed possible and offers the following examples: "While I am in some sense commending someone or something in calling him or it a good rock-climber or a good carving knife I need not even pretend to be endorsing the requirements in question. I may be a convinced vegetarian and think it perverse to go up mountains the hard way. Again one may say, 'That is a good sunset, but the beauties of nature leave me cold'" (1977, 55). Mackie rejects the view that such examples are of an "inverted commas" use of the term *good*, where in using the term *good* we mean "what *others* view as good." This kind of explanation, he notes, is common among philosophers who stress that the term *good* always denotes "egocentric commendation." He maintains that it would be "stretching the account" of egocentric commendation to say that "the carving knife is one such as I would favor if I wanted to slice meat; the sunset is one such as I would favor if I were one for the beauties of nature" (1977, 55).

Mackie is correct in that the statement "The carving knife is one such as I would favor if I wanted to slice meat" does not necessarily denote *personal*, or "egocentric," commendation. I can utter that statement without myself having a pro-attitude toward the knife. Still, Mackie allows that what is common to his examples "is that in each there is, somewhere in the picture, some set of requirements or wants or interests, and the thing that is called good is being said to be such as to satisfy those requirements or wants or interests" (1977, 55). It will be important to keep this link in mind as we explore whether Mackie's examples can be accommodated by the thesis that we understand instrumental goodness in terms of our own flourishing.

The link between the idea of interests and the term *good* serves as the focal point of Paul Ziff's thoughtful analysis of the meaning of *good*. Ziff's proposal is that we understand the term *good* as follows: "If an element of an utterance is modified by 'good' then if the utterance is to be nondeviant the element modified by 'good' must there serve to characterize something that may or may not answer to certain interests" (1960, 213). By "certain interests" Ziff does not mean that the interests must be ones that someone *actually* has. It is enough that the object in question *would* be a good one to a person who had the relevant interests. To illustrate, consider the statement "That is a good potato, but I detest potatoes." Ziff acknowledges that in uttering this statement, "There is in general no reason at all to suppose that interests or the interests of the speaker must be in question" (1960, 233). For Ziff, the question "*Whose* interests?" is an "essentially irrelevant" question. He remarks, "The answer to the question 'Whose interests?' is this: whichever one has the interests in question. . . . The relevant question is whether what is in question does or does not answer to the indicated interests" (1960, 236).

Ziff here goes beyond Mackie in pointing out that the interests "somewhere in the picture," as Mackie put it, need only be interests we imagine someone as having. But before we look at whether Ziff's semantic analysis of *good* can be reconciled with our earlier thesis that we understand "good" with reference to our own flourishing, we should consider the objection that Ziff does not go *far enough* in resisting the link between people's interests and their identification of objects as good. James Griffin questions whether there really are interests of *any* kind at stake every time we identify an object as good. He asserts, "A few nouns modifiable by 'good' apply to things without a function or role or purpose, and there is then no interest being served. A good Roman nose is merely one that has the defining characteristics to a high degree" (1996, 40). So should we conclude that, in some uses of the term *good*, there simply are no interests whatsoever lurking "somewhere in the picture"?

A fuller examination shows that this would be the wrong conclusion. Take Griffin's example of the Roman nose judged to be good because it has the defining characteristics of a Roman nose to a high degree. As we learn the names of objects and concepts, it is certainly very useful to be able to point to examples that illustrate clearly the objects and concepts we are trying to learn (or teach to others). A "good" Roman nose would serve as instrumentally useful in this task. This fact does not by itself establish that representative Roman noses came commonly to be called "good" *because* they were instrumentally useful. Yet this explanation seems the most plausible.

In support of this plausibility, consider the difference between the two statements "That corpse is good" and "That cadaver is good." Ziff notes that, while the first statement sounds very odd indeed, the second does not; and he offers the following explanation as to why this is so. We typically use the term *cadaver* when the context involves medical training or other activities for which a lifeless body serves some purpose. A good cadaver in this context will be one that answers to the interests of medical students who need to study bodies that resemble closely the kinds of patients they are likely to treat in the future. If someone does utter the statement "That corpse is good," this will probably be a deviant use of the term. For, unless some context exists where some special interest is at issue, the speaker's utterance will amount to a deviation from the regularities found in the use of *good* by speakers of the language.

The reference to a "good Roman nose" does not sound odd; and it surely is not a deviant use of the term, for many people use the term in this way. So do we call a representative Roman nose "good" for the same general reason that we would call a cadaver "good": namely, because it is useful for certain purposes we can identify? This conclusion is roughly the one I want to defend. But before doing so formally, there is one further point I need to unpack.

Sometimes speakers of the English language do, I admit, use the term *good* to denote features of an object or event that do not answer directly to anyone's interests—even their imagined interests. For example, *good* is sometimes used simply to denote "large." One might refer to a "good-sized ice cream scoop" or a "good amount of rain." Here the speaker simply means a "large scoop" or a "large rainfall." Indeed, a farmer might say that a "good amount of rain fell yesterday"—whether the rain was needed for his crops (and thus contributed to his own flourishing as a farmer) or whether his fields were already flooded. Suppose the farmer has a young son who is just beginning to learn the English language and who hears his father describing the rainfall to others both in terms of a "large" amount of rain and a "good" amount of rain. If the son already knows the meaning of *large*, he may naturally think that *good* simply signifies the same quality as *large*. That is, the son may think that the same set of examples by which he came to understand the concept "large" are indistinguishable from the set of examples that give content to the concept "good." The son may then begin to use the term *good* as a synonym for *large*.

If the farmer's son echoes his father in speaking of a "good amount of rain," it will be difficult to charge him with a deviant use of the term *good*. After all, many English speakers use the term *good* to refer to a "large" amount of rain. Yet it remains plausible for us to explain the use of *good* in this context as a *derivative* use of the term—"derivative" in that the usage stems from contexts where *good* does involve people's interests. Plausibly, we first started using *good* as synonymous with *large* in describing amounts of rain because large amounts of rain typically were useful for our projects of growing crops. Indeed, another commonly used synonym for *large* in modern-day conversations is *healthy*. In the midst of a thunderstorm, it would not be unusual to hear someone shake her head and marvel at the "healthy amount of rain we are getting"—irrespective of whether rain levels for the year were above or were below the optimal amount for crops, drinking water supplies for the area, and so on. Like the term *good*, the term *healthy* is often used today as a synonym for *large*—without any accompanying pro-attitude or any reference to someone's real or imagined interests. However, plausibly this use of *healthy* has been derived from usage where the term referred to something that *did* contribute to our flourishing and to the achievement of our projects and interests. And the most plausible explanation for the use of *good* as a synonym for *large* is also that this usage has been derived from contexts in which, for example, a large amount of rain did answer to identifiable interests.

Returning to Griffin's example of a "good" Roman nose, it is not difficult to construct similar lines of explanation. In describing a Roman nose, the terms *typical* and *representative* would be understandably synonymous with the term *good* if the context was an artist's attempt to capture in art form a "Roman look," or if the context was an attempt to explain to others by means of example what one had in mind when talking of a Roman nose. Admittedly, there are contexts, like the one Griffin envisions, where the term *good* is used as a synonym for *representative* and where this characteristic of an object serves no use—even an imagined use—in the mind of the speaker. However, the plausible explanation remains that the synonymous use of *good* and *representative* stems from contexts in which the representativeness of an object was viewed as good because it *did* serve certain identifiable interests.

So, with this qualification to Ziff's analysis of "good" as "answering to certain interests," let me now address the question whether this analysis of "good'" undermines my earlier explanation that we understand instrumental "goodness" in terms of our own flourishing. It will be remembered from section 1.2 that, in viewing an object as good, I need not see it as promoting *my* flourishing. It is enough, we noted there, that I see it as promoting the interests of someone whose interests I make my own. Seeing an action in this way ensures that I have a pro-attitude toward the object in question (with this pro-attitude accounting for why I view the object as good). But certainly this kind of explanation will not serve us here as we seek to account for cases where we identify an object as good by merely *imagining* someone to have certain interests.

So I will need to modify at this point my original proposal of section 1.2 that I as an individual understand other things as "good" because I see them as fostering "my own flourishing and/or the flourishing of others whose interests I make my own." To accommodate Mackie's and Ziff's examples, let me now modify that account so that an individual understands "good" in terms of "my own flourishing and the flourishing of others whose interests I recognize as possible."[9]

This modification preserves the central tenet of my account in that it still allows us to understand the term *good* as necessarily referencing our own flourishing. Consider Mackie's example of the vegetarian who commends a carving knife as good. The vegetarian recognizes that the knife serves the interests of *someone*—specifically, someone who wants to carve a piece of meat thinly, evenly, easily, repeatedly, and the like. The use of *good* here is a functional use; the knife is good because it helps the meat-eater to accomplish certain purposes. Even though the vegetarian does not share these specific purposes, he still must think the accomplishment of purposes (in general) a good thing. This much follows from the fact that, as Mackie allows, he *commends* the knife in some sense. And why should the vegetarian think the accomplishment of purposes in general a good thing? The answer must be that he himself has accomplished certain purposes—and experienced the accompanying thoughts and feelings that come with accomplishing, as opposed to failing to accomplish, one's intended purposes.[10] Similar explanations, of course, are available when we consider the urbanite who views a sunset as good or the chairlift enthusiast who recommends a mountain walking trail as good. Thus we are again left with an account of the "good" according to which we use our own experiences of flourishing as a reference in coming to see objects and events as good.

Perhaps one may think that the ease of our accommodation of Mackie's examples owes to the fact that Mackie has allowed too much in saying that there is "some sense" in which the vegetarian commends the carving knife. Ziff suggests that the standard definition given by dictionaries and philosophers alike of *good* in terms of commendation is unfortunate (1960, 229–32). He offers various examples where the term *good* is used without any sense of commendation—for example, when one says that "the good seats are all reserved."

In response, we should again keep in mind the point—which Ziff himself stresses—that in calling seats "good" we are imagining them to answer to certain interests. If it is theater seats that are in question, we view them as good in that they are useful to someone who wants a good view of the stage, wants to hear the actors clearly, and so forth.[11] Admittedly, Ziff is correct in saying that the statement "The good seats are all reserved" does not by itself convey my commendation of anything. However, it is also true that, in viewing the seats as "good," I would commend the seats to someone who had the interests of seeing the stage, hearing the actors, and so forth (assuming, of course, that I wanted to advance, not thwart, her interests). And so there remains, as Mackie says, "some sense" in which I commend the seats when I refer to them as good—even if I do not have an overall pro-attitude toward the seats that would lead me to commend them, full stop.

To summarize the points of this section, I have expanded in two ways my account of how references to our own experiences of flourishing allow us to form the judgment that something is good. First, for those things we assess as good, we need not always commend them in the sense of having an overall pro-attitude toward them. It is true that the meaning of *good* remains linked to the idea of "answering to someone's interests." But where the interests do not belong to anyone about whom we care (e.g., an imagined person), a pro-attitude will not automatically accompany our recognition that something answers to the interests in question. Second, there are admittedly times when people use the term *good* to denote something *other* than answering to someone's interests. However, such use of the term (e.g., as meaning "large") is derivative in nature—derived from usages of the term *good* in which it *is* linked with someone's interests.

At the beginning of this section I noted two broad categories of goodness: instrumental goodness and noninstrumental goodness. My original question was whether there are examples of either kind of goodness that would undermine the working thesis that we understand the term *good* only by referencing in some way our prior understanding of what it is to flourish. The examples of instrumental goodness we have considered do not undermine this working thesis. Let me now turn to the question of whether instances exist in which we come to view some object or activity as having *noninstrumental* value, quite apart from any consideration of whether that object or activity answers to our or anyone else's interests.

## 1.4  Noninstrumental Goodness

Noninstrumental goodness is not the same thing as *intrinsic* goodness.[12] Still, in exploring questions of noninstrumental goodness I will focus some of my discussion on questions of intrinsic goodness. Suppose it is plausible to think that people do come to believe—without referencing in some way their own flourishing—that some things are intrinsically good (i.e., that goodness lies within the things in question). It then would be a short move to conclude that they believe these things to be noninstrumentally good (i.e., good as an end). But do people indeed come to think of some things as intrinsically good, without having referenced in some way their own flourishing?

Such a conclusion seems obviously false when we consider how we form a pro-attitude toward something. We consider something, observing it via our senses or imagining it. "Considering" it may involve reflecting on its anticipated effects on our own or others' well-being; reflecting on the intrinsic qualities of the thing itself; or merely observing the thing at a quick and unreflective glance. As we consider the thing, we have certain mental experiences. If the mental experiences are positive ones—that is, ones we would associate with our own flourishing—then we come to have a pro-attitude toward the object. So in this way it seems rather obvious that we do reference our own experiences of flourishing in making the evaluative judgment that something is good.

But is this too quick a conclusion? It might be objected that I have improperly separated the mental experiences we have when considering some object (or some activity or event) from the object itself. That is, I have distinguished (1) our positive mental experiences from (2) our considerations of, or engagements with, some object, event, or activity. And then I have argued that the former—not the latter—gives rise to the pro-attitude we have toward the things in question. But this suggests, so the objection might go, that we can speak of the former in isolation from the latter. And this is not correct. We do not simply have positive mental experiences, or enjoyments, full stop. Rather, we enjoy *objects* and *activities* and *achieving things*. Consider Robert Adams's comments on the way we enjoy things other than our first-person experiences: "*What we enjoy* . . . is not limited to states of consciousness, but also includes actions, and objects to which we are related. Swimmers enjoy swimming by doing it. Nature lovers enjoy woods by walking in them, and birds by hearing and seeing them. . . . None of this enjoyment is without experience, but it is not only the experiences that are enjoyed" (1999, 95). But is Adams correct that, in these examples, what we enjoy are actually *objects* and *pursuits* of goals, as opposed to the first-person *experiences* associated with (believing that one is) observing these objects and pursuing these goals?

My response is that, strictly speaking, we do not enjoy a walk in the woods or the completion of a challenging swim. This much is clear from the fact that the enjoyment I receive from reflection on a completed swim remains the same if we suppose that I have been hypnotized into (falsely) believing that I have completed the swim.[13] Rather, it is the first-person *mental experiences* associated with taking a walk or completing a swim that, strictly speaking, are enjoyable to us.

Admittedly, in describing the activities through which we experienced enjoyable mental sensations, we might say colloquially that we "enjoyed a swim" or "enjoyed a walk." And Adams's examples rightly call attention to the fact that our enjoyable experiences are often occasioned—and indeed made possible—by those times when we *focus our attention* on some external, impersonal object or activity.

On this last point, it is common knowledge that people can often best enhance their own well-being by focusing on things other than their own well-being. Even motivational hedonists—who claim that only our own pleasures and pains motivate us—would be wise to recognize this point. Henry Sidgwick highlighted this aspect of human nature in his description of the "paradox of Hedonism"—namely, the concern that "pleasure, if too predominant, defeats its own aim" (1981, 48). He commented,

Many middle-aged Englishmen would maintain the view that business is more agreeable than amusement; but they would hardly find it so if they transacted the business with a perpetual conscious aim at the attendant pleasure. Similarly, the pleasures of thought and study can only be enjoyed in the highest degree by those who have an ardour of curiosity which carries the mind temporarily away from self and its sensations. In all kinds of Art, again, the exercise of the creative faculty is attended by intense and exquisite pleasures: but it would seem that in order to get them, one must forget them: the genuine artist at work seems to have a predominant and temporarily absorbing desire for the realisation of his ideal of beauty. (1981, 49)

Happily, as Sidgwick's last sentence indicates, humans are quite capable of focusing their attention on these external things. In such instances does one need, as Sidgwick indicates, to *forget* that first-person experiences are the only things pleasurable in and of themselves? This requirement is too strong, if by *forget* we mean that one must cease to be aware of the fact that first-person experiences are ultimately the only things that directly affect the phenomenology of flourishing. I need not forget my arguments of this section in order to focus on completing a swim or on making a free throw in a game of basketball. I can readily focus on making a free throw while still aware (1) that my enjoyment is linked directly to my own mental states and even (2) that my enjoyment would diminish if, instead of concentrating on the basket and saying to myself, "Make the basket!" I instead concentrated on my mental states and said to myself, "Enjoy the moment more!"

The broad point is that we can focus our attention on some activity or on the intrinsic qualities of some object. And while focusing our attention on these things we can come to have a pro-attitude toward them. These points do not undermine my conclusion, though, that the pro-attitude we have toward them stems from the fact that we associate them with the positive mental experiences we have as we consider or engage with them.

As a rejoinder to my conclusion, perhaps one might insist that there is more to be made of my acknowledged point that people desire things other than their own flourishing. In making this rejoinder, one might attempt to build on Joseph Butler's discussion of the desires we have for objects. Butler provided a helpful general insight in distinguishing between "self-love" (which he linked with a person's "general desire of his own happiness") and the "variety of particular affections, passions, and appetites to particular external objects" that we may have (1970, sermon 11, §5). He rightly went on to note that our desire for some object is every bit as much *our* desire as is self-love, stating that the gratification of a desire to see my neighbor prosper produces in me a pleasure "as much my own pleasure as the pleasure self-love would have from knowing I myself should be happy some time hence" (1970, sermon 11, §7). So far, there is nothing that challenges the conclusions of this chapter. We can indeed focus our attention on objects; we can desire them. This point is consistent with the conclusion that our pro-attitude toward objects and activities stems from the positive nature of the mental experiences we have as we consider or engage with objects and activities.

Butler further reminded us that the desires we have toward external things are "distinct from the pleasure arising from them" (1970, sermon 11, §6). He commented that "there could not be this pleasure were it not for that prior suitableness between the object and the passion"—that is, if there were not "an affection or appetite" for the object (1970, sermon 11, §6). These remarks still do not amount to any objection to the conclusions of this chapter. Butler's general points are simply that we experience pleasure—that is, positive mental experiences—as our desires are fulfilled; and this pleasure that comes with a fulfilled desire is possible only if one has the desire in the first place. All this seems uncontroversially true. However, the idea of a desire existing *prior* to certain positive mental experiences may give the impression that one can desire an object (or activity) *prior to any* positive mental experiences associated with one's consideration of it. Such an implication would indeed undermine the conclusions of this chapter. For, if a person can have a desire—or pro-attitude—toward some object *prior* to having positive mental experiences associated with her consideration of it, then we need not appeal to these positive mental experiences in order to explain why she has a pro-attitude toward the object (such that it would lead her to think of the object as good). But can we properly draw out such an implication from the points Butler makes?

This implication does not at all follow from Butler's remarks; and such a conclusion is at any rate false. Butler's focus is again on the point that, if it were not for an existing desire we had for some object, then we would not receive pleasure as we interact with the object in the way we desire to interact. This point merely shows that our desire for an object might exist prior to any (pleasurable) mental experience we receive when the desire in question is later *realized*. However, this does not show that, in *forming* the desire in the first place, we do so without reference to our experiences of flourishing.

A desire that some state of affairs obtain involves—at least in the kinds of cases that will interest us for the purposes of this project—an experience of being impelled.[14] If I have a desire to visit Paris, I feel a certain urge to change the world (i.e., make it so that I *am* in Paris) until I believe that my desire has been realized. Even if my desire is something I do not (through second-order reflection) welcome, all things considered, and even if I end up resisting the desire, I am nonetheless impelled to some degree by the desire to act. Public language does not seem useful in trying to clarify further the nature of this feeling that comes with desiring something. But our own experiences of desiring things will hopefully make the common phenomenology clear enough.

Let us return to Butler's comments, which, we saw, might be taken to suggest that we form desires for objects or states of affairs *prior* to any pleasurable mental sensations we have as we observe or imagine the objects or states of affairs. Though Butler is correct that we can distinguish a desire from the pleasurable mental states that result when we believe that desire is fulfilled, we must also remember that a desire is a mental experience in its own right. It is a feeling of being impelled. Granted, there will be substantial variation in the "feeling tones" within the range of desires we have. When we desire that a charitable organization we support dig wells in third world communities where there is no access to clean drinking water, we may have a similar feeling to that which arises when we read the noble act of substitution by Sydney Carton at the end of *A Tale of Two Cities*. By contrast, when we desire to cheat in a game of cards, we may have a feeling similar to times in our childhood when we felt shame while acting in disobedience to our parents. But the point is that *all* our desires carry the feeling of being impelled, whatever other differences exist among the mental experiences associated with our various desires. Even with the desire to cheat at cards, there is still some action we feel impelled to take, even if we do not welcome this desire or approve of this action, all things considered. Accordingly, there is some feeling of release that we anticipate if the desire is fulfilled, along with some level of frustration that we experience until we come to believe that it has been fulfilled (or until we cease to have the desire).[15] The feeling of being impelled—and the accompanying dichotomy between *(a)* frustration accompanying the belief that the world is, or might be, one way and *(b)* release accompanying the belief that the world is, or might be, a different way—is (almost always) part of what it is to have a desire.[16]

What is important for our larger discussion is that our ability to form a desire or pro-attitude toward some object presupposes our ability to appreciate, phenomenologically, the contrasting feelings associated with (what I have termed) "frustration" and "release." This appreciation of the distinction between frustration and release is one example of the more general appreciation of the distinction between experiences of flourishing and experiences of failing to flourish. So we are again unable to avoid the conclusion that we form a pro-attitude toward an object only by associating that object with our mental experiences of flourishing (in contrast to our mental experiences of failing to flourish).

## 1.5 The Morally Good

Thus far my general conclusion has been that the meaning of *good* is linked to the idea of answering to someone's interests. In this section we will see that the question of *how significant* one's interests are proves key in identifying the narrower range of things that might be called "morally good."

In discussions of ethical matters, there seems to be a common assumption that a particular kind of goodness is at stake: *moral* goodness. From my own everyday experiences, when people speak of some matter as a "moral issue," they typically do so with only a vague reference to some set of considerations that are thought to be normative. Admittedly, in some cases a person may have formed a definite view that morality is linked with some specific, identifiable consideration(s)—for example, that a moral issue is one in which God has commanded or willed that we act a certain way. But often we hear statements such as

"Legally you'd be in the right; but morally you'd be in the wrong" or "This matter is not merely a political question, it's a question of morality." And the reference to "morality" in these cases seems to amount to some unspecified appeal to obligations or principles or rights or agreed-upon standards or perhaps something else. These vague references are really not surprising when we consider that even trained philosophers have widely differing views on the nature of normativity.

If we leave aside deontological issues of rights, obligations, and so forth, focusing instead only on goodness, how should we distinguish *moral* goodness from other types of goodness? My answer is that morality ends up a fuzzy-edged concept, not allowing for a sharp distinction between the moral and the nonmoral. For purposes of my larger project, I do not think the distinction between moral and nonmoral goodness is of any importance. But given that many people do ascribe a special importance to the "morally good," I shall offer a very general way to make the distinction (while also accounting for the special status often afforded to the morally good).

When philosophers think of an act or state of affairs as *morally* good, they often claim that its value stems from being an act or state of affairs of a certain kind. R. M. Hare remarked that "moral statements are made about actions for *reasons*, namely that the actions have certain non-moral properties. An act is wrong, e.g., *because* it is an act of hurting somebody for fun" (1997, 126). Hare (along with many other philosophers) follows Kant in thinking that the properties in question are *universalizable*—that is, they make reference only to persons of a certain *type*, not to specific individuals by name. Thus, if it is morally good for me to give money to my starving neighbor, this entails that it would be good for anyone in my position to give money to anyone in my neighbor's position. In section 6.1 I shall discuss whether the properties involved in moral judgments really are universalizable or whether there is a better way to characterize them. (To anticipate, I think there is a better way.) However, our focus in this section is on the way in which one might distinguish judgments about moral value from other types of evaluative judgments. Though I again do not think that much, if anything, hangs on this distinction, we are considering at present how this distinction is commonly made. And it is admittedly useful to look at how universalizable properties might be seen as serving as a basis for identifying certain things as morally good.

Even if we suppose that moral judgments are made in virtue of perceived universal properties, the first thing to note is that this would not by itself be enough to distinguish moral judgments from other evaluative judgments. A person might believe that it is always a good thing to serve white wine with fish. This judgment, while universalizable in the relevant sense, is one of *taste*. Also, a person might believe that the statement "Thank you," accompanied by an offer of a handshake, should always be returned with the statement "You're welcome" and a grasp of the hand. Such a universal judgment, rather than being moral, seems to be one of *etiquette*.

A common attempt at this point to distinguish moral judgments from nonmoral judgments is to say that moral judgments have the property of, as Hare puts it, "overridingness" (see Hare 1963, §9.3; Hare 1981, 53f.). Hare illustrates overridingness by imagining a conflict "between the aesthetic principle that one ought not to juxtapose scarlet with magenta, and the moral principle that one ought not to hurt one's wife's feelings, in a case in which my wife has given me a magenta cushion to put on my scarlet sofa in my room in college" (1981, 55; cf. Hare 1963, §9.3). In such a case, we would of course think that the moral principle should override the aesthetic one.

So does it help us distinguish moral principles from nonmoral principles by saying that moral principles are the ones that are overriding? This move is actually no help at all. In terms of providing a definition of *moral*, the claim that moral considerations are overriding is, by itself, an empty one. We need to know *why* they are overriding.

In answering this question, it is first important to notice the connection between the ideas of good taste or etiquette and our familiar notion of flourishing. The reason one makes an evaluative judgment that people should always serve white wine with fish is perhaps that one believes that red wine overpowers the flavor of fish. Or perhaps one believes that fish dishes are best appreciated with a chilled drink. Whatever the reason, a universalizable evaluative judgment of taste will be made in virtue of what one believes will promote enjoyment and well-being—in sum, will promote flourishing—of some kind in all people who may be in some particular situation. Likewise, rules of etiquette are designed to promote human flourishing. Etiquette guidelines help us relate smoothly to one another in ways that comfortingly reinforce agreed-upon social structures; and they help us avoid embarrassment and uncertainty in social situations.

Having seen that evaluative judgments of taste and etiquette are justified by appealing to that which helps us flourish, let me now give an answer to the question of what distinguishes these judgments from *moral* judgments. The only real answer here is straightforward, if very general: moral judgments involve the *really important* aspects of people's (or creatures') flourishing. A certain color scheme in the living room might be judged to be good as a matter of taste. In aiding our aesthetic enjoyment of our homes, it promotes our flourishing. A thank-you note might be judged to be good as a matter of etiquette, for it goes some way toward promoting healthy relationships and thus our flourishing. Moral judgments are made along these same lines. The difference is that, in making a *moral* judgment that some object or event is good, we see the object or event as *significantly* promoting our flourishing.[17]

Matters of taste have the potential to become moral issues if what is at stake involves a significant enough aspect of human well-being. Consider the case of Gwynne, who hosts a dinner party to which her coworkers are the invited guests. With fish on the menu for the evening, Gwynne might believe that, as a matter of taste, one should always serve white wine with fish. The reason, let us assume for now, is that white wine brings out the flavor of fish better than red wine does. But suppose Gwynne discovers she is out of white wine, just two hours before the dinner is scheduled to be served. She could manage a quick trip to the local wine shop and still complete her dinner preparations; but adding this extra task would make her preparations difficult and very stressful. If in the end Gwynne decides to forego the shopping trip and just serve the red wine she has in the cupboard, her choice of wine will not be "good" as a matter of taste. Yet surely no one would view her choice as a *morally* bad one.

But suppose that the reason Gwynne thinks it good to serve white wine is that the particular fish dish she is serving has the peculiar effect of causing slight indigestion for those who eat it—unless the fish is accompanied by the acidity of a dry, white wine. Does Gwynne's decision to serve the red wine constitute a *morally* bad decision? We probably will still be inclined to say that it does not. But what if her dish tends to cause moderate indigestion for those who eat it and—to explain in our example why the guests would drink red wine along with the fish—that Gwynne, but not her guests, knows that it has this effect? What if her dish tends to cause severe indigestion? At some point Gwynne's decision becomes an obviously moral one (again, as the term *moral* is employed in common usage). If we imagine Gwynne as knowing that the combination of fish and red wine will probably hospitalize her coworkers with severe stomach cramps, then Gwynne's decision to serve red wine will reflect a morally objectionable attitude of indifference toward her coworkers' well-being.

Where, then, do we draw the line in these examples between matters of taste and matters of morality? The answer is that there is no obvious place to draw the line; and different people will draw the line in different places—according to what they perceive as being crucial to our flourishing. As I suggested earlier, morality is a fuzzy-edged concept. In almost any example of an evaluative judgment regarding taste, we can make the judgment into a moral one by supposing that a great deal of human flourishing is at stake. Take a living room's color scheme that one judges to be aesthetically "good" because it promotes a feeling of cheer. The goodness or badness of the color scheme becomes a moral issue if we suppose that alternative color schemes somehow bring on long-term clinical depression. If any designer privately knew this and chose not to paint with a cheerful color for her client, the public consensus would surely be that she was guilty of a bad moral decision and not simply bad taste. In identifying a criterion as to when people cease to call an issue one of *taste*, and instead call it a *moral* issue, we can give only the general qualification that a moral issue is one that is judged to be *really important* to the flourishing of someone's life.

Matters of etiquette can similarly rise to the level of moral issues when the effects of keeping (or breaking) rules of etiquette are seen as significantly promoting (or undermining) people's flourishing. In commenting on the overlap between moral considerations and those of etiquette, D. Z. Phillips asks us to consider "behavior while eating food where gracelessness of sufficient extremity becomes the indecent and the gross." Phillips remarks that "the censure due in such cases is certainly a moral censure. What can be said of the style of a man in such circumstances constitutes a comment on his moral character" (1977, 147).

To see again the difficulties with trying to specify the point at which a violation of a rule of etiquette becomes a morally bad thing, consider the rule that profanity should be used sparingly, if at all, in social settings. We would typically consider the use of profanity at a formal dinner party a breach of etiquette, but probably nothing more. By contrast, we would all agree that a string of profanity publicly directed at a small child at a children's birthday party would be a moral outrage. Yet a coach of a professional sports team who loudly castigates a player with plenty of profanity during a team practice will not do anything morally wrong in the eyes of the players, who may view the coach's behavior as at most marginally ill-mannered. The difference between a breach of etiquette and a bona fide "moral" wrongdoing has to do with the extent to which the other party is affected. If a coach knew that a particular player was very fragile emotionally—perhaps because mourning the death of a parent—and that any criticism would at present cause a great deal of distress, then the coach's profane chastisement *would* be viewed as a morally bad thing. The line between a severe breach of etiquette (where the other party is said to be offended) and a *moral* offense (where the other party can likewise be said to be offended) is one of degree. We can again say no more than that moral offenses are ones that *really* hurt others.

Philippa Foot offers an example from Dostoevski's *The Brothers Karamazov* that may appear to cast doubt on the thesis that people always view moral considerations to be of more importance than considerations of etiquette. The example involves Father Zosima; and Foot's summary of Dostoevski's character is as follows:

> As a young man Zosima had provoked another officer, simply because he was jealous of him, and forced him to issue a challenge. However, realising that his conduct has been disgraceful he waits until the other man has shot at him and then, when it is his turn to shoot, throws away his pistol and apologises. The seconds are furious about this breach of the rules, and the following exchange takes place:
> I stood facing them and now I addressed them all seriously:

"Gentlemen," I said, "is it really so surprising these days to meet a man who can admit he has done something stupid and apologise publicly for the wrong he has done?"

"But you cannot apologise in the middle of a duel" my second shouted at me angrily. (Foot 1978a, 185)

Foot's suggestion is that the seconds might recognize that morality calls for an apology; and they might also care about morality. Nonetheless, it is entirely possible that they view adherence to dueling rules as more important.

Does this example show that people can give matters of etiquette more importance than matters of morality? Toward answering that question, I think we should ask why the seconds are outraged. We will assume that the outrage does not simply stem from the shock of what has happened; rather, the seconds reflectively find it objectionable to follow the call of morality to apologize in the middle of a duel. Why are the rules of dueling so important to preserve? Perhaps the seconds would say that Zosima's honor is at stake, as well as the honor of the other officer and perhaps the stability of the institution of dueling itself. Why is honor so important, along with an institution that affords individuals the means to preserve their honor when it is challenged? The answer is no doubt that honor is considered an integral part of a flourishing life by those in the social circle of Dostoevski's characters.

It seems plausible, then, to respond to Foot's example by maintaining that the seconds *do* think of adherence to, and preservation of, dueling rules as moral issues. If they would fail to call it a moral issue, this is simply because the term *moral*—whose meaning, like other words, stems from its conventional use among competent speakers of the language—does not in most people's view extend to considerations of the kind of honor that would be preserved in a duel. After all, even in Western cultures where dueling has been actively practiced, the social circle of practitioners has typically been quite limited. If, as Foot suggests, the seconds recognize that morality requires an apology in the midst of the duel, then they understand by "morality" the issues that the *larger society* recognizes as moral. If the society had been composed entirely of people who, like the seconds, viewed dueling rules as fundamental to the preservation of healthy relationships of integrity, then the upholding of dueling rules *would* surely be seen as a "morally" good thing. As evidence for this conclusion, consider how in some Eastern cultures issues relating to honor play a very prominent role in the kind of acute guilt, praise, and shame we commonly associate with moral behavior. A public accusation of dishonor in such a culture would be widely viewed as a severe threat to one's social standing and overall welfare. Accordingly, an unwarranted accusation of dishonor would be viewed as a serious moral breach. In other cultures, though, it might be viewed as an ineffective, almost comical, way of trying to undermine another person ("You think I lack *honor*? So what?")—and thus at most a breach of etiquette on par with any general act of public name-calling.

We noted earlier in this section that defining moral issues in terms of their *overridingness* is empty. Still, the insight behind this attempt to define the "moral" is that the issues to which our use of the term *moral* refer will be those issues that we consider of utmost importance to our flourishing. Is smoking a moral issue? If enough people view it as having consequences of great enough importance to our flourishing, then the term *moral* can indeed, by linguistic conventions, be attributed to the decision whether to smoke. If not, then the term *moral* will not apply. Of course, one might wish to wage a personal campaign that we *should* view the issue of smoking as a moral issue. But this campaign amounts to an argument that smoking is a vital enough issue to the well-being of people that it merits inclusion among the issues that we think of as "moral" issues. Without widespread support for this campaign, the meaning of *moral* will not extend to the decision whether to smoke. After all, an individual has not by herself the power to change the conventional use of public language.

### 1.6 Closing Moore's Open Question

My account of the concept "good" in this chapter has been reductive. I have contended that we understand this concept in terms of a further, epistemically prior understanding of what it is to flourish. The idea that we can define *goodness* in other terms has been challenged by various philosophers, most notably G. E. Moore. Moore insisted that the concept "good" is not composed of various parts that might be individually described so as to give a clearer picture of the thing as a whole—as when we describe the parts of a horse to give someone unacquainted with horses a better idea of what a horse is. Instead, he maintained "that 'good' is a simple notion, just as 'yellow' is a simple notion; that, just as you cannot, by any manner of means, explain to any one who does not already know it what yellow is, so you cannot explain what good is" (1993, §7). For Moore, "good" was a simple, unanalyzable concept; and to attempt to define it in other terms was to commit the famed "naturalistic fallacy."

The term *naturalistic* is notoriously difficult to define without begging some question or other. Still, a fairly standard working definition is given by Moore himself as "that which is the subject-matter of the natural sciences and also of psychology" (1993, §7). In the next chapter I will offer a naturalistic analysis of the *nature* of the good. Our concern in this chapter is with the meaning of *good*. My conclusions in this chapter are also naturalistic in that I think the concept "good" can be spelled out in terms of answering to someone's interests, a situation we understand by relating it to our own positive mental experiences as our interests are furthered.

In truth, it is not most pointedly *naturalism* to which Moore objected. Rather, his objection was to any form of reductionism.[18] The good is, again for Moore, an unanalyzable concept; and we come to form beliefs about things being good by a kind of moral intuition. As proof that the concept "good" could not possibly be given a reductive analysis, Moore pressed his famous *open question* argument against the reductionist. Sticking with naturalistic reductions, Moore's argument proceeds as follows. Take any natural property $X$, such as "maximizes happiness" or "satisfies desires" or "promotes flourishing." For someone who understands the concept "good" and the concept $X$, it will always be intelligible to ask: "I accept that a certain action is $X$, but is it good?" (1993, §13). The fact that this is an intelligible question shows, according to Moore, that "good" cannot be given a reductive, conceptual analysis in terms of any naturalistic property.

What should we make of Moore's open-question argument? Before offering my own answer to Moore, I should mention one popular naturalistic response to Moore that, I shall argue, ultimately proves unsatisfactory. This popular response is to claim that a naturalistic definition of *good* need not reveal something that is known to every competent user of the term *good*. One can be a competent user of the word *water* even if one does not know that the composition of water is $H_2O$; and one can identify gold even if one does not know that gold is atomic number 79. Similarly, so this line of response goes, one can grasp the sense of, and competently use, the term *good* even if one does not understand that goodness, on closer analysis, is identical to a naturalistic property (such as "maximizes happiness").

This response makes use of Gottlob Frege's famous distinction within the philosophy of language between *sense* and *reference* (see Frege 1997). The term *water* and the term $H_2O$ both make the same reference. That is, they both refer to the same substance. Our current, best understanding of the meaning of the word *water* is, of course, $H_2O$. However, this fact in no way kept those who lived before the scientific discovery of hydrogen and oxygen molecules from being able to identify the substance water and competently use the term *water*. These earlier people had at least *some* sense of what water is, being familiar with what water looks like and how it behaves: a colorless liquid that can freeze, dissolve salt, and so forth.

Moore's point against naturalism is that, if the term *good* really were reducible by conceptual analysis to some description in natural terms, then we could never reasonably question whether an object with this natural property also had the property *good*. Such a matter would already be settled. The naturalistic response to Moore we are now considering insists: from the fact that we can competently use the term *good* in describing things, it does not follow that the meaning of *good* is permanently settled. The description "good" *fixes the reference* for some property we might go on to analyze further—just as calling the liquid in some glass "water" fixes the reference for a substance we might go on to analyze further. Upon examination, we might find that there are *additional* descriptions of, respectively, this property *good* and this substance *water*. In the case of water, we find that this additional description is "$H_2O$"; in the case of good, we find that this additional description is something naturalistic (such as "maximizes our happiness" or "fulfills our desires"). Just as we should think of "$H_2O$" as our clearest statement of the meaning of *water*, so the naturalistic response to Moore goes, so we should think of the naturalist's stipulated naturalistic property as our clearest statement of the meaning of *good*.

Let me now summarize our naturalist's response to Moore's open-question argument before stating why I think the response is flawed. The response is, again, that we can all be competent users of the term *good* and still engage in a meaningful discussion as to whether the essence of goodness is best captured in further, naturalistic terms. After all, it was at one time for scientists an open question whether *water* and $H_2O$ referred to the same thing. An early nineteenth-century chemist might have grasped the sense of *water* and the sense of $H_2O$; but it would have been at the time an open question to the chemist whether these two descriptions referred to the same thing. So, from the fact that we can debate whether the term *good* and, for example, the term *maximizes happiness* both refer to the same property, it does not follow that the naturalist is incorrect when she explains that each of these terms does indeed fix the reference for a single property. True, we will not arrive *by conceptual analysis* of the term *good* at the conclusion that *good* and, say, *maximizes happiness* refer to the same property. So our naturalist will not affirm what we might call *definitional*, or *analytic*, naturalism. Nevertheless, our naturalist can affirm (by a posteriori exploration) what is popularly called *synthetic* naturalism—a thesis that in no way is undermined by our ability to question whether naturalistic terms really do explain the essence of the property of goodness.

Although synthetic naturalism offers an interesting line of response to Moore's open-question argument, it turns out to be a deeply flawed response. The reason has to do with how we come to understand the term *good*. Synthetic naturalism supposes that a person can grasp some sense of *good* without necessarily grasping the sense of *maximizing happiness*, or *fulfilling desires*, or whatever the preferred naturalistic explanation is of goodness. Or, at least, one can grasp the sense of these separate terms without recognizing that they both refer to the same property. To use one of Frege's examples, I can hold in my mind one concept of "the morning star" and another concept of "the evening star" without recognizing that they both refer to the same object (i.e., the planet Venus). Analogously, argues the synthetic naturalist, we can arrive at a concept of goodness without appealing to the concept of some naturalistic property—even though there exists in the end only a single property whose reference is fixed both by the description *good* and by this naturalistic description.

However, this analogy does not hold. If the arguments of this chapter are correct, we come to understand the concept of goodness by referencing in some way our own experiences of flourishing. Thus it is emphatically *not* the case that we could ever grasp the sense of *good* without also having an appreciation for what it is to flourish. In the example of water and $H_2O$, one can grasp the sense of *water* without grasping the sense of $H_2O$. But for any competent user of the term *good*, her concept of goodness will be derivative of her understanding of flourishing. The concept "promoting flourishing" does not simply fix the reference of a property that may or may not be identical with the property of goodness. Rather, we arrive *by conceptual analysis* at the truth that the property of goodness is used by speakers of the language to identify that which promotes flourishing (i.e., that which answers to someone's interests). Admittedly, a competent user of the term *good* may not be aware of the philosophical point that her own concept of goodness is actually derivative of her epistemically prior concept of what it is to flourish. But my arguments have been that, on *some* level of consciousness, we must draw on our contrasting experiences of flourishing and failing to flourish in order to appreciate the contrasting concepts "good" and "bad."

The upshot of this discussion is that synthetic naturalism does not represent a satisfactory response to Moore's open-question argument. For it does not acknowledge the conceptual connection between goodness and flourishing on which we draw, at some level of consciousness, in forming our conception of goodness.

In contrast to synthetic naturalism, what term best characterizes the type of naturalism I have sought to outline? The term *analytic naturalism* is the obvious alternative; and it is indeed true that, on my account, the meaning of *good* is necessarily linked with the meaning of *flourishing*. However, the term *analytic naturalism* seems perhaps to suggest too simple a link between something that is good and something that promotes flourishing. As we saw in section 1.3, the link between goodness and flourishing needs a good deal of spelling out when it comes to such complications as an imagined person's flourishing (e.g., when I refer to the good seats in an empty theater) or a derivative use of the term *good* (e.g., when I refer to a good amount of rain). I prefer the term *conceptual naturalism* as a description for the account of the meaning of *good* that I have put forward. On my account, talk of things that are "good" can be reduced by conceptual analysis—again, with the nuances outlined in the first four sections of this chapter—to talk of things that promote people's flourishing.

A statement Moore made about naturalism helps clarify how my naturalist account differs from a strict, analytic kind of naturalism. In arguing against a naturalistic analysis of "good," Moore at one point remarked that "no difficulty need be found in my saying that 'pleasure is good'; but one need not mean "that 'pleasure' is the same thing as 'good,' that pleasure *means* good, and that good *means* pleasure" (1993, §12). This remark from Moore would not constitute any challenge to my own account of the meaning of *good*. I am in no way committed to saying that *good* is synonymous with *flourishing* and that the two terms can be used interchangeably. That is, I am in no way claiming that talk about goodness can be reduced to talk about flourishing *and* that talk about flourishing can be reduced to talk about goodness. Against any proposal involving the latter kind of reductionism, we can note that the concept of flourishing may have a number of facets: phenomenological, anthropological, psychological, and so forth. Only some of these facets may be adequately captured by the notion of "good."

Having settled the kind of naturalism at stake in my discussion, let me return to Moore's argument against naturalism. If the kind of conceptual naturalism I have advanced is correct, then Moore's open-question argument is rendered ineffectual. Suppose the meaning of the term *good* is linked, as I have maintained, with the idea of answering to someone's interests, or promoting someone's flourishing. We might now apply the form of Moore's open-question argument and consider the possibility that someone might ask: "I accept that action *A* promotes my flourishing (or the flourishing of someone whose possible experiences I relate to my own), but is *A* good?" Is this an open question?

The answer is that it depends on how the question is read: whether as a question about the *meaning* of "good" or about the *nature* of good things. If the question is read as asking the kind of question Moore intended to ask, then the question is decidedly *not* an open one. Moore intended the question as a test for claims about the meaning of *good*. Indeed, Moore began his critique of naturalism by acknowledging the possibility of giving a naturalistic description of the *nature* of good things. That is, he did not object to the idea of using naturalistic terms to answer the question "What sorts of things are good?" Rather, his objection aims at naturalistic answers to the question, "not what thing or things are good, but how 'good' is to be defined" (Moore 1993, §5. Cf. §9 and §12). His focus here is on the concept of goodness itself. My own answer to the relevant question here is again that we understand the concept "good" ultimately in terms of our own experiences of flourishing.

To assess this answer, we would need to ask whether the following question is open: "I know what it is for something to promote flourishing, but are things that promote flourishing good?" If the conceptual analysis of "good" that I have advanced is correct, this question is decidedly *not* an open one. For, if the arguments of the first four sections of this chapter are correct, *goodness* is simply a general term we use to denote the fact that some object or event promotes our flourishing (i.e., furthers our interests) or the flourishing of others whose experiences we relate to our own. So any competent user of the terms *flourishing* and *good* cannot fail to see—at least, when properly aware of how we humans are able to form our concept of goodness—that something that is "good" will, by definition, be something that promotes someone's flourishing. Thus my conclusion again is that Moore's open-question argument is ineffectual against the conceptual analysis of "good" that I have advanced.

Unfortunately, the form of Moore's open-question argument may be read as asking something *other* than the question of the previous paragraph. Consider again the following articulation of Moore's open-question argument: "I accept that action *A* promotes my flourishing (or the flourishing of someone whose possible experiences I relate to my own), but is *A* good?" If this question is understood as asking about the *nature* of the good—either a substantive question of whether some actual object is good or a formal question as to what would need to occur for an object to be good—then the question is indeed an open one. But in the present context it would be improper to ask such questions about the nature of the good. After all, it will be remembered, these sorts of questions are the very ones Moore originally insisted he was *not* pressing the naturalist to answer.

Perhaps in the simplest of cases we could close Moore's open question, even while reading it as a question about the nature of the good. If

I believed that some action *A* promoted my own flourishing, and if this was the only relevant consideration in my assessment of *A*, then I would naturally view *A* as being good. If I believed that some action *A* promoted the flourishing of someone whose interests I had made my own, and if we again assume this to be my only consideration, then I would see *A* as good. And if I believed that *A* promoted the flourishing of someone with interests I merely imagined, then, all things being equal, I would once again view *A* as good (though I would not have an accompanying pro-attitude toward *A*). However, in the judging of whether some action, object, or event is good, things are rarely so simple. Two main complications arise in typical judgments.

First, there is the question of where our (and others') true flourishing actually lies. Does, for example, inheriting a huge amount of money at the age of twenty typically help someone to flourish? People will have different answers to this question, depending on whether they associate a person's flourishing with the ease of his life or with the development of his character; with his immediate happiness or with the development of his long-term relationships; and so on. Disagreements here are over the question of how a given individual might flourish. The second complicating question involves the matter of *whose* flourishing we are considering. In making an all-things-considered judgment as to whether some action *A* is good, we may well view *A* as promoting *my* interests— but not the interests of someone else about whom I care. In such a case, whether I judge *A* to be, all things considered, a *good* action will depend on such things as whether my values run more toward egoism or toward altruism.

So any number of possible complications can arise when we try to answer the substantive question "I know that action *A* promotes my flourishing (or the flourishing of someone whose possible experiences I relate to my own), but is *A* good?" Because of these complications, this question admittedly will typically be an open one for competent users of the terms *good* and *flourishing*. But this fact has no bearing on the matter of whether the *concept* "good" can be understood by reference to the concept "flourishing." This conceptual matter is, as I have argued, closed. Moore's open-question argument is no objection at all to the conceptual analysis of "good" I have offered. Any appearance to the contrary stems from the failure to maintain the distinction between questions about the meaning of "good" and questions about the nature of the good.

## 1.7 The Place of Semantic Analysis

In the next chapter I will explore the question of which things are good—that is, the question of the nature of the good. One way of focusing this discussion would be to build on the conclusions of this chapter. *Goodness* is a term denoting that something answers to someone's interests. Straightforwardly, an analysis of the nature of goodness would then focus on the question of what *does* in fact answer to people's interests, or promote their flourishing.

Discussions historically about the nature of goodness, however, have often called for (or assumed) a metaphysically richer understanding of the good. This point seems especially true of ethical frameworks offered by Christian theists. Commenting on the view that "God *just is* the ultimate Good," David Baggett and Jerry Walls remark that this view "has a venerable history within Christianity. Thomists, Anselmians, theistic Platonists, and theistic activists, including such contemporary analytic philosophers as Alvin Plantinga and Robert Adams, all concur that on a Christian understanding of reality, God and the ultimate Good are ontologically inseparable" (2011, 92).[19]

But why should the Christian theist embrace something like a Platonic ontology of the Good, revising the Platonic picture at points so that God can play certain roles that the Good plays in Plato's explanation of how our universe operates? Plato was of course interested in such questions as how our experience of the universe is one of sameness and of difference. His theory of forms is one quite particular attempt at an explanation. But why follow Plato in thinking that "the Good" has some ontological status other than a reference to the state of affairs of someone flourishing?

I would want to extend a similar caution about what Christian theists should and should not read into God's recorded declaration in Genesis that the world God created was good.[20] Admittedly, this declaration *could* be interpreted as a pronouncement that every living and nonliving thing possessed a property of "goodness," irrespective of any impact on anyone's flourishing.[21] But why privilege such an interpretation? The Hebrew root word translated as "good" in the Genesis passage in question, *tôḇ*, has very wide connotations. I would say they are hopelessly wide, if one's aim is to extract ontological implications about the good from the use of this evaluative word. One dictionary of biblical Hebrew words notes that *tôḇ* "means 'good' in the broadest sense possible. It includes the beautiful, the attractive, the useful, the profitable, the desirable, the morally right."[22] And if we look more broadly at the six hundred or so passages in our English Bibles in which the word *good* is used, we find an array of contexts, with no attempt to offer philosophical precision as to what the word does and does not denote. As another dictionary of biblical words indicates, the uses of the word *good* throughout the Bible "are clearly prephilosophical in content." They "generally reflect ordinary uses of the term" and "do not seek to clarify 'the good' in distinction from other moral categories, such as 'right' or 'appropriate,' or to develop some kind of value theory or alternative philosophical hypothesis."[23] My summary point, in looking at God's evaluative use of the term *good* in Genesis, as well as the use of that term through the Christian scriptures, is that a variety of philosophical positions on the meaning of *good*—and on the nature of the good—cannot automatically be ruled out. One could of course *begin* with an ontology (Platonic or otherwise) of the good that leads us to conclude that, for example, God's evaluation of the whole of creation in Genesis must be an allusion to a property of our world not reducible to the way it answers to the interests of sentient creatures and beings. But I cannot see how one could plausibly begin with this recorded evaluative statement in Genesis and *draw out* such a conclusion.

This chapter of course contains my own methodology for reaching conclusions about the meaning of *good*; and I think these conclusions provide at least some prima facie indication as to the nature of the good (which is the subject of the next chapter). However, authors like Adams, Baggett, and Walls warn about putting too much stock in the kind of semantic analysis outlined in this chapter. They point to examples of the kind discussed in the previous section—for example, *water* and $H_2O$ referring to the same thing, though a competent user of the term *water* may not know this. A competent user of the term *good* may not mean anything having to do with God. However, these authors stress, it might still be the case that the best analysis of the nature of goodness will yield the conclusion that the good "just is" God.

But, again, why should we think that there is *more* to the nature of goodness than—following the semantic analysis of this chapter—states of affairs in which people flourish, or have their interests answered to? Baggett and Walls disclose, "We are inclined to think that the ultimate ontological inseparableness of God and the Good is something of an axiomatic Anselmian intuition; a vision apprehended, not just the deliverance of a discursive argument" (2011, 93). In response to this intuitive appeal, I would point out that the appeal seems to work most naturally with a Moorean conception of the good as a simple, unanalyzable concept. However, I have of course argued in this chapter that we *can* analyze the concept of goodness. Specifically, I have argued that we understand this concept by drawing from our understanding of our contrasting experiences of flourishing versus failing to flourish. While semantic analysis does not decisively settle the matter of how we should understand the nature of goodness, surely we would do well not to ignore the direction at which semantic analysis points.

Adams considers our common use of the term *good*, but he concludes that a semantic analysis points in a different direction than I have concluded. He begins by noting Plato's reference to the Good in the *Republic*. "Nobody is satisfied to acquire things that are merely believed to be good, however, but everyone wants the things that really *are* good and disdains mere belief here. . . . Every soul . . . divines that the good is something but it is perplexed and cannot adequately grasp what it is" (Plato 1992, bk. VI, §505d–e, 179). Explicating Plato's idea of people "pursuing" the good, even while not "adequately grasping what it is," Adams remarks that "presumably they are competent users of the word 'good' (or ἀγαθός in Greek), and understand (at least roughly and implicitly) whatever is given by the sense of that word, but do not know the nature of the good" (1999, 16). So far, I myself might adopt these points and suggest that people have a pro-attitude toward their own flourishing and others about whom they care and that people accordingly pursue this flourishing, even though the substantive formula for a life of unambiguous flourishing continually proves elusive.

Adams concludes that competent users of the term *good* search for something different when they search for the good. He first makes clear that he is talking only of a particular meaning that *good* has in certain contexts.

> Beauty is clearly a species of good for Plato, and the role assigned to the Beautiful in the *Symposium* is recognizably a version of the role that belongs to a more general (and still transcendent) Good in the *Republic*. What sort of good is at issue here? It is not *usefulness*, or merely instrumental goodness. It is not *well-being*, or what is good for a person. It is rather the goodness of that which is worthy of love or admiration. We have no word that in common usage signifies precisely and uniquely this kind of goodness; I shall refer to it often (though not always happily) as "excellence," and sometimes . . . simply as "goodness" or the "good." (1999, 13–14)

Adams then suggests that the way we speak of goodness in this context "treats it as a *property*, and as one that objects of evaluation possess (or lack) independently of whether we now think they do. . . . Our keeping an eye out for possible corrections of our views is an important part of the seriousness of evaluative discourse. These considerations strongly favor *realism* about the good; as candidates for the role of the good, that is, they favor properties possessed *objectively*" (1999, 18).

Does our use of the term *good* typically treat goodness as an objective property? If so, then does this semantic analysis point us in the direction of the kind of analysis of the nature of the good Adams favors: one in which God serves the role of an *exemplar* of goodness/excellence, with finite things being good inasmuch as they resemble this exemplar of personified, infinite goodness?

To clarify what is at stake in our discussion, I do not at present want to provide a full range of reasons for concluding that goodness lies in particular states of affairs, linked with people's flourishing. (I will provide further arguments for this conclusion in the next chapter, when I offer my own account of the nature of the good.) At present our concern is solely with the implications of a semantic analysis of *good*. My claim has been that, since *good* is a term used to denote that something answers to someone's interests, then the search for those things that *are* in fact good will be, prima facie, a search for those things that do in fact further someone's interests, or promote someone's flourishing. However, if a better semantic analysis is that we use *good* to denote a "property possessed objectively," then the search for good things plausibly becomes, prima facie, a search for how things in and of themselves measure up to some standard or resemble some exemplar. But do we often think of things as possessing the property of goodness "objectively"?

As an initial acknowledgment, if we look at the structure of people's sentences when they describe objects, we often find the pattern Adams suggests. We refer to a "good piece of music" or a "good floral arrangement." And when contemplating the value we place on these things, I acknowledge that our attention may be focused simply on the intrinsic qualities of the thing itself. However, I would quickly draw attention back to the point, discussed in section 1.4 in connection with the "paradox of Hedonism": our pro-attitude toward these objects stems from the mental experiences we have as we contemplate them. A semantic analysis of *good* cannot merely explore the structure of sentences that commonly contain this term in colloquial use.[24] It also has to explore how we came to *have* the concept "good," which we may then apply in various ways.

The critic at this point may say, "Fair enough. Perhaps we *learn* the concept 'good' by referencing in some way our experiences of flourishing. But the fact is: we can be aware of this point and still use the term to refer to things we think have value in virtue of their intrinsic properties."[25] My response at this point is twofold. First, I have doubts as to how often people really do value objects, quite apart from any perceived effects the objects have on their own or others' flourishing. Second, in examples where people *do* insist that objects are intrinsically valuable in their own right, the intrinsic properties of these objects usually are just not plausible candidates for inherent value. Let me expand in turn on these two lines of response.

Is it common for us to value things, quite apart from any perceived effects on anyone's flourishing? Thomas Nagel offers his own view on this matter. He does not focus his discussion so much on whether we commonly think of *objects* or *actions* as being intrinsically valuable. Rather, he thinks a strong case can be made that it is the *achievement* of having created certain objects or performed certain actions that people frequently recognize as intrinsically good. Nagel concludes that we fre-

The Meaning of *Good* 51

quently assign intrinsic value to creations and achievements "apart from their value *to* individuals" who experience or use them:

> Examples are provided by the intrinsic value of scientific discovery, or artistic creation, of space exploration, perhaps. These pursuits do of course serve the interests of the individuals directly involved in them, and of certain spectators. But typically the pursuit of such ends is not justified solely in terms of those interests. They are thought to have an intrinsic value, so that it is important to achieve fundamental advance, for example, in mathematics or astronomy even if very few people come to understand them and they have no practical effects. The mere existence of such understanding, somewhere in the species, is regarded by many as worth substantial sacrifices. (1979a, 129–30)

Before contending here that part of our motivation to pursue scientific discoveries stems from the way we recognize the intrinsic value of these pursuits, Nagel acknowledges early in the passage that we do think that these pursuits typically "serve the interests" of certain people. His contention, though, is that this consideration is not sufficient to explain why we value things like scientific discovery as we do. But let us not pass too quickly over this consideration, ignoring some of the less obvious ways in which research in the sciences might be defended on the grounds that it is good *for* people.

Advancements in science can have positive effects on public morale. More specifically, it can foster public confidence in a government's or a scientific community's ability to meet the challenges of the future. And when advancements come as a result of public funding and collaboration between agencies, a sense of solidarity within communities large and small is often created. As one example here, consider the effects of the completion of the Human Genome Project. Also, there is a sense in which citizens live vicariously through individuals in the areas of science (and art, literature, sports, and so forth). If I feel linked in some way to those individuals who make scientific breakthroughs, then their achievements in a sense feel as though they are my achievements. Consider, for instance, the intense pride felt by citizens of the United States and the USSR during the so-called space race of the 1950s and 1960s when successful explorations into space were conducted within their respective nations. In addition, because advancements in science, mathematics, and astronomy have often brought with them important, though unexpected, benefits, it seems reasonable to defend research in these areas by pointing out that we simply do not currently know the ways in which this research may prove to have great practical significance to future efforts to solve problems we have yet to identify. In adopting a pro-attitude toward scientific achievement, most people surely have at least some awareness of most of these ways in which science does, or at least may, aid human flourishing. Once we exclude all the ways in which scientific (or artistic) achievement might aid human flourishing, I think most people would be at a loss to explain why achievements are valuable "for their own sake."

Still, I acknowledge that people do at times report thinking that objects and achievements have intrinsic value. Consider a person who assigns value to a prominent, old tree in the middle of a town center. When public debates arise about whether to cut down the tree to make way for a new shopping mall, the person may advocate preserving the tree. His motivation, let us suppose, is not that he will enjoy seeing the tree or even that he will enjoy knowing that the tree remains in the town center. Perhaps he will soon be moving from the area and does not plan on keeping up with the developments of the town.

In accounting for this example, it may be the case that the person's view is, in some sense, an unreflective view. For instance, the person may have been told by a parent or some other trusted authority that the tree is valuable in its own right, and the person may simply have formed the belief that this is so—without further reflection on why this should be so. Alternatively, the person's attitude toward the tree may be explained in terms of our tendency to personalize objects as we interact with them. Both children and adults may talk to a tattered teddy bear, saying "Sorry, old fella," when a button eye comes off in the wash, and saying "This will fix you up" when we are sewing the eye back on. W. D. Ross commented that, when we speak of "good" activities and objects, we are "half-personalizing" them and "transferring to non-persons the meaning of 'good' appropriate to persons" (1930, 66).

Notwithstanding these possible explanations, the person who values the old tree may still insist that he has reflected on the matter and that what he values about the tree are the intrinsic qualities of the object. I want to address the plausibility of a tree's intrinsic qualities having value. But I do not want to restrict my discussion to trees. So we might ask at this point: What range of objects can most plausibly be cited as examples in which people will claim merely to be recognizing value that already exists within an object? Let us look at a list that Adams provides. In his explanation of the kind of "goodness" at stake in his own semantic analysis of the term, he remarks that his interest is in "the type of goodness exemplified by the beauty of a sunset, a painting, or a mathematical proof, or by the greatness of a novel, the nobility of an unselfish deed, or the quality of an athletic or a philosophical performance. It is the goodness of that which is worthy of love or admiration, honor or worship, rather than the good (for herself) that is possessed by one who is fortunate or happy, as such (though happiness may also be excellent, and worthy of admiration)" (1999, 83). If we examine the intrinsic qualities of the things on Adams's list, is it plausible to think that they have intrinsic *value*?

Let us begin with mathematical proofs, which are indeed sometimes described by mathematicians as elegant. What intrinsic quality might we identify as itself elegant, or excellent, or good? Perhaps the suggestion will be that we recognize the *simplicity* of a mathematical proof. But why should we view simplicity as a kind of elegance? Presumably, the reasons have to do with the (contingent) human need to make sense of the world around us;[26] the desire to find order and patterns; and the reassurance we feel when we find symmetry and, indeed, simplicity. Aside from these effects that perceived simplicity has *on* us, is it plausible to think that there is something intrinsically valuable to *simplicity itself*? I myself find no force behind an intuitive appeal to simplicity as something that is of value in its own right.

Similar points could be made about the beauty of a painting or a sunset (or a tree). While we may describe a painting as sublime, "sublimity" is not an intrinsic quality that a painting can have. On a standard definition of *sublimity*—as "majestic, noble, and inspiring awe"—to say that a painting is sublime is to say something about the way the painting reminds us of thoughts and values and experiences toward which we already have a pro-attitude. If we look for something intrinsic to a painting itself, we may find things like a subtle use of color in the drawing of a forest or an accurate representation of proportions in a portrait. But of course some humans may regard subtlety and proportionality as unimaginative and uninspiring. In some possible worlds, all humans—and indeed all creatures—would find this so. Is it plausible to think that intrinsic qualities of proportional representation and subtlety of (what appears to us as) color have value in their own right? Again, I myself do not find any intuitive appeal here.

Consider next Adams's example of a great novel. It is true that we view some novels as more excellent than others—often because they contain vivid descriptions or intricate plot twists. Yet we surely value these qualities only because of the effects these qualities contingently have on us. If vivid descriptions did nothing but produce fear and confusion within us, and if intricate plot twists had the sole effect of giving us splitting headaches, our understanding of what would constitute an excellent book would be very different. Likewise, if we consider a great piece of music—an example Adams cites elsewhere (1999, 149)—it is true that we may view Mahler's second symphony as especially creative. And the piece does contain innumerably more chord progressions and melody motifs than does, for example, Elvis Presley's "Blue Suede Shoes." However, it again seems an entirely contingent matter that we should judge as especially creative the surprising chord progressions and melodic turns of Mahler's second symphony. For many of us, multi-layered countermelodies may evoke a complex set of simultaneous emotions, and an innovative chord progression may challenge us as we anticipate how dissonant sounds will finally be resolved. But it is certainly possible to imagine creatures for whom creativity is always measured by the simplicity of artwork—just as sometimes simple elegance is for us a sign of creativity. For this society of creatures, perhaps almost everyone is capable of writing long, complex symphonies—whereas only a few souls (those seen as true creative geniuses) are able to condense the complex melodies running through their heads into clear, simple tunes like "Blue Suede Shoes." In short, complex novels and music inspire us, challenge us, remind us in new ways of our commitments, and so forth. Yet, beyond these kinds of effects that complex novels and music have *on us*, there seems to be nothing left to explain why we would *commend* them. Is there value to such intrinsic qualities as vividness and complexity, which we might grant novels and symphonies as exhibiting? I once again fail to find the intuitive force behind such a claim.

Adams's examples of athletic and philosophical performance are, to my mind, only slightly more intuitively appealing candidates for intrinsic value. Whatever intrinsic qualities an athletic or philosophical performance might have—perhaps the explosiveness of an ice skater's jump or the determined effort of a philosopher's systematic defense of her position—we can imagine scenarios in which we would not view such qualities as good. For example, if all human bodies had only a small fraction of their current capabilities to regenerate physically and mentally, then we might well view such performances as lavish and imprudent squanderings of precious resources that should be reserved for other tasks. Accordingly, we might then come to view the ability and inclination to perform strenuous physical and mental feats as lamentable aspects of human nature. Is it nevertheless plausible to argue that strenuous effort is itself something of value? Admittedly, it is difficult to imagine worlds where strenuous effort would not have *instrumental* value in at least some contexts. It is not obvious to me that strenuous effort itself has (noninstrumental) value, though I confess my immediate intuitions are not quite as clear as with the previous examples.

Even less clear, I think, will our intuitions typically be about the last of Adams's examples: namely, unselfish deeds. We typically—if not always—associate unselfish deeds with presumed benefits to others. That is, we think of an unselfish act as one in which a person is deferring her own interests to the interests of others. Inasmuch as we care about others, we will have a pro-attitude toward these others whose well-being presumably is being furthered by the selfless deed. And unless we have read Nietzsche and concluded that an aggressive "will to power" constitutes our avenue to true flourishing we will think that the selfless person is shaping her character in a way that will serve her well in the future. It seems difficult to screen off these considerations (about the effects of selfless deeds *on* people) so as to focus our intuitions on the *deed itself*. I confess I do not immediately find it intuitively obvious either to deny or to affirm the suggestion that selfless deeds have value in and of themselves.

Appeals to value do of course largely come down to our intuitions.[27] In the next chapter—specifically, section 2.1—I will make my own intuitive appeals in defending a particular view about final value. At present, I want only to draw two conclusions. These conclusions are again in response to the critic who says: "Even if the arguments of sections 1.1–1.4 are correct in that we *learn* the concept 'good' by referencing our own experiences of flourishing, toward which we have a natural pro-attitude, we can still appropriate this term and use it to describe things we judge to have value in their own right, quite apart from their impact on anyone's flourishing."

My first conclusion has been that the term *good* is surely used much more often to denote that something (e.g., scientific discovery or artwork) is answering to someone's interests than to denote that something has intrinsic qualities that are valuable in and of themselves. While a semantic analysis of *good* certainly does not settle the issue of the nature of the good, perhaps we will want to take a semantic analysis as possibly providing clues as to what kinds of things really are good. If so, then our most common use of the term *good* surely gives us most reason to suppose that the things that are in fact good will be the things that do in fact answer to people's interests.

Still, there do remain cases—though again, I think, a minority of cases—where people's use of the term *good* reflects their belief that some object or achievement has intrinsic value quite apart from its impact on anyone's flourishing. In response to such cases, my second conclusion has been that the truly intrinsic qualities of these things—such as simplicity, complexity, proportionality—are often not plausible candidates for final value.

Admittedly, in some cases—for example, where we value selfless deeds—there is arguably some intuitive appeal to the suggestion that something can have intrinsic value in its own right, quite apart from its effects on anyone's flourishing. But in cases that are not immediately obvious, let us not apply our intuitions too quickly in trying to reach a conclusion about noninstrumental value. We can sharpen our intuitions by surveying the range of existing theories about that which makes something good. In the next chapter I shall discuss some of the leading theories and advance one particular theory about the nature of the good.

CHAPTER TWO

# The Nature of the Good

The discussion of the previous chapter involved the *meaning* of the term *good* within our public language. We saw there that our common use of the term is possible because we understand "good" in terms of our shared experiences of personally flourishing, toward which we have natural pro-attitudes. We describe things as good because they promote our own flourishing, or the flourishing of others whose interest we make our own, or (in cases where we describe something as good without having a pro-attitude toward it) the flourishing of those whose real or imagined interests we consider but do not make our own.

We turn now to explore the *nature* of the good. The account of the nature of the good that I will offer in this chapter will primarily be a *formal* account, as opposed to a *substantive* (or *material*) account. To illustrate this distinction, a formal theory of the nature of causation would not tell us what actually causes muscle spasms or economic recessions. Rather, a formal theory would tell us what would need to occur in order for us rightly to describe one state of affairs as causing some other state of affairs (such as a muscle spasm or an economic recession).[1] Similarly, a formal account of the nature of goodness would tell us what it is for something to be a source of goodness. A substantive account would identify these sources.

In Part II of this book I will provide a substantive account of the good, offering a description of the good life and of the choices that make this good life possible for us. In this current chapter I want to offer a primarily formal account of the nature of the good, providing arguments in support of a particular understanding of noninstrumental value. This account will be welfarist in nature. I will argue that something is good only inasmuch as it is good *for* someone. Further, I will argue that our welfare is directly affected solely by the intrinsic qualities of our mental experiences. My account thus has some important connections with certain historic versions of hedonism.

## 2.1 Hedonism

The form of hedonism from which I wish to draw insights is *not* what is sometimes called *motivational* hedonism. As the name suggests, this (very implausible) form of hedonism claims that our motivation when we perform intentional actions is always the attainment of pleasure and the avoidance of pain. Instead, what is relevant to our discussion here is *ethical* hedonism, which offers a theory of value according to which pleasure—in contrast to unpleasure—stands as the sole good.[2] Classic versions of ethical hedonism need a great deal of revision if they are to be at all plausible.[3] Yet the general approach of ethical hedonism is to understand a person's flourishing in terms of her mental states. (Or, if a hedonist prefers not to talk in terms of flourishing, then mental states at least explain that which makes the person's life go well for him.)[4]

In section 4.1 I will explain how my own (substantive) account of human well-being has connections to perfectionism. Perfectionism is sometimes viewed as contrasting sharply with hedonism, as it offers an *objective* approach to explaining what it is about a person's life that makes it good. On a perfectionist account of the good, my life is good inasmuch as it exemplifies some ideal. Despite my own view that there *are* objective answers to questions about what the human good life consists in, I do *not* want to follow standard perfectionist frameworks on a particular matter. Specifically, on (many, at least) perfectionist theories, the affirmation that "my life is good if it exemplifies some ideal" implies that "whether or not my life contains positive experiences for me is a separable matter." Put another way, exemplifying the stated ideal is *itself* enough to establish the good life. Against this perfectionist element, I want to side here with hedonists in linking conceptually a good life with a person's experiences. With reference to the two senses of *experience* discussed in section 1.2—namely, "participation in an activity" versus "mental experiences with certain feeling tones"—I again mean to focus on experiences in the second sense of the term. This *subjective* approach to defining a good life identifies certain mental states of the person (subject) alone as having noninstrumental value.

In chapter 1 I argued the epistemic point that we come to view things like artistic creations and space exploration as good ultimately by referencing our own experiences of flourishing. My (ontological) claim in this section is that our flourishing consists in our subjective experiences, which therefore constitute the only things that *are* noninstrumentally good.

There are two broad steps to my conclusion that noninstrumental value consists solely in the mental states of subjects. First, on my understanding of a flourishing life, I am committed to a *welfarist* understanding of value, according to which ethics must ultimately be concerned with how well lives go. Second, I am committed to a thoroughly subjective approach to welfare, where one's flourishing ultimately depends solely on one's mental states.

My argument for taking the first step of welfarism largely consists of an appeal to reflective intuitions. (I noted at the end of chapter 1 that, in making judgments about value, we will inevitably need to rely on our intuitions.) I myself find it intuitively compelling that any adequate answer to the questions "Why is this a good (or bad) thing, and why should (or should not) I bring this thing about?" must include an answer of the form, "Because someone will benefit (or be harmed)."[5] L. W. Sumner's defense of welfarism includes this same intuitive point. "If something will improve the conditions of no one's life, make no one better off, then what ethical reason could be given for recommending it? And conversely if something will harm no one, make no one worse off, what reason could be given for condemning it?" (1996, 192). Beyond this appeal to our intuitions, is the onus on the welfarist to provide further arguments for his position?

Sumner notes that the objector to welfarism may insist that, in addition to a person's welfare, there remain personal goods such as achievement or knowledge or liberty that remain basic ethical values. He then offers a point about where the burden of proof lies in this debate.

> To my mind, the value of these states of affairs is adequately captured by the role they play in enriching our lives; there is no remainder which requires independent acknowledgement beyond this prudential payoff. I can offer here no proof that installing these items as separate, non-welfarist basic goods is redundant, but I do think that at this point it is fair to shift the argumentative burden to the pluralist. Since welfarists can already make sense of the ethical point of promoting and protecting these personal goods, and since foundational values should not be multiplied beyond necessity, some reason is needed for according them an independent status. (1996, 202)

Some of the attempts to demonstrate nonwelfarist value have already been discussed in chapter 1. We acknowledged there that people may sometimes ascribe value to nonwelfarist, personal goods (e.g., scientific knowledge) and to impersonal goods (e.g., an aesthetically beautiful sunset). Yet I concluded that we can seemingly offer plausible arguments that, on closer analysis of the things in question, the only reason to value such things has to do with the (contingent) effect they have on us.

All our intuitions surely align with at least the initial welfarist claim that the positive welfare of people is *a* good. Hence, the arguments against welfarism will take the shape of claiming that other things are goods *as well*. But I think we can again offer plausible appeals to our intuitions that, on closer analysis, the intrinsic qualities of things like paintings and symphonies are really not to be valued. This is so even while it remains true that our attention may need to be focused on the intrinsic qualities of such things in order for us to have any pro-attitude toward them. I think this closer analysis at least makes the intuitive appeal of the welfarist critic—who claims that value exists in such things as paintings and symphonies, independent of its effects on us—less than clear and forceful. On the other hand, I think the intuitive appeal of welfarism remains very clear and strong: if someone cannot tell me *any* person, creature, or being who is in *any* way made better (worse) off by some object, event, or state of affairs, then I am at a loss to see why I should think it good (bad). For those whose intuitions follow along these lines, I think Sumner's point about burden of proof becomes persuasive. We really do need some further reason for multiplying the foundational value of subjects' well-being. I for one simply find no further reason.

I stated earlier that there are two broad steps to my conclusion that noninstrumental value consists solely in the mental states of subjects. Having discussed the first step of welfarism, let me now turn to the specific kind of welfarism I wish to defend: a purely mental-state account of welfarism (i.e., "mental statism"). In the remainder of this section—and indeed this chapter—I shall elaborate on, and defend, the claim that our welfare consists solely in our subjective experiences.

One might inquire at this point about the welfare of those living things *without* subjective experiences. Richard Kraut observes: "Plants do not have minds. And yet some things are good for them: to grow, to thrive, to flourish, to live out the full term of their lives in good health. Whatever impedes this—diseases, drought, excessive heat and cold—is bad for them" (2007, 9). While Kraut shares my own concern to focus on questions of what human flourishing consists in, he nevertheless calls attention to the corresponding way we can talk about what is "good for" a nonsentient life form. "When we finish talking about the good of plants and turn next to a discussion of the good of human beings, what changes is that which is good for each; different things are good for these two groups, because the nature of the members of these groups differs. But the meaning of the expression 'good for' does not alter. The relata are different; the relationship is the same" (2007, 94). So is my own attempted argument for mental statism too narrow as a welfarist account of the nature of the good?

In response to that question, let me first acknowledge that it is not a deviant use of the term *good* to speak of what is "good for a plant." Kraut remarks that "for most living things, to flourish is simply to be healthy—to be an organism that is unimpeded in its healthy functioning" (1997, 90). Given that plants can flourish in this sense, it does not seem overly strained to talk about water and certain nutrients "answering to a plant's interests," to use the language of chapter 1. Admittedly, then, there is a sense in which a comprehensive analysis of goodness will, even supposing the truth of welfarism, extend beyond the mental states of sentient, living things.

Nevertheless, my own interest in this book is in the metaphysics of goodness insofar as goodness denotes *noninstrumental value*. And I see no reason to think it (noninstrumentally) valuable that a life form should flourish instead of fail to flourish, if that life form is incapable of appreciating, phenomenologically, any difference between its life going well and not going well. Borrowing again Nagel's language, if there is not something "that it is like to *be* that organism—something it is like *for* the organism" (1979b, 166), then is there really anything of (noninstrumental) value lost if harm comes to that life form? Cancerous cells and poison ivy can have negative, instrumental value for humans and other animals. Is there really a *trade-off* when such things are killed, a noninstrumentally valuable state of affairs lost in spite of a greater, instrumentally valuable gain? Such a conclusion strikes me as very implausible, though again there is nothing to appeal to at this point beyond our intuitions. My own intuition remains squarely that, if someone tells me that an event occurred in our world in which no life form suffered any positive or negative mental experiences of any kind, no pleasure or unpleasure, then I have not yet been given any reason for thinking that this event has made the world better or worse (i.e., made it contain more valuable states of affairs or less of them).

The critic may ask, "But what is supposed to be so intuitively obvious about all positive mental states being uniquely of noninstrumental value?" My answer is that positive mental states are clearly valuable *to someone*: namely, the person having them. And this value is not (merely) an instrumental value. This conclusion seems obvious from (1) reflection on our own pleasurable mental experiences; and (2) inferences we draw about other creatures who likewise are capable of pleasurable and unpleasurable mental experiences. We experience certain mental states *as* better than others. A pleasurable mental state is experienced as better than an unpleasurable one. This point is enough to draw the axiological conclusion that certain mental states have more value—they are better—than others.[6] Parallel lines of argument cannot be made with respect to the senses in which we might describe a plant as flourishing. Thus, in my exploration of noninstrumental value, I again turn my focus to the mental states of sentient creatures and beings.[7]

There is some debate on the general question of what mental states *are*, as well as how they can contribute to our well-being. Historically, hedonists have been the most influential defenders of mental statism.[8] The kinds of mental states of interest to hedonists are of course pleasure and unpleasure. But what exactly qualifies a given mental state as a pleasure or an unpleasure?

Sumner notes that on this question one can be an *internalist* or an *externalist*.[9] An internalist would understand a pleasure or pain as a mental state with a certain *feeling tone* to it; whereas an externalist would focus on a person's reaction to, or attitude toward (e.g., appreciation or dislike), the sensation associated with the mental state. Sumner also notes that, while Bentham consistently offered an internalist account of pleasure, other hedonists of the eighteenth and nineteenth centuries sometimes equivocated between internalist and externalist accounts of pleasure and pain. Sidgwick, for example, assumed an internalist definition of pleasure in saying that "all pleasures are understood to be so called because they have a common *property* of pleasantness, and may therefore be compared in respect of this common *property*" (emphasis mine) (1981, I, 7, §2, 94). Yet he also offered this externalist definition: "Let, then, pleasure be defined as feeling which the sentient individual at the time of feeling it implicitly or explicitly *apprehends to be desirable*" (emphasis mine) (1981, II, 3, §1, 131).

Most modern ethicists adopt an externalist approach in analyzing pleasure and pain. Two broad considerations seem mainly to account for this tendency, though I shall argue that neither consideration is convincing.[10] First, we find pleasure in a wide variety of activities: reading, exercising, resting, playing music, watching birds, sipping tea, and so forth.[11] (Similar observations could be made about the varieties of painful activities.) The "feeling tones" associated with these enjoyable activities differ accordingly. What these feeling tones have in common, says the externalist, is that we have a positive attitude toward them.[12] But there is no single "pleasurable feeling tone" we might point to that is intrinsic to all pleasurable experiences.[13]

In response to this kind of argument from heterogeneity, Roger Crisp insists that critics of internalism have failed to notice that there *is* a single type of experience to all the examples we might list of pleasurable sensations: specifically, "they feel enjoyable" (2006b, 109). Crisp's response draws on the determinable-determinate distinction. As a way of reviewing this distinction, blue is one determinate of color (just as navy is one determinate of blue). If an object has the property of blueness, it also has the property of being colored (with this relation of course being asymmetric). Importantly, "colored things" are types of things, just as "blue things" are types of things. Crisp's suggestion is that the internalist *can* point to a single type of experience—an enjoyable experience—in explaining the commonality of all those activities that bring us pleasure.[14] The key is to understand this single type of feeling as a determinable, not as a determinate.

> There is something that it is like to be experiencing enjoyment, in the same way that there is something that it is like to be having an experience of colour. Likewise, there is something that it is like to be experiencing a particular kind of enjoyment (bodily enjoyment, perhaps, or the enjoyment of reading a novel), in the same way that there is something that it is like to be having an experience of a particular colour.... The mistake in the heterogeneity argument is that it considers only determinates. Enjoyable experiences do differ from one another.... But there is a certain common quality—feeling good—which any externalist account must ignore. (Crisp 2006b, 109)

While there are of course different feeling tones associated with the variety of activities that occasion our positive mental experiences, I think Crisp is right in saying that these positive experiences do seem to be of a particular kind.[15] As noted in chapter 1, we are able—without relying on further, more primitive concepts—to distinguish clear instances of flourishing from clear instances of failing to flourish. Whatever the biological story as to how humans are capable of having mental experiences with these contrasting phenomenologies, the fact remains that we are so capable. It is our appreciation of this contrast, we again saw in chapter 1, that allows us to form an understanding of the distinction between the concepts "good" and "bad."

In forming the concepts "good" and "bad," we admittedly will need to reflect on the contrasting mental experiences we have had that we might describe as being pleasurable versus unpleasurable. Importantly, though, our pleasurable experiences exist prior to our (second-order) reflections on them. I grant that we categorize our positive experiences as "good" because we have a certain kind of attitude toward them. Nevertheless, if we are asked what *makes* them good, or *why* they should all be thought of as good, our answer surely will *not* refer to our *attitudes* toward these experiences. Rather, the feeling tones themselves of the experiences serve as the explanation as to why we should think them good.[16] I shall discuss shortly some of Fred Feldman's reasons for preferring "attitudinal pleasures" to "sensory pleasures" in accounting for what makes a life good for the one who lives it.[17] We can note here that he defines sensory pleasures as "feelings in which the feeler takes intrinsic attitudinal pleasure in the fact that he himself is then feeling it" (2004, 57). Again, though, while Feldman has perhaps given us a good way to *identify* sensory pleasures, an attitude we have toward a mental episode is surely not what necessarily *makes* that episode a pleasure.

Having seen that the argument from heterogeneity does not undermine an intrinsic analysis of pleasure and unpleasure, let us turn to the second objection often raised against it. This objection focuses on the different ways in which a particular pleasurable or painful feeling tone can affect the well-being of different people. While a feeling tone associated with sexual pleasure is typically enjoyed for its own sake, the aging Lothario may experience less and less life satisfaction (to use one popular description of well-being) from his romantic encounters. Conversely, for the masochist physical pain may be a source of growing enjoyment. Some ethicists insist that a lesson we can draw from such examples is that it is one thing to speak of the intrinsic qualities of a pleasurable or unpleasurable sensation but quite another thing to speak of our reactions or attitudes toward this sensation. While a given sensation with pleasurable (or unpleasurable) properties may or may not increase (or decrease) our well-being, a positive (or negative) *reaction* to—or *attitude* toward—this sensation *will* always increase (or decrease) our well-being. Thus, it is argued, the externalist model offers the better account of how our mental states affect our welfare.

This objection ultimately proves unconvincing. Inevitably the objection—whatever its subtle variations—assumes that the internalist must be committed to an overly narrow understanding of a mental experience. Consider a case Eric Cassell relates in his explanation that *suffering* is a broader phenomenon than *pain*. He comments on a young woman whose treatments for breast cancer left her with more than mere physical pain. "We know why that woman suffered. She was housebound and bedbound, her face was changed by steroids, she was masculinized by her treatment, one breast was twisted and scarred, and she had almost no hair. The degree of importance attached to these losses—that aspect of their personal meaning—is determined to a great degree by cultural priorities" (1991, 39). Sumner notes that, for Cassell, suffering is "a response of the whole person, which takes into account both the subjective experience itself (in the narrow sense) and its meaning or significance. It follows that episodes of pain which are intrinsically indistinguishable (being of the same kind, having the same intensity, and lasting for the same duration) may cause quite different degrees of suffering to different subjects, or to the same subject at different times" (1996, 103). But should we really think that two people who suffer in different ways from, for example, cancer might have "intrinsically indistinguishable" episodes of pain?

Any plausibility to this conclusion stems from viewing the "intrinsic" nature of pain as something like a "physical" pain—in contrast to the suffering that stems in part from the meaning and value one attributes to one's situation. But to contrast pain and suffering in this way is, in the context of the present discussion, artificial.[18] A physical pain is, after all, a mental sensation—the designation *physical* simply refers to the bodily nature of the phenomena we identify as giving rise to the sensation.[19] Equally, the value or meaning we *assign* our physical states (and our situations in general) affects our well-being only insofar as these assignments are tied to mental sensations with certain intrinsic properties.

Too narrow a view of "sensory pleasures" seems to affect Fred Feldman's discussion of their adequacy (or, in Feldman's view, their *in*adequacy) in accounting for that which makes a person's life go well for her. Feldman's preference is again to talk in terms of "attitudinal pleasures." He offers the following example to illustrate that attitudinal pleasures are distinct from sensory pleasures. "Suppose you are in intense sensory pain and feeling no sensory pleasure at all. Suppose you notice that the pain is becoming less intense. You might be pleased that the pain is becoming less intense. I would describe your situation by saying that you take attitudinal pleasure in the fact that your sensory pain is becoming less intense. In this situation you might still feel no sensory pleasure at all, even though you are taking attitudinal pleasure in a certain fact. All you strictly 'feel' is diminished pain" (2004, 56). My response is that you will feel more than what Feldman has indicated. Your *reflection* on your diminishing pain has a certain *feeling tone* to it; it *feels* a certain way to reflect on your changing condition. Feldman seems to want to resist this conclusion. His further thought experiments include a case where a neuroscientist is working on a drug that temporarily makes one unable to experience sensory pleasures or pains:

> He tries it on himself. It seems to work. . . . He cannot feel sensory pleasure or pain. He is at first thrilled. This suggests that his research has finally been successful. He takes great attitudinal pleasure in the fact that he is feeling neither sensory pleasure nor sensory pain. Some time passes. The effect of the drug seems not to be wearing off. He begins to worry. Maybe this drug has caused a permanent change to his nervous system. That would be terrible. Now his attitude toward his own mental state begins to change. He takes much less attitudinal pleasure in the fact that he is feeling neither sensory pleasure nor sensory pain. (2004, 65)

Feldman takes this example as evidence that attitudinal pleasures are distinct from sensory pleasures and that the former can vary without concomitant variation of the latter. But how are we meant to understand the neuroscientist being "thrilled," and later "worried," upon reflection of his circumstances—all the while "feeling neither sensory pleasure nor sensory pain"?[20]

What Feldman's discussion seems to point up for us is simply that *some* sensory pleasures (and unpleasures) take place as we reflect on objects or states of affairs (including our own mental experiences).[21] The feeling tones that arise as we reflect on something then form *part of the overall mental experience*, or episode, we have at any slice in time.[22] Whereas Feldman wants to stress the distinction between sensory pleasures and attitudinal pleasures, I would instead stress the point that *some* sensory pleasures arise without any kind of second-order reflection, while *other* sensory pleasures arise only when we reflect on objects or states of affairs (including our own mental experiences). Thus I will maintain that the intrinsic nature of a mental experience is what affects a person's well-being—while acknowledging that a mental experience we have at some slice in time may have various feeling tones to it (some of which arise in the context of second-order reflection of some kind).[23]

These points help address part of Philippa Foot's argument that a good life must surely consist in more than merely pleasurable experiences. She begins by recalling "a talk by a doctor who described a patient of his (who had perhaps had a prefrontal lobotomy) as 'perfectly happy all day long picking up leaves.' This impressed me because I thought, 'Well, most of us are not happy all day long doing the things we do,' and realized how strange it would be to think that the very kindest of fathers would arrange such an operation for his (perfectly normal) child" (2001, 85). Foot seeks to draw the conclusion from this example that "when we talk about a happiness that is supposed to be humanity's good we cannot intend pleasure or contentment alone" (2001, 86).

The beginning of my response to Foot's example is to ask about the sense in which the doctor's patient was "perfectly happy." Seemingly, the idea is that the patient experienced certain pleasurable mental states and no unpleasurable mental states. Colloquially, perhaps the phrase "perfectly happy" does not seem an unusual choice of words. But strictly speaking it surely is not in all ways apt. There clearly are degrees, or measures, or grades of pleasurable experiences—even if a thoroughgoing analysis of the ways one pleasure might be "better" than another would be a tall task. Foot hits on as good an allusion as any when she speaks of a missing "depth" to certain pleasurable experiences. She explores the ways in which the pleasurable experiences of children lack this dimension of depth that adults can have—and indeed need—for the kind of happiness we hope they will have.

I am in accord thus far with Foot's discussion of depth of experiences. But she then offers the following conclusion: "We are mistaken if we think of happiness as something 'in the mind' in principle detachable from a person's resources of experience and belief, as if a mental state were like the surface of a pond that could be described in terms of the coming and going of water beetles there, without any reference to what was lower down" (2001, 86). But why should a mental statist suggest that mental experiences are "in principle detachable" from a person's beliefs and valuations? As the earlier discussions in this section have shown, many of our mental experiences depend greatly on what reflective attitudes we take toward objects and toward our mental attitudes themselves. Foot reflects on how her own enjoyment of gardening "owes, I find, little to pleasant sensation or movement and much to awareness both of immediate achievement ('That's got it well dug in!') and the prospect of good things to come" (2001, 84). But my response here is along the same lines as discussed in connection with Cassell's and Feldman's examples: the kind of "awareness" Foot mentions contributes to the feeling tones within her current mental experience as she is gardening. Her examples rightly show how certain sensory pleasures contribute more to a human's highest flourishing than do others.[24] And they rightly show that these more desirable pleasures may be possible for humans only as they develop and exercise certain capacities: for reflection, for imagination, for virtue, and so forth. However, I do not see anything in her examples that undermines the mental statist's thesis that our well-being is a matter of the pleasant or unpleasant mental experiences we have.

Returning to Feldman, to his credit his externalist account of pleasure at least emphasizes that one's life-enhancing attitudes toward one's sensory pleasures are indeed *pleasures*. (My critique has been that these attitudinal pleasures are but *one grouping* of pleasant experiential feeling tones one might have, even at a given slice in time.) It certainly will not do to say that one's welfare is directly affected by the *value* or *meaning* one assigns some sensory pleasure one has. Rather, it is once again the mental sensations that arise with our valuations that directly affect our welfare. Consider a case of two teenagers who both value sexual abstinence before marriage. We can suppose that they value abstinence above all other lifestyle choices. As it turns out, however, both teenagers are weak-willed on this matter. And subsequent sexual experimentation with each other brings for each teenager the recognition that he or she is living in a way contrary to what he or she most values. The first teenager is good at putting matters out of mind. While this first teenager experiences uncomfortable sensations of guilt whenever reflecting on the matter, these reflections are only occasional throughout the day. By contrast, the second teenager feels a continual sense of shame, and even revulsion, at the physical functions that play a part of sexual encounters. In other words, the second teenager experiences the same kinds of negative feelings, only with greater frequency and with greater intensity. If we consider only the impact of these mental experiences themselves, then the second teenager's life—vis-à-vis the first teenager's life—is clearly going worse for the one who lives it. Yet these two people, we suppose, equally value sexual abstinence.

It might be objected that the emotional trauma experienced by the second teenager, but not by the first, shows that the second teenager *does* value sexual abstinence more than the first and that this is the reason why it is more difficult for the second teenager to put matters temporarily out of mind. But this need not be so. We can simply stipulate that, in our example, the sole difference between the two teenagers is that one is a "live in the moment" person, while the other is a deeply reflective person. Here we suppose that the respective reflections by each teenager bring with them the same feeling we might associate with guilt. In this case, the greater suffering of the second teenager comes simply from the fact that the second teenager thinks about the matter more frequently and with more focus than the first teenager. Yes, the valuing of their past encounters affects the mental experiences they now have as they remember these encounters. But it is the *current mental experiences* associated with their reflective valuations—rather than the valuations themselves—that directly affect their welfare.

Although one's well-being is directly affected by mental states with intrinsic qualities—as opposed to our attitudes, including valuations, of these mental states—there are nonetheless reasons for emphasizing the ways in which our attitudes affect some mental states and not others. Returning to Sumner's discussion of how "physical pain" can affect people differently, one of his concerns is that we not lose sight of "the features peculiar to strictly physical pleasures," in contrast to those experiences—such as walking with a loved one—that we find pleasurable in large part because we "attach a prior value" to them (1996, 108). And this is fair enough. The activities that occasion the various mental states that contribute to our well-being are indeed different in significant respects. In distinguishing physical pleasures from other sources of enjoyment, Sumner remarks that "whereas the former are liked just for their phenomenal qualities, the latter depend on our attitudes toward states of the world" (1996, 107–8). Still, to repeat my line of response to Foot, this point shows only that, with respect to the phenomenal qualities of those mental states that enhance our flourishing, a necessary condition for the presence of *some* of them will involve our assignment of value or meaning. The point does nothing to undermine the thesis that the phenomenal qualities of mental states—whatever the reason for the presence of those mental states—is solely constitutive of well-being.

At times one's attitude toward, or desire for, or valuation of, one's current mental experiences may change all the feeling tones that together compose that current, mental experience. But the internalist need not claim that the only way for attitudes (or desires or valuations) to change one's overall mental experience at some point in time is by changing all the feeling tones, or individual sensations, that compose that feeling tone. In his critique of internalism, Chris Heathwood seems to assume that internalism *does* involve this claim. As a beginning point, Heathwood remarks that the examples that most clearly support externalism are those involving sensations that some people like and others dislike. "The sound of fingernails scratching on a chalkboard is extremely unpleasant to many people, but not at all unpleasant to others. If unpleasantness is intrinsic to sensations, then one of these groups has to be *mistaken*. If this sound really is intrinsically unpleasant, then those whom it doesn't bother and who therefore judge it to be not at all unpleasant, are wrong. That is hard to swallow" (2007b). But surely Aaron Smuts is correct in his response that this objection "confuses sensory input with sensory experience. The same input, the sound, is experienced differently by different people" (2011, 262). Heathwood anticipates that the internalist might insist "that such cases always involve intrinsic changes in the sensation." And he offers the following example to show that this response just will not do.

> Imagine a professional wine taster whose job it is to categorize wines along a list of dimensions. After the hundredth taste of wine, she may no longer get any pleasure from it, but might still retain all

her sensitivity and powers of discrimination, and continue to classify the wines correctly. But if internalism is true, she wouldn't be experiencing the same taste sensations she would have been experiencing had she been enjoying the wine. She might thus be unable to classify the wines properly. But that can't be how it works. Surely she can know what a wine tastes like whether she is enjoying it or not. (Heathwood 2007b)

This example again is to rebut the internalist rejoinder that cases like the chalkboard example "always involve intrinsic changes in the sensation." But surely the internalist need not claim that the "taste sensations" change for the wine taster. Rather, it is the overall mental experience that changes. Whereas the chalkboard example conflated "sensory input" with "mental experience," the example here conflates "taste sensation" with other sensations (or feeling tones) that contribute to one's overall mental experience at a given slice in time.[25] Smuts remarks of the weary wine taster that "the taste sensation might be largely the same, sans hedonic tone, but the taste experience is far different. The internalist does not have to say that the taste sensations must be different, only that the taste experiences have got to be" (2011, 263). The summary point to draw from these discussions is then succinctly put by Smuts: "Our attitudes can clearly have a causal impact on the pleasantness of experiences" (2011, 263). This point allows the internalist to account for the fact that a pleasurable or unpleasurable feeling tone can affect in different ways the well-being of different people.

It should be clear at this point that a sharp separation between our mental experiences and the attitudes (or valuations or desires) we have toward our mental experiences is simply unwarranted. Yet this perceived separation may partly explain why purely mental-state accounts of well-being are so unpopular among philosophers today. Many of the arguments against purely mental-state accounts of well-being—that is, mental statism—seem to assume an (overly narrow) working definition of first-person "experiences" along the lines of the kind of "physical pleasure" that the classical hedonists tended to equate with utility. Consider, for example, how Robert Adams defends his claim that, when we enjoy a swim or a walk in the woods, "None of this enjoyment is without experience, but it is not only the experiences that are enjoyed" (1999, 95).

In defending this conclusion Adams imagines a swimmer who, after a long, arduous period of training, manages to complete a painful, anxiety-filled swim of the English Channel.[26] We might naturally suppose that she will savor her achievement at various times in the future. However, Adams asks us to suppose

> that she died of some unrelated cause so soon after the swim that she did not have time to accumulate moments of retrospective pleasure equivalent in duration and intensity to the unpleasantness she had endured. It would be misguided to argue that in that case she would have enjoyed her life more on the whole if she had not made the swim. More important than the duration and intensity of the moments of retrospective pleasure, when we are considering whether she enjoyed her life more by making the swim, is "what it meant to her"— what difference her knowing that she had done it made to the value that she set on her life as a whole. (1999, 96)

Adams acknowledges, rightly, that the swimmer must have at least *some* moment of knowledge of her achievement; otherwise "her achievement would contribute nothing to her *enjoyment* of life" (1999, 96–97). Given this acknowledgment, it may seem curious that Adams should maintain his insistence that "it is not only experiences that are enjoyed." His rationale for this conclusion is that "enjoying life is not simply a matter of 'feeling good' or having pleasant experiences. It is also, and much more, a matter of the zest or interest with which one engages in the activities of life" (1999, 95). Perhaps this point goes some way toward showing the inadequacies of an overly narrow sense of pleasure that perhaps hedonists historically have sometimes sought to link with welfare. But it leaves untouched the central thesis of mental statism. In Adams's example, valuing one's own swimming accomplishment contributes to one's well-being in the same general way that physical happenings in the body contribute to (or detract from) one's well-being: namely, by leading to certain first-person mental experiences. We may engage in debates over which mental states really *do* enhance our flourishing (and I shall offer my own substantive proposal in section 4.2). But however this debate is to be decided, the thesis of mental statism remains that one's welfare is enhanced only by first-person experiences of *some* kind and derivation.

I should note one final point before moving on to consider a leading alternative to mental statism. While I have defended the thesis of mental statism that pleasurable mental states alone are intrinsically good, I have said nothing about how we might *compare* good states of affairs. In Feldman's discussion of hedonism he notes that, in "Default Hedonism" (i.e., a basic form of hedonism from which we might then add nuances), we "assign an amount of intrinsic value to each episode of pleasure and to each episode of pain. In the case of pleasure, the amount of intrinsic value in such an episode is always a positive number equal to the number of hedons it contains. As a result, 'bigger' pleasures are said to be intrinsically better. This means that more intense pleasures are intrinsically better than less intense ones, durations being equal. Similarly, longer-lasting pleasures are better than briefer ones, intensities being equal" (2004, 27–28). I do not want to commit myself to this formula, for I am dubious that logical relations always hold between the values of comparative states of affairs. Granted, there seem to be obvious cases where it is difficult, if not impossible, to deny that one state of affairs is *better* than some other state of affairs. For example, a world where one person experiences almost exclusively positive mental experiences is surely, ceteris paribus, better than a world where that person experiences almost exclusively negative mental experiences. But it seems clear enough from various examples that transitivity cannot always be affirmed when comparing worlds where people's welfare is at issue.[27] World B may have more value or be more good than world A, with world C being better than world B—and yet it can be wildly implausible to affirm that world C is better than world A. So, rather than venturing into questions of how we might compare good states of affairs, I want to commit myself in this section only to the view that a person's life is a good (or bad) one for her solely in virtue of her mental experiences—with the intrinsic nature of these mental experiences determining their goodness or badness.

## 2.2 The Inadequate Alternative of Desire Satisfaction

Among modern accounts of what makes a person's life good for the one who leads it, the leading alternative to mental statism urges that our welfare hinges on whether states of the world realize our *desires* or *prefer-*

*ences.* Measured in terms of the number of defenders among current philosophers, desire-satisfaction accounts of welfare are dominant over purely subjective accounts. Given the severe and rather obvious shortcomings of such desire-satisfaction accounts of welfare, it is somewhat surprising that they enjoy such widespread support. Before highlighting these shortcomings, we can note two reasons—both helpfully catalogued by L. W. Sumner—for the popularity over the past century of desire-satisfaction accounts of welfare.[28]

The first reason involves the development of economics as a science. The classic hedonist accounts of well-being made popular in the nineteenth century by such philosophers as Mill, Bentham, and Sidgwick emphasized the role of pain and pleasure. These mental sensations are of course a matter of private experience and therefore unhelpful to economists who seek to quantify a person's or society's "economic welfare." What *is* measurable, however, is the amount of money a person is willing to pay for some market item. If the level of one's willingness to pay for an item is then linked to the level of *desire* one has for that item, and if one's level of desire is then accepted as a good indication of how satisfied one will be when one gets the item, we end up with a way of publicly measuring one's economic welfare. In short, one's welfare is measured by the extent to which one's preferences—as revealed through one's monetary choices—are realized. By focusing on people's revealed desires, then, economists have a way of assessing how a given economic state of affairs affects people's well-being.

A second reason behind the current popularity of desire-satisfaction accounts stems from their usefulness within certain frameworks of political theory. Sumner explains that desire-satisfaction accounts are consonant with "the liberal spirit of the modern age." "Unlike objective theories, on which the sources of our well-being are dictated by unalterable aspects of our nature, the desire theory offers us the more flattering picture of ourselves as shapers of our own destinies, determiners of our own good. In this way it internalizes within a conception of welfare the paradigmatically liberal virtues of self-direction and self-determination. . . . It is little cause for wonder, therefore, that all of the principal recent advocates of the desire theory have also been political liberals" (1996, 123). Desire-satisfaction accounts of welfare may lend support to political theories we may want to embrace. And they may give us a way to assess the impact of various economic policies. Yet whatever the usefulness of desire-satisfaction accounts, the question we must now ask is whether they are descriptively plausible accounts of welfare. And the answer to this question is clearly "no."

The central thesis of desire-satisfaction accounts is that our well-being consists in having our desires realized. One problem with this approach to welfare is that we often find ourselves pleasantly surprised by events we had not desired—and possibly even had dreaded. When children first encounter the proverb that "it is more blessed to give than to receive," it is usually in the context of being forced by a parent to give away a toy the child wishes to keep for his own. Perhaps the child will need to be forced more than once to act in this way that seems to the child so contrary to his own interests. When the child does come personally to appreciate the "joy of giving," this moment will be marked with a first-person experience of delight and satisfaction. Clearly, this feeling will contribute to the child's own well-being. Yet the experience is one that the child did not desire beforehand. Admittedly, once the child experiences this joy of giving, he perhaps *does now* have a desire to (continue to) give things to others. However, surely the enhancement of his well-being has not been *because* his newly formed desire is being realized. His new desire is a result of his initial, joyful experience—which contributed (and, we suppose, continues to contribute) to his welfare. At best, his new desire helps us mark those experiences that he believes are contributing to his well-being. But his well-being does not *consist in* the realization of this new desire.

Equally problematic are those cases in which one *does* have a desire for something, only for the realization of that desire to result in disappointment. The familiar sayings "Be careful what you wish for" and "It's not what it's cracked up to be" point to this unhappy fact about human strivings. To close the gap between what we *think* will enhance our well-being and what actually *does* enhance our well-being, desire-satisfaction proponents typically stipulate that the relevant desires must be rational, or fully informed, or in some sense idealized. Thus, to mitigate cases in which people desire states of affairs that will not actually satisfy them, Richard Brandt suggests that we focus on a person's "rational" desires, defined in terms of those desires that would survive cognitive psychotherapy (1998, chap. 6). John Rawls offers the view: "In brief, our good is determined by the plan of life that we would adopt with full deliberative rationality if the future were accurately foreseen and adequately realized in the imagination" (1999, 370). And Peter Railton proposes that "an individual's good consists in what he would want himself to want, or to pursue, were he to contemplate his present situation from a standpoint fully and vividly informed about himself and his circumstances, and entirely free of cognitive error or lapses of instrumental rationality" (2003, 54).

The right kind of amendment along these lines can perhaps successfully close the gap between our desires for states of affairs and the actual effects these states of affairs will have on our well-being. But in closing this gap, the account of welfare on offer ceases to be a desire-satisfaction account. Rawls and Railton both speak of what a person *would* want, if fully informed in the relevant way. If we adopt this approach, we must press the question of what a fully informed person is fully informed *of.* For the "fully informed" condition to guarantee that one's welfare will indeed be enhanced by a given desire, it is the effects of the fulfillment of that desire that one must accurately foresee. That is, one must accurately foresee whether one's life will in fact go better if the desire in question is fulfilled. But now we have moved to something other than a desire-satisfaction account of welfare. The thesis of desire-satisfaction accounts is that one's welfare is enhanced when one's (informed) desires are fulfilled. And now, in specifying which desires are informed in the relevant way, the desire-satisfaction proponent must stipulate that they are the ones that *really will* further one's well-being.[29]

Ironically, this conclusion fits well with mental statism. For if a fully informed person foresees that particular, fulfilled desires *really will* further his well-being, he presumably foresees that he will be contented, cheerful, inspired, and so forth. And these are mental states. So the amended desire-satisfaction approach to well-being may end up measuring well-being in the same way that mental-state accounts do. At the very least, the amended desire-satisfaction approach gives us no reason to think that well-being is *not* ultimately a matter of one's mental states. "Informed desires" may perhaps track one's welfare, but they play no ultimate explanatory role in one's welfare. Again, in explaining why the fulfillment of informed desires will further a person's welfare, we end up assuming that welfare rises or falls independently of these desires.

Traditional desire-satisfaction accounts are also rendered implausible when we consider the spatial and temporal range of our desires. Sumner notes that Carl Sagan was keenly involved in the search for extraterrestrial life. He then remarks, "Suppose that twenty thousand years from now, some intelligent alien civilization encounters one of our probes in deep space and deciphers the messages which it carries. Sagan's desire will then have been satisfied, though he will know nothing of it" (1996, 125). With such a desire as this one, it seems exceedingly difficult to see how the person's life goes better as a result of his desire being realized in some distant place and at some distant time. Again, the mental statist insight seems an important one that our well-being must somehow be tied to our first-person mental *experiences*.

Perhaps the desire-satisfaction proponent might attempt to solve this problem (i.e., the problem of the spatial and temporal range of our desires) by suggesting that the *current* satisfaction of our desires makes our lives go well for us. But although this move may solve the general problem of the spatial and temporal range of our desires, it does little to solve the gap between our desires and what actually does benefit us. Even the desires we have at the time of our mental experiences will not always be sensitive to the impact these mental experiences have on our well-being. Consider an example provided by Daniel Haybron: "Perhaps you have lived with a refrigerator that often whined due to a bad bearing. If so, you might have found that, with time, you entirely ceased to notice the racket. But occasionally, when the compressor stopped, you did notice the sudden, glorious silence.... All the while it had been, unbeknownst to you, fouling your experience as you went about your business. In short, you'd have been having an unpleasant experience without knowing it" (2008, 205).[30] So it seems clear that we can have mental experiences that affect our well-being, even while we are having no desires about these mental experiences.[31] A necessary connection simply does not exist between the two; and without this necessary connection, the desire-satisfaction theory we are considering fails.[32]

## 2.3 L. W. Sumner

In part to clarify further my own account of welfare by contrasting it with other accounts, and in part to assess a thoughtfully conceived alternative to my own account, I want to consider an account of welfare put forward by L. W. Sumner. Sumner's account of welfare seems to fall somewhere between desire-satisfaction accounts of welfare and the kind of mental statism I am defending in this chapter. On Sumner's account, "Some condition of a subject's life is (directly or intrinsically) beneficial for him just in case he authentically endorses it, or experiences it as satisfying, for its own sake" (1996, 172–73). The key concept in this analysis is *authenticity*, which Sumner explains can be violated when a subject's endorsement of some condition of her life involves (1) a lack of relevant *information* or (2) a lack of full *autonomy*.[33] When a subject endorses the condition of her life, then (with the proviso that her endorsement is made with relevant information and is made from a point of view that is truly *hers*) her life goes well for her.

Sumner summarizes his account of welfare in terms of "authentic happiness." Lest one conclude that his account is firmly within the family of desire-satisfaction accounts—where "authentic evaluation" replaces "desire"—Sumner insists that "more is involved in being happy than the bare positive evaluation; you must also experience your life as satisfying or fulfilling" (1996, 146). So Sumner's account shares with my own account what we might call the experience requirement—the requirement that some condition does not contribute to our welfare unless it enters our experience. Sumner's endorsement of this requirement ensures that his account is, in important respects, subjective. The account is also—like desire-satisfaction accounts—objective in that, as Sumner puts it, the account "incorporates an information requirement" as a condition for authenticity and is therefore in important respects "a state-of-the-world theory" (1996, 175).

My own account views welfare *solely* in terms of mental states with intrinsic qualities. Against an account of welfare that seeks to affirm the experience requirement while *also* maintaining the requirement that one's life experiences be "endorsed," I would press the following point. If a positive evaluation of one's life is not *sufficient* for well-being, why should we think it is *necessary*? Sumner thinks it is necessary because he resists the claim that one's happiness is a matter simply of one's mental states.[34] However, I would stress again the point made in section 2.2 that valuing or endorsing some condition in one's life is one of the factors that help determine what a person's mental experiences *are* as she goes through life. That is, valuing or endorsing some activity or mental experience will give rise to certain feeling tones that then partly *compose* one's ongoing mental experiences. I can accept Sumner's point that a reflective endorsement of some aspect of one's life will, ceteris paribus, contribute to one's well-being. Importantly, though, the contribution comes from the impact this endorsement has on the nature—that is, the intrinsic qualities—of one's first-person experiences. Perhaps Sumner's description of an "authentic endorsement of one's life" translates into a particular kind of positive feeling tone, unique to those occasions when one is able to make such an endorsement. But as we saw in our earlier discussion of Feldman's account of attitudinal pleasure, this kind of acknowledgment does nothing to undermine the thesis of mental statism.

Sumner's account also is susceptible to the kind of objection leveled earlier at desire-satisfaction accounts: namely, that there can exist a gap between what we desire (or authentically endorse) and what actually contributes to our well-being. Sumner seems to acknowledge that his authenticity condition does not guarantee closure of this gap. But he resists the kind of perfectionist appeal I myself would want to make—and indeed will make in section 4.1—to there being things that *really do* (and really do not) promote the welfare of all human beings. In commenting on the appropriate response to subjects who authentically endorse lifestyles that strike us as trivial or ill advised, Sumner advises, "Where the authenticity requirements are satisfied we have no reason to think that the choice in question is bad for the person who has made it. However distasteful we may find her choice, for all we know it is the lifestyle which will be most fulfilling for that person in her full particularity" (1996, 199). I think there *is* reason to think that a person's seemingly ill-advised endorsements do not in fact align with her true well-being. The reason stems from certain conclusions I will reach in chapter 4 about the common avenue to long-term flourishing for all people. But Sumner cannot go in such a direction because of his commitment to *neutrality* as a condition for an adequate account of welfare. Of this "key test" for any adequate account of welfare, Sumner remarks, "Neutrality requires that a theory not exhibit any bias in favour of some particular list of goods or some favoured way of life. Objective theories have difficulty with this requirement, since they typically stipulate a pattern of the good life for all members of a particular natural kind (such as us)" (1996, 181). As we noted at the beginning of this chapter, Sumner contends that any theory of the nature of welfare must be *formal* and must not confuse the *sources* of welfare with an account of what it is to *be* a source of welfare. In section 4.1 I will outline the substantive, Christian account of welfare I myself endorse; and it will become clear at that point why I do not think we can actually maintain this kind of distinction Sumner wants to make. But for now we might ask what principled reason there is to prefer purely formal accounts of the nature of welfare to accounts that make substantive references to sources of well-being for people.

Put another way, is it appropriate to construct an ethical framework around starting assumptions about where people's welfare *really* lies? An answer to this question perhaps depends on what dangers one seeks to avoid. Sumner's concern seems to be avoiding paternalism. In his discussion of the possibility of ill-advised authentic endorsements, Sumner suggests that "an open mind and a willingness to attend to the specifics of people's particular circumstances seems less patronizing than simply assuming that the lifestyle in which they are engaged, besides failing to measure up on some other value dimension, is also necessarily bad for them" (1996, 199). In response to this concern, however, I do not see how we can avoid making *some* starting assumptions about what *really makes* for human welfare. In commenting on the value of agency, Sumner states that "autonomy is an intrinsic prudential good: something whose presence in our lives makes them go better in itself" (1996, 205). Yet this statement seems quite an assumption to make about human welfare—certainly not one that all people would agree needs no argumentation or further qualification. And indeed, one of the goals of this chapter is to provide arguments that mental states are the only things of intrinsic, noninstrumental value.

Admittedly, there are certain aims we might have in constructing a theory of welfare where autonomy would be a necessary ingredient. Sumner remarks at one point that, "in the absence of autonomy, a person's welfare is indeterminate or unknowable" (1996, 205). If our aim is to track a person's welfare as best we can without relying on any outside assumptions as to what actually makes one's life go well, then perhaps a focus on what a person authentically endorses is the best we can do.

If these epistemic considerations are what Sumner has in mind when he states that "a person's endorsement of the conditions of her life is *determinate* of her well-being" (emphasis mine) (1996, 205), then his point is well taken. But Sumner seems also to mean by this statement that a person's endorsement *will determine* his well-being. And as the discussions in this chapter have shown, one's endorsements do not play this role. Thus, while epistemic considerations may render Sumner's account of welfare useful in certain contexts, it is not a descriptively adequate alternative to my own account.

To conclude this section, let me summarize the respective senses in which Sumner's account of welfare is both more and less subjective than my own account. I have noted that my account, being a mental statist account, is purely subjective in the sense that only first-person experiences are noninstrumentally good for a person. Sumner's view is that, whatever the intrinsic qualities of our mental states, we must *also* endorse our lives in some way in order for our lives to go well for us. Because mental statism omits any reference to facts about our mental states (such as whether they are endorsed), beyond their felt qualities, there is a clear sense in which mental statism offers an account of human welfare that is purely subjective in a way that Sumner's account is not. On the other hand, Sumner himself defines "subjective" theories of welfare as those that "make our well-being logically dependent on our attitudes of favour and disfavour" (1996, 38). Under this definition of *subjective*, my own account of welfare will certainly not be purely subjective, for it includes the claim—which I again will detail in chapter 4—that all people's well-being is, as a matter of fact, achieved only through mental experiences of a certain sort. Sumner would agree with this assessment of my own account's (lack of) subjectivity. He remarks, "A theory which stipulates that welfare consists in some distinctive feeling, regardless of the place which this feeling is actually assigned in the lives of reflective subjects, is only doubtfully subjective" (1996, 93). I have of course given my reasons for thinking that any purely subjective account of welfare—under Sumner's description of "subjective"—is unpromising as a descriptively adequate account of welfare. Again, the persistent problem is the gap between what actually *will* make our lives go better and our reflections as to what we *think* will make our lives go better.

2.4 Nozick's Experience Machine

A purely mental-state account of welfare—which again I am defending—is very much out of favor with most moral philosophers these days. In the final three sections of this chapter I want to defend mental statism by responding to various objections that our welfare cannot plausibly be a matter solely of our first-person experiences.

It would be very implausible for anyone to claim that first-person experiences play *no* contributory role in our welfare. Instead, the common objection to mental statism is that our experiences are not the *only* things that contribute to our well-being. In recent decades, much of the discussion of experience-based accounts of welfare has been influenced by Robert Nozick's description of an "experience machine."[35] Nozick's well-known thought experiment is as follows: "Suppose there were an experience machine that would give you any experience you desired. Superduper neuropsychologists could stimulate your brain so that you would think and feel you were writing a great novel, or making a friend, or reading an interesting book. All the time you would be floating in a tank, with electrodes attached to your brain. Should you plug into this machine for life, preprogramming your life's experiences?" (1974, 42). From the presumption that at least many people would not opt to use the experience machine, Nozick draws three conclusions about what matters to us in addition to our experiences. First, "we want to *do* certain things, and not just have the experience of doing them." Second, "we want to *be* a certain way, to be a certain sort of person," and we cannot say of a person who spends her life plugged into the machine that she is, for example, courageous or kind. She is neither courageous nor cowardly in character, neither kind nor cruel; she is simply a receiver of mental sensations. Third, we desire to have "*actual* contact" with the world—as evidenced by the tension some feel between facing up to difficult situations and opting to ease one's experiences through, say, drugs (Nozick 1974, 43).[36]

Nozick's thought experiment is widely viewed as providing decisive reason to reject mental statism. The general point Nozick draws from his reflections on the experience machine is that we desire many things in life *besides* the mental sensations associated with first-person experiences. Previously, I have stated my agreement with those classical hedonists who have insisted that welfare is singularly enhanced by mental sensations with intrinsic qualities. And it is widely thought that one cannot affirm both (1) Nozick's general point about the range of things we desire and (2) the hedonist's point that welfare is solely a matter of having certain first-person experiences. James Griffin is representative of those who see these two affirmations as inconsistent: "Bentham, Mill, and Sidgwick all saw utility as having to enter our experience. But we desire things other than states of mind: I might sometimes prefer, say, bitter truth to comforting delusion" (1986, 13).[37] I do not wish to deny that people desire things other than having first-person experiences. What I *do* wish to deny is that this point has any direct bearing on whether one's welfare is solely a matter of one's first-person experiences.[38]

Consider some of Griffin's further comments on the importance we place on *doing* things and *being* a certain way.

> If I accomplish something with my life, it is not that I want to have a *sense* of accomplishment. That is also desirable, but it is different from, and less important than, the first desire. And if I want to accomplish something, it is not necessary that I want my accomplishment to enter my experience—say that I know about it. That too is desirable, but it is still not the first desire. If either I could accomplish something with my life but not know it, or believe that I had but not really have, I should prefer the first. (1986, 19)

Probably many people will share the sentiments of this last sentence. For various reasons, we may indeed desire *to accomplish* certain things with our lives—not just *believe* that we are accomplishing these things. However, let us press the question of what actually enhances one's welfare (i.e., makes one's life go better for the one who lives it). Surely, it is the *belief* that we are accomplishing certain things. Suppose that I have as a goal for my life the writing of a self-help book that will help lift people from states of depression. If I am successful in doing this, but am completely unaware that my book has been of any help to anyone, in what sense is *my* welfare enhanced? I may believe my efforts to have been completely in vain, and, as I think of all the people I (mistakenly) believe are still in need of help, I will experience the same sadness and melancholy that, we suppose, motivated me to write the book in the first place. I cannot see how *my* well-being is enhanced by the mere fact that I have accomplished what I desired to accomplish. To enforce the point, we might suppose that my goal is *not* accomplished because, let us say, my publisher never actually publishes my manuscript. Nevertheless, if I *believe* that my book is helping others (and we can suppose my perverse publisher shows me fake letters from people thanking me for my "help"), then I will experience delight, comfort, and so forth. Surely when we are considering *my* welfare—that is, what is good *for* me—the sole consideration directly relevant is whether I have positive mental experiences associated with *believing* that I have helped others. The actual accomplishment of my goal leads to an increase in my welfare only on the condition that I form true beliefs about this accomplishment.

What enhances my well-being is a different question from the question of what my desires *aim* at.[39] We can maintain a purely mental-state explanation of the former without needing to do the same with the latter. It is a failure to recognize this point that has seemingly led so many philosophers to insist (wrongly) that Nozick's experience machine provides decisive reason to reject mental-state accounts of welfare.[40] Joel Feinberg, for example, states that "because the objects of a person's interests are usually wanted or aimed-at events that occur outside his immediate experience and at some future time, the area of a person's good or harm is necessarily wider than his subjective experience and longer than his biological life" (1993, 179). And James Griffin, as we saw in his remarks quoted earlier, rejects the "experience requirement" for utility on the grounds that "we desire things other than states of mind." The assumption, of course, is that those who affirm a purely mental-state account of well-being must also be committed to the idea that we *desire* only mental states. Yet there is nothing in the claim that "one's welfare is enhanced only through one's first-person experiences" that commits the mental statist to the idea that the *objects* of one's desires are only one's own experiences.[41]

A similar line of response can be given to Peter Unger's well-known example of how some of our desires aim at states of affairs completely removed from us: "Consider life insurance. To be sure, some among the insured may strongly believe that, if they die before their dependents do, they will still observe their beloved dependents, perhaps from a heaven on high. But others among the insured have no significant belief to that effect.... Still, we all pay our premiums. In my case, this is because, even if I will never experience anything that happens to them, I still want things to go better, rather than worse, for my dependents. No doubt, I am rational in having this concern" (1990, 301). Again, the defender of mental statism need not be troubled by this sort of example. We can all agree with Unger's contention that, in taking out life insurance, "what motivates us, of course, is our great concern for our dependents' future, whether we experience their future or not" (1990, 302). Yet a mental statist need not claim that it is the anticipation or thought of having certain experiences that *motivates* us whenever we act. A mental statist simply claims that, as a matter of fact, our own welfare *is* enhanced solely by our own mental states.

Perhaps the objector might seek to strengthen her case against mental statism by raising the issue of what we *value*. In Unger's example, the emphasis seems to be on the fact that we assign great (noninstrumental) value to our loved ones' well-being. And indeed Griffin, in his earlier example of preferring *actual* accomplishment to a *sense* of accomplishment, remarks: "That would be, for me, the more valuable life" (1986, 19).

For the discussion that follows, I think it will be most useful not to focus on Unger's phrase "for me." This qualification may lead us to think of "valuing something" as synonymous with "desiring something." And if we take "valuing" to be the same as "desiring," then our previous discussion (related to Nozick's experience machine) of desiring external things will cover cases of valuing external things. Let us instead understand "valuing" to involve the belief that an external thing has intrinsic value in its own right.

I acknowledged in chapter 1 that people may at times believe that some activity or object (e.g., an old tree) has noninstrumental value, quite apart from its impact on how well people's lives go for them. Given the arguments of this chapter, I of course believe that people are simply mistaken in such instances. But I acknowledge the point that Griffin and Unger make: people may at times assign noninstrumental value to objects and states of affairs other than their own experiences of flourishing.

It is not altogether clear to me what specific problem this point is meant to raise for mental statists. Unger insists that it is "rational" to value a loved one's future well-being. Perhaps he is suggesting that mental statists are committed to describing the behavior in his life insurance example as *ir*rational. Griffin also is not fully clear on the alleged problem that arises from scenarios where people value things besides their own experiences. He remarks that, if we view mental states as solely desirable, "we should then have, puzzlingly, to accept that when, with eyes wide open, I prefer something not a mental state to a mental state and so seem to value the former more than the latter, I get greater utility from what I value less" (1986, 10).[42] Perhaps there is an objection in the air something along the lines of: "Even mental statists surely find themselves sometimes valuing external states of affairs over their own positive experiences. It certainly is not irrational to do so, even in situations where one knows that the former will come at the expense of the latter. Does not this scenario then leave mental statists in a puzzling situation: (1) on the one hand they claim in theory that only mental states have noninstrumental value, and (2) on the other hand in practice they sometimes, like all of us, value external states of affairs more than their own first-person experiences?" I have defended the thesis that the intrinsic feeling tones of people's mental experiences are the only things that make their lives go better. Would it be puzzling—even irrational—for me to pursue some purpose with the knowledge that this pursuit will have a negative overall effect on the feeling tones of my own mental experiences?

In response, let me begin by noting that the "external objects or states of affairs" the objector imagines us valuing might be personal or impersonal. The responses available to the mental statist will differ accordingly. If we suppose that the valued external object is personal—for example, the well-being of a loved one in Unger's life insurance example—then the mental statist can point out that she need not claim that it is only *her own* experiences that are of noninstrumental value. Rather, a mental statist need only affirm the more general thesis that it is solely mental experiences (of *some* sentient being) that have noninstrumental value. The question of *whose* experiences—and subsequent flourishing—should count as valuable, or good, is a matter I will take up in chapter 4. But for the present discussion, there is nothing about mental statism that precludes the proponent of it from explaining Unger's life insurance example in terms of a person purchasing life insurance because she values the future experiences that her loved ones will have. Granted, if mental statism were combined with ethical egoism, then the mental statist could not accommodate the fact that she, the mental statist, no doubt values (noninstrumentally) the well-being of her loved ones. But a mental statist need not be an egoist. As chapter 4 will make clear, the framework for ethics I endorse does not include the thesis of egoism (of either the ethical or the psychological variety). In sum, if the external state of affairs one values is personal, then our proponent's valuing of *other* people's personal experiences over her own is no more puzzling than the idea that one can be altruistic.

Let us turn now to situations in which a person is said to assign value to *im*personal objects over one's own first-person experiences. Perhaps the objection will be that this belief is common even among mental statists, despite their theoretical commitments that only mental states have noninstrumental value. In what sense is this scenario "puzzling," to use Griffin's description?

A mental statist might hold the belief in question uncritically—as when one simply accepts the declaration of a trusted authority that an old tree in the center of town is valuable in its own right. The holding of this kind of unreflective belief would not be puzzling. Still, we might suppose that the mental statist reflects on the matter and comes to recognize that the (noninstrumental) value she finds herself placing on the tree conflicts with her theoretical commitment to a purely welfarist, mental-state account of the good. The mental statist might realize the error of her previously unreflective assumptions and find that she no longer thinks of the tree as having noninstrumental value. But even if she finds that she cannot shake the belief that the tree has inherent value, this only shows that she is incapable of reconciling, through an act of the will, two beliefs of hers that she recognizes to be contradictory. And it is not too uncommon an occurrence for us to find that we are unable to rid ourselves of deeply entrenched beliefs for which we acknowledge there is little good evidence. Certainly, our mental statist is in no more awkward a position than anyone else who finds herself with a belief for which she cannot reflectively provide evidence that is satisfactory by her own standards.

Of course, we might further stipulate that the mental statist comes to think that there *is* good reason to believe that the tree has noninstrumental value. Perhaps our proponent will think that intuitions are reliable guides on matters of value; and she finds herself with strong intuitions for mental statism *and* for a tree having noninstrumental value. Though she will perhaps be tentative that she has arrived at the best categories for approaching questions of value, she may nevertheless hold fast to both intuitive judgments—for the kinds of pragmatic reasons that led scientists to affirm that light is both a wave and a particle. This seems to me the most awkward situation in which the mental statist might find herself. But any "puzzling" aspect of this scenario still does not seem to constitute any kind of argument against mental statism.

## 2.5 The Badness of Death

Taking stock of where we now stand, we have seen that Nozick's thought experiment involving an experience machine does not serve to undermine the mental statist account of welfare I have been advancing. Nozick's central point is that people *desire* things other than to undergo first-person experiences. In rebuttal, I pointed out that a mental statist need not deny that people *desire* things other than their own first-person experiences. The thesis of mental statism is simply that our first-person experiences happen to be the only things in which our well-being consists. We then considered the objection that, although the thesis of mental statism assigns noninstrumental value alone to our first-person experiences, in practice even the mental statist may perhaps think of external objects and states of affairs as more valuable than her own experiences. However, we found that this objection does not in the end amount to any real challenge to mental statism.

A cluster of further, potential objections to the mental-statist position that I have defended can be generated from discussions about how one's death—or, in some discussions, events after one's death—can affect one's welfare. Specifically, I want to consider three kinds of claims that may seem to undermine mental statism as I have outlined it: *(i)* that events *after* my death can affect my well-being *now*; *(ii)* that my death affects my well-being, though at *no particular time*; and *(iii)* that my death affects my well-being at times *after* my death.[43]

*(i) The claim that events after my death can affect my well-being now*

The thrust of arguments that lead to this first claim do not actually rely heavily on the unique context of one's death. Rather, references to postmortem events merely help in reaching the more general conclusion that my well-being at time $t$ can be affected by later events at some time $t_{+1}$. By focusing on specifically postmortem events, critics of mental statism draw our attention to the ways in which our lives (purportedly) can be affected by events that are clearly later, that are clearly external to us, and that resonate with our intuitions about how we should honor the dead. If my current welfare really can be affected by events that take place at a later time, then my current welfare would seem to depend in part on factors besides my current, first-person experiences. Such a conclusion would undermine mental statism as I have articulated it.

One obvious way to claim that my current welfare can be affected by later events—or, even more generally, events outside my ken—is simply to *assume* a desire-satisfaction account of well-being.[44] Given that some of my current desires (e.g., for my children's long-term happiness or for cold fusion someday to meet the world's energy demands) will either be frustrated or realized after I am dead, then, if my current well-being depends on the realization of my current desires, my current well-being will of course be affected by events after my death. But in any discussion about the merits of desire-satisfaction accounts of welfare, we must make sure that the desire-satisfaction proponent does not simply beg the question in providing an argument for his position.

To see how assumptions might be mistaken for actual arguments, consider Joel Feinberg's well-known advocacy of the idea that I can be harmed by others even if I never learn of the harm they do to me. As a preliminary point before looking at an example Feinberg provides, we can note that the term *interest* has more than one meaning. On the one hand, the term can be used synonymously with *desire*. When I say that I have a "keen interest in the new faculty position that has been recently vacated," I am expressing a desire to fill that position. On the other hand, I can refer to my "interest" as denoting my welfare. When I ponder whether the new faculty position "*really is* in my interest after all," I am considering what will truly be good for me.

Consider now Feinberg's remarks on the harm that can be done to a person's interests. "If someone spreads a libellous description of me among a group whose good opinion I covet and cherish, altogether without my knowledge, I have been injured in virtue of the harm done my interest in a good reputation, even though I *never* learn what has happened. That is because I have an interest, so I believe, in having a good reputation *as such*, in addition to my interest in avoiding hurt feelings, embarrassment, and economic injury. And *that* interest can be seriously harmed without my ever learning of it" (1993, 180). Feinberg makes two references in this passage to "a good reputation" being part of "my interest." In each of these references, it is unclear to me whether he means to use *interest* in our first sense (as denoting a desire) or in our second sense (as denoting one's welfare). With that said, one way of reading the passage would be as an argument that starts from the premise that

(1) I have an "interest" (desire) to possess a good reputation

and then concludes that

(2) My "interest" (welfare) lies in possessing a good reputation.

Such a line of argument, of course, would not actually be any kind of real argument at all. It is true that, if one *assumes* as an additional premise a desire-satisfaction account of welfare, then one may think of (2) as naturally following from both (1) and this further assumption. However, it is only by failing to notice the double meaning of the term *interest* that we might be tempted to think that (1) itself constitutes sufficient evidence to conclude (2). Thus there seems to be no real argument in the passage from Feinberg; there is merely the assertion of a desire-satisfaction account of welfare (from which it would admittedly follow that a person can be harmed after death). I argued in section 2.2, though, that a desire-satisfaction approach to welfare is a decidedly inadequate one.

L. W. Sumner is not convinced that we will find it intuitively plausible to view our well-being as something that cannot be affected by future events. He offers an example meant to illustrate that, while later events cannot change one's *happiness* at earlier times, they can nonetheless surely affect one's *welfare* at earlier times:

> Consider the woman who for months or years has believed in, and relied on, the devotion of a faithless and self-serving partner. Her belief concerning a crucial condition of her life—a state of the world—was false.... If you ask her during this period whether she is happy, she will say that she is; if you ask her whether her life is going well for her she will say that it is. If you ask her how she sees the same period after the delusion has been exposed, she will probably say that it now seems to her a cruel hoax and a waste of that part of her life. Clearly she *now* thinks that her life was not going well *then*; she has retrospectively reevaluated her well-being during that period. But will she now deny that she was *happy* then? (1996, 157)

Sumner's last sentence contains the central point he wants to make with this example: namely, that the example does not undermine the thesis that happiness is a purely mental state. On this point we will agree. However, his preceding sentence is most relevant for my larger discussion. Sumner takes happiness to be one source of welfare; and while he allows that our *happiness* may be a purely mental state, he insists that we will surely view our *welfare* as not solely determined by our mental states.

So what should we make of Sumner's description that the woman "*now* thinks that her life was not going well *then*"? If her welfare at the earlier time was affected by her partner's infidelity—even though at this earlier time her mental experiences were not affected by any belief that her partner was unfaithful—then we would have a case where one's welfare is not solely a matter of one's first-person experiences. But is Sumner's description accurate that the woman in the example now thinks that her life was not going well *then*? I think this description begs the question against mental statism and in favor of a desire-satisfaction proponent's account of why the woman's life was not going well for her.

Sumner is right in pointing out that we often reevaluate earlier times in our lives after learning new information or acquiring new values that we did not have at these earlier times. And Sumner is even correct that there is *a sense* in which, as we reassess our earlier lives, we can form the conclusion that they were not "going as well" as we had earlier thought. However, the sense of "going well" here is an *instrumental* sense related to the goals we had and/or now have. The woman in Sumner's example sees that, during the earlier periods of her life, her activities and commitments were not actually conducive to achieving many of her life goals.[45] Now lamenting this fact, she of course recognizes that her earlier activities and commitments were not conducive to her long-term happiness. But none of these points serve to undermine the mental statist's thesis that first-person experiences alone contribute noninstrumentally to well-being. As Sumner correctly points out, there is nothing to suggest that the woman in his example should deny that her later realizations affected her happiness—or, for that matter, *any* descriptions of her mental states—at earlier times. So, absent any further, general arguments as to why we should favor a desire-satisfaction account of well-being over mental statism, our common experience of reevaluating earlier periods in our lives does not serve to undermine mental statism.

One may still wonder whether mental statism becomes counterintuitive once we turn our focus to the particular way in which we commonly think of the deceased. Most people tend to take very seriously the wills and last requests of people who die. When someone fails to carry out the stated requests of the deceased—or worse, when one reneges on a promise explicitly made to the deceased—we generally react with repulsion. Now, if mental statism is correct, then we cannot harm the deceased by failing to fulfill the desires they had while they were alive. So how are we to account for the common thought that we should carry out someone's dying wishes?[46]

A number of considerations may contribute to this common thought. Our attempts to carry out someone's dying wishes may sometimes simply stem from a commitment to a larger goal that we happen to share with that person. Alternatively, we may think it important that the societal practice of honoring deceased people's wishes and written wills continue, not least because we hope that *our* wishes will be honored when we die. We may also think of the expectations family and friends have toward one another in terms of obligations, which friends and family members continue to have when a loved one dies. Or we may consider the prospect of *not* honoring a deceased person's wishes as a kind of alienation from ourselves: we could not convincingly both tell ourselves we truly loved (and still love) the person *and* fail to stand with them in this manner. In sum, there seem to be plausible explanations—without relying on desire-satisfaction models of welfare—as to why we generally feel that we should honor the wishes of a person after she is dead.[47]

*(ii) The claim that my death affects my well-being, though at no particular time*

Thomas Nagel, among others, has questioned whether something can be good or bad for a person only if it is good or bad for her at a given time. Nagel acknowledges that "there certainly are goods and evils of a simple kind (including some pleasures and pains) that a person possesses at a given time simply in virtue of his condition at that time." But he concludes that "this is not true of all the things we regard as good or bad for a man. Often we need to know his history to tell whether something is a misfortune or not; this applies to ills like deterioration, deprivation, and damage. Sometimes his experiential *state* is relatively unimportant—as in the case of a man who wastes his life in the cheerful pursuit of a method of communicating with asparagus plants" (1993, 65). If a person's "experiential state" is sometimes "relatively unimportant" in determining whether things go good or bad *for* that person, then of course mental statism would be exposed as inadequate. But is Nagel correct in his conclusion?

Nagel's primary argument for his conclusion consists in providing "an example of deprivation whose severity approaches that of death":

> Suppose an intelligent person receives a brain injury that reduces him to the mental condition of a contented infant, and that such desires as remain to him can be satisfied by a custodian, so that he is free from care. Such a development would be widely regarded as a severe

misfortune, not only for his friends and relations, or for society, but also, and primarily, for the person himself. This does not mean that a contented infant is unfortunate. The intelligent adult who has been *reduced* to this condition is the subject of the misfortune. He is the one we pity, though of course he does not mind his condition—there is some doubt, in fact, whether he can be said to exist any longer. (1993, 65)

So Nagel acknowledges that the person now before us is not to be pitied because he has certain gifts of intelligence or artistry that are not being fulfilled. The person now before us *has no* high gifts of intelligence and artistry that either he or we might lament as going untapped. But Nagel challenges us to consider the whole history of the person when determining whether things are going well for him. "If, instead of concentrating exclusively on the oversized baby before us, we consider the person he was, and the person he *could* be now, then his reduction to this state and the cancellation of his natural adult development constitute a perfectly intelligible catastrophe" (1993, 66). We might describe Nagel as providing a counterfactual analysis of the person in that Nagel is discussing the kind of person our subject *could* have been. Yet the appeal to counterfactual considerations is problematic when used as an analysis of a person's welfare.

Admittedly, Nagel's analysis reveals a *sense* in which we can view a severe brain injury—or indeed a person's death—as a catastrophe. But the mental statist can grant this point without conceding that a person's welfare is affected by anything beyond her (temporally located) mental experiences. Toward fleshing out this point, consider Jens Johansson's helpful summation of the two ways we might interpret the question: When is death bad for the one who dies?

(Q1) When is the intrinsic value for S of $w$ (in its entirety) lower than the intrinsic value for S of $w^*$ (in its entirety)?

(Q2) When is S intrinsically worse off in $w$ than S is at that time, or those times, in $w^*$? (In other words: At which time, or times, is S's well-being level lower than it would have been then if S's death hadn't occurred?) (2013, 258–60)

(Q1) asks us to compare someone's welfare levels in one world with the person's welfare levels in some alternative, possible world. From Nagel's example, if we grant that there is one subject who has certain experiences in the actual world (in which the accident occurred), and then grant that the same subject would have had other, presumably more life-enhancing experiences in the next closest possible world in which the accident *didn't* occur, then we can perhaps grant that subject S would be better off in the alternative, possible world than in the actual world. *When* would the subject be better off? Well, this question would not admit to any answer, other than "atemporally."[48]

I previously noted that I myself am hesitant to venture into the kinds of questions of comparative value represented by question (Q1). But I will acknowledge here that there seem to be clear cases where one world would have more value than another. And I would not quibble with the suggestion that a person may be worse off in a world in which she dies or has a serious brain injury at a young age than she would be in a world where she lives to an old age with greater brain functions. Again, as to *when* the person would be better off, I agree that the only answer can be: atemporally (or eternally).

All the same, these points do not serve to undermine mental statism. The mental statist can make comparisons of value between possible worlds while still asserting that a person's well-being in any world and at any time is a matter of her mental experiences in that world at that time. An objection to this assertion would need to identify (in reference to [Q2] above) specific points or periods of time in our actual world where a person's well-being is *not*, contra mental statism, a matter of the intrinsic qualities of the person's mental experiences at that time.

Can the critic of mental statism perhaps try to use Nagel's example to make just this kind of objection? We previously discussed the claims by Feinberg and others that our well-being at time *t* can be affected by *later* events (e.g., events after one's death). Perhaps the critic now might argue that *earlier* events can affect a person's well-being at some time *t*—and affect it in more direct ways than the trivial sense in which past events of course affect what experiences a person comes to have. Perhaps it will be argued that Nagel has been too quick to conclude from his example of the brain injury victim that "the intelligent adult"—as opposed to the brain-injured person we now see before us—"is the one we pity." The critic might insist: "The person in Nagel's example whose lack of well-being I lament is precisely this person who lies before me! And I can tell you *when* this person's well-being is being adversely affected by the previous event of the brain injury: at all those moments when I'm witnessing this person continue to exist with only a shadow of his mental capacities functioning properly."

Whatever the initial, intuitive appeal of this reaction, counterfactual considerations (such as what a person's welfare *would* have been if a brain injury had not occurred) simply cannot play a role in an account of a person's actual welfare. Aside from the positive arguments for mental statism, as outlined in earlier sections of this chapter, we can also offer a type of reductio ad absurdum response to the critic's suggestion here that counterfactual considerations can play a role in accounting for a person's well-being at any given time. Suppose that the person in Nagel's example has lived to the amazing age of 110 and then, because of a brain injury, is reduced to the state of a contented infant for the last three months of his life before dying. Would we intuitively regard this turn of events as a catastrophe? Clearly not. But why not? Perhaps the answer will be that we judge a 110-year-old, unlike the subject in Nagel's actual example, to have already had a "good innings": he has had a chance to marry, have children, and plot a career path.

But has the 110-year-old really had a good innings? It is true that he has spent most of his adult life with mental abilities far greater than those of a two-year-old. But his mental properties were nonetheless not what they *could* have been had he regularly practiced mental exercises, regularly consumed optimal amounts of fish oils, and regularly done any number of other things that increase brain function. Neuroscientists tell us that we humans typically use only a certain percentage of our brain capacities. If the door is opened in our discussion of welfare to allow appeals to counterfactual scenarios, we might imagine the possibility of the human race discovering the keys that unlock the full potential of the human brain. We might further imagine advancements in medicine such that the average age expectancy becomes a Methuselah-like 969 years—most of which is spent at the fitness level of a modern-day thirty-five-year-old. In such a society perhaps it would be the norm to have fifteen to twenty generations of children, becoming a better and better parent as one continued to learn from past mistakes. And perhaps the deeply meaningful years of a marriage would typically be the ones after the first hundred years or so—when each spouse learned (through his or her high-functioning brain) to become so in tune with the other's thoughts and needs that the couple then lived in a harmony barely imagined by most couples today.

In such a society it would not be appropriate to say of a 110-year-old brain injury victim that he had had a good innings.[49] If married, he would have experienced only a small fraction of his expected years with his wife—again, missing out on the really good years. (If as yet unmarried, then not even that.) Certainly in a society like this one, a 110-year-old's brain injury would be, as Nagel puts it, a "perfectly intelligible catastrophe." And I see nothing at all about human nature that precludes the possible existence of such a society.

What this discussion points up is that, while we can of course make comparisons between possible worlds (and between the welfare states of a person in each of these possible worlds), counterfactual possibilities do not play any plausible role in determining whether a person's life goes well for him at times in the actual world. Further, even if these comparisons *were* (contrary to fact) relevant in determining whether a person's life was going well for him, it is quite by chance that our intuitive reactions to these comparisons should elicit feelings that the person's life *is*, as opposed to *is not*, going well for him. There are an infinite number of comparisons among possible worlds we might consider—an infinite subset of which might make us pity the person we are considering and an infinite subset of which might make us rejoice in the person's good fortune. In this light the designation that a person's life, in virtue of counterfactual considerations, must be going "well" or "poorly" for her becomes an arbitrary designation.

In an attempt to exclude the far-fetched counterfactual scenarios I have sketched, while still holding on to the initial, intuitive suggestion that *some* counterfactual scenarios should play a role in our assessment of a person's well-being, one might perhaps point out that most people today have the capacity to live a hundred or so years, but no one has the capacity to live 969 years. Thus, given the state of human technology and advancement at present, we are able to make our (socially influenced) judgments that, all other things being equal, a man's life goes well for him if he lives 110 years with typical, adult mental functioning; but his life does not go well for him if he loses this function early in his adult life. Yet even if one thinks that this consideration may undermine the rejoinder I gave related to arbitrariness, observe what has now happened. Our judgments about whether *one* person's life goes well for her have become dependent on the life expectancies—and expected well-being levels—of *others*. But surely the question of how *others'* lives are going (or are expected to go) does not directly affect how well *my* life is going.[50]

In sum, we have found in this section that Nagel's line of reasoning does not provide grounds for concluding that a person's experiential states are sometimes "relatively unimportant" in determining whether that person's life is going well for him. Admittedly, a brain injury or a person's death may provide grounds for making the comparative judgment that the person's life goes better for her in some alternative, possible world where the brain injury or death does not occur. And in making this judgment we admittedly do more than look only at the person's mental states at any one particular time in the actual world. Yet any (atemporal or eternal) truth of this kind about the comparative value of states of affairs has no bearing on the mental statist's claim that a person's well-being at any point or period of time is solely determined by the mental states she actually has at that point or period of time. If we try to amend Nagel's line of reasoning by appealing to our purported intuition that an earlier severe brain injury surely affects negatively the well-being of a person we see lying helplessly before us at definite points of time in the actual world, then (in addition to the positive arguments for mental statism) reductio ad absurdum arguments should defuse any initial, intuitive force this appeal might have.

*(iii) The claim that my death affects my well-being at times after my death*

Instead of appealing to intuitions in support of the claim that past events can make our lives intrinsically better or worse off, Ben Bradley has provided an interesting argument that the particular event of one's death is in fact "bad for the person who dies at all and only those times when the person would have been living well, or living a life worth living, had she not died when she did" (2009, 74). Bradley shares my rejection of arguments by desire-satisfaction proponents like Feinberg that death (or events after one's death, like the spreading of slanderous accusations) can harm someone retroactively. Yet Bradley wants to insist that "death makes an impact on its victim's well-being, by reducing it to zero" (2009, 44). Bradley views the postmortem person as continuing to exist—even though the person doesn't exist *now*, "much in the way that objects may exist without existing *here*" (2009, 81).[51] Just as the past event of a toe-stubbing can affect one's well-being now, so the past event of one's death can affect one's well-being (at those times when she would otherwise have been alive).

What is particularly interesting for our purposes is that Bradley is a self-described mental statist. However, the implications of his position (on the impact death has on our well-being) undermine the kind of mental statism I am seeking to defend. Toward seeing how Bradley's understanding of mental statism differs from my own, consider his statement on the reason why a toe-stubbing affects my well-being at later times: "It seems to me that the reason we say that my stubbing my toe at $t_1$ is bad for me during the seven days following $t_1$ is that my life would have been going better for me during that time had I not stubbed my toe" (2009, 88). We of course do not want to revisit Jens Johansson's question (Q1) from the previous section, which involves the comparisons of possible worlds. Is a toe-stubbing really bad for me for seven days because my life would have gone better for me if I had not stubbed my toe? This may initially strikes us as an odd thing for a mental statist to say. Surely it is more in line with mental statism to say that, following a toe-stubbing, my life goes bad for me in that for seven days I experience the negative mental experiences associated with physical pain.

But Bradley quickly clarifies that a toe-stubbing (or a death) is *instrumentally* bad for me. Moreover, Bradley explains that his claim is *not* that a toe-stubbing (or a death) is instrumentally bad for us because it causes something intrinsically bad (like negative mental states). Rather, his claim is: "Death is typically bad for us in virtue of what it takes away from us" (2009, 47).[52] Specifically, death *prevents* us from having those positive mental experiences that we would otherwise have. Lacking any property of being pleased, and lacking any property of being in pain, my well-being is zero (as it might be measured on a hedonic calculus of some kind). Death thus affects my well-being during those times I would otherwise have been alive: it causes my well-being to be zero.

Bradley and I are both mental statists in that we both affirm that a person's well-being is a matter of the intrinsic nature of one's mental states. However, Bradley will interpret this affirmation as meaning that the intrinsic features of a person's mental states are the only things that can (noninstrumentally) make her life go better or worse for her. I on the other hand will insist, for reasons to which I shall shortly come, that we should also maintain that a person only *has* a welfare at a given point in time if she has mental states at that time.[53]

So, does a person who dies (and who, let us allow with Bradley, exists even though she does not exist *now*) have a welfare? Bradley suggests two reasons for thinking that the answer is "yes," as seen in his description of his postmortem self. "I lack the property of being in pain, and I lack the property of being pleased. This—perhaps in conjunction with my satisfying the responsiveness requirement R, in light of there being some time at some world at which I feel pleasure or pain—is what, on hedonistic grounds, explains my zero well-being level" (2009, 106). The two reasons are thus related to (1) the properties his postmortem self has; and (2) a responsiveness condition. Let us take up these two points in turn.

We might anticipate that Bradley's appeal to the "lack of property of being pleased (or in pain)" will be featured merely in order to show that a postmortem person's welfare is *zero*. But Bradley also uses it to help establish that the postmortem person *has* a welfare. From the fact that the postmortem person lacks the properties of being pleased and being in pain, Bradley maintains that we can conclude that the postmortem person has corresponding *intrinsic* properties that help mark the person out as someone with a welfare. Bradley's argument on this point is as follows.

> It would seem that the "negative" property, *not being pleased*, is an intrinsic property too, if being pleased is intrinsic. Not being pleased seems to satisfy the leading criteria for intrinsicness; it is, for example, shared among all duplicates . . . , and it can be had by something whether that thing is lonely or accompanied. In general, it seems that if F is an intrinsic property, then lacking F is an intrinsic property too. . . . If this is right, then if I have a well-being level at a time at

which I am not located, it must be at least in part because of some intrinsic properties I have then. (2009, 107)

The appeal to (allegedly) intrinsic properties such as "not being pleased" as a partial basis for one having a welfare is initially difficult to reconcile with Bradley's preceding comments that "when I am sitting in a chair and having no pleasant or painful experiences, I have a well-being level of zero. But this is not because of any pleasure or pain I am feeling then, nor in virtue of any other paradigmatically intrinsic property I have then. . . . Rather, it's because I *lack* certain intrinsic properties" (2009, 106).[54] Presumably, the *lack* of properties helps establish that his well-being is *zero*, while the intrinsic nature of the corresponding negative properties helps establish that he *has* a well-being.

A key problem with this line of argument, though, is that it opens the door to most anything having a welfare. Following Bradley's analysis, an old shoe has an intrinsic property of "not being pleased." Bradley does not seem troubled by this implication. He remarks, "I think it may be completely harmless to attribute a zero well-being level to a shoe"; after all, "The distinction between zero well-being and no well-being is a distinction with no import" (2009, 104).[55] I agree with Bradley that this distinction has no import *for a person with a welfare* as to how her life goes for her. That is, I agree that, for a person alive today, her life will go no better or worse for her if she dies than if she falls into a permanent comatose state in which she experiences no mental states associated with pleasure or unpleasure. But I disagree that the distinction between "zero well-being" and "no well-being" has no import, period.

Specifically, I think the mental statist should maintain that a person has a welfare at a given time only if the person has mental states at that time—even if these mental states do not admit to any positive or negative calculation on any hedonic scale. My worry is that, if something (e.g., an old shoe) can have a welfare in virtue of its intrinsic *properties* (like "not being pleased"), then the connection between mental statism and welfarism becomes less secure. As outlined in section 2.1, I think much of the plausibility of mental statism is derived from the intuitive force of a welfarist understanding of value. If the mental statist insists that, to have a welfare at a given time simply *is* to have mental states of a certain kind,[56] then the link between welfarism and mental statism is secure (though we may have to rule out alternative, subjective theories of welfare like desire-satisfaction theories). However, if having certain properties (like the property of "not being pleased") is sufficient to ensure that a subject has a welfare, even though the subject has no mental experiences, then we lose any necessary connection between welfarism and a person's mental states. As a mental statist, Bradley will of course want to insist that the only things that can move a subject's well-being up or down are mental states. But this claim seems to me less obviously true if, in principle, properties beyond a subject's mental states can provide sufficient conditions for that subject to *have* a welfare. If a shoe can have a welfare, does, for example, a functional account of welfare now become more plausible, whereby the shoe's well-being can be increased the more it is worn? If so, then so much for the original, intuitive appeal of welfarism.

Despite thinking it "may be harmless to attribute a zero well-being level to a shoe," Bradley does seek to provide a reason for attributing a welfare to a postmortem person but not to an old shoe. (And now we have come to Bradley's second reason for concluding that his postmortem self has a welfare.) If Bradley can indeed rule out a shoe having a well-being, then the worries I outlined in the previous paragraph subside. But will his second reason for attributing welfare to a postmortem person allow him to do so?

Steven Luper has argued that a deceased person obviously cannot have a welfare because such a person is not *responsive*. For Luper, a subject has the property of responsiveness at $t$ "if and only if its well-being may be affected at $t$—rising if certain conditions are met, and falling if certain other conditions are met" (2007, 244). Bradley acknowledges that "surely something resembling Luper's notion of responsiveness is required" in order to distinguish a dead person from an old shoe. But Bradley plumps for a wider understanding of this notion: "In calling a thing responsive, we are making a claim about its modal features: we are saying it is the sort of thing that *can be benefited or harmed*. So perhaps the difference between a dead person and a shoe is this: a person who is dead at t nevertheless has a positive or negative well-being level at some time, at some possible world. The same cannot be said of a shoe, which seems to be the sort of thing that could not possibly have a welfare level" (2009, 104).[57] Bradley's own responsiveness condition is indeed broad enough to allow for a deceased person to have a welfare, while ruling out an old shoe having a welfare. The problem is that, even if we restrict our discussion to possibilities in our *actual* world, this broader responsiveness condition is still implausibly broad.

Consider that, at some point in the earth's evolutionary history, living organisms first started experiencing mental sensations. If we call the first such thing "multicelled organism X" (where this refers to a type, not a token), then presumably we can use Nagel's language in saying that, unlike all prior living things on earth, there was something that it was like to be an organism X. (I will want to say that at that point organism Xs began to have a welfare.) Perhaps the capacity of organism Xs to have a mental life was the result of evolutionary processes that took millions of years. And perhaps for a thousand years there were full-fledged organism Xs that roamed the earth but that had not yet been lucky enough to pull together all the conditions needed for a mental life. For all those organism Xs that predated the first lucky organism X with a mental life, it was of course *possible* that they could have a well-being. This supposition is made plausible by the fact that things did fall into place for our first, lucky organism X. Yet should we really say of all these earlier organism Xs that, even though they lived their entire lives without any mental sensations whatsoever, they *did have* a well-being, since it was *possible* that they could have had a mental life susceptible to increase or decrease? Surely the answer is "no."[58]

If Bradley's responsiveness condition for welfare does not rule out clearly implausible candidates, then we should conclude that this condition is not sufficiently narrow. We have already seen that his complementary condition—namely, the intrinsic property of "not being pleased/pained"—is not sufficiently narrow. I see no reason to think that the two conditions, in combination, might be sufficiently narrow. I thus see no reason for amending my working description of mental statism (which includes the point that something has a welfare at time$_t$ only if it has mental states at time$_t$.

Let us remind ourselves what is at stake in the discussion of Bradley's argument that deceased people can be harmed by their deaths (during those times when they otherwise would have been alive). His own mental-statist position involves affirming that mental states alone can make one's life better or worse for the one who lives it. On that point all mental statists should agree. Bradley wants to resist thinking that mental statism need, or should, have the implication that a subject *has* a welfare at a given time only if the subject has mental states at that time. If Bradley is correct, then I will at least fall back on our common affirmation that the intrinsic qualities of one's own mental states are the only things that can move one's well-being level up or down. But I do not think Bradley is correct in resisting this further implication of mental statism. My care in assessing Bradley's line of argument stems from my worry that, if mental statism is divorced from this further implication, the force of the mental statist account of welfare—along with the intuitive force of welfarism itself—lessens.

## 2.6 Is Schadenfreude a Special Problem?

The objections to mental statism from the previous two sections have insisted that factors aside from the pleasurable nature of one's mental states can affect one's well-being. In section 2.4 I considered the point that people desire and value things besides their own pleasurable experiences. And in section 2.5 I considered whether events—such as a slanderous accusation after one's death, or an accident that reduces one to near-death, or the event of one's death itself—can make a person's life go better or worse for her. In these discussions the critic of mental statism might concede that pleasurable mental experiences do, ceteris paribus, make our lives go better (rather than worse) for us. It is just, the critic will say, that other events can also affect our well-being. But perhaps the critic of mental statism will *not* grant the point about the necessarily positive value of pleasurable mental states. In the current section I want to address this claim that pleasurable mental states are not always positive constituents of well-being.

The objection leveled at mental statists here is that they ignore the contexts in which pleasure might occur. Aristotle insisted that, "since activities differ in degrees of decency and badness, and some are choiceworthy, some to be avoided, some neither, the same is true of pleasures; for each activity has its own proper pleasure. Hence the pleasure proper to an excellent activity is decent, and the one proper to a base activity is vicious" (1999, X, 5, §6, 1175b). It is not immediately obvious why any pleasure should be thought of as vicious, or bad. It is no help to pursue Aristotle's further comment that "the pleasures agreed to be shameful are not pleasures at all, except to corrupted people" (1999, X, 5, §11, 1176a).[59] The point remains that the person in question still has experiences that are pleasurable *for her*.

Of course we can recognize that some pleasures clearly further a person's well-being *more* than other pleasures do. I again do not want to focus on the issue of how we might calculate and compare good states of affairs. But surely the pleasurable experience associated with a successful marriage proposal adds more to a person's well-being than does the experience of shaking a stranger's hand. (And I shall submit in sections 4.1 and 4.2 that a specific kind of mental experience holds the key to our long-term flourishing.)

Also, we will want to remain clear that it is the *noninstrumental* value of pleasurable mental experiences that is at issue. We can all agree that some activities and pleasurable mental experiences are *instrumentally* bad things. For example, the person who experiences a mental "high" from taking a drug may then begin an addictive quest to recreate that experience—at cost to his family, friends, and his own long-term happiness.[60] The controversial issue is the mental statist's claim that all pleasurable mental experiences have positive, noninstrumental value.

In his well-known discussion of base pleasures, G. E. Moore has us imagine a world "in which the greatest possible pleasure would be obtained by a perpetual indulgence in bestiality." He then presses the point against Sidgwick and like-minded hedonists that, "if the greatest possible pleasure could be obtained in this way, and if it were attainable, such a state of things would be a heaven indeed, and . . . all human endeavours should be devoted to its realisation. I venture to think that this view is as false as it is paradoxical" (1993, §56). In response to Moore, I would want to stress that it is merely an *empirical* fact that humans do not obtain the kinds of ultimate flourishing represented by "heaven" from base sexual escapades. Again, I shall say a great deal in Part II about the ways in which humans, from a Christian perspective, can and cannot flourish in the long term. But the empirical observation that humans flourish more through some activities and mental experiences than through others does not undermine the thesis of mental statism.

Nor is the mental statist's position necessarily undermined if she acknowledges that, of course, most of us will feel revulsion to an activity like bestiality. This revulsion can plausibly be explained by a number of factors: our reflective consideration that people surely will not flourish in overall, healthy ways through such activity; our evolutionary, nonreflective reactions to things that are likely to undermine our survival; our socially conditioned reactions to activities considered taboo; and so forth. I do not see that our negative attitude toward Moore's example reveals any intuition that the pleasurable mental experiences themselves associated with a base activity do not have noninstrumental value. What *would* count against mental statism is an argument that mental experiences of pleasure deriving from "base" activities (as Aristotle put it) are not states of unequivocally positive, noninstrumental value. Is such an argument forthcoming?

To focus our discussion, let us select one particular mental experience widely thought to be a prototypical instance within the category of pleasures to which we should resist attributing noninstrumental, positive value: namely, schadenfreude. Arthur Schopenhauer commented that "there is no sign more infallible of an entirely bad heart, and of profound moral worthlessness than open and candid enjoyment in seeing other people suffer" (1915, 156–57). Surely we will all agree that such enjoyment can be *instrumentally* bad for others and for oneself. But how might the critic of mental statism argue that the pleasurable mental experiences associated with schadenfreude do not have positive, *noninstrumental* value?

Many philosophers have simply asserted that our intuitions surely prevent us from following the mental statist in defending the positive, noninstrumental value of pleasurable mental experiences at another person's misfortune.[61] (The intuitions to which the critic of mental statism appeals will of course be in contrast to the welfarist intuitions I defended in section 2.1.) Sometimes the denial of welfarism is straightforward. W. D. Ross, for example, concludes that "four things, then, seem to be intrinsically good—virtue, pleasure, the allocation of pleasure to the virtuous, and knowledge (and in a lesser degree right opinion). And I am unable to discover anything that is intrinsically good, which is not either one of these or a combination of two or more of them" (1930, 140).[62]

Other times, we have to dig just a bit deeper to see the denial of welfarism. Consider C. D. Broad's discussion of why we must surely reject the noninstrumental value of malice (which we can read as synonymous with schadenfreude):

> Suppose that I perceive or think of the undeserved misfortunes of another man with pleasure. Is it not perfectly plain that this is an intrinsically bad state of mind, not merely *in spite of*, but *because of*, its pleasantness? Is it not plain that any cognition which has the relational property of being a cognition of another's undeserved misfortunes and the hedonic quality of pleasantness will be worse in proportion as the pleasantness is more intense? No doubt malice is a state of mind which on the whole tends to increase human misery. But surely it is clear that we do not regard it as evil, simply as a means. Even if we were quite sure that all malice would be impotent, it seems clear to me that we should condemn it as intrinsically bad. (1930, 234)

Given the intuitive appeal I think welfarism has, I will immediately want to ask, "If the pleasures of malice are bad, *for whom* exactly are they bad?" I would indeed venture a broader argument (based on the substantive account of the good life I shall offer in Part II of the book) that these pleasures are bad for the person who holds them—but only in the sense that they will be *instrumentally* bad for him. It is not at all clear to me why *any* pleasure would *itself* make a person's life go worse for him.[63]

Beyond an appeal to nonwelfarist intuitions, which I for one do not at all find compelling, are there actual *arguments* against the mental statist's conclusion that the pleasures associated with schadenfreude have positive, noninstrumental value? In looking for such arguments, I should note that I am supposing that our welfare is determined by the intrinsic qualities of our mental experiences. If we allow for a *desire-satisfaction* account of well-being—and of the good—then admittedly a person's life would not go well for her insofar as she desired *not* to have the experiences of schadenfreude that she found herself having. Equally, if we allow for an externalist version of mental statism, where pleasure involves our attitude toward (or desire about) our mental sensations, then there conceivably *is no* real pleasure for the one who feels shame at the recognition of her own enjoyment of another's misfortune. But in section 2.2 we rejected desire-satisfaction accounts of well-being, and in section 2.1 we established the internalist conclusion that mental states contribute to a person's well-being in virtue of their intrinsic qualities.

If we move beyond an intuitive denial of welfarism, and beyond a denial of internalist versions of mental statism, are there again actual arguments against thinking that the pleasures associated with schadenfreude have positive, noninstrumental value? I think that the most promising form of argument—though it ultimately fails—will draw from other examples where the mental statist *will* plausibly agree with certain intuitive starting points. I have in mind cases where, it is argued, extrinsic considerations can change the *intrinsic* value of some object or state of affairs. If we open the door to such scenarios, then the critic of mental statism might claim that the intrinsic value of a pleasurable mental state (e.g., one associated with schadenfreude) can be affected by extrinsic considerations (e.g., viewing this pleasurable mental state with disdain or shame).[64] And from this conclusion about the alterability of a mental state's *intrinsic* value, it would be a short step to a plausible conclusion about the alterability of a mental state's *noninstrumental* value.

How might one argue that extrinsic considerations can change the intrinsic value of an object or state of affairs? Consider Shelly Kagan's suggestion that a painting has more intrinsic value in virtue of its uniqueness (1998, 282–83). Thus the *Mona Lisa* would have less value if Leonardo had painted ten near-identical copies of it. Similarly, the pen used by Lincoln to sign the Emancipation Proclamation seems more intrinsically valuable than another pen whose history does not involve such a significant event.[65] The property of "being used by Lincoln to sign the Emancipation Proclamation" is not something *intrinsic* to the pen. Yet, Kagan suggests, we think of the pen itself as having great value. Of course the fact itself that we value Lincoln's pen or the *Mona Lisa* does not establish that such objects *have* intrinsic value.[66] But perhaps one might argue that the best explanation of our valuing these objects is that the objects *do* have intrinsic value.

The promise of this line of argument abates, however, when we recall the discussion from section 1.4. We saw in that section that people might value or enjoy a walk in the woods or a game of basketball. I acknowledged in that section that, while we are making evaluative judgments about these activities, our attention may very well be focused on these activities themselves or on the intrinsic qualities of objects as we engage in these activities. However, I also stressed that the explanation of our pro-attitude—as opposed to some other attitude we might have—toward such things lies in the fact that we have pleasurable mental experiences as we focus our attention on them. I want to make a similar point here in response to Kagan's claim that the extrinsic properties of some object can affect that object's intrinsic value. My response is that the extrinsic properties of, say, a pen or painting may well affect whether we find ourselves valuing (or, for that matter, having another kind of pro-attitude toward) that pen or painting. Still, whether in light of an object's intrinsic *or* extrinsic properties, the point remains that a full explanation of the pro-attitude that may accompany an evaluative judgment of an object needs to make reference to the pleasurable mental experiences that accompany our consideration of that object.

The key issue for our larger discussion is whether the goodness of an object or state of affairs can be affected by extrinsic considerations. If so, then the claim might be made that extrinsic considerations (e.g., the distaste we may feel at others' or our own episodes of pleasure in witnessing another person's misfortune) can affect the intrinsic value of some state of affairs (e.g., these episodes of pleasure associated with schadenfreude). Continuing my response from the previous paragraph, let us consider cases where we value some object or state of affairs at least partly in virtue of the extrinsic properties it has. The critic of mental statism will claim that our positive valuation of the object or state of affairs serves as evidence of the intrinsic value of the *object or state of affairs*. The mental statist will claim that our positive (rather than negative or nonexistent) valuation of the object or state of affairs serves as evidence of the *pleasurable mental experiences* we have while considering the object or state of affair's extrinsic properties. I do not see how our positive valuations of, say, Lincoln's pen lend greater evidential support for the critic's conclusion than for the mental statist's conclusion. If we judge this matter a stalemate, and if we then look for further considerations whether to side with or reject the critic's conclusion, we come once again to what seems to me the strong intuitive appeal of welfarism, discussed in section 2.1. Combined with the further arguments in that section that our lives go well for us in virtue of the intrinsic nature of the mental states we have, I think we have decisive reason to reject the claim that extrinsic considerations can affect the intrinsic value of some object or state of affairs (such as a mental state).

We have thus far in this section considered arguments against mental statism that (1) appeal to our disapproving or disvaluing of certain pleasurable experiences (like bestial pleasures or the pleasures associated with schadenfreude) and then (2) attempt to conclude that these pleasurable experiences do not have positive, noninstrumental value. I have argued that the jump from (1) to (2) cannot be made without simply challenging the mental-statist conception of the good as a whole. The particular pleasurable mental states associated with objects or activities we disvalue do not pose any special problem for the mental statist. Perhaps we should not therefore be surprised that arguments against mental statism that focus on such distasteful pleasures as schadenfreude so often take the form of mere appeal to some immediate intuition that we should resist assigning value to these pleasures.

Before concluding this section, let me turn briefly to the arguments the *mental statist* might offer—beyond the arguments of the previous sections in this chapter—in support of the positive value of pleasures associated with schadenfreude. Interestingly, some defenders of this position have noted that the *critic* of the position might actually be assuming the *truth* of the position in arguing against it. Recall Ross's judgment that the "allocation of pleasure to the virtuous" is intrinsically good. Ross later elaborates that it is an "independent good" that there should be "the apportionment of pleasure and pain to the virtuous and vicious respectively" (1930, 138). Irwin Goldstein wonders why we should find the pleasures enjoyed by the vicious so distasteful. With respect to the "mass murderer retiring to days rich in undeserved pleasure," Goldstein claims that "we denounce the pleasure *because* of its good; moral degenerates luxuriating in health, happiness, or long life seems repugnant for the same reason" (1989, 269).[67]

While interesting, this line of argument is not conclusive, even as an ad hominem argument. As Stuart Rachels notes, the critic may say: "I don't denounce the villain's pleasures because they're good. I denounce them because he enjoys them; and, for that reason, they're not good" (2004, 259). Rachels instead offers the following argument that pleasures are good, even when enjoyed in contexts that we might condemn:

Intense pleasure is good when taken in a neutral object (such as a silly joke), and intense pleasure is good that lacks any objects (as in generalized euphoria). Think of such pleasures that do not accompany laudable or culpable behavior; are neither deserved nor undeserved; and stem from neither error nor insight. These pleasures are good merely because they feel good. But, if so, then altering their extrinsic properties shouldn't affect *that* value. Therefore, pleasures are good irrespective of what they're taken in; of what accompanies them; of what they depend on; and of whether they're deserved. (2004, 259–60)[68]

Rachels anticipates that the critic might then object that the pleasures of generalized euphoria are not good merely in virtue of how they feel. Rather, the critic might insist, these pleasures are good because they feel a certain way *and* because they are not taken in bad objects. But Rachels's response to this objection is: "Given that such euphoria has no object, object-talk is irrelevant to its value. Its goodness resides in its feel; describing what it's like suffices to account for its value. And experiencing such pleasure suffices for us to understand its value. This response, I think, is better than the objection. If so, then the argument supports [the thesis]: pleasures are good even in bad company" (2004, 260).[69] Even setting aside my previous reasons, as outlined in the previous sections of this chapter, for affirming mental statism, I am inclined to think that Rachels's response is indeed better than the objection on this specific point about pleasures taken in objects or activities we might disvalue or dislike. Still, whatever the force of Goldstein's and Rachels's arguments *for* the value of pleasures even within objectionable contexts like that of schadenfreude, the defensive point of this section remains that cases of schadenfreude do not serve as a special problem for the mental statist. Though we may object to, or disvalue, some mental state of pleasure enjoyed by others or ourselves, this point can be accounted for within the mental-statist position and does not by itself serve as evidence against that position.

To summarize in the broadest terms the arguments of this chapter, I have rejected nonwelfarist accounts of the good, arguing instead that something can be good only if it is good *for* someone. In assessing competing welfarist theories, I have defended a purely mental-state account whereby one's welfare is solely a matter of (the intrinsic qualities of) one's mental states. These discussions have been largely formal ones. Looking ahead to Part II of this book, I will offer a more substantive account of the particular mental states that hold the key to our attainment of the good life.

In this latter half of the book I will also explore the kinds of decisions we can make that lead us toward this good life. But before offering this substantive account of decision making and the good life, I need to lay some further groundwork. Specifically, I need to discuss why humans are moved to make decisions. An examination of human motivation will therefore be the focus of chapter 3. Arguably, humans are moved not only by (axiological) considerations of what is *valuable* but also by (deontological) considerations of what is *right* or *wrong*. So our discussion in the next chapter will lead us also to consider the relationship between the good and the right. I will offer a particular account of this relationship, consistent with my broader conclusions about human motivation. These conclusions will again serve as groundwork for my substantive discussions in Part II about attaining the kind of good life I believe is possible for every person.

CHAPTER THREE

# Motivations, the Good, and the Right

## 3.1 Sticking to Humean Guns

Since at least the time of Socrates, philosophical discussions of affective attitudes like feelings, desires, and passions have largely been in the context of how they might be reined in. In the *Gorgias*, Plato records Callicles as asking: "How can a man be happy who is the servant of anything? On the contrary, I plainly assert, that he who would truly live ought to allow his desires to wax to the uttermost, and not to chastise them; but when they have grown to their greatest he should have courage and intelligence to minister to them and to satisfy all his longings" (1871, §491, 80). Against this picture of simply indulging one's desires, Socrates—and Plato and Aristotle after him—advocated temperance. Socrates stressed the need for self-mastery, or "ruling over oneself," a phrase he spelled out in terms of a person being "a ruler of his own pleasures and passions" (Plato 1871, §491, 80). To his credit, Socrates did not advocate simply *eliminating* or *suppressing* one's desires; he advocated making them responsive to the more stable system of values one has. Nevertheless, desires are ultimately reined in by a higher-order mechanism, *reason*, which plays the key role in improving one's appreciation of values, virtues, and what makes for a good life.

The link between reason and moral progress perhaps reached its most extravagant height in Immanuel Kant, who identified the very act of the will with the exercise of practical reason in the application of certain rules: "Only a rational being has the power to act in accordance with his ideas of laws—that is in accordance with principles—and only so has he a will" (2004, chap. II, §412, 76). The alternative, for Kant, of exercising reason in this manner is utter subjection to one's passions. Inasmuch as morally good actions involve willful choices, it is not surprising that Kant went on to link proper, moral actions with rational actions.

By contrast, David Hume's analysis of intentional actions provides a way for us to see morally significant choices as choices between competing desires or attractions. Admittedly, Hume seemed not to appreciate all the ways in which reasoning can affect our desires. He relegated reason to the dual roles of determining *how* we might achieve our desires and identifying *what* features a particular object or event has. And as regards this second role, the reader of Hume can be left with the impression that reason simply uncovers features toward which one has preexisting attractions or aversions. But surely we should note that the process of identifying features of an object or event—thinking through the further things it makes possible or precludes, learning about the impact it has on others, and so forth—can greatly affect what attractions or aversions we have to the object or event in question.[1]

Nevertheless, I think Hume is right to complain that the history of Western moral philosophy is marked by the tendency to overstate the role that reason—vis-à-vis our desires—can and should play in our decisions. "Nothing is more usual in philosophy, and even in common life, than to talk of the combat of passion and reason, to give the preference to reason, and to assert that men are only so far virtuous as they conform themselves to its dictates. Every rational creature, 'tis said, is oblig'd to regulate his actions by reason; and if any other motive or principle challenge the direction of his conduct, he ought to oppose it, 'till it be entirely subdu'd, or at least brought to a conformity with that superior principle" (Hume 1978, II, iii, §3, 415). Hume viewed it as misleading to think of reason as an *alternative* to desires when discussing human motivations. Reason—and perhaps we should say any *belief* in general, whether arrived at by a process of reasoning or not—is motivationally inert. An analysis of some *desire* will always be the kind of analysis that explains the motivation to perform any intentional action.[2]

I think Hume's framework for explaining motivations is correct. If we ask why a person is motivated to perform some action, the obvious initial answer is that the action is attractive to her in some way. More precisely, when she focuses her attention on the action (or on some object related to the action), she experiences positive mental sensations with certain feeling tones to them. In section 1.4 I discussed the impelling force of a desire, which I characterized in terms of the dichotomous feeling tones of "release" and "frustration."[3] On the Humean model that I now want to defend, being motivated to perform some action will always be a matter of having some desire that impels one to perform that action.[4]

One standard objection to the Humean model is that *beliefs* sometimes motivate us when we perform various actions, as evidenced by the fact that our belief that some action is good or right always seems to track with a motivation to perform that action. While conceding that many of our beliefs (e.g., that dolphins tend to be larger than porpoises) carry no internal motivation to perform any action, many moral philosophers nevertheless insist that other kinds of beliefs *do* themselves impel us to act. We might designate these beliefs as "moral beliefs." Or, if we want to avoid possible complications arising from the term *moral*, we might focus—despite my own reservations about talking in terms of *reasons*—more broadly on beliefs about "what there is reason to do."[5] While philosophers have offered various explanations as to why these beliefs (purportedly) carry their own internal motivation, the plausibility of internalism in general stems from the way our beliefs about a reason for acting seem to coincide with a felt push to act.

Suppose I form the belief that it is wrong for me to cheat on my taxes. Or suppose I judge that there are reasons for me to contribute to a medical mission to a third world country. Or suppose I become convinced that I should visit my sick aunt. It would be simply incredible if I were to claim that, despite having these beliefs, I felt no accompanying motivation to act. We need not go as far as some moral philosophers in suggesting that a belief that I have most reason to perform some action is tied to an intention to perform that action. I may think that, all things considered, there is most reason for me to visit my sick aunt. Yet I may end up giving in to my desire to attend a ballgame. Weakness of the will is a genuine possibility and indeed a common occurrence.[6] Nevertheless, it remains incredible to claim that I earnestly believed that I should visit my aunt but felt absolutely *no* motivation to do so. The same goes for the belief that it would be wrong to cheat on my taxes or the belief that there are reasons to contribute to a medical mission. If our motivations really do consist in the feeling tones associated with a *desire*, to the exclusion of (purportedly) motivating moral *beliefs*, then how do I account for the coincidence between such beliefs and felt motivations?

In responding to this question, I think it important first to distinguish between the beliefs about an action's or state of affairs' *goodness* and its *rightness*. We have already seen in chapter 1 that the affirmation that something is "good" is linked with thinking that it answers to someone's interests. On the other hand, the concepts "right" and "wrong" seem to be tied to such further concepts as obligation, guilt/innocence, and social sanction. Explanations why motivations track with moral beliefs will differ according to whether the belief is about something being good/bad or about it being right/wrong. Let me start with beliefs about what is good or bad.

The first point to make about beliefs involving goodness is that they do *not* in fact always coincide with motivations. If I think that something is good because it answers to my own interests, then of course I will have a pro-attitude toward it. If I think that something is good because it answers to the interests of someone whose interests I have in some way made my own, interests I feel are "tied to my own," then again I will have a pro-attitude toward it. Put another way, if the person whose interests are in question is a person whose life I desire to go well for him—in such a way that my own unhappiness increases with the belief that he is unhappy—then I will of course have a pro-attitude toward those things that answer to his interests. This point applies for individuals I can personally identify (e.g., my child, or a friend) and for individuals whose interests can (unlike characters from novels) genuinely be affected, yet whom I cannot name specifically (e.g., the people in Malawian communities who, according to a news report I read, are lamentably without access to clean drinking water).

If, however, I identify something as good because it answers to the interests of someone whose well-being I do not desire be maintained or furthered, then I will not, ceteris paribus, have a pro-attitude toward it. A person may genuinely wish ill of a work colleague who is having a birthday. If so, the person could still identify a surprise birthday party for the colleague as a "good" one—that is, as answering to the interests of the colleague—all the while being in no way motivated (indeed, quite the opposite) to contribute in any way to that party.

So one's affirmation that something is good coincides with a motivation only if the person whose interests one is considering is oneself or someone else whose life one desires to go well for him. In these cases there is no reason to suppose that the motivation stems from something internal to one's *beliefs*. Rather, it is the positive feeling tone associated with a desire that readily explains why a motivation would accompany these beliefs about the goodness of some action or state of affairs.

A different set of considerations arise when we turn to the belief that an action or state of affairs is right or wrong. The corresponding concepts right/wrong seem to be linked to a cluster of other concepts, including blameworthiness and punishment. If I always do what is right, it seems that I cannot rightly be *blamed* for anything; and when I do something wrong, I do seem to become a candidate for blame. Accordingly, when I do something wrong there seems to be a basis for *punishing* me; if I always do what is right, I seemingly cannot appropriately be punished. These further concepts linked to rightness/wrongness thus involve social sanction.[7]

Social sanction provides the starting point for understanding why a belief that some action is right (or wrong) coincides with a motivation to perform (or avoid) that action. The mental experiences that make our lives go well (or not well) for us are greatly affected by (our beliefs about) others' attitudes toward us. Accordingly, we desire that others approve our actions and commend us, while desiring that others *not* condemn our actions and reprove us. Hence, if I believe that some action is wrong for me to do, my desire for my own flourishing, combined with my belief that in doing that action I become a candidate for reactions of rebuff (which would undermine my flourishing), ensures that I have a motivation not to perform the action. A corresponding story could of course be told about a motivation to perform actions that I believe to be right.

As with a belief that some action is good, a belief that some action is right or wrong does not automatically mean I will attempt to perform that action. The phenomenon of weakness of will is enough to establish this point. Also, a belief about the rightness or wrongness of an action does not entail that, all things considered, I believe it is an action I should actually perform. Aside from the (debated) issue of having conflicting obligations, it seems obvious enough that supererogatory acts (e.g., wading into a dangerously swollen river to help rescue a stranger caught in its currents) can sometimes trump obligatory acts (e.g., keeping a promise to meet a friend for lunch). Believing an action right or obligatory does not automatically mean I think I should, all things considered, perform it. The belief does, though, ensure that I will have *some* motivation to perform it, just as thinking some action wrong ensures that I will have some motivation to refrain from performing it. The motivation is again linked to the effects that social sanction—both positive and negative—has on our well-being.[8]

I have thus far discussed the link between social sanction and motivation in quite general terms. It seems obvious enough that we desire agreement and encouragement from others, and not conflict and reproach. Yet the motivation provided by the threat of social sanction has certain unique features, which are not appreciated merely by noting the positive and negative feeling tones that all desires broadly have in common. In the following section I want to explore these unique features. Also, social sanction seems only one source of the normative pressure we can feel to act a certain way. And so, to appreciate more fully why social sanction motivates us, we will need a framework for understanding more generally the phenomenon of normative pressure, or force.

## 3.2 The Source of Normative Force

As I drive along in my car, a passenger friend may say to me, "There's a stop sign over there." In certain contexts this remark would merely elicit from me the kind of feeling that comes when we learn a piece of trivial information. Perhaps my friend is noting to me that his new spectacle lenses now allow him to see objects quite far away. However, if my friend's remark is a way of saying to me, "You should stop," the feelings with which I find myself are markedly different. The idea that I *should* do something, that I *ought* to do it, introduces a phenomenon that is crucial to any ethical framework.

When told that we ought to do something, we feel as though something from the outside is impinging upon us. We lose a sense of freedom: the freedom to chart our own course and act according to our own preferences. Some demand has been placed on us, as when a loud knock at the door interrupts our time of restful reading on the couch. It feels as though we are suddenly in an arena with fixed rules and penalties, even though we did not necessarily have a say either in the formation of these rules or on the matter of whether we would participate. How does this normative force, this pressure to act a certain way, arise?

While it is quite fashionable these days to talk of *reasons* in connection with normativity, I shall not do so. Perhaps the appeal to reasons is beneficial within discussions of, for example, the requirements of rationality. And inasmuch as the appeal to reasons helps to make people's actions intelligible, giving us a way to understand their thought processes, then references to people's reasons serve a useful purpose indeed. At the same time, the appeal to reasons in offering an account of people's *motivations* is, I think, an unpromising methodology.

In explaining why someone acted (intentionally) in a particular way, we will need to appeal to features of the person's psychology. Granted, in trying to retain the terminology of reasons, we could restrict our discussion of reasons to "the reasons a person *has*" or to a person's "subjective reasons." Nevertheless, we would still be left with the crucial question whether the motivation within a so-called "motivating reason" can always be spelled out in terms of a *desire(s)* or whether the internal features of a *belief* can themselves sometimes explain why a person is motivated to perform some action. I know of no convincing argument for the conclusion that a belief could motivate us. Such attempted arguments often take the form of citing some principle of rationality and then arguing that any rational person who forms some particular belief—such as a means-end belief—will be motivated to perform an action.[9] But as far as I can tell, there simply is never any real explanation offered as to why rationality should *move* us to act.[10] (Stating *that* rational people are guided by means-end beliefs is different from showing *why* the activity of practical reasoning should itself impel us to act.) A Humean approach to "motivating reasons"—where the pleasant and unpleasant feeling tones we experience as we contemplate or pursue certain projects move, or impel, us to pursue some projects and not others, with beliefs simply explaining why we pursue a given, desired project through one action rather than through another action—is far more compelling as an account of what moves us to act.

It might be objected here that, instead of juxtaposing desires and beliefs as I have done, we should think of a reason as the *combination* of some belief(s) and desire(s) one has. Consider, for example, Niko Kolodny's analysis of the reasons for love: "[Love] partly consists in the belief that some relationship renders it appropriate, and the emotions and motivations of love are causally sustained by this belief" (2003, 146). Especially given that my broader concern in Part II will be the motivations that prompt us to participate in loving relationships, one might object that an explanation of a person's motivations to relate to others cannot merely focus on one's *desires*, to the exclusion of one's *beliefs*.

In response, I would certainly want to acknowledge that our beliefs about a relationship can affect the desires we have to relate to the person in question. And there is indeed room to explore the ways in which various beliefs *should*—if ideal, loving relationships are to be formed and maintained—affect one's desires to interact with others. However, the fact remains that desires and beliefs have differing "directions of fit." Briefly, beliefs are representational in nature. As Mark Platts puts it, "Beliefs aim at being true, and their being true is their fitting the world." If we find that some standing belief of ours does not align with the way the world is, our belief must change accordingly if it is to be a bona fide belief. On the other hand, desires, Platts continues, "aim at realization, and their realization is the world fitting with them" (1979, 257). If we find that the world does not align with some desire we have, our desire need not—and indeed typically does not—disappear. Rather, we are moved, or impelled, to change the world in an attempt to make it fit with our desire.[11] Given that desires, and not beliefs, are what move us to act, they remain the particular kind of mental state on which we must focus in exploring *motivation*, including the kind of motivation we experience as normative pressure.

In Kolodny's discussion of the reasons for love, he comments that love is "rendered *normatively appropriate* by the presence of a relationship" (2003, 146). I would not object to this phrase, provided we do not understand our participation in some relationship as itself the source of any normative pressure we feel. Strictly speaking, it will be some *desire(s)* we have—for example, the desire to maintain that relationship in its current shape—that will move or impel us to continue interacting with the other person. To the person who no longer has any desire to maintain a certain type of relationship with a particular person, there simply is no scope for her to be moved, or impelled, to continue in the relationship. We might say that she "should" continue in the relationship because we think it the case that good states of affairs really will fail to materialize if she discontinues the relationship. But my point here is that *she* will not feel any normative pressure to relate to the other person in ways that continue their relationship. Following Hume, I think the point remains that the mental state of a desire is where we must look in explaining human motivation—including the motivation we associate with normative pressure.

I recognize that some philosophers will view this fixation on human psychology as misguided. Consider Philippa Foot's depiction of a person who throws away his supply of cigarettes:

> He does so because he wants to give up smoking. And he wants to give up smoking because he wants a healthy old age. The series goes on—A for the sake of B—but it can't go on forever. Must it not end with something that the agent "just wants"; in other words, with some "conative" element in his individual psychological state? The question is meant to be rhetorical; but the answer to it is "No." . . . Why do we say that what gets the whole thing going must be a desire or other "conative" element in the subject's "psychological state"? Suppose instead that it is the recognition that there is reason for him, as for anyone else, to look after his future so far as circumstances allow? Why should not this be where the series of questions "Why?" comes to an end? (2001, 22)

In response, it may be worth making the preliminary point that I do not see the issue of a *series* as any key issue here. Admittedly, a person may want to give up cigarettes because she wants to live a healthy life. Perhaps it is only after reflecting on her long-term health prospects—and perhaps even reflecting on her *desire* that she live to a ripe old age—that she finds herself with the desire to quit smoking. Perhaps the person's initial desire arises because she is becoming uncomfortable at the prospect of losing a certain kind of freedom if she becomes captive to addiction. But of course her desire may arise from *no* further considerations. She may simply wake up one day feeling repelled at the prospect of smoking another cigarette, unable to offer any explanation to someone who asks, "But why this sudden disgust?" We find ourselves with desires in all kinds of contexts—sometimes because of some further desire and/or some further reflection, sometimes not. So the key issue is not where the "series of questions 'Why?' stops." Whether there is or is not a series leading to some particular desire, the key question is whether we need to appeal to (the psychological phenomena of) this desire in order to explain a person's motivation in intentionally acting.

Foot finds such an appeal unnecessary. Addressing the "Why?" in the case of the person who gives up smoking, she comments, "No special explanation is needed of why men take reasonable care of their own future; an explanation is needed when they do not" (2001, 23). If our concern is the requirements of rationality, then Foot's point is well taken. However, I cannot see any necessary link between the rationality of some action and the psychological phenomenon of feeling impelled to perform some action. Outside of an analysis of this psychological phenomenon, I cannot see what we could possibly analyze as a way of shedding light on what human motivation itself consists in.[12] A desire, I take it, is the name we give to this psychological phenomenon of feeling impelled. And so it seems obvious to me that we must unpack the nuances of desires if we are to shed light on the ways humans are motivated.

With various conditions to come later, I contend that normative pressure to perform an action can be spelled out in terms of the negative feeling tones we experience as we consider states of affairs that may arise if we do not perform that action. *Negative feeling tone* here refers to the aspect of desires I earlier characterized as "frustration"—in contrast to the positive feeling tone of "release." (Alternatively, we might perhaps use the terms *dissatisfaction* and *enticement* to describe the respective feeling tones of a desire.) Negative feeling tones seem, phenomenologically, to *push* us to act, whereas positive feeling tones seem to *draw* us. The account of normative pressure I want to advance allows for a very wide range of motivations that fall within the category of normative pressure. But I do not think our experience of normative pressure aligns with *all* motivations constitutive of desires. Specifically, the *positive attraction* we feel toward some action or state of affairs does not, I think, provide for the kind of mental experience we associate with normative pressure. I think any time we feel pressure that we *should* or *ought* to do something, the force we feel is something other than mere attraction. I think the pressure in question is, in one way or another, the *"push"* of the negative feeling tones of a desire. One happy outcome of this account of normative force is that, if this force simply *is* the negative feeling tones of a desire, then the motivational force that accompanies normative judgments (about what we should or ought to do) is no more mysterious than the motivational force provided by desires.

There is a broad objection to this approach to explaining the nature of normative pressure; and much of the remaining discussion in this chapter will be directed to it. Let me mention first, though, two kinds of objection with which I am *not* going to engage. First, I am not going to engage with proposals that, in order to understand normativity, we need to focus on what reasons exist for a person *being motivated*. In his discussion of the reasons we have for acting, Derek Parfit remarks that "when we have a reason to do something, this reason is not provided by, and does not require, the fact that after Internalist deliberation we would want to do this thing. This reason is provided by the facts that also give us reason to have this desire" (1997, 130).[13] A discussion of the reasons for having a desire may help us understand why a person acted; and it may perhaps lead to discussions of what does and does not count as a rational action or a rational recognition of reasons. Foot's reference to a "series of questions 'Why?'" leads us toward such discussions. But whatever the explanatory reasons or the cause of some motivation, motivation itself (i.e., the force that moves us to act) consists in the pleasurable and unpleasurable feeling tones of a desire. Accordingly, in offering an account of normative force, I want to emphasize that I shall be focusing only on the motivational force of a desire.

Second, I am not going to engage with investigations of normativity that connect the concept "ought" to judgments we make *in light of* our desires (rather than to the desires themselves). Jonathan Dancy notes that "the decision that one option is more pleasant, and from that point of view better, is not itself the decision that this is 'what I shall do'" (2004, 118). Dancy then relies on this point in distinguishing "enticing reasons" (which "take us to 'bests'"—namely, to that which we judge is the best, or most good, thing to do) from "peremptory reasons" (which "take us to 'oughts'"—namely, to that which we judge is the thing to do) (2004, 116). Enticing reasons have an "evaluative focus" and can help us answer the question "What shall I decide to do?" By contrast, peremptory reasons have a "deontic focus" and help in answering the question "What should I decide to do?" (2004, 111, 116). Perhaps one might rely on this line of contrast to claim that we do not arrive at the concepts "should" and "ought" merely by making evaluative judgments about well-being[14]—let alone, even more minimally, experiencing positive and negative mental states. Instead, what "takes us to" the idea that we should, or ought, to do something is our all-things-considered judgment about what is to be done. Or perhaps what takes us to these deontic concepts is our belief that something is to be done because of deontic considerations that it would be wrong to do (or not to do) it.

In response, let me again emphasize that my concern is with the normative *force* we feel—a force that we experience as being impelled to act. Thus, even in cases where our judgment itself (about what to do) helps explain our motivation to act, it is still the mental state of a desire—as that which moves us to act—that will be our concern.[15] As for the normative force we feel from deontic considerations of what is right or wrong to do, I shall argue that this normative force is actually a subset of the more general, impelling force of a desire (which sometimes, though not always, involves a more reflective evaluation of some sort). So my account of normative force will once again focus on the motivational nature of a desire—even in cases where the context of one's motivation involves a belief that there is some action that would be wrong to do (or not to do).

Now that I have noted the kinds of issues with which I shall *not* engage, the discussion here of beliefs about what is right and wrong usefully leads us to the broad kind of objection that I *do* want to address at length.¹⁶ The general, Humean approach to motivation leaves us with the matter of explaining why normative pressure seems, phenomenologically, to come from the *outside*, placing demands on us whether we like it or not. This phenomenology seems especially keen at times when we believe some action is wrong for us to do, whether or not we would like things to be as we believe they are. If motivation is a matter of *our own* desires, the critic will ask, then how is it that normative pressure feels as if it comes from the outside, sometimes unwanted by us? In the course of spelling out my own explanation of the source of normative pressure, I shall remain mindful of the need to account for this sense of being *confronted* with what one believes to be true about some situation.

My central claim is that a normative judgment will involve our consideration of some state of affairs toward which we have a negative attitude.¹⁷ Our consideration of an unwelcome state of affairs can occur in two broad ways. First, our attention can be drawn to some unwelcome outcome. Our negative experiences here stem from the thought that if we do not do something we "should" do, we will run the risk of this unwelcome outcome occurring. This first broad avenue to normative pressure is fairly straightforward, though we should perhaps clarify the conditions under which an unwelcome outcome motivates us to avoid that outcome.

When I consider the prospect of eating an earthworm, listening to loud country music, or sitting through a two-hour seminar on time-share opportunities, I experience negative feelings. As I make my daily decisions, these outcomes are among the ones I want to avoid. Often, it is my imagined lack of enjoyment, should an outcome materialize, that leads to my current negative feelings as I contemplate that outcome.¹⁸ Alternatively, I might have a negative feeling toward some outcome because, for example, I imagine that it will lessen the enjoyment of someone toward whom I have affection. But whatever the explanation of my negative mental experiences when I consider some state of affairs, these negative experiences serve to motivate me to avoid that state of affairs.

At least, these experiences serve to motivate me when certain conditions are met. Importantly, I will need to be aware of an alternative possibility in which the unwanted state of affairs would be avoided. If I simply had negative associations with some state of affairs but lacked any idea that that state of affairs could be avoided, my negative associations would not motivate me to act in any way. I would be in a position similar to that of an infant who is cold. The infant might be described as unhappy because of the uncomfortable temperature; but the infant has no idea what might be done to change the situation. In coming to judge that I "should not" do something, the idea is present (at some level of consciousness) that there exists some possible, better alternative.[19] Even if I am not focusing my attention on this alternative, it remains in the background in the sense that I have *some* level of awareness of it. Also, I will need to have some idea that *I* might do something to help prevent the unwanted outcome. Otherwise, I may experience anxiety similar to that of a soccer parent watching helplessly as her child lines up a penalty kick in the big match. But I will not experience genuine normative pressure that motivates me to perform an action.

Thus the first broad avenue to normative pressure remains fairly straightforward. In these kinds of cases, forming the judgment that I ought (or ought not) to do something is a matter of grasping features—which I do not welcome—of some state of affairs. When others tell me that I ought (or ought not) to do something, they are pointing out to me, or at least reminding me of, the features of some state of affairs (and perhaps also reminding me why it is not in my interest to welcome these features). For others to make a statement concerning what I ought (or ought not) to do, they must have some idea of an alternative possibility by which I might avoid the unwelcome state of affairs.[20] Otherwise they might lament, object to, or commiserate with my plight, but they would have no thought about my doing one thing over against another.

The second broad avenue to normative pressure is more complicated. The process begins by identifying some state of affairs toward which we have a *pro*-attitude. As with the first broad avenue to normative pressure, the process will *end* with us identifying some *un*wanted outcome and experiencing the negative feeling tones toward that outcome constitutive of normative pressure. But on this second broad avenue to normative pressure, the first step in the process is to identify some state of affairs that one welcomes. Certain conditions must then accompany this identification if it is to lead eventually to feelings of normative pressure. Chiefly, it will need to be the case that the welcome state of affairs is at some risk of failing to occur.

Consider an example in which *no* risk exists to a welcome state of affairs. Suppose David has climbed into a seat on board the world's highest, fastest roller coaster. The attendant has locked the bulky safety harness down against David's torso, and a conveyer belt is now moving David's car slowly up toward the top of the first hill. David remains excited at the prospect of rushing down this first hill. Is he motivated to act in any way? The answer is surely "no." There is an inevitability to the world changing (as the conveyor belt continues to lift the roller-coaster cars until gravity takes over) so that it lines up with David's desire (to speed down the hills of the roller coaster). David is very aware that, even if he wanted to escape his fate, he could not possibly wriggle out of the locked safety harness or shout loudly enough for the roller-coaster operator to hear him back on the starting platform. For the next few minutes, he is truly along for the ride. Of course, in our example David very much desires to ride the fast parts of the roller coaster. If we want to use the language of reasons, this anticipated enjoyment serves as a reason for him to stay on the roller coaster. But this pro-attitude he has toward remaining on the roller coaster does not *motivate* him to stay on the roller coaster. He is not at present motivated to do anything (aside from perhaps raising his arms as a way of demonstrating his lack of fear to his girlfriend).

Thus far in our second avenue to normative pressure we have noted that a person identifies some wanted outcome, he believes that this outcome is not guaranteed, and he believes that he can help ensure the outcome. We can now add that the feelings associated with normative pressure are the feelings that come when a person reflectively considers the prospect of *missing out* on the wanted outcome.

To illustrate this type of reflective consideration, suppose Tom convinces Lucy to attend the cinema one evening, despite Lucy lobbying that they should attend a folk dancing festival. Sitting in his theater seat, Tom is engrossed as he watches the film. It seems right to say that the attractiveness of the film—that is, the pleasant mental experiences he has as he views the film—motivates him to continue watching it. While engrossed in the film, he is not reflecting on any possible decision *whether* to watch the film. And without any consideration of the possibility of *not* watching the film, he experiences no negative feeling tone (which might motivate him to perform some action). Put another way, he experiences the "release" aspect of a desire but not the corresponding "frustration" aspect of a typical desire.[21]

We can now change our illustration to show how the negative aspect of a desire *can* arise and motivate one to act. Suppose that Lucy is not as enamored with the film as is Tom. Halfway through the film she nudges Tom and says, "Do you want to leave? We can still catch the last half of the folk dancing festival." Tom is now jolted out of his nonreflective state of enjoyment as his attention is called to the matter of whether or not to stay.[22] Tom will think through (some of) the implications—that is, the pros and cons—of staying at the cinema versus not staying. Thinking through such implications is simply part of making sense of the options to which Lucy has alluded. His attention is no longer simply on *the film*; rather, his attention is on his positive experiences thus far in watching the film and on the further positive experiences he anticipates having if he stays. Put another way, his thought processes will include the idea that he will *miss out* on certain states of affairs if he leaves the cinema. The negative feeling tones associated with this consideration will then serve as a motivation impelling him to stay (even while other considerations may of course impel him to leave). Thus normative pressure here is linked to the idea of "opportunity cost"—a term I borrow from economics that alludes to the real cost of any capital outlay as being the lost outcome(s) that would have resulted had the capital been used in an alternative way(s). Normative pressure is felt when one is confronted with the things of value that will be lost, or missed, if one acts (or does not act) in a certain way.

We noted earlier that our second avenue to normative pressure begins with identifying some welcome state of affairs. Accordingly, when we evaluate some action, trying to determine whether it is indeed something we ought to do, we sometimes think of what there is to be said *for* that action. That is, we sometimes reflect on what we find attractive about that action. In the case of Tom, he might reflect on good experiences he anticipates he will have if he continues to watch the film. But such reflection does not, strictly speaking, itself produce the kind of normative pressure associated with the idea that we should, or ought, to do something. This normative pressure comes only as Tom recognizes that he will *miss out* on this enjoyment if he agrees to leave the cinema halfway through the film. Thus, in our second broad way in which normative pressure arises, just as was the case in the first broad way, normative pressure is constituted by the negative aspect of a desire. That is, normative pressure is constituted by the feelings that arise when we consider an unwelcome outcome.

In saying that a person does not want to miss out on some welcome outcome, it may be that one does not actually think that this welcome outcome will consist of experiences that in and of themselves will be primarily positive. Instead, the welcome outcome may simply be *less bad* anticipated experiences, as one makes comparative judgments. We might alter our example of Tom and Lucy by supposing that Tom really dislikes the film. But the thought of the folk dance festival, which he imagines would amount to sheer torture, drives him to resist leaving the film. Thus Tom does not anticipate having any experiences, if he stays at the cinema, that would be on balance positive in nature. Rather, his motivation stems from the extremely adverse reaction he has to the thought of spending an evening watching folk dancing. The welcome outcome, which he reflectively does not want to miss out on, consists of the experiences at the cinema that he believes will be comparatively less bad than those to be had watching folk dancing.

Of course, we could change again the example by supposing that Tom really does like folk dancing and that he imagines he would have an enjoyable time if he left the cinema and watched the last half of the dance festival. But we could now suppose that Tom has greatly looked forward to seeing the film, is engrossed in the film at present, and is desperately keen to see how the plot lines are resolved. Tom may thus conclude that, all things considered, he should stay. At the same time, I think it is right to describe Tom as feeling normative pressure to stay *and* normative pressure to leave. There is nothing uncommon about identifying multiple, welcome outcomes that are mutually exclusive. We may feel the "push," or negative aspect, of a desire when considering the possibility of missing out on any of these multiple outcomes. This point remains whether or not we feel the push more strongly when it comes to one of the outcomes—and whether or not we go on to act so as to avoid missing out on that outcome.

Having outlined now the second of our two broad avenues to normative pressure, one may wonder whether normative pressure perhaps *always* involves this second avenue. Do comparisons—and weighing of opportunity costs—indeed accompany *every* instance of reflection that leads to a conclusion that we ought to perform one action over another? The answer is "no." The feelings constitutive of normative force can sometimes arise when we consider only the negative consequences of an option (which is again the first avenue to normative pressure previously discussed). If the passenger in a car I am driving on the highway points to a policeman at the side of the road holding a radar gun, I may quickly conclude that I ought to slow down. Seemingly only the unwelcome, possible consequences of failing to slow down motivate me to slow down. I do not reflect on the *positive* consequences of slowing down: the things I could do with the time and emotional energy I save from not being pulled over for speeding; the things I could purchase with money that would otherwise go toward a speeding fine; and so forth. Admittedly, when setting the cruise control in the car, I might do a quick cost-benefit analysis about the speed at which it is wise to travel, given my goals at the time. But when a friend suddenly points out that a radar gun is tracking me, all I can think of is the unwelcome, possible outcome of being pulled over—an outcome whose likelihood is of course increased if I fail to slow down. So not all our negative attitudes toward outcomes arise from weighing an opportunity cost. And of course *both* avenues to normative pressure might at times be engaged, as when I am mindful of the opportunity cost of being fined for speeding *and* experience an immediate, uncomfortable surge of adrenaline when I see a radar gun tracking me.

We might also note that sometimes our attention can be focused on an action we think we *should do* and sometimes our attention can be focused on an action we think we should *not do*. Admittedly, almost any prohibition *against* performing some action can be recast as a demand *to* perform some other action(s), and vice versa. Still, it remains true that our thought processes are sometimes focused on an action we believe we ought to *refrain* from performing and sometimes they are focused on an action we believe we ought to endeavor to perform. In cases of the former, we often characterize our experiences as resisting temptation. In cases of the latter, we typically seek to overcome, among other things, inertia.

As a point of clarification within my larger discussion, I note that the following two distinctions do *not* run parallel: (1) the distinction between focusing on something we *should* do versus something we should *not* do; and (2) the first versus the second broad avenue to normative pressure that I have identified in this section. Let me illustrate each of the four combinations generated by these two distinctions.

1. Focusing on an act we *should* do, where normative force arises through the first broad avenue of identifying an unwelcome outcome.
   *Example: A car driver immediately depressing the brake pedal when a passenger yells, "Stop at the sign!" while pointing to a policeman monitoring the intersection.*

2. Focusing on an act we *should not* do, where normative force arises through the first broad avenue of identifying an unwelcome outcome.
   *Example: A grammar school boy who refrains at the last second from shooting a spitball when a friend yells, "Wait!" while motioning that the teacher is looking at them.*

3. Focusing on an act we *should* do, where normative force arises through the second broad avenue of identifying a welcome outcome on which we do not want to miss out.
   *Example: A teenager who is thoroughly bored with the conversation at a Christmas dinner but who keeps saying to herself, "Continue with the conversation" as she reminds herself of a promised new video game from her parents if she remains cheerful and engaged throughout the family gathering.*

4. Focusing on an act we *should not* do, where normative force arises through the second broad avenue of identifying a welcome outcome on which we do not want to miss out.
   *Example: A dieter who stops himself from reaching for the extra drink or dessert, cognizant of the goal he has set himself for the weigh-in at next week's weight loss support group.*

Given again the way in which almost any prohibition *against* performing some action might arguably be recast as a demand *to* perform some other action (and vice versa), I do not want to stake too much on the firmness of this distinction. But if there is a firm distinction between judging that one *ought* to perform an action and judging that one *ought not* to perform an action, the point for my larger discussion is that this distinction cuts across the distinction of the first and second broad avenues to normative force.

In highlighting earlier the merits of the Humean model of motivation, I also noted that Humeans need to account for the way in which normative pressure seems, phenomenologically, to come from the *outside*, placing demands on us whether we like it or not. There seem to me at least two broad, key factors that contribute to this phenomenon, as well as perhaps more minor factors that at times can play a role. One such minor factor is that we sometimes desire quite different things. At a given moment, the anticipated outcomes from doing *and* from not doing an action may be in certain respects unwelcome. Consider a teenage girl who decides to break up with her controlling boyfriend. She may very much welcome separation from this person whose character she has discovered to be abhorrent—even while *also* feeling, confusingly, dismayed at the idea of this separation. Thus, while one "part" of her welcomes the outcome of separation, another "part" of her does not welcome it. She may become frustrated with herself over the fact that she continues to feel attached to him even though she reflectively feels that, all things considered, breaking up with him is clearly the outcome she should, and does, welcome. Inasmuch as her negative feelings about an outcome (i.e., the outcome of being separated from a controlling boyfriend) may be opposite to the bulk of her feelings and to her better judgment, these residual feelings—which are a source of normative pressure that she *shouldn't* leave the boyfriend—may seem to come from the "outside." At least, they may seem so from the perspective of that "part" of her that *does* welcome the outcome (just as the normative pressure *to leave* the boyfriend may seem foreign to that "part" of her that is resisting leaving).

I want to focus, though, on what seem to me the two major factors contributing to the way normative pressure feels as though it comes to us from the outside. The first factor will tend to be more prominent in evaluations of what is good and bad, whereas the second factor will be more prominent in deontic conclusions of what is right and wrong.

The first factor involves a particular feeling tone that accompanies our experiences of normative pressure. Perhaps the best way to begin to describe this feeling tone—which can also arise in contexts other than normative pressure—is to note that it commonly leads us to say, "I didn't make the rules."

It is a contingent matter that the possibility of an unwelcome outcome should loom at a given time. The world could contain such resources and providential ordering that no danger existed of missing out on anything we desired or evaluated as good. It is a contingent matter that we should face decisions whether to avoid unwelcome outcomes. Contingent on what? All too obviously, the contingency does not arise from anything we had a say in creating or organizing. We *find ourselves* in positions where we will need to act in order to prevent unwelcome outcomes (of being pulled over for speeding, of missing the second half of a film, and so forth). We did not ask to be put in such positions. We did not ask to be in a world where we cannot *both* speed and be guaranteed always to get away with it. But in such a world we all are.

Admittedly, we may make decisions that affect the *particulars* of the decisions and potential outcomes we face. Deciding to go to the cinema, for example, I help determine what my options will be halfway through the movie and what I will miss out on if I leave to attend a folk dance festival. Deciding to exceed the speed limit, I set the stage for a later decision—with attendant consequences—whether to slow down as I see a policeman monitoring motorists' speeds. Someone might declare in such cases that I have "gotten myself into the situation" or have "made my own bed." Yet the broader point is that I have no say in whether these *kinds* of decisions, with possible unwelcome outcomes, arise—whatever the particulars of those decisions and whether I contribute to their shape.[23] We are faced in life with the fact that we cannot have it all, that undesirable scenarios exist and are sometimes unavoidable.

In sum, we do not have a say in whether we will find certain scenarios in life possible, unwelcome, and potentially avoidable through our actions. Given that we cannot avoid having desires of some kind, and given that we cannot avoid believing that the world may conflict at times with these desires, we will all feel the world at times impinging on us. We are not allowed a happy, utopian state to pursue our own projects while continuing fully to flourish. We must *react* to the world, to those situations into which we have not asked to be placed. The phenomenology that normative force comes to us "from the outside" is, I suggest, largely a product of the fact that decisions about avoiding unwelcome scenarios are decisions with which we find ourselves *faced*.

A second major factor in the "outside" feeling of normative pressure is seen most clearly in cases where one forms the belief that it is wrong to do (or not to do) something. A full articulation of the point I wish to make will take us into the final two sections of this chapter, in which we will explore the meaning and nature of "rightness" and "wrongness." But let me sketch in the remainder of this section this second major factor contributing to the outside feeling of normative pressure.

It is well established that we can form definite cognitive attitudes even when we are unaware through introspection that we have such cognitive attitudes. For example, although adults typically cannot consciously recall events that occurred when they were under three years old, many of these events are nonetheless remembered. The continuing effects of these memories (though again not *conscious* memories) are profound, with these memories influencing our perceptions of, and affective feelings about, our circumstances.

As small children we desperately need expressions of love and approval from parents and others around us. While small children may not grasp moral concepts such as obligation, culpability, rightness, and wrongness, they are certainly capable of appreciating aspects of (negative) social sanction that are connected to these concepts. Small children will be able to appreciate, for example, that "Daddy is angry" or that "Mommy is not responding to me in the loving way she normally does." Of course very small children will not use *terms* like *angry* and *loving*; but they are clearly able to appreciate negative experiences they have as they perceive the disapproval of those around them. As we mature to adulthood, we will often—noting the point from the previous paragraph—be unable through introspection to articulate, or even become consciously aware of, the beliefs we have. Therapists may help in bringing more of our beliefs to conscious awareness. But there will inevitably remain any number of unconscious beliefs—including beliefs about the manner and conditions of others' approval—that continue to affect our emotions and subsequent belief formation.

From early childhood, the authority figures in our lives tell us of the importance of eating vegetables, brushing our teeth, wearing a hat on a cold day, obeying the laws of the land, and so forth. These rules and guidelines of what J. S. Mill called "customary morality" are repeatedly enforced through social sanction. The associations we make between social sanction and rule breaking (or other kinds of prohibited behavior) are exceedingly complex. After all, our relationships within social networks are themselves hugely intricate; and the ways others express approval and disapproval to us can take any number of blatant or subtle forms. One upshot of these points is that we will typically not be able consciously to appreciate all the associations we make between (1) some action we believe to be wrong and (2) anticipated social sanctions if we perform that action.[24] Understandably, then, we may come to associate the breaking of a guideline with negative experiences of social disapproval, even while we may only scarcely be able to begin articulating all the instances in our pasts that have led us to make this association.

Let us return to the example of the motorist who approaches a traffic sign. In our earlier discussions of this example, we have imagined that the motorist may perhaps consider only the unwelcome outcome of being pulled over by a policeman. And we have imagined that the motorist, if given time to reflect, may also consider a planned purchase on which she would miss out if she were forced to pay a fine for a traffic violation. Let us suppose now that the motorist—upon seeing a stop sign and deliberating whether to come, inconveniently, to a full stop—sees that no police officer is in sight. Indeed, there is open space in all directions and the motorist can see that it is not possible that a hidden police officer might be observing the road intersection. Moreover, we suppose that the motorist clearly sees that there are no cars or pedestrians in the area—and thus that no danger of an accident exists. The motorist is completely alone. The motorist may even be a professional ethicist—perhaps a utilitarian—who holds the view that it is in no way irresponsible or morally objectionable to disobey minor traffic rules in such a clear case where no harm can come to others. In short, we imagine in this example that the motorist cannot identify anything specifically, should she fail to stop, on which she would miss out or more generally that would constitute an unwelcome outcome. Yet the motorist may still experience a hesitancy, a nagging feeling, that prevents her from unambiguously moving past the thought that she ought to come to a full stop.

The most plausible explanation of such a state of dis-ease is surely the association the motorist makes between breaking rules and social sanction. (A desire to avoid the kinds of negative experiences we associate with social sanction seems clearly the most plausible kind of desire that could be motivating our motorist. And a Humean account of motivation offers, again in my view, the only actual explanation of human motivation.) Given our deep need to relate positively to others, the idea of others disapproving of an action we perform is a very unwelcome outcome. If we want to cast these considerations in terms of "missing out," the belief that we may miss out on the goodwill of others can cause significant feelings of dis-ease. These points remain even if we note that our beliefs about unwelcome outcomes can occur at various levels of consciousness. Thus we can have a belief that we may miss out on the approval of others, even while we cannot consciously identify any specific *person's* disapproval or the precise *reason* we think this person (or persons) might disapprove. Indeed, the complex ways our associations (between breaking a rule and social sanction) are made seemingly ensure that we will typically not be able to appreciate fully, through introspection, why we think the failure to perform some action will result in the unwelcome outcome of social sanction.

For our motorist, the normative pressure she experiences in thinking she "ought to stop" at a stop sign stems, plausibly, from a combination of (1) her desire to avoid social sanction and (2) her belief that she must stop in order to avoid this unwelcome sanction. Still, the complex ways that associations are formed between social sanction and prohibited behavior all but ensure that she will have far less than both (1) a conscious recognition of the states of affairs at which her motivating desires are actually aiming (i.e., the avoidance of disapproval from past, present, and imagined people in her life) and (2) a fully conscious appreciation of why she believes that a failure to obey this traffic rule will invoke disapproval from some person(s). Understandably, then, the normative pressure she experiences in thinking she *ought* to stop at a stop sign will very much feel as though it is impinging on her from the outside.

In sum, there seem to be two key factors as to why normative pressure—that is, the feeling associated with the belief that we ought to do something—often seems as though it comes to us from the "outside." The first factor involves the way we find ourselves, as we make axiological judgments and strive for good outcomes, in a position not of our own choosing. Unwelcome outcomes abound if we do nothing; and in trying to avoid *one* unwelcome outcome we very often run into *another* unwelcome outcome. We thus continually face the restrictions and contingencies of our world, and this creates a feeling of having guidelines thrust upon us from someone or something outside us. The second factor involves the way we typically are not remotely able to identify all the associations we make between social sanction and an action being, we believe, wrong—even while the anticipation (at various levels of consciousness) of social sanction remains the most plausible explanation of our motivation to avoid that action. Hence, with plausible explanations available as to the phenomenology of normative pressure feeling as though it impinged on us from the outside, the Humean is free to emphasize the obvious merits of appealing simply to desires in explaining the source of normative pressure.

My discussion of this second factor, as noted earlier, introduces the larger point about the link between normative pressure and our judgments that some action is *wrong*. In the following section I shall examine further the concepts "right" and "wrong"—before exploring in section 3.4 the potential of finding any objectively correct answers to questions about either the right or the good.

### 3.3 The Concepts "Right" and "Wrong"

The terms *right* and *wrong* are sometimes used as descriptions that have nothing to do with ethical matters. For instance, we may use them as synonyms for *correct* and *incorrect*—as when we say, "You're right! J. L. Mackie was the one who espoused an 'error theory' about most people's moral judgments." Our concern in this chapter is for the concepts often called *moral* rightness and wrongness. We can think of these concepts as mirror images of each other. To say that some action is wrong necessarily implies that it is not right. And while the term *right* can sometimes be used to indicate merely that an action is not wrong (i.e., is permissible),

I will use the term in the stronger (and more common) sense as indicating the wrongness of not acting. Thus, to say that some action is right is just to say that it would be wrong not to perform it.

The concepts "right" and "wrong" differ from the concepts "good" and "bad" in several ways. One difference involves the sense in which the rightness or wrongness of an act seems to be an all-or-nothing proposition. We can naturally think of an act as being (instrumentally) more and more *good* as it provides more and more flourishing for someone. For instance, to visit my sick aunt and ensure her comfort for a day is a good act. To visit and ensure her comfort for two days is a better act in the sense of leading to more and more intrinsic goodness in the world (which comes in the form of positive mental states). In the same sense, my act of ensuring my aunt's comfort *and* providing peace of mind to my aunt's traveling family would be a better act than merely ensuring my aunt's comfort.[25] However, it would be odd to think of some act as possibly being "more *right*" (or more wrong) than some other act. If I have acted rightly, then seemingly I have not violated anything. If a violation—say, of some oath or of some rule—*has* taken place, then an act may be described as wrong. Perhaps another act might violate the same rule at further points (e.g., exceeding the speed limit for ten minutes versus five minutes) or might violate more than one rule (e.g., an act of speeding *and* of reckless endangerment versus an act merely of speeding). But the concepts themselves of rightness and wrongness do not seem to admit to degree in the way that goodness and badness do.

A further distinguishing feature of the concepts "right" and "wrong," as noted briefly in the previous section, involves the cluster of further concepts to which they are linked. These further concepts include innocence/guilt and praiseworthiness/blameworthiness. If I always do what is *right*, it seems that I am innocent and not guilty of anything; and if I do what is *wrong*, it seems that I *am* now guilty of something. Also, if I always do what is right, there seems no basis for assigning *blame* to me—whereas when I do something wrong, I do seem to become a proper candidate for blame. Accordingly, when I do something wrong there seems to be a basis for *punishing* me; if I always do what is right, a basis for punishment does not exist. A further concept associated with right/wrong is the concept of an *obligation*. If I always do what is right, it seems that I have met all my obligations to others, and no one is entitled to press a claim against me. Also, it seems difficult to imagine how I could do anything *wrong* if I do not violate any obligation I have.

Continuing the exploration of the link between the concepts "right/wrong" and the cluster of concepts involving blame, punishment, and obligation, let me note one more way in which the concepts "right/wrong" differ from the concepts "good/bad." Much of chapter 1 explored the kinds of experiences we humans must have if we are to come to understand the distinction between good and bad. Briefly, we come to understand the difference between good and bad ultimately by referencing the difference in our own experiences of flourishing versus failing to flourish. Appreciating what it means for some things (and not others) to answer to our interests, we are able to arrive at the concept of a property, "good," as indicating that something answers to someone's interests.

Our ability to understand the concepts "right/wrong" requires more than that we simply have pleasurable and unpleasurable mental experiences. Our positive and negative experiences must be of a certain kind. Specifically, they must stem from certain sorts of interactions with others in which we bear the brunt of what I have been calling, generally, *social sanction*. I have used this term at times within this chapter; let me now clarify what I take it to signify. The term *sanction* can denote approval and prescription. The term can also signify the opposite ideas of disapproval and proscription. Our experiences of, and ability to distinguish, these senses of *sanction* serve as a necessary step in developing an understanding of the concepts "right" and "wrong."

We of course begin to understand the dynamics of social sanction from a very early age. As noted toward the end of the previous section, small children may be unable to grasp concepts such as obligation, culpability, and blameworthiness, but they can appreciate that "Daddy is angry" or that "Mommy is not responding to me in the loving way she normally does." Again, small children will not use terms like *angry* and *loving*, but they are clearly able to appreciate the difference between demonstrations of disapproval and warm expressions of love. (Regrettably, some small children miss out on bonding with an adult and cannot appreciate the difference between connecting lovingly with that adult and having that adult withdraw in some way. Such children, unless such appreciation is somehow learned later on, will be unable to grasp concepts like right and wrong.)

I want ultimately to advocate a social understanding of obligations and of our understanding of the concepts "right" and "wrong." I think J. S. Mill was essentially correct when he stated, "We do not call anything wrong, unless we mean to imply that a person ought to be punished in some way or other for doing it; if not by law, by the opinion of his fellow-creatures; if not by opinion, by the reproaches of his own conscience" (1987, chap. 5, 321). Some moral philosophers of course have denied that social sanction is necessarily linked to the concept of an obligation or to the concepts of right and wrong. Those who do defend this link may go on to deny that social sanction serves as the *whole* basis for understanding these concepts. In what follows, however, I want to argue that the concepts of obligation and right/wrong are more tightly, and singularly, linked to social sanction than even social requirement theorists like Mill seem to acknowledge.

Mill noted that the original meaning of *recht*—from which came the English words right and righteous—pointed to "physical straightness; as 'wrong' and its Latin equivalents meant twisted or tortuous" (1987, chap. 5, 320). Thus, in saying that something is *right*, we seem to be saying that it lines up with a standard of some sort. If we were to talk about the sense of *right* as synonymous with *correct*, we might say that a right belief or statement is one that aligns with the truth of the matter. But in talking about the sense of right often called *moral* rightness, and connected to the cluster of concepts mentioned earlier in this section, we need to ask: With what standard does a (morally) right action align, or measure up?

One common answer among moral philosophers would be that a right action is one that conforms to some guideline, such as a rule or law or moral principle. But I do not think this answer is precisely correct. A standard of rightness (and wrongness), I want to argue, is better described as some person's or group's *expectation*. Such an expectation may of course be *expressed* as some rule or other guideline. And the content of an expectation may be that some existing rule or guideline be followed. But it is only in fleshing out the idea of an expectation that we can make sense of the cluster of concepts—such as blame, punishment, obligation—surrounding moral rightness and wrongness.

A distinguishing mark of so-called *moral* rightness—vis-à-vis the sense of *right* as synonymous with *correct*—is the normative pressure we feel in forming a judgment that it is right for us to perform some action. In the previous section, I connected normative pressure with the anticipation of an unwelcome outcome. The normative pressure that accompanies specific judgments that some action is *right* (or *wrong*), though, does not arise as we consider just *any* unwelcome outcome. As indicated in section 3.2, I contend that the normative pressure associated with such deontic judgments is most plausibly explained in terms of our consideration of unwelcome outcomes *involving social sanction*. (Thus the impelling force that accompanies deontic considerations of what is right or wrong to do is a subset of the more general, impelling force of normative pressure; and normative pressure is—per the discussions of the previous section—a subset of the more general motivation of a desire.) In this current section I want to argue more fully that the "wrongness" of an act amounts to nothing more than that some individual(s) intends to sanction (in the negative sense of *sanction*) those who perform that act. Put another way, a *wrong action* is an action that contravenes *someone's proscription* against performing that action. Accordingly, and to anticipate the discussions of section 3.4, there will be no answer to the question whether some action is *wrong, period* (i.e., wrong irrespective of anyone's intent to sanction). Let me now offer a fuller line of argument for these conclusions, beginning with a clarification of what it means for someone to intend to sanction.

We sometimes encourage others to perform certain acts, while still allowing them—with no threat of any kind of sanction—room to decide whether they will perform those acts. Parents, for example, may encourage their children to spend a free hour reading rather than watching television. But if the hour is genuinely a free one in the sense that the parents agree that it is an hour of leisure, with the children given the final say in what activities they will pursue, then the parents convey the intention not to hold it against the children if their actions are not as good as the parents have encouraged. Admittedly, the line between permissible actions (where no sanction results) and punishable actions can at times become fuzzy. From the fact that a child frequently chooses television over reading, a parent may inevitably then relate to the child as one who (among other things) does not always use his leisure time in the wisest manner. And this might plausibly be taken as a kind of sanction. However, the distinction itself between permission and prohibition is clear enough, even if in some cases it becomes difficult to say when permission ends and aspects (like punishment) of prohibition begin.[26] It remains my contention that a wrong action denotes someone's intent to sanction those who perform that action.

*Intent* seems to me the correct term here. We would not want to link prohibition to a negative *feeling* of some kind that others have toward the person who performs some act. I may direct my toddler not to smear paint on his face, with a promise of some punishment if he does. Yet I may find the proscribed act adorable when I am issuing my warning, when the act is committed, and while I am administering the punishment. Yes, I will have *some* negative feelings toward both the act and my toddler: a slight, negative feeling from the recognition that his act of defiance is instrumentally bad for character development, and a slight, negative feeling that he has rejected my counsel. But the overwhelming feeling may remain a positive one, as I savor the delightful antics of a toddler (even while proscribing these antics because I recognize that they may lead to unsociable habits). Further, I do not think there will be any particular, negative feeling—such as resentment—to which we could point as present in *every* case of sanction. So "prohibition," and by extension "wrongness," are better linked with someone's *intention* to sanction than with any feeling toward the person who performs (or toward the performance itself of) some action.

I use *intention* in the sense of signaling an intent to do something in the future, rather than in the sense of performing an intentional action. We might ask whether an act should be considered wrong if the would-be sanctioner does not (try to) go through with some sort of sanction against the person who performs the proscribed act in question. I think it most natural to say that an act remains wrong up until the time when the sanctioner ceases to intend to sanction those who perform that act. Admittedly, the notion of "ceasing to intend" to do something could be explored further. As part of the discussion one could explore how concepts like "commitment" or "disposition" might help us understand what it means to exert the social pressure associated with sanction. But we again seem to have a clear enough grasp of what others are doing when they proscribe an action. And an "intent to sanction" seems to me the best way of characterizing a proscription.

We might ask whether an act is proscribed, and by extension wrong, if the would-be sanctioner does not *communicate* her intent to sanction those who perform that act. I think our answer should be that the act is indeed a wrong one. We can quickly add that the matter of the wrongness of an act does not settle the matter of how we should make all-things-considered judgments about the blameworthiness of a person who performs that act. For almost any would-be sanctioner, someone else acting wrongly is merely a prima facie consideration for judgments about blame, punishment, and assessments of that person's character. Further circumstances—such as a nonculpable ignorance that the action in question has been proscribed—can mitigate against the sanctions that would otherwise be administered.[27]

Let me now address an obvious objection to spelling out the concept "wrong" in terms of the intention of some individual(s) to sanction. An objector may emphasize that a wrong action is one in which the agent violates some *obligation* and often, if not always, someone else's *rights*. And a right is not, at least in all cases, something we *confer* on others. Rather, we recognize that others *have* certain rights, that they *own* certain things—whether or not anyone intends to sanction the person who would violate these rights and make an improper claim to these things they own.

In response to this objection, I indeed recognize the link between doing something wrong and failing to meet an obligation. I would even accept that the failure to meet an obligation will always constitute an infringement on that which someone owns or to which someone has a right. As Richard Swinburne points out, "The original meaning of 'obligation' is something owed, and of 'duty' a debt" (1989, 20). In recognizing that we owe someone a debt, we recognize that that person *owns* something and thus has a *right* to it. But my response to the pending objection is to press the question: What is it to own something?

It will not do here simply to explain the concept of ownership in terms of having a *right* to something. To have a right to some physical object *is* to own it, or have the final say about its use. To have a right to act in some way or to be treated in some way *is* to be the one who has the final say on whether one acts or is treated by others in some way.

Thus, appealing to a person's right gets us no further than appealing to a person's ownership. We are seeking a (noncircular) explanation of what it might mean to own something.

I accept that owning something involves having ultimate control over it, in the sense of having the final say about its use. More exactly, though, ownership involves the idea that one *should* have ultimate control over it, so that those who interfere with this control become subject to blame, punishment, and so forth. In the end, I do not think we will find any elucidation of the concept "ownership" beyond the following: to recognize that a person owns something is to recognize that some individual(s) intends to sanction those who deny that person's use of it. For whatever reason—for example, individual preference, a belief that some principle is being satisfied, and so on—individuals may come to have a pro-attitude toward a person's deciding how something should be used. They may then resolve to react in some negative way toward those people who would interfere with that person's use of it. Search as we may, I do not think we will find anything above and beyond this occurrence in spelling out what it is to "own" or "have a right to" anything.

One consideration leading to this conclusion is, again, that we understand the concept "wrong" only by its necessary, conceptual connection to further concepts having to do with social sanction: blaming, punishing, and so forth. An additional consideration involves ontological parsimony: if we have no good reason to affirm a non-natural property of objective, moral "wrongness," then our fallback position should be to suppose that such a property does not exist. As I will argue more fully in section 3.4, the property of wrongness, which ex hypothesi exists independently from anyone's perspective, becomes superfluous in explaining why people proscribe various actions. Gilbert Harman has pointed out that, in scientific observations and judgments, presumed facts (e.g., the existence of protons) do help us explain a scientist's observations (e.g., of a vapor trail). But as Harman noted, we do not need to appeal to some (objective) fact about the "wrongness" of an action in order to explain our reaction to, for example, a cat being set on fire and our subsequent judgment that this action is wrong (1977, 6–7).

Again, I will say more in section 3.4 about the superfluity of the property of objective "wrongness" in accounting for our moral judgments and intuitions. My conclusion in that section will continue to be that, if we raise the metaphysical question of what makes it the case that some action is wrong, the answer will simply be that that action is sanctioned by some individual(s). Nevertheless, I concede that many people do not typically *mean* by references to "wrong" and "right" that some action has been sanctioned. In everyday use, these terms are often seemingly invoked to refer to something more objective than the intent of some person(s) to sanction. How do we account for the way the terms *right* and *wrong* are commonly used?

J. S. Mill's discussion of customary morality remains a good starting point for the kind of explanation I wish to advance. In discussing the way we seek to preserve our own interests and the interests of those about whom we care, Mill notes that we will have strongly negative attitudes toward threats to our security. To ensure security we recognize that these negative attitudes, and accompanying intentions to punish those who threaten security, must be shared by others in our community if we are to ensure well-being. Mill then notes how this matter vital to our well-being—which in truth is a matter of "expediency"—quickly becomes a "moral necessity": "Our notion, therefore, of the claim we have on our fellow creatures to join in making safe for us the very groundwork of our existence, gathers feelings round it so much more intense than those concerned in any of the more common cases of utility, that the difference in degree . . . becomes a real difference in kind. The claim assumes that character of absoluteness, that apparent infinity, and incommensurability with all other considerations, which constitute the distinction between the feeling of right and wrong and that of ordinary expediency and inexpediency" (1987, chap. 5, 327–28). When interacting with others and making requests of them, it is natural (and practically wise) to focus especially on those actions that affect most significantly the things on which we place greatest value—such as people's well-being.[28] We must settle these matters first before we debate the pros and cons of those actions that affect more peripherally the things we value. When an action is viewed as a significant enough threat to those things we most value, we agree to sanction those people who perform that action.[29] (Violators of our proscriptions will acquire a social standing within our community: they will stand as guilty within the community, worthy of blame, and so forth.) Yes, the act of sanctioning comes at a cost: our own time and resources in administering punishments; fractured relationships between ourselves and those we sanction; and so forth. But the cost of *not* proscribing the action is, we calculate, even greater. In proscribing those actions we view as crucially damaging the things we value, we convey the idea that those actions are to be avoided, no matter what might be said for them. Following Mill, our decision to proscribe actions may indeed be a matter of "expediency." But the gravity of our negative attitudes—backed up by threats of sanction—toward those actions we view as crucially undermining the things we value gives our prescriptions a "character of absoluteness."

It is also worth noting at this point a further contributing factor to the absolutist feeling that accompanies our everyday thoughts about right and wrong actions: namely, the *language* used to proscribe actions and convey intentions to sanction. When proscribing some action that threatens crucially valuable things, like the safety of ourselves and others we love, we do not typically make statements like "My own preference is that the action not be performed, and I intend to react negatively to those who perform it." Such a mild expression may allow room for would-be offenders to contemplate whether the sanctions are a price worth paying. In order to deter others effectively, we phrase our proscriptions in absolutist terms—for example, "This is wrong"—to elicit agreement that the action in question is to be avoided, no matter what might be said for it. Given that we receive from an early age proscriptions about certain matters (viz., those considered really important by our parents and by society) in absolutist terms, it is little wonder that we can come to associate the terms *right* and *wrong* with proscriptions that (somehow) transcend anyone's personal viewpoint.

As matters move from acknowledged "expediency" to perceived "necessity," the meaning of *wrong* changes accordingly for its users. People will come to associate the term with the idea of "not-to-be-doneness." This is arguably what most people mean today when they say that some action is "wrong." Let me say why we should regard this common usage as a *derivative* one.

We discussed in chapter 1 how a person can think of impersonal objects as good, even though we all come to understand the term *good* by referencing our own experiences of flourishing. The interests of an impersonal object may not have any meaningful parallels to our own interests that, when answered to, provide for our mental experiences of flourishing. Nonetheless, we may use the term *good* to commend the intrinsic qualities of an impersonal object, even while it remains the case that our understanding that some things in life might be commended (versus opposed) is derived from our own experiences of flourishing (versus failing to flourish). We might say something similar here about the derivative use of the term *wrong*. We understand this term by referencing our own experiences with the dynamics of someone proscribing an action (including others' disapproval once we have performed that action). Still, we might come to use this term as a way of expressing our belief that some actions are "in principle punishable" (or blameworthy or guilt-conferring), irrespective of whether anyone proscribes that action and accordingly intends to punish those who perform that action. Such use of the term *wrong* would be derivative in that, although the term is being divorced from anyone's proscription, it remains the case that the meaning of the term for us is tied to our experiences of what it is like for *actual* persons to proscribe an action. If we did not retain that experiential link to punishment (or to blameworthiness, disapproval, and the like), then we would lose the necessary connection between our concept "wrong" and our concept "punishment"—which would amount to emptying the concept "wrong" of its content.

In contrast to this *derivative* use of the term *wrong* it is not infrequent to hear the term used in a further, *deviant* sense. Specifically, the term *wrong* (or *right*) can be used as a synonym for *bad* (or *good*). I have of course already outlined important differences between these twin sets of concepts. Briefly, while the terms *right/wrong* are grasped only by also grasping a cluster of concepts including blame, punishment, and obligation, the same cannot be said for the terms *good/bad*. As we saw in chapter 1, these terms are grasped, not through necessarily experiencing the dynamics of proscription and punishment, but rather more generally through grasping the distinction between flourishing and failing to flourish. Thus, if the term *wrong is* being used as a synonym for *bad*, we have a deviant use of the term.

Such use of the term *wrong* is again not uncommon. A person may linger over a dessert cart at a restaurant. When his fellow diners press him to make a decision, he may explain that he wants to be sure he makes "the right choice." What he means is that he wants to make the "best," or "most good," choice—that is, the choice that will bring him the most pleasurable experiences. His fellow diners, observing that all the desserts look appealing, may insist that "there really is no wrong choice." They do not mean that every choice is *permissible* and that none of the choices would make him subject to *blame*. They simply mean that none of the choices constitutes a *bad* choice: each option will bring him overall pleasurable experiences.

So the term *wrong* can be used in a deviant sense. It can also be—and seemingly typically *is*—used in a derivative sense. And I have offered reasons why we should not be surprised at this common, derivative usage of the term *wrong* as denoting something along the lines of "not-to-be-doneness." As I stated a few paragraphs ago, when we consider Mill's explanation of the easy move from "expediency" to "necessity," and when we consider the language that becomes most effective when training our children, it is little wonder that people in a society will come to associate the terms *right* and *wrong* with proscriptions that (somehow) transcend anyone's personal viewpoint.[30] But a proscription is always *someone's* proscription.

## 3.4 Moral Facts and the Place of Objectivity

I anticipate the objection from various quarters that moral wrongness must surely refer to something more *objective* than mere social sanction. Consider Robert Adams's comments on the role social sanctions might have within a "premoral" society. "We can imagine a morally underdeveloped society in which people speak of the chief, for example, as issuing commands, and of themselves as having obligations arising from the chief's commands, without ever raising a question about the moral validity of these commands and obligations. Even if we asked them whether they have a 'real' obligation to obey the chief's commands, and whether it would 'really' be wrong to disobey them, we may suppose, they would hardly know what to make of our questions" (1999, 243). I confess to not knowing what to make of these questions either. I admit that such questions can be *asked*. What I dispute is that they have any answers.

In the previous section I acknowledged that people often do ask the question "Is this action *really* wrong?" Even though our understanding of the term *wrong* is inevitably derived from our subjective experiences of social sanction, it is nevertheless common for people to mean by the term *wrong* something along the lines of "not to be done, period." We are at present interested in what facts, if any, would make our pending question true or false. Returning to the questions Adams raises about the chief's commands, perhaps we can ask whether the chief really did issue these commands (with the accompanying threat of social sanction for those who disobeyed). And we can ask whether *other* people have proscribed a different range of actions. But beyond finding answers to these types of questions, there are no further facts to help settle the question of whether a given action is "really wrong."

Part of my argument for understanding "wrongness" in terms of social sanction stems again from the kind of explanation Mill offered as to how social sanction based on "expediency" can come to be associated with "moral necessity." However, David Baggett and Jerry Walls warn against drawing implications too quickly from any analysis of how we humans came to grasp the concept "wrong." They begin by offering a helpful summary of Alasdair MacIntyre's early work on the origins of ethical concepts.

> Early on, MacIntyre, the consummate philosophical historian, tells a tale according to which we shouldn't be surprised that moral language about obligations today lacks force and coherence. For such language has been severed from its original foundations and now its remaining fragments persist without sufficient social foundation. The original foundation for the notion of obligations, he argues, was a rigid hierarchical social structure in ancient Greece, where individuals within the community had clearly defined roles and social expectations within the *polis*. What naturally developed were obligations imposed by society to perform well in those specific roles. With the breakdown of such social hierarchy, obligations were less tied to social relations and came to be seen more and more as obligations *simpliciter*. (2011, 107)

So far, we seem to have strong *support* for the kind of social beginnings Mill outlined that gave rise to our current, common understanding of "wrong" along the lines of "not to be done." But Baggett and Walls warn about being too quick to draw conclusions about the (lack of) necessary, or objective, features of moral wrongness. "We can see the feet of the genetic fallacy at the door . . . ; how the language of moral obligation originally came about does not settle the question of the metaphysical status, essential nature, or real authority of moral obligations themselves" (2011, 108). This point is fair enough. However, what reasons do we have for thinking that, as a metaphysical point, "*real*" obligations can exist and certain actions can be "*really* wrong"—independent of the social analysis (of intent to sanction) that I have outlined?

Baggett and Walls press the distinction between a *definition* of some moral concept and an *analysis* of that concept (2011, 40, 47, 112–16). Perhaps it will be suggested that I have merely offered an account of how the terms *wrong* and *obligation* came to be defined—with the ontological status of these things still a matter for discussion. Indeed, Baggett and Walls may suggest that the ways in which terms and concepts like *obligation* and *wrong* developed point to a human recognition (at some level) of realities that transcend any social roles, expectations, or intentions to sanction. But a story involving social roles—roles that lead to expectations and intentions to sanction—certainly seems adequate to explain how we came to have the concepts "obligation" and "wrongness." If there is evidence that wrongness possesses an ontological status at which our socially formed concept of wrong merely points, what is that evidence?

The repeated claim of Baggett and Walls is that "the normative force needed to explain the authority of moral obligations needs an account" (2011, 109). In section 3.2, though, I provided an account of the source of normative force; and it relied on no metaphysical assumptions beyond the relatively uncontroversial point that people have internal desires and beliefs. What is it that Baggett and Walls think needs accounting for exactly? In their critique of naturalism, they rhetorically ask at one point: "How would naturalism explain obligation itself?" (2011, 11). But of course I have already offered an account of an "obligation," urging that it (and associated concepts of "rights" and "ownership") is nothing more than some person(s)'s expectations, backed by the intent to sanction.

Baggett and Walls will view these accounts I have offered as inadequate. Their foundational reason seems in the end to be the sheer obviousness that certain actions are (objectively) wrong. Citing the moral intuitions to which C. S. Lewis appealed in his moral argument for

God's existence, they contend: "It's wrong, for example, to torture innocent children for fun, and we plainly recognize it. . . . Reflection yields legitimately difficult questions in ethics, yes, but a great many ethical truths remain obvious. Just as it's clearly enough wrong to put profits before people, so is it clearly enough right to accord people basic respect" (2011, 9). But is it obvious that, for example, the act of torturing a child for fun has some (intrinsic or at least objective) property of "wrongness"? I do not at all see how this point is supposed to be obvious.

Let me quickly add that, of course, I find such an act reprehensible and repulsive. I for one will volunteer my intention to sanction anyone who would do such a thing. (And we should keep in mind that "sanction" need not refer to refined chastisement; severe forms of punishment and retribution fall under the umbrella of "sanction.") I am also reassured to note that our society stands ready to sanction—and sanction severely—anyone who would perform such an act. And I think it easy to construct a case, from the Christian perspective, that God stands ready to sanction anyone who would perform such an act. Surely these declarations are sufficient to convey that I take the horrific act of child torture as seriously as anyone else. What is added if I declare, "Also, such an act is just plain wrong!"? Perhaps people commonly expect to hear such a declaration from anyone who views child torture with the utmost seriousness. And a person's reluctance to make this declaration may, for some people, signal that the person somehow feels ambivalent about the topic—as though there existed a "gray area" in which child torture might not in all contexts be intolerable. But this is decidedly *not* my reason for resisting the declaration. Despite its common, colloquial use, the declaration simply is not available to us. The meaning, nature, and normative force of "wrongness" cannot be divorced from social sanction.

C. S. Lewis's appeal to the objective nature of rules or laws—an appeal on which Baggett and Walls attempt to build—centered on the way people use language when quarrelling. Lewis noted the way we commonly phrase our arguments: "How'd you like it if anyone did the same to you?"; "That's my seat, I was there first"; "Give me a bit of your orange, I gave you a bit of mine"; "Come on, you promised." He insisted that the appeals here are "to some kind of standard of behaviour which he expects the other man to know about" (2001b, 3). Indeed, the act of quarrelling itself "means trying to show that the other man is in the wrong. And there would be no sense in trying to do that unless you and he had some sort of agreement as to what Right and Wrong are" (2001b, 4).

Lewis's favorite example involves the sense of *fairness* all people (ex hypothesi) seem to have, even young children. "Whenever you find a man who says he does not believe in a real Right and Wrong, you will find the same man going back on this a moment later. He may break his promise to you, but if you try breaking one to him he will be complaining 'It's not fair' before you can say Jack Robinson" (2001b, 6). Lewis submitted that cultures from around the world understand the binding force of the "laws of human nature." They are considered *laws*, Lewis reasoned, "because people thought that every one knew it by nature and did not need to be taught it" (2001b, 5). Lewis's name for this transcending standard of behavior is the *Tao*, a norm that educators from cultures around the world have long recognized, and "a norm to which the teachers themselves were subject and from which they claimed no liberty to depart" (2001a, 60).

Do children recognize this "moral law" and employ it in their quarrels? I myself have not come to this conclusion. Admittedly, children often advance claims such as "That's not fair!" in the course of their quarrels. But in engaging children further on the question of what fairness amounts to, I myself have not detected anything like a pattern that resembles C. S. Lewis's depiction of the *Tao*.[31]

While my own evidence is only anecdotal, social scientists have for some time researched the moral reactions of children and adults from a variety of cultures. As Kristján Kristjánsson notes, a common conclusion social scientists have drawn from their research is that there exists among humans a "universal sense *of* (or *for*) justice" (2006, 111).[32] At first reading, such a conclusion seems to support Lewis's line of argument. Yet conclusions about humans possessing a sense of justice cannot be drawn without normative import from the social scientists conducting their studies. Kristjánsson explains, "There is no non-evaluative royal road to understanding what justice means, be it for children or for adults. . . . [No] empirical theory of justice can avoid resting on a normative premise" (117).

Kristjánsson discusses several leading theories of social scientists about how humans develop their sense of justice.[33] He observes how, inevitably, "Normative considerations steer the design and interpretation of empirical research into the development of justice conceptions by providing assumptions both about what counts as a conception of justice in the first place (and what does not), and about what counts as a better (or worse) conception of justice" (2006, 112). Seemingly, social scientists who have charted the moral sensibilities and development of humans from childhood through adulthood "have normally gone about their business in the conviction that they are merely trading in empirically discernible facts about human growth" (15). The problem, as David Carr has also convincingly shown, is that "any such facts are entirely fictions" (2002, 117). Social scientists do not record purely descriptive facts about people's development of a sense of justice and fair play. They construct questions and interpret answers through preexisting lenses of normative terms and concepts.

Thus, for example, when assessing William Damon's stage theory of the development of justice conceptions in children, Kristjánsson observes: "What we notice at once is the primacy-of-justice thesis: all conceptions of resource allocation must be justice conceptions; all distributive principles must be justice principles (or as Damon would put it, principles of 'positive justice'). But why presume that other moral concerns, such as pity, benevolence or utility, cannot play a role here also, or even non-moral ones, such as pure self-interest?" (2006, 117). So how could a social research project reach conclusions about people's moral sensibilities—drawing merely from the empirical data of people's responses to, for example, resource allocation? Such a project would have to avoid privileging any particular framework of ethical concepts, and it would have to avoid presupposing a theory about human motivation. Such a project seems quite a daunting task.

A purely empirical fact that, I think, probably *can* be established is that children have an understanding of *proportion*. If an adult gives a form of preferential treatment to one child over another, the slighted child will be quick to pick up on this fact and will typically feel unaffirmed, marginalized, and indeed very hurt. More generally, children from the earliest age are deeply affected—positively or negatively—by relationships that are harmonious or strained. As they grow out of infancy, children seem to have a keen sense that certain practices (e.g., refusals to share; refusals to reciprocate acts of kindness proportionally;

refusals to consider others' well-being) fracture a healthy group dynamic and in general undermine the well-being of themselves and/or others.[34] And of course children will in general react strongly to anything they perceive as undermining their own well-being and the well-being of others toward whom they have affection. These facts about children's needs and desires seem a plausible basis for explanations about children's reactions to the kinds of behavior Lewis mentions. If so, then this explanation is preferable to the more complex (in terms of metaphysical types) explanation Lewis offers involving a non-natural "moral law" that children and adults recognize.

Whatever the moral intuitions that children do or do not have, I must acknowledge with Lewis, Baggett, and Walls that adults' reflections on ethical issues do often seem to defy a reduction to considerations of social sanction. Indeed, much of our moral deliberation as adults arguably involves a concern to *critique* the demands that humans may place on one another. At times this concern may stem simply from one's own desire to escape the sanctions that others impose or threaten. One does not welcome the restrictions that accompany the proscriptions of others, and one searches for a way to push back against these proscriptions. Or perhaps one may yearn for some "objective" list of obligations that unifies people's beliefs about behavioral standards and helps ensure that our relationships operate smoothly. However, I acknowledge that it is common for a person genuinely to *believe* (not merely to desire) that others' proscriptions either are or are not appropriate—that is, that others' proscriptions either do or do not align with what one's obligations *really* are.

I do not think our search for facts about how to live is in vain. Although I resist the metaethical view that non-natural facts exist about an action's "wrongness" or "rightness," I think there remain a number of facts we can identify as we think through how we ought to live.[35] Accordingly, I think there are plenty of resources available to account for the way in which we deliberate about correct answers to ethical issues. We simply need to be clear about what kinds of facts are and are not available. In the remainder of this section I shall focus on this matter.

Although it is common to talk about "moral facts" and "moral beliefs" in a discussion such as ours, I hesitate to do so for two reasons. First, the adjectival term *moral* is used colloquially in varied and often extremely vague ways. It is common to hear such statements as "Well, legally you'd be right; but morally you'd be wrong." This single statement is uttered by people who have widely ranging values, religious beliefs, commitments, and decision-making procedures. On a personal note, I am usually left not knowing *what* the person meant when making the statement—other than it probably was not what was meant by the previous person I heard making the statement! Accordingly, the varied associations that the term *moral* seems to carry in everyday conversations invite misunderstanding when specifying that a discussion is to be about *moral* matters.

Second, when we do try to distinguish moral facts or beliefs or actions from nonmoral ones, the designation *moral* ends up being rather arbitrary. I argued in sections 3.2 and 3.3 that the normative pressure associated with judgments about right and wrong is a subset of the more general normative pressure that accompanies *any* judgment about what we "ought" to do. (And I accounted for normative pressure in terms of the more general impelling force of [the negative aspect of] a desire.) Hence, we have no basis for designating beliefs about rightness and wrongness—or about goodness and badness—as "moral beliefs" on account of their (often alleged) unique connection to motivation. On what other basis might we distinguish moral beliefs or facts from nonmoral beliefs or facts? Following the discussion of section 1.5, when we consider those actions that are good/bad or that ought to be done, perhaps we might reserve the term *moral* for the ones that *crucially* affect how people live. But given the obvious arbitrariness of drawing this line, I much prefer just to talk about "facts" (rather than "moral facts") in discussing those questions about how to live that are generally associated with ethical inquiry.

It again seems clear that much of our ethical inquiry is an attempt to acquire correct answers to questions—that is, to align our beliefs with certain facts we think exist. But it remains a curiosity to me that so much ethical analysis this past century has focused on identifying and defending some single, universal answer to the question "What are we doing when we make moral statements?" Expressivists like A. J. Ayer are surely right insofar as some moral statements we make are simply expressions of our own emotions or desires. A comic who tells a joke about a recently deceased celebrity may be met with groans from the audience, with some individual decrying (as he suppresses laughter): "That's just wrong!" Perhaps the audience member could have a vague appreciation for some unwritten social norm about respect for the dead. But plausibly the audience member's statement is simply an expression of an emotional reaction we might characterize as mild disdain.

At other times, our so-called moral statements are plausibly interpreted, following R. M. Hare, along the lines of a prescription. A toddler may have a pattern of snatching his older sister's toys, which then leads to the sister's strategy of remonstrating every time he snatches a toy—"That's not fair! You mustn't do that!"—as an attempt to break her brother's habit. Admittedly, it is possible to theorize that the sister has awareness at some level of consciousness of some "moral law," with her statement being a reference to some fact about that moral law. But, for reasons discussed earlier, surely it is more plausible to think that the sister is simply prescribing a certain pattern of respectful behavior for her brother (and perhaps for herself as well, following Hare).

I in no way want to attempt a taxonomy of noncognitive theories about our moral statements. The point is that it may well be true that *some* moral statements we make are most plausibly interpreted along noncognitivist lines. It seems at least as clear, however, that *all* our moral statements cannot plausibly be so interpreted. Our statements often reflect judgments about what we *believe* to be the better, or best, or obligatory course of action. We assume that these beliefs would be true beliefs even if we had been brought up to think differently. And we argue with others who hold contrasting beliefs, recognizing that we cannot *each* be correct in what we are claiming.

These points were obvious enough even to J. L. Mackie, who of course denied that moral facts, or "objective values," exist that might correspond to our moral beliefs.[36] As we look to identify facts that our moral language might at times reference, and that actually exist, we can focus either on beliefs about what is right/wrong or beliefs about what is good/bad. Let us start with the former beliefs.

We noted in the previous section that, in order to keep the necessary link between the concept "wrong" and the cluster of further concepts including blame and punishment, we must tie wrongness to *someone's* (or some group's) proscription of that action. If we reflect on the everyday claims people make that a given action is wrong, it seems clear that the "someone" (or group) in question can vary a great deal. A person might raise various objections to some action; and when those proposed objections are refuted by an interlocutor, the person's final retort might be "Well, I still think it's wrong!" Plausibly, the person will be simply stating the fact that she herself disapproves of the action (and, more pointedly, disapproves of those who perform that action). At other times people may have their own family or community in mind when they insist that some action is right or wrong. For example, upon hearing a provocative lecture that there exist no compelling moral principles that obligate us to treat the elderly with any more respect than anyone else, a person may shake her head and say, "Sorry, that's not the way we did things when I was growing up." At still other times, a person may have her own country firmly in mind. For instance, a person might be told by a foreign exchange student that many people in the student's home country acknowledge an obligation not to renege on arranged marriages. The person might then respond by saying, "In *our* country we *don't* think it would be wrong to disregard parents' wishes on an issue as important and personal as marriage." In all these cases, one's moral statements are plausibly read as declarations that some person or group is proscribing or permitting certain actions.

For those with religious backgrounds, comments about the rightness or wrongness of an action will often amount to allusions to the proscriptions of God. Hence, Robert Adams's suggestion is certainly plausible that, for many people, part of what it *means* to say "Action *x* is wrong" is that "Action *x* is contrary to the commands of a loving God."[37] Put another way, the concepts "wrong" and "right" come for many people to be tied to one particular person's (or, for Christians, one tri-personal being's) proscriptions.

How might we critique the claims made by a person or group that some action is wrong? We have already noted (in discussing Adams's example of the chief) the two kinds of appeals available to us as we critique the claims of others that some action is wrong. One avenue of disputing claims about wrongness and rightness would be to question whether a person or group *really has* proscribed some action. Such disputes are common of course when it comes to conclusions about what God has and has not proscribed—for example, same-sex marriages within the church established by Jesus Christ. The other avenue of disputing claims would take the form "Yes, I know that *you* (or some group) have proscribed this action and is accordingly prepared to take punitive measures toward those who perform the action, but I (or God or my community) intend no such negative sanctions toward those who perform the action."[38] Outside these two broad avenues for challenging someone's claim that some action is right or wrong, I do not think we can make sense of the search for objective facts about wrongness—again given my conclusion that we have no good reason to affirm that there exists some non-natural property of "wrongness" not reducible to someone's intent to sanction.[39]

Admittedly, the claims people actually make, along with attempted challenges to these claims, do not always follow neatly these two avenues of investigation. When people describe an action as "wrong" (or "right"), they may not at all be clear on who exactly is proscribing that action (or otherwise why the action is wrong). Consider a homeowner who responds to a recently passed statute that he must sell his home to the government to make way for a new highway. The homeowner might say, "I don't care what law has just been passed, I have a right to live in my own home and it's wrong for them to try to take it!" The homeowner's statement might plausibly be interpreted as an expression of his own anger, frustration, and other such emotions. The statement might perhaps be a bona fide statement about his own commitment to react negatively to those who would force him (and perhaps others) to sell their homes. Plausibly, his statement might be a statement about the government's own historic stance (as seen in previously passed laws) proscribing—rather than instigating—the taking of property from citizens who possess certified deeds to that property. (Thus his statement would be a reference to the inconsistency within the government's laws.) Perhaps the homeowner's statement reflects more than one reference to a person's or group's proscriptions.

Alternatively, perhaps there really is no reference at all—at least in the homeowner's mind—to any particular person or group. Plausibly, the homeowner's appeal is to some sense of wrongness that transcends anyone's perspective. Here the homeowner *means* by "wrong" something along the lines of "not-to-be-done." Perhaps the homeowner, though not using the language of moral philosophers, nonetheless thinks of the wrongness of the government's act along the lines of a non-natural, moral fact. If so, then at this point I think we have to adopt Mackie's conclusion that the homeowner is simply in error. That is, there is no moral fact that would render his statement "The government is wrong, full stop," either true or false.

Still, although the use of the term *wrong* along the lines of "not-to-be-done" is common, let us not conclude that most ethical searches for (objective) correct answers are vulnerable to Mackie's error theory. Let us consider the beliefs people have about what is *good or bad*. We have already noted that sometimes the terms *right* and *wrong* are actually used—again, deviantly—to denote "good" and "bad" (e.g., making the "right" choice at the dessert cart). Perhaps our homeowner means to convey that the government's action is incontestably a *bad* one and therefore, on account of axiological considerations, ought not to be executed. Certainly there are objective facts about goodness and badness. As argued in chapter 2, noninstrumental goodness (and badness) are matters of the mental states of sentient creatures or beings. Confining our discussion to the mental states of humans, there are—from the Christian perspective, and to anticipate my discussion in chapter 4—facts about how humans flourish and fail to flourish.

The search for objective facts on so-called moral matters will often be an attempt to ascertain facts related to the goodness or badness of some action or state of affairs. We may search for facts about how people flourish. Again, in chapter 4 I will offer a view about what our ultimate flourishing consists in—and how we can attain it. This view may not of course be shared by everyone. Still, there are indeed facts about how people *do* flourish, irrespective of anyone's viewpoint on this matter.

In searching for answers about how people flourish, we may ask such questions as: Are the various, pleasant experiences of a given person at a given time commensurable? Are the pleasurable experiences of an adult better than the pleasurable experiences of an infant? Are any nonhuman animal's pleasurable experiences better than any human's pleasurable experiences? Are people's good experiences at least roughly quantifiable and additive, in such a way that we can sometimes calculate when one group's sum total of good experiences is more than another group's sum total of good experiences? How significant is the freedom of self-expression to a person's overall flourishing? Is such freedom equally vital to all persons' current flourishing? How significant are other freedoms, such as the freedom from oppression, from arbitrary incarceration, or from extreme poverty? There arguably are correct answers to such questions; and a good deal of public debate over so-called moral matters involves these kinds of questions.

Debates also exist as to *why* something is good, even while all parties have concluded that it *is* good. For example, people may agree that it is better to distribute resources equally than unequally. But why is it good to distribute resources equally? Given the arguments of chapter 2 that only pleasurable mental states are *noninstrumentally* good, equal distribution at most could be an instrumentally good course of action. It may, for example, foster better (experiences of) relationships within the general public, along with forestalling resentment toward the person or organization distributing the resources. But of course some will have a different view and will see equal distribution of resources as a good thing in and of itself. We can then debate the point about why—about the sense in which—equal distribution is good.

The search for objective facts about people's flourishing can often be mingled with considerations of the rightness/wrongness of an action. For instance, when we ask questions about the importance (to people's well-being) of various freedoms, we may be trying to settle questions about the merits of going to war. At times our inquiry will be focused merely on questions of goodness: Will a particular group of people oppressed by some regime be, all things considered, better off if they revolt against that regime? At other times we may be also trying to determine whether violence against the regime should be considered *wrong*. That is, we may be trying to determine whether we will proscribe such violence and/or whether such violence violates the principles of some established "just war" theory.

Let us return now to our (understandable) felt need to be able to critique the demands that humans might place on one another. Robert Adams rightly notes that we often praise the courageous moral reformer who opposes—Athanasius *contra mundum*—the prevailing views of a culture we consider to be immoral. Adams seeks a way to critique the views of any society while retaining his focus on the cluster of concepts related to *wrongness*—including blame, punishment, and obligation. He states, "A genuinely moral conception of obligation must have resources for moral criticism of social systems and their demands" (1999, 243). And again, "What is essential to the role of wrongness is that blame in some form is appropriate when an agent is fully responsible for a wrong action" (1999, 236). Seeking an objective vantage point from which to critique human views of where our obligations lie, Adams moves to a "*transcendent* source of the moral demand" (1999, 244); and so his moral framework focuses on the commands of a loving God. This seems fair enough, inasmuch as God's perspective indeed transcends any perspective of those creatures living in a created universe. But why go further and seek *objective* facts about moral matters by focusing on *wrongness/rightness*?

I would ask the same question of Baggett and Walls. They in general endorse Adams's conclusion that the property of being "contrary to the commands of a loving God" is the property that "best fills the role designated by the concept of wrongness." This property makes something "essentially wrong" (2011, 116). Interestingly, by "essential wrongness" Baggett and Walls do not mean some property that exists independently from *all* perspectives. They are interested—as is Adams—in a perspective that transcends all *human* perspectives: specifically, God's perspective. But now the phrase "*essential* wrongness" becomes curious, at least to my ears. However the essential, or necessary, nature of some action's wrongness is to be settled, it is at least clear that Baggett and Walls do want an objective way to settle deontic questions such as where a person's obligations lie. They express the concern that "human social requirements fail to cover the whole territory of moral obligation and can, moreover, conflict with each other without a clear way for such conflicts to be adjudicated" (2011, 118). But, once again, why seek objective facts about moral matters by focusing on *wrongness/rightness*? Why not seek objective facts relating to *goodness/badness*?

Perhaps we might still salvage an appeal to "essential wrongness" by noting that God's essential character is such that he will always prohibit, say, torture of children in any possible world. Thus God's intent to sanction torturers becomes a necessary, or essential, fact. I would not quarrel with this way of spelling out the claim that torture of children is "essentially wrong." But of course the reason God would prohibit torture is that the action has such significantly bad effects on the victim (and on the torturer). The search for God's commands about torture may be epistemically useful as a guide to answers about how humans do and do not flourish. But if God is prohibiting child torture *because* it is bad for us, this only reinforces the point that our search for objective answers about how we should live ultimately lies within discussions of goodness/badness.

Suppose we viewed the question "What ought I to do?" as ultimately settled by considerations of goodness and badness.[40] Our critiques of others' claims on us could take the form: "I know that you or this person or this group proscribes my action, but that action furthers the overall well-being of myself and/or others about whom I care." Plausibly, we could cast our search for "objective moral answers" in terms of our search for what is, all things considered, most good for some person or group. Consider the common subjects of debate currently within applied ethics: abortion, euthanasia, just war theory, treatment of animals, genetic engineering, and so on. Our search for objective facts in these areas can amount to a search for who, and in what way, people (or animals or beings) would benefit or be harmed by some action. We may of course disagree about what to do in virtue of these facts. I may, for instance, care more about animals than you do and thus may want to prioritize the well-being of orangutans more than you do. But here the search for objective facts has ended, and the revealing of our differing desires has begun.

I do not want to suggest that the search for facts about who has proscribed some action is not at times vital. In section 5.4 I shall discuss more fully the role of God's perspective and commands, which, within a Christian ethical framework, are sometimes what helps determine which actions will be (instrumentally) good for us. And again as an important epistemic point, a search for God's perspective and commands may be our best way to *ascertain* facts about how we flourish. These points notwithstanding, one of the outcomes of this current section has been that the most interesting "moral facts" involve facts about how we and others flourish. These facts about people's (or animals' or beings') flourishing—that is, facts about what is *good/bad* (as opposed to what is right/wrong)—are the facts on offer to the one who searches for a genuinely *objective* answer to some moral question.

*Part Two*

# A Christian Framework for Choosing the Good Life

CHAPTER FOUR

# Others and the Good

Part II offers a substantive account of what a good human life looks like, as well as how we can attain it. After unpacking a Christian understanding of that in which a good life consists, I will go on to explore the conditions that must be met for this good life to be realized. I will arrive at an analysis of those decisions, available to all people, that allow us to enter into the good life; and I will discuss the kind of freedom we need to have as we make those decisions. This substantive account of the good life will, I hope, provide a framework for better understanding certain facts we can all recognize from day-to-day life as key to all people's well-being, whatever their individual differences. And the uniquely Christian resources within this account will provide a way of solving some otherwise intractable difficulties in how we might achieve the good life.

My conclusion at the end of chapter 2 was that our well-being is a matter of our mental states. In this current chapter I want to specify those mental states in which I believe our well-being consists. In the first three sections of this chapter I shall outline and defend the claim that a particular kind of mental experience holds the key to our long-term flourishing. I shall then explore in the remainder of the chapter the actions that lead one to have this kind of (sustained) mental experience.

## 4.1 Perfectionism

The substantive account of human well-being that I will defend is very much an orthodox Christian one. Notwithstanding the differences among us as individual humans, the Christian tradition has always affirmed that our long-term flourishing is secured in the same, broad manner. In section 4.2 I will say why I think our everyday experiences provide strong hints that the Christian picture of human nature is true. In this current section I want to describe briefly what this picture of human nature *is*.

In chapter 2 I advanced a welfarist, mental-statist account of noninstrumental value. This was a *formal* account of the nature of goodness. I noted at the beginning of that chapter that a formal account of the nature of goodness would tell us what it is for something to be a source of goodness, whereas a *substantive* account would identify these sources. What follows in this chapter—and for much of Part II of this book—is once again a substantive account of the good.

In truth, it was never really possible for my earlier, welfarist account of goodness to remain purely formal. L. W. Sumner, in his analysis of welfare, contends that any theory of the nature of welfare really should remain formal. Sumner explains that this kind of theory should not confuse the *sources* of welfare with a description of what it is to *be* a source of welfare (1996, 135–37, 180–81). Only this latter description, he emphasizes, is a true account of the *nature* of welfare. However, in my previous discussion of Sumner (section 2.3), I alluded to the fact that it will simply not be possible for me to keep a list of the sources of flourishing separate from a description of the conditions for being a source. This is because the account of the nature of welfare I wish to explore presumes that there is only *one* ultimate source of flourishing.

The Christian understanding of God is that God is the sole, ultimate source of any flourishing that God's created order might enjoy. Indeed, the Christian tradition as a whole has continually reaffirmed Augustine's summation: "Thou madest us for Thyself, and our heart is restless, until it repose in Thee" (2008, bk. I, 7).¹ Thus, on the account of well-being that I am offering in this chapter, a formal answer to the question "What is it for anyone to flourish?" will need to be something along the lines of "To draw from, or be imbued with, the life of God." And this answer clearly makes material reference to the *source* of our flourishing.

However the formal-substantive distinction applies to my own account, let me now offer my description of the Christian understanding of human nature, which is rooted in the Christian understanding of God.² The doctrine of the Trinity describes God as a tri-personal Being. In affirming that "God *is* love" (1 John 4:8, 4:16), Christians are committed to spelling out the ontology of God in terms of a set of loving, interdependent relationships among Father, Son, and Holy Spirit. Christians also understand God as a self-sufficient Being who is the source of life. Indeed, God is seen as life *itself*: both in the sense that his existence is necessary and in the sense that everything in our universe is not only created but also continually sustained by him.³

According to Christian teaching, humans have a special place in the world in virtue of being created in the "image" of God. One of the important ways we are said to reflect God is that we, like the persons of the Trinity, flourish as we participate in loving relationships. C. Stephen Layman makes this point succinctly: "God creates the human race for a certain end, namely, for harmonious relationships with God and with the other creatures God has made" (1991, 52). With various qualifications to come, I wish to defend the idea that any human's well-being consists in being in right relationship with God and with others.

In my earlier discussion of hedonism (section 2.1), I mentioned that my account of human well-being is in some respects a perfectionist account, while in other respects it is decidedly *not* perfectionist. Before specifying these respects, let me first say a bit more about what perfectionism *is* and briefly note its origins as an influential theory. The term *perfectionism* again describes an approach to assessing that in which a *good life* consists.⁴ On the perfectionist approach, the goodness, or value, of a person's life is a measure of the extent to which her life exemplifies a specified ideal. Sometimes this ideal is seen as unique to each individual. Rousseau, for example, remarked that "aside from the nature common to the species each individual brings with him at birth a distinctive temperament, which determines his spirit and character. There is no question of changing or putting a restraint on this temperament, only of training it and bringing it to perfection."[5] More typically, however, perfectionists historically have pointed to some aspect of human nature in general in describing what it is that makes for an ideal life for any individual. Aristotle and, arguably, Plato offered such accounts; and both adopted the same method for identifying the aspect of human nature that holds the key to a person leading a good life. This method is to single out the property (or properties) of human nature that is *unique* to humans.

Plato's suggestion of this method can be seen in the *Republic*, where Socrates discusses the "function" of things like pruning knives, eyes, ears, and human souls. The function of each thing "is what it alone can do or what it does better than anything else" (1992, bk. I, §353a). Given that "anything that has a function performs it well by means of its own peculiar virtue"—a point Socrates tentatively acknowledges—we now have a link between a person's function and a person's good. For, as Plato maintained elsewhere, what makes a thing good—whether the thing is a pruning knife or a person—is its possession of a virtue, or *aretê*, specific to a knife or person.[6] Thus Plato's suggestion seems to be that a person's good consists in those qualities and abilities that he possesses alone or, at least, in unparalleled degrees.

Aristotle followed Plato in linking the "function" of human beings with how "the best good" for any human life is achieved.[7] Just as "the carpenter and the leather worker have their functions and actions," so also humans qua humans have a function (1999, 1097b, §11). Aristotle identified this function by exploring what is distinctive of humans:

> What, then, could this [function] be? For living is apparently shared with plants, but what we are looking for is the special function of a human being; hence we should set aside the life of nutrition and growth. The life next in order is some sort of life of sense perception; but this too is apparently shared with horse, ox, and every animal. The remaining possibility, then, is some sort of life of action of the part of the soul that has reason. . . . We have found, then, that the human function is activity of the soul in accord with reason or requiring reason. (1999, 1097b–98a, §11–14)

For Aristotle, humans genuinely flourish (that is, they attain *eudaimonia*) when their function or work (*ergon*) is done well over a whole life. And we identify their function, again, by examining the activities in which they can uniquely engage.

The appeal to unique functions in explaining what makes for human flourishing is open to clear objections. Whether some *other* creature does or does not have the faculty of reason (or any other faculty humans have) is surely irrelevant to the question of whether our development of this faculty holds the key to *our* flourishing. Also, as Thomas Hurka points out, the criterion of uniqueness can be difficult to apply (1993, 10–11). For instance, it is true that other animals have digestive systems. Yet, strictly speaking, no other animal's digestive system has precisely the same structure that ours does. It is therefore unclear why we should follow Aristotle in concluding that our human function of "nutrition and growth" is shared by other living things. Finally, and decisively, some unique human attributes seem morally trivial and even, as Bernard Williams has argued, morally repugnant (1993, 59–60). If humans have, for instance, a unique capacity to kill things for public amusement, surely we will not want to conclude that we will genuinely flourish only if we develop this capacity. In the end, then, the uniqueness criterion does not provide a plausible way of determining that in which human flourishing consists.

Of course, one might adopt a perfectionist account of human good without relying on a uniqueness criterion to explain how a human life is perfected. Hurka's suggestion is that we focus on the properties that are *essential* to humans—that is, those properties that a human possesses necessarily (1993, 11f.). Hurka recognizes that the simple form of this essence criterion allows for too many properties. After all, all humans are necessarily self-identical and necessarily mammals if mammals. And these properties are clearly not plausible criteria for determining whether a human life is a good one. Hurka's solution to this problem is to amend the essence criterion so that human nature—the perfection of which makes for a "good human life"—is equated with "the properties essential to humans and conditioned on their being living things" (1993, 17).

This version of perfectionism bears a certain resemblance to my own account of what makes for a good human life. I have assumed the

Christian understanding that all humans are created in the image of a relational God. Accordingly, I will want to depict human flourishing as consisting in *one* ideal: participation in loving, self-giving relationships with God and others. Like any theory of the good that contains such a perfectionist element, it is open to the objection that the diversity of human attributes and interests renders implausible the proposal that any single ideal can constitute ultimate flourishing for everyone. James Griffin, for example, remarks that, while accomplishment and autonomy are valuable to most people, a particular person might be made so anxious by any ambition or by being autonomous that it will be best for her not to seek such things. And "even if we confined attention to the natural range of normal human capacities," Griffin continues, "there would still be no single ideal. The natural and normal range would include an artist creating beauty, a researcher discovering truth, a politician realizing the good, a citizen tending his own garden. There is no one balance of prudential values in all of these lives.... And when we add the reality that most of us, as a result of the accidents of upbringing, have developed our native capacities to different degrees, then the perfectionist account of well-being seems not at all plausible" (1986, 58–59). There seem to be two points within Griffin's objection to perfectionism. First, the variety of activities from which different people receive fulfillment cannot be encapsulated under a single "ideal human life." Second, even if we suppose for the sake of argument that there *is* a single, ideal life, many people will not be in a position to achieve this ideal life.

In response to the first point, we should acknowledge that Christianity does understand God's goal for each person to be conformity to Jesus Christ. And it is true that all people who grow in the image of Christ will manifest certain general features, identified in Galatians as the "fruit of the Spirit."[8] Yet if we grant that all aspects of life in this world (e.g., beauty, laughter, craftsmanship, and so forth) reflect in some way aspects of the creator of this world, then we begin to see that there exist an enormous variety of ways in which we creatures might conform to the image of our creator. It is thus a mistake to think that imitation of Christ must take the same form for all people. Indeed, we recognize Christian saints as much for their individuality, if not their idiosyncrasies, as for those character traits they share.[9]

An appreciation for the variety of ways an individual might imitate Christ goes some way toward meeting the concerns Susan Wolf has raised in her well-known critique of the idea of a moral saint. Wolf's primary concern is that a moral saint—whom she identifies as one "whose every action is as morally good as possible" (1982, 419)—would not have time for well-rounding activities like painting, reading philosophy, or gardening. However, Wolf's conception of the "morally good" is clearly not nearly so wide as that outlined in section 1.5, where the *morally* good was identified simply as that which crucially promotes a person's flourishing. Given that God has created people with differing talents and interests—which translate into differences as to how their ultimate flourishing can be achieved—the pursuit of the morally good need neither look the same in all cases nor exclude such things as artistic pursuits for some individuals.

A further point, having to do with the nature of relationships, can also be made that goes further in addressing Wolf's concerns about the moral saint. As Brian Hebblethwaite rightly reminds us, "Christian discipleship is rather a matter of relation—of growth in faith and love that permits the Spirit of Christ to work through us and build us up into Christian personalities and groups of very different people" (1992, 5). Thus, Hebblethwaite continues, "as has often been pointed out, the imitation of Christ cannot be thought of as a matter of 'uncreative copying'" (1992, 5). Rather, any ethic of moral character should stress "not only the type of general qualities and virtues that, when habitual, come to constitute the Christian character—but also the individual personality, the unique 'character' in the other sense of that word, which is the product of an individual life story lived in and through particular and unrepeatable sets of interpersonal relations, including, supremely, the relation between that individual and his Lord" (1992, 5). If we picture the life of the moral saint in terms of relating to God through the joint pursuit of certain purposes, or goals, then we can view God as inviting each person to pursue with him a set of goals unique to that person— according to the unique set of experiences and gifts that person has been given. And again, if we suppose that the various avenues to joy and fulfillment—such as creative craftsmanship and laughter—have analogues within the nature of God, then it is not unnatural to think of God as seeking to build relationships with some people in part through activities like wood carving and the honing of a joke for an upcoming speech.

Inasmuch as people are created so that they flourish as they engage in such things, it seems *unavoidable* that God, who seeks to bring life to his creatures, would will their engagement in these activities as part of their "perfection." Also, if exercising the freedom to choose occasionally between whittling a piece of wood or practicing a comic routine—or, for that matter, between whittling and spending the afternoon raising money for Oxfam—is necessary for a person to maintain mental health and the capacity for healthy relationships, then the making of these choices is contrary neither to the will of God nor to a life as a moral saint. In short, because Christian discipleship is fundamentally a relationship with God, then God may well seek to develop relationships with people through a whole host of different pursuits, according to their individual attributes and interests. And there is at least one obvious reason why God would want to create people with differing attributes and interests: namely, so that we finite creatures could learn about the various qualities of God as we learn about each other.

We noted earlier the two points within Griffin's objection to perfectionism: (1) that there does not exist a single "ideal human life"; and (2) even supposing there *is* an ideal life, many people will not be in a position to achieve it. Having seen that the perfectionist element within my own account of a good human life can comfortably survive Griffin's first objection, let me now address his second point. Griffin speaks of the "accidents of upbringing" and of the fact that we develop our "native capacities to different degrees." His point is well taken. Even if, as I have argued, each person's flourishing takes a unique form according to the specific gifts and experiences he has been given, who among us has the opportunity to develop her gifts to their fullest capacity? Though God may have unique plans for each person in line with what will bring about her highest flourishing, who among us fulfills God's most perfect will for her life?

This line of thought, however, is not really an objection to perfectionism. It is merely an observation that many people may have, given the contingencies of this earthly life, very limited ability to approximate the ideal life that a perfectionist theory of well-being might describe. At the same time, because the Christian religion emphasizes the possibility of life after death, a Christian perfectionist account of well-being *can* affirm that all people have the opportunity to attain a life of what I will call "ultimate flourishing."[10] For those who at present find such a life unattainable, the Christian tradition has always affirmed God's ability continually to "meet us where we are" and to lead us toward the kind of ideal life understood to exist within the heavenly community.

What emerges from these discussions is that a Christian account of the nature of the good shares the perfectionist emphasis that a human life is good to the extent that it exemplifies a particular ideal. An ideal life will, for every person, have certain common features—for example, it will manifest particular Christ-like traits such as love, joy, peace, patience, and so forth. At the same time, our account of a good life differs from any simple form of perfectionism that fails to acknowledge the different ways a person might flourish (according to her attributes and interests) and that identifies too narrow a range of pursuits—for example, ones involving reason—as the key to every person's flourishing.

Having now responded to the two points within Griffin's objection to perfectionism, let me briefly address an objection from L. W. Sumner. As discussed in section 2.3, Sumner emphasizes the themes of autonomy and authenticity in offering an account of human welfare. While I argued against some of Sumner's conclusions in that earlier section, he is nevertheless right to worry about any perfectionist account of welfare that ignores the question of a person's own attitudes of favor and disfavor toward her condition. "Objective values are quite literally alien to us because they emanate from a standpoint which is external to us as individuals, and because their status as values requires no affirmation or endorsement of them on our part" (1996, 214). A perfectionist account of welfare would certainly be implausible if it was consistent with the idea that a person's life goes better for her under certain conditions, *whether she likes it or not*.

My own account of welfare, however, will avoid such an unqualified conclusion. Admittedly, as we noted in our previous critique of desire-satisfaction accounts of welfare (section 2.2), a person will not always desire ahead of time those things in which she finds joy and satisfaction. (We can remember our example of the child who learns the joy of giving.) And the Christian picture of growth within a divine-human relationship certainly involves self-discovery, which itself inevitably involves times of facing up to tough truths about oneself.[11] Thus a person in a positive relationship with God may well find that a particular experience of God—involving a tough truth—carries feeling tones more in line with embarrassment and shame than with appreciation and enjoyment. In such cases, we will need to say that at *some* point the subsequent, life-enhancing experiences (at times $t_2, t_3, t_4 \ldots$) made possible by this difficult experience at time $t_1$ will render it true that the initial experience at time $t_1$ will contribute positively (and instrumentally) to the person's welfare (which, again, we measure in terms of mental states with intrinsic qualities). Presumably, as part of a person's maturity—growing in true beliefs as well as in life-enhancing experiences relating to God—a person will *recognize* that her long-term welfare is being enhanced by this process that involves facing up to uncomfortable truths about herself.[12] So my account of welfare is safeguarded against the concern Sumner rightly raises toward the idea that a person's welfare can be enhanced by certain conditions, whether or not the person appreciates or endorses these conditions.

Having outlined in this section the perfectionist element within my account of the good, let me now turn to the respects in which my account differs from most established perfectionist theories of the good. First, we can note that some perfectionist theories are offered as purely formal accounts of the good. For example, in Hurka's proposal that a human life becomes perfected by possessing *essential* human properties, he reminds us that that this explanation does not tell us "what properties *are* essential to humans" as living things (1993, 17). By contrast, my own account, as previously discussed, cannot fail to make reference to the material source of a good human life in offering an account of the nature of such a life.

Second, a purely formal perfectionist theory—which views a life as perfected by possessing certain properties, whatever those perfecting properties are—may lead to the conclusion that there is noninstrumental *value* in the *attainment itself* of perfecting properties. Such a conclusion, however, is very much at odds with the conclusions from chapter 2. The conclusions of that chapter were that our own well-being is (noninstrumentally) enhanced only by pleasurable mental experiences.

Beginning with the Christian picture of God, my account of well-being does not see the life within the Trinity as good because of the *mere fact* that the three persons of the Trinity relate to each other. Rather, the kind of life within the Trinity that is critical for discussions of noninstrumental value involves the *experiences* of the persons of the Trinity as they relate to one another. Presumably, there is (following Nagel) "something that it is like to *be*," respectively, the Father, the Son, and the Holy Spirit. With respect to the ongoing life within the Trinity, I do not see why *life for life's sake* would be a good thing—if it made no difference to the experiences of the persons (subjects) of the Trinity. Accordingly, it is this Trinitarian experience of fellowship that, strictly speaking, constitutes the kind of life into which God seeks to draw us.[13] In the next section, I want to begin to explore what I think is a common, identifiable mental experience that corresponds to the common, perfectionist ideal outlined in this section of relating rightly to God and to others.

## 4.2 The Mental Experience of "Connecting"

I noted in section 1.2 that, though there are borderline experiences between flourishing and failing to flourish (such as strenuous exercise), the conceptual distinction is clear enough between the two kinds of experiences. Among those mental experiences that enhance our well-being, some mental experiences obviously enhance our well-being *more* than others. Furthermore, some mental experiences, while noninstrumentally good for us, are nonetheless instrumentally bad for us in that they either prevent future pleasurable experiences or engender future unpleasurable experiences. Is there any type of mental experience that provides for our highest flourishing, along with ensuring that this flourishing continues in the long term? I think there is.

The project of identifying a single kind of mental experience as *the* key to our well-being faces a challenge similar to the one Sidgwick put to Bentham some years ago. In describing pleasure and pain, Bentham asserted that they are "names of homogenous real entities" (1996, 53 n. c). By contrast, Sidgwick objected to the idea that there exists a single "quality of feeling" to every instance of pleasure, remarking that the only "common quality" he could find in all instances of pleasure involved the fact that the person who felt pleasure found it "desirable" (1981, II, ii, §127).[14] In defending Bentham's general claim about the nature of pleasure, one might appeal to Roger Crisp's determinable-determinate distinction (as discussed in section 2.1) and maintain that any pleasurable experience, taken as a whole, has an overall pleasurable tone to it. One could in this way affirm a common feature of various sorts of pleasurable experiences—such as good health, hunger satisfaction, sex, skilled labor, and artistry, to use a few examples from Bentham's own list (1996, chap. 5)—without falling back on Sidgwick's externalist appeal to the way we find our experiences "desirable."

I will not rely on Crisp's maneuver here because the discussion points on which I want to focus in this current section are narrower than my discussion of pleasure in chapter 2. *Within* our pleasurable experiences, I want to pick out a certain feeling tone that holds the key to our flourishing. So we come again to the objection from Sidgwick: namely, that any number of different feeling tones can contribute to our mental experiences and seem to enhance our flourishing. In the current section and the one that follows, I want to suggest reasons for thinking that the feeling tone I have in mind plays a necessary role in any mental experience that contributes positively to our well-being. In the following section I will also say why, from the Christian perspective, this feeling tone will prove sufficient in ensuring our well-being.

I want to characterize the feeling tone in question in terms of *connecting* with others.[15] I think this term best captures what the Christian theist will want to say about the phenomenology of relating to others in loving, self-giving ways—which, mirroring the relationships within the Trinity, represents the ideal for our own relationships.

In section 1.2 I noted that the experience of flourishing is best viewed as a basic concept we have that is not analyzable in terms of further, more basic concepts. I want to suggest something similar about our understanding of what it is to "connect" with someone else. Admittedly, there will be unique features to each mental experience we have as we relate to a particular person at a particular time. I might experience a feeling we associate with appreciation as I reflect on past interactions with a friend. A moment later I may experience a feeling we associate with anticipation as I turn my attention to a future, planned project with the friend. And of course our relationships with different people produce greatly varying combinations of feeling tones that will make up our mental experiences. Still, I think we can recognize a common phenomenology to all our experiences of relating positively to someone else—whether the other person is a lover, a friend, or even a stranger. Positive relationships give rise to a certain feeling of intimacy. Although this feeling is difficult to describe further using public language, it seems easy enough to recognize when we reflect on the best examples of human relationships in this life. Aristotle captured certain elements of this intimacy in his discussion of how the well-being of parents can be affected by the well-being of their children. He commented that a child can become "another self" for a parent. Likewise, within a friendship one friend can become "another self" for the other.

Aristotle recognized that intimate fellowship is characterized by caring about the other person's interests as if they were one's own. He noted our common view of a friend as "one who shares his friend's distress and enjoyment" (1999, IX, 4, §1, 1166a). Aquinas used even stronger language in describing the "union" that takes place in loving fellowship: "In so far as he reckons what affects his friend as affecting himself, the lover seems to be in the beloved, as though he were become one with him: but in so far as, on the other hand, he wills and acts for his friend's sake as for his own sake, looking on his friend as identified with himself, thus the beloved is in the lover" (1947, I-II, 28, 2). While Aquinas's language is quite dramatic, it nonetheless is suggestive of the way two people's welfare really does rise and fall together in the best examples of human, loving relationships. How such ideal, loving relationships are formed will be something I examine later in this chapter. My present concern is the phenomenology of such a relationship. And on this matter, there seem to be two elements: the feeling associated with loving someone else, and the feeling associated with (believing that one is) being loved by someone else. To talk about the feelings associated with this mutual giving and receiving of love is, in my terminology, to talk about "connecting" with someone else.[16] Again, my purpose in this discussion is to defend the plausibility of the claim that our long-term well-being hinges on whether we experience the feeling tone(s) associated with connecting with others. The plausibility comes partly from considering the powerful effects of both giving and receiving love in the best examples of relationships in this life. Let me start with the effects we feel when we give love.

The Christmas season often serves as a time in which we try to teach our children the "joy of giving." We want them to discover what we ourselves have discovered: that giving to others leads to immense personal rewards in the form of mental states we associate with "knowing that a needy child has been helped" or "seeing a smile on Aunt Ethel's face." In truth, children have already experienced the joy that comes with loving others and caring for their needs. Toddlers often delight in taking care of a favorite teddy bear or in making sure that their dollies are well rested, well fed, and well dressed. The point of teaching them the joy of giving at Christmas time is to turn their attention to those people—for example, less fortunate children or house-bound Aunt Ethel—upon whom they would not automatically focus their attentive care. We want our children to discover that greater benefits often await us even in those situations where it may initially seem that the gifts we offer (of material possessions or our time) will come at an overall cost to us.

How powerful can the effects of loving others be on the one who offers love? Consider a parent's love for an infant. While we hope that our newborn children will someday return our love, there is no expectation that at the time they will—or indeed can—do anything except involuntarily receive what we give them. Nonetheless, the positive experiences of meeting the physical and emotional needs of an infant can be as rewarding as any experience we have in this life. And in general, loving and caring for others is widely—and rightly—viewed as therapeutic. When other humans are not available as recipients for our affection, we turn to a teddy bear when we are young or a cat when we are old. The mental experiences of caring for someone (or something) seem to have profoundly healing qualities to them; and there exists a terrible void when we do not have others to love.

In looking for a kind of experience that might rival, in terms of mental impact, the best examples of offering love to others, I think we can point only to those experiences where we *receive* love from others. The belief or feeling that we are deeply loved and accepted seems key for humans in averting such substantially life-diminishing mental experiences as those we associate with, for instance, feelings of abandonment, rejection, inadequacy, and isolation. Indeed, humans simply will not be mentally healthy if they do not feel that they are substantially loved by others. So powerful is our need for love that people can draw comfort merely from a brief meeting with a stranger who seems to understand their point of view as they recount a hurtful predicament.

Importantly, the belief *alone* that we are understood by someone does not produce positive mental experiences. I will think myself disadvantaged if I believe I have adversaries who know me well (and who will therefore be more effective in their plotting against me). And I will feel unnerved to discover that an acquaintance understands me quite well if her knowledge of me has been gained by stalking me or by some other surreptitious means. The belief that we are understood leads to a positive mental experience only if it exists within a mutually loving relationship—or at least holds the promise of one, as when a connection with a stranger arouses excitement that we might at some point engage in cooperative pursuits with him or with others with similar interests and perspectives.

What this points up for the Christian theist is that the mental states associated with feeling loved are positive inasmuch as they mirror (or anticipate) certain aspects of the kind of ideal relationships for which we were created. We might think of the experiences of connecting with strangers as *shadows* of the ideal.[17] Yes, the mental experiences that come with being understood are often positive in nature. But this is because, in being understood, we anticipate certain aspects of the ideal, mutually loving relationships for which Christian theists affirm we were created. Following this same pattern, our mental experiences arising from the loving acts we *bestow* on others will also be positive experiences only as they mirror ideal, loving relationships. After all, a parent may experience resentment as she offers loving service to an ungrateful and increasingly rebellious child. And a person may wish that she had *less* of a continued attraction to, and desire to care for, an ex-lover who is the source of painful memories.

It is possible of course to offer various theories as to why humans, through offering love and receiving it from others, should have profoundly life-enhancing mental experiences. The Christian theist understands humans as being created by God in such a way that they flourish by being in the kinds of relationships that mirror the mutually self-giving relationships within the Trinity. As noted in the Introduction, I am not attempting with this book to provide conclusive arguments for the truth of Christian theism—or specifically the claim that our eternal well-being hinges on the state of our relationship with God. Still, I do think that the profoundly healing effects of connecting deeply with others serve as some evidence that our eternal well-being really will hinge on the states of our relationships with others and with God. In drawing general conclusions from human experiences as to how a lasting sense of well-being is attained, my own (limited) data come primarily from the testimony of friends in the fields of counseling and medicine. But I would venture the conclusion that almost all instances of mental disease (which in many cases give rise to physical maladies) have as their root cause some absence of a completely healthy relationship(s) with family, friends, and one's wider community. Typically, it is the most important relationships in a person's life that, when they become unhealthy, lead a person to the therapist's office. Still, it is *some* absence of healthy relationships that arguably lies at the root of all visits to the therapist's office.[18] Indeed, it is difficult to imagine a case in which a person would be less than joyful if absolutely all the relationships in her life were flourishing wonderfully.

In the following section I shall offer more theological reasons for thinking that our well-being hinges on the state of our relationship to God. I shall then conclude the section by addressing the objection that, even if the mental experiences of "connecting" that arise as we relate to God and others are important for our well-being, they are not *sufficient* to ensure it.

## 4.3 Are Relationships the Key to Our Well-Being?

Although God is relational by nature, and although the Christian perspective I am endorsing is that *our* flourishing consists in relating rightly to others, it would be too strong to claim that the flourishing of *any* possible creature God creates could occur only through participation in personal relationships. There could be creatures who flourish in isolation and who, like amebas, even reproduce asexually. Though in a minimal sense their flourishing would depend on their being related to God (after all, in the Christian worldview all creatures will be sustained in existence by God), it is not necessary that their flourishing depend, as human flourishing does, on their being in loving relationships with others. There might conceivably be creatures, for instance, that flourish as they reflect *other* aspects of God—such as aesthetic ones. Christian hymns of worship sometimes speak of human limitations to appreciate the beauty of God. And it is entirely possible that there could be other creatures whose ultimate flourishing chiefly consists in their much greater capacity to recognize and contemplate the aesthetic aspects of God's nature. Still, the Christian view of *human* flourishing that I wish to explore sees it as an essential fact about any human that he or she will ultimately flourish only by relating to God and others in loving, self-giving ways.

A comparison with Robert Adams's views is instructive here. Adams has proposed that human well-being consists in enjoyment of the excellent, where "excellence" for a finite thing involves its resembling God, who is infinite, personified excellence.[19] Though this proposal shares with my own account certain central, Christian affirmations—such as that human flourishing ultimately depends on one's relation to God—it differs from my own account in important respects. As we saw in chapter 1, Adams, following Plato, understands the Good (or, as Adams calls it, the "excellent") in terms of "that which is worthy of love or admiration" (1999, 13). For Adams, something can have goodness—which is an intrinsic quality—whether or not anyone is enjoying it.

By contrast, I argued in chapter 1 that the meaning of "good" cannot be divorced from the question of whether that which is said to be good is promoting someone's interests or well-being. In chapter 2 I made a similar affirmation about the *nature* of goodness, arguing, in contrast to Adams, that "what is good" cannot be separated from "what is good *for*" someone.

Differences in theistic, ethical frameworks can often (if not always) be traced to differing conceptions of the nature of God. Perhaps the heart of the differences between Adams's account of goodness and my own account involves the different aspects of God we wish to emphasize. While Adams emphasizes the intrinsic qualities of God that are worthy of "love and admiration," my own starting point in describing God is to emphasize the point that God is life itself. On my account, then, God is the source of goodness because God brings life—that is, states of flourishing—to finite creatures like us. Adams may be correct that any contingent being or thing that is good will resemble God in some way.

But on my understanding of what goodness amounts to, this translates to the claim that any creature's flourishing will occur only as it resembles some aspect of the flourishing life of God. My point remains that a good life for us does not *consist in* resembling God; rather, a good life consists in having the mental states constitutive of flourishing.

I use the term *life* in a broad sense when speaking of the life God brings to us. Clearly, we will flourish only if our bodies are animated. But the Christian tradition sees God as offering to people life in a much wider sense than mere animated existence. The right kind of relationship with God is affirmed to bring with it life-enriching experiences of peace, joy, and so forth—states fully realized in heaven. Certainly, there can be circumstances in one's earthly life where physical death actually promotes one's ultimate flourishing. Martyrdom is one obvious example of continuing on the path to fullness of life (i.e., the kind of life in heaven for which Christians affirm we were created) despite one's earthly existence coming to an end. And of course there are subtler examples—such as times of facing up to difficult truths about oneself—where hardship and discomfort are the best, and perhaps only, means toward achieving in the long term this life of ultimate flourishing for which we were created.

Taking up the point that my notion of a flourishing life includes a wide number of aspects, one might question whether all the things that seem to enhance our lives really do fall under the compass of "God giving life to us." Think, for instance, of the enjoyment a person gets from whittling a piece of wood on a lazy Saturday afternoon or practicing a comic routine for an upcoming amateur night at the local pub. True, some theists may find these activities to be a means of strengthening their relationships with God. But surely, so the objection goes, some people flourish simply when they engage in these activities—irrespective of any effects these pursuits may have on their relationships with God.

Before responding directly to this objection, let me note a preliminary point. On the Christian view that we exist only in virtue of continued divine conservation, there is of course a minimal sense in which we could not exist in complete separation from God. Further, the Christian doctrine of prevenient grace includes the idea that God is, in various ways, "at work" in the lives even of those who expressly are rejecting God. Although the Christian tradition has had different ways of spelling out the nature of God's continued communication to, and interaction with, all people (again, even those people who wish to distance themselves from God), it still follows from the Christian understanding of prevenient grace that all people will experience *some* of God's life-giving resources. Moving beyond these minimal claims, though, our interest is in the question of whether secular pursuits themselves might sometimes be the immediate cause of our mental experiences of flourishing.

The objector may suggest that an affirmative answer to this question should be obvious. The repetition of mindlessly carving a piece of wood can lead to a feeling of relaxation; and the unexpectedness of a clearly delivered punch line can lead to laughter and a momentary forgetting of any problems we might have.

In response, I do not wish to deny that the repetitive act of whittling a piece of wood or the hearing of an unexpected comedic punch line can cause physical reactions in the brain that give rise to positive mental experiences. But such things are *partial* causes. They are not sufficient to elicit mental experiences associated with peace and laughter, irrespective of the states of one's relationships with others. To illustrate, moments of laughter tend to grow much scarcer when feelings of isolation become acute. A well-conceived and well-delivered joke will fail to amuse someone in the throes of depression. Conversely, viewing an unimaginative comedic film can be the occasion of great amusement if the viewing takes place among a group of friends who are enjoying each other's company. These points add plausibility to the Christian claim that our participation in positive relationships will determine whether we have lasting, positive mental experiences associated with such things as relaxation and amusement. Perhaps within the heavenly community people will need activities jointly to pursue if their relationships with one another are to be as rich as is possible.[20] But the types of activities they pursue will not hold the key in determining whether their pursuits lead to positive mental states. The positive nature of their relationships will hold the key.

Consider how we often react to situations in which our positive mental experiences do not have the feeling tone associated with "connecting" with others. For example, a person might experience feeling tones we seek to capture with the term *awe* (upon seeing the Grand Canyon and finding oneself unable to capture one's experience with public language). Or one might experience feeling tones that we associate with "positive nervous energy" (when facing a task one both wants to undertake and fears to some extent). These experiences might possibly be used by the critic to underscore the point that *other* feeling tones—besides the feeling tone of "connecting" with others—can enhance our flourishing. What we should find interesting, though, is the way we typically look for others to share in these experiences with us. When a comic tells a good joke, people often laugh *as* they search for eye contact with others. "Are there others who relate to what I'm experiencing?" they seem to be asking. We humans have remarkably strong desires that others share, or at least understand our involvement in, the activities we enjoy—such as watching a good movie, seeing the Grand Canyon, performing well at a piano recital, or accomplishing an athletic feat.[21] In an attempt to ensure that our mental experiences include the feeling tone of connecting, we may even interact with impersonal objects as though they were the kind of sentient creature with whom we can connect. Thus a person might talk to the automobile he is attempting to fix, pretending that he has with the automobile the kind of give-and-take relationship that can exist between personal agents. A person might form an emotional attachment to an old tree she is campaigning to save from housing developers, perhaps imagining (and believing at some level of consciousness) that the tree has a mental life, with a corresponding welfare akin to ours and an ability to appreciate the efforts of campaigners to protect its welfare.

The main takeaway point from the previous two paragraphs is that the human need for relationships is such that relationships must surely play a contributing role in any experiences of flourishing we have. But perhaps now the critic will raise the pending objection first mentioned in the previous section: even if it is *necessary* to be rightly related to others in order to flourish, it is still implausible to think that our relationships are *sufficient* to determine whether we will flourish. After all, severe physical trauma to one's body can cause intensely negative mental experiences that we associate with physical pain. And does not this show, so the objection goes, that *other* conditions are needed—such as physical health—if we are to flourish?

In response, the Christian theist can point out that it seems an entirely contingent fact about humans that, for example, harm to their physical bodies should rob them of the benefits that would otherwise come with relating to others. People we meet in pain typically are capable of *moments* when the physical trauma to their bodies does not preclude their having positive mental experiences. For example, a hospital patient recuperating from painful surgery may, upon hearing a joke from a visitor, involuntarily laugh and experience a brief moment of relief. Similarly, upon seeing the door to her room swing open (possibly heralding the visit of another friend), the patient may experience the kind of pleasant feeling we associate with anticipating good news. We sometimes talk in terms of a person "forgetting" that she is in pain. In these moments, the physical trauma to the patient's body does not prevent her from having the kinds of life-enhancing experiences ultimately made possible, as argued earlier, through her positive relationships with others. And it seems an entirely contingent fact about humans that their positive mental experiences in the midst of physical trauma should be only fleeting in nature. It is conceivable that physical trauma might *not* in practice detract from our flourishing—given, for example, scenarios involving much deeper relationships that foster much greater comfort; or involving a greater mental ability that allows us to focus our full attention on these relationships irrespective of our surroundings and circumstances; or involving, most obviously, a different kind of physical body. So it seems plausible for the Christian theist to insist that, given certain conditions (perhaps realized by God in an afterlife), our relationships with God and others really can be the sole determining factor as to whether we flourish.

Admittedly, it may initially seem counterintuitive to deny that, in addition to our participation in relationships, other contingencies should have at least *some* impact on the positive or negative nature of our mental experiences. Thus, if sharing a laugh with a friend is good, then doing so while seated in a massage chair is even better—whereas doing so while stubbing a toe is a bit worse. However, the theist's response will again be that it is a contingent matter that extrarelational factors should have any bearing on whether our lives go well for us. Even if we assume that the resurrected bodies of the redeemed in heaven are receptive to the difference between a massage and a toe-stubbing, it is a contingent matter that this difference should have any more impact on their well-being than the difference between standing with hands to one's sides or hands on hips.

In chapter 5 I will say more in support of the claim that God will in fact ensure that all contingencies—beyond our decisions about how we want to relate to God and others—will not stand in the way of our ultimate flourishing. These contingencies will include such things as physical maladies and unhealthy emotional reactions, which can sometimes rob us in this life of peace and joy. For now, in order to make this claim about God at least plausible for the current discussion, it may be worth briefly sketching the role that relationships play in the Christian understanding of heaven.

In some religions, heaven may be viewed as containing enjoyable things that are separate from, and are rewards for, one's obedience to God's directives. Such rewards might include exotic foods or sexual pleasures. However, the Christian explanation of heavenly rewards will take into account the understanding that humans—created in the image of God, who is triune and therefore relational in nature—find ultimate fulfillment in being in right relationship with God and others. Accordingly, the rewards of heaven will be understood in terms of people enjoying the kinds of personal relationships for which they were created. Put another way, the Godly relationships established with others *are* the reward; heaven is simply the place where these relationships can continue for eternity.

As to our experiences in *this* life, I have acknowledged that positive mental experiences can arise from individual pursuits disconnected from the kind of interchange that characterizes a relationship. We can experience relaxation through the activity of whittling; and laughter can come with exposure to adroit comic timing. Actually, there seem to be sound theological reasons for this fact. The Christian tradition has a long history of discussing the "hiddenness of God"—that is, why God does not make more obvious his existence and other religious truths. One broad and frequently cited reason is that religious ambiguity provides scope for moral choices and for human cooperation in learning about God.[22] Applying this general theme, the Christian theist will view the fact that individual pursuits (e.g., whittling, watching a sunset, listening to a comic routine) can provide positive mental experiences as part of the religious ambiguity in our world. Accordingly, spiritual wisdom will involve the recognition that any activity that can be pursued in isolation does not itself hold the key to our long-term well-being. If we try to secure our well-being through various pursuits, we will find diminishing returns unless we share these pursuits with others. And given the Christian claim that we find long-term fulfillment only through a relationship with God, the same holds true if we attempt to secure our well-being by sharing activities only with (finite) people.

I am inclined to think it is a necessary fact about humans that their long-term fulfillment hinges on the state of their relationships. However, for the sake of argument we might grant that this is a contingent matter. Perhaps a string of inspiring nature scenes or a running catalog of jokes could forever distract us from our dysfunctional relationships. Even if such scenarios are possible, the Christian theist can press the point that God's providence will ensure that our eternal destiny in fact depends on the relationships we have formed. God will press the truth upon us of how we relate to him and others. This "judgment" will involve removing the nonrelational contingencies of our lives so that we experience the effects either of participating in the kind of ideal, loving relationship into which God invites us or of refusing to participate in such genuinely loving relationships.

Some of the points of this past paragraph will be taken up in more detail in section 5.6, where we will see how our everyday choices move us in the long run either toward settled, benevolent dispositions or toward settled, purely self-interested dispositions. My aim at present is to indicate that the Christian theist has resources for accounting for the fact that we find pleasure in individual pursuits like painting or reading. This fact does not render implausible the Christian claim that it is the state of our relationships with God and others that ultimately determines whether we experience peace and laughter for eternity.

## 4.4 Making Others' Interests Our Own

If our ultimate well-being does consist in the mental states arising from our participation in (ideal) loving relationships, we should now ask how such relationships are established. I noted in the previous section that writers like Aristotle and Aquinas point us in the right direction when they observe that, in the best examples of human relationships, a child or friend can become "another self" for me. Part of the insight here is that we have the facility to make other people's interests our own. Yet this scenario of "making someone else's interests my own" stands in need of clarification. Most immediately, a question arises whether the scenario is one in which I pursue (or, at least, am disposed to pursue) the other person's welfare as *she* sees it or as *I* see it. Of course, there are certain asymmetrical relationships in which one person (e.g., a parent of a child, or a caretaker of an adult with diminished mental capacities) has certain responsibilities toward the other person that, we would all agree, can justify the overruling of the other person's stated preferences. But let us confine our discussion to adult peers.

On some matters relating to another person's well-being, the person's own avowals about where her interests lie will constitute our only reliable source of information about those interests. For instance, if we want to paint the bathroom a color that will bring Sue aesthetic enjoyment, our only guideline will be her testimony. If she tells us that she prefers magnolia to earthen cream, then, outside some imaginative scenario where we are privy to psychological research on the effects of long-term exposure to magnolia, we are in no position to overrule her preferences on the grounds that we know what is *really* best for her. On other matters, however, we can find ourselves with a definite view as to where the other person's best interests lie—whether or not the other person agrees. We may believe in certain situations that we have true information about the other person's best interests that she has not considered, or cannot consider, or will not properly consider. In such cases we face a choice whether to promote the other person's well-being as *we* think it is best promoted or as *she* thinks it is best promoted.

If a person's welfare were a matter of whether her own current desires were realized, then our decision in such cases would be an easy one. However, we saw in section 2.2 that a person's welfare—and thus her ultimate interests—does not simply lie in the satisfaction of her desires.[23] Thus, if my decision to make another person's interests my own is to be a positive thing *for* the other person, then this decision will not automatically involve promoting the other person's interests as she prefers. On the other hand, the idea of promoting a person's interests in a manner that overrules her stated preferences smacks of paternalism and the accompanying devaluing of her point of view as a personal agent. Limits of course exist to this danger of paternalism. When we are trying to do what we believe is best for someone else, it is clear that that person's life will not go well for her if we continually drag her kicking and screaming toward some goal that we—but not she—recognize as good. Rather than paternalistic overruling, persuading the other person to pursue this goal with us is likely to have the happier outcome. Still, there are many times when it is reasonable to think that we can help a person's life go well in the long term by pursuing a course of action at odds with what the person currently would have us pursue. At such times, what would it mean to make someone else's interests our own?

There seems initially to be plausibility to *both* the following perspectives: (1) that we should promote others' interests as *they* see them; and (2) that we should promote others' interests as *we* see them. Before we explore the possibility that these two aims might somehow be reconciled within a single project, let us establish that both perspectives really do carry substantial force. If one or the other perspective were to lose its force upon closer examination, then we would have no need to attempt a reconciliation. So are there substantial reasons to maintain each perspective? Let me begin with the importance of pursuing others' interests as they see them.

Interpersonal relationships involve a kind of dynamic different from that of a playwright reading through a dialogue he has written. A playwright, as a single personal agent, simply cannot generate the kind of "give-and-take" necessary for true, interpersonal relationships. The playwright may identify strongly with one of the characters, perhaps having even constructed the character in an autobiographical fashion. But his identifying with a character in no way generates the kind of dynamic distinctive of interpersonal relationships. For the playwright is, after all, relating to *himself* when he reads through the dialogue he has written. There simply are no other bona fide personal agents in the picture to whom we might think of him as relating interpersonally.[24] And an interpersonal relationship of course requires two distinct personal agents.

The "give-and-take" dynamic of genuine interpersonal relationships will be examined in some detail in section 4.6. But at present we can note that when I relate to another personal agent I am relating to someone with a distinct center of consciousness and point of view. Consequently, unless I somehow could gain full access to, and appreciation for, her mental inner workings, I will not always fully grasp her thought processes. She will rank preferences and arrive at reasons for acting in ways that I will not always be able to predict.

If we acknowledge this point of other personal agents having a point of view and reasons for acting that are distinct from our own, then we will need also to affirm the importance of pursuing other people's interests as they see them. Other people will, of course, have their own views about where their own interests lie. Yet, as we have seen, I will not be in a position fully to understand a person's thought processes as she ranks preferences and arrives at reasons for acting. And without a full understanding of these matters, I am not in a position to pass definitive judgment on her decisions as being unwise, imprudent, and so forth. Admittedly, we may find in some instances that a person's stated preferences and reasons for acting seemingly reveal a lack of wisdom and prudence by any conceivable standard. In such cases we may conclude that the realization of the person's preferences cannot possibly promote her well-being in the way that other available options will. But it also seems clear that plenty of instances will exist in which the private nature of a person's preferences and reasons for acting prevents us from passing definitive judgment that we should override the person's requests on the basis that we know what is actually good for her. At least, this point will be clear to us if we remain mindful of the possible differences between the person and us on two matters. First, there is the difference between another person's well-being and my own. Importantly, the shape of a person's well-being will partly arise from the person's own preferences and commitments to projects. Second, there is the point that the person's well-being might be furthered in more than one way—including a way that the other person grasps, though I do not.

Where there exists doubt as to whether the other person's requests will or will not actually further her well-being, we would do well to keep in mind Robert Adams's point that the project of your own good is a project that "belongs to you in a way that it does not belong to me" (1999, 376). At the very least, Adams makes the intuitive point that people have a uniquely vested interest in their own welfare—and thus perhaps the right to have their views on the matter given special consideration. How far can we push this point, particularly on issues where there is much at stake with respect to the other person's well-being, and where it becomes less and less plausible to think that the person's stated preferences might actually further the person's well-being? I doubt if we could arrive at anything approaching a precise answer. But the point remains that, in making someone else's interests our own, it may well be vital at times, as we maintain an interpersonal relationship with the person, to promote her interests as *she* sees them—even though we have a different perspective as to how her interests can best be promoted.

Given that substantial reasons exist for maintaining the importance of promoting others' interests as *they* see them, let me now turn to consider whether telling reasons also exist for promoting others' interests as *we* see them. Against the conclusion that such reasons exist, one might attempt to extend some of the arguments of the previous paragraph and make a case that we should seldom, if ever, overrule someone else's informed, stated preferences. Adams, after making the point that the project of your own good "belongs to you in a way that it does not belong to me," continues by stating, "and it is yours rather than mine to determine the shape of the project" (1999, 376–77). Building on this general thought, there are various arguments one might utilize in defending the conclusion that it would be bad—and even wrong—to overrule someone's preferences and requests as to how his or her own well-being should be promoted. For instance, one might draw from natural law theories or from contractarian theories in arguing that people have the right to determine the manner in which they will receive their allotment of public resources. Or one might argue that personal autonomy has overriding value. My general response to such lines of argument stems from my conclusions about the nature of noninstrumental value, as outlined in chapter 2. If, as I have argued, certain kinds of mental states are the only things of noninstrumental value, then natural rights and personal autonomy will ultimately be valuable only insofar as they contribute to these mental states.

What, then, should we do in a situation where we believe that, by pursuing someone else's well-being as she sees it, we will not (compared to other available options) ultimately be promoting those mental states in which her well-being solely consists? It seems clear in such a case that deferring to the person's stated preferences would hardly be the loving act. Perhaps someone will object to this conclusion by questioning how often we could really *know* that a person's overall well-being will best be achieved through an alternative course of action. But this is no good objection. The most we can *ever* do in promoting a person's welfare is to do that which we believe—whatever the strength of that belief—will promote her welfare. If we believe that, among the courses of action available to us, a certain course of action will most probably promote a person's well-being, then this course of action will be the one we pursue if our goal is to promote the person's welfare. Again, our welfarist conclusions from chapter 2 were that things like autonomy and respect for someone's preferences will be good and of value only insofar as they contribute to someone's well-being. Thus, if we reach the all-things-considered judgment that we will best further a person's welfare by overruling her stated preferences, loving care for the other person demands that we do so. If I choose to pursue one course of action over another while believing my action will make the person comparatively *worse off*, then surely I have not made the person's interests my own.

Perhaps someone will object by saying that we ourselves may often want to exercise autonomy, even when others are sure they know what is "really best for us." And if we are to treat others as we would want to be treated, should not we, as we make their interests our own, afford them the same level of autonomy we would want? But this objection misses the point. The reason we often prefer autonomy ourselves is that we think *we will flourish* by exercising it and not listening to other people—for instance, we believe that we know better than they do, or we believe that we will ultimately learn more from the mistakes we ourselves make, or we enjoy the feeling of independent decision making. As we make judgments about how others will flourish, we can incorporate the consideration that others might prefer autonomy as we prefer it. The point of the previous paragraph is that, if we make an *all-things-considered* judgment that we will best further another person's welfare by overruling her preferences, then we should do so if we are truly seeking what is best for the person.

So there seem to be strong reasons to think that, in forming a positive relationship with another person, we should promote her interests as *we* think they are best promoted. At the same time, we concluded earlier that genuine, interpersonal relationships require us to give room to the other person in determining her own preferences and projects. There seem, then, to be strong reasons to keep *both* perspectives on the question of promoting someone's interest as she sees it or as we see it. And indeed I do not think we should attempt to dispense with either perspective. Instead, we should explore the possibility of reconciling the two perspectives in such a way that a decision "to make someone's interests my own" incorporates both of them. Such is the goal of the next section.

## 4.5 Divine Coordination

As we begin to work toward this goal, we must first be clear on what is involved in someone having an "interest." Thus far, we have used the term *interest* synonymously with a person's well-being. In this sense of the term, something is in my interest if it is good for me. There is, once again, another sense of the term, which is more closely associated with being interested in some activity or state of affairs. In this second sense, I have an interest in something if it is one of my projects or areas of concern. The distinction between these two senses of *interest* is perhaps best seen when I have an altruistic interest (in the second sense) in, say, labor laws in Indonesia that protect more vigorously the rights of workers, even while dismissing the idea that such laws might somehow be tied up with my own personal welfare, or what is in my own best interest (in the first sense). For ease of discussion, let us refer to these two senses of *interest* as, respectively, interest$_{(2)}$ and interest$_{(1)}$.

Within an ongoing interpersonal relationship, many of the decisions I make will be whether to join the other person in the pursuit of her interests$_{(2)}$. She may have interests$_{(2)}$ in campaigning for Indonesian workers' rights, watching foreign films, writing a novel, and so forth. In deciding whether and how I will relate to her, I will face a stream of choices as to whether I will join her in pursuing her chosen projects (or, at least, work to enable her to pursue them herself). Furthermore, the room we must give others as personal agents—as we allow them to rank preferences and arrive at reasons for acting, which we do not fully understand—pertains to all of their interests$_{(2)}$, whether or not these interests$_{(2)}$ are self-directed.

These considerations may lead us to think that the key to the formation of ideal, loving relationships is the decision to make someone else's interests$_{(2)}$ our own. This conclusion, however, would be the wrong one to draw. As I shall go on to argue, we establish ideal, loving relationships by focusing on promoting other people's welfare, or interests$_{(1)}$. Still, we will need a grasp of each of our two senses of *interest*—that is, personal welfare versus chosen projects—if we are to achieve the reconciliation of perspectives that is the goal of this section. This goal again is how I might promote someone else's welfare *both* as I think best and as she thinks best. The question how to promote others' interests$_{(1)}$ is a subset of the larger question of how to promote their interests$_{(2)}$. And we will need a way of achieving a reconciliation of perspectives on this latter question in order to achieve a reconciliation of perspectives on the former question.

These differences in perspectives can, and often do, plague even the best examples of human relationships. Each person within a relationship may be completely committed to promoting the other person's welfare. Still, there remains the question of how this goal is best achieved. A man with an elderly mother may face the difficult decision of whether to facilitate his mother's move to a retirement home (which he judges to be in her best interests$_{(1)}$) or to show support for the idea that she should continue to live by herself in her own home (which is her persistent request). While this example seems primarily to involve how best to promote someone else's welfare, or interests$_{(1)}$, there are of course cases that include others' projects, or interests$_{(2)}$. The man may have a son who he believes is best served in the long term by continuing his university education but who asks for permission to drop out of school and use his university fund to launch a project digging wells for third world communities. In this instance, even if the man shares the project, or interest$_{(2)}$, of the son, there may remain disagreement about how this project should be achieved. The man may also have a wife who is embroiled in a dispute with other members of their extended family. Despite thinking that the situation would improve for everyone if his wife reexamined her own attitudes, he also knows that his wife wants and expects him to agree with her perspective when she shares it with him. In this instance, there may remain disagreement with his wife as to both how he should promote *her* interest$_{(1)}$ and how he should prioritize his concerns for the interests$_{(1)}$ of everyone involved in the dispute.

In these examples of the man's interactions with his mother, his son, and his wife, there is a cost to promoting their interests$_{(1)}$ as *he* thinks they are best promoted. If the man does not share the projects, or interests$_{(2)}$, of his loved ones, or if the man *does* share these projects but does not agree on *how* they should be pursued, then the cost will of course involve the loss of projects they can pursue together. Further, costs will come in the form of the feelings his family members will experience as a result of his actions: they will probably feel unsupported, perhaps even betrayed. Sadly, then, in attempting to further the overall welfare of his loved ones, the man will probably be undermining his own relationships with them. Even in the best examples of human relationships—marked by a steadfast concern for the other person's welfare—there remains the threat of differing perspectives as to how each person's welfare is best promoted. And with such differing perspectives comes the frequent result of hurt feelings that we all recognize in even our best experiences of participating in loving relationships.

If we think of this difference in perspective in terms of a "gap," we can acknowledge that a gap need not *necessarily* arise on any particular occasion when I form a belief about how someone else's interest$_{(1)}$ (or indeed interests$_{(2)}$) is best promoted. However, as a relationship progresses over time, more opportunities obviously exist for this gap to appear. Furthermore, even if a situation has not yet arisen in which I find myself in disagreement with someone else about how her welfare is best promoted, we will both need to recognize how disagreements *would* arise under various, possible circumstances. At least, we will need to be aware of this "under the surface" disagreement if our relationship is to be one of true intimacy. After all, we relate to others only superficially unless we have a certain depth of knowledge of who the other person really is (i.e., her values, commitments, point of view, and the like). A chief reason that an intimate relationship takes time to develop is that it is through a progression of different circumstances that we come to know more fully the other person's projects and commitments. True, we can often predict what someone will do in new circumstances. If my daughter observes as a toddler my consistent willingness to defer to her choice of cartoons during family television viewing, she may correctly believe as a teenager that I will defer on some particular occasion to her choice of a sitcom over my own preferred alternative. However, if she believes as a teenager that I will *always* defer to her choices, she will be faced with adjusting her understanding of me when she finds that I will not always defer to her choices in this manner. Growing in shared experiences with someone typically takes the form both of having our expectations confirmed and of being surprised at times. Profound surprises, which can occur years into a relationship, can lead us to say such things as "I guess I never really knew him."

So, in intimate relationships characterized by a thorough knowledge of the other person, we will not only know the other person's past commitments. We will also know the person's tendencies in hypothetical situations. It is our beliefs about how the other person will act in future, imagined situations that give us the feeling of security that is one hallmark of a positive relationship. If our beliefs are not *true* beliefs, we face the perpetual prospect of disillusionment when some new situation reveals the gap between the person's actual commitments and our expectations of her commitments. And again, even if a new situation does not materialize to expose this gap, our ignorance of the gap shows that we do not know the other person as we might. In a deepening relationship between two people, in which they grow in their knowledge of one another, they will inevitably come to know the gaps in perspective as to how each person should promote the other person's interest$_{(1)}$ (as well as interests$_{(2)}$).

What is needed of course is a way of reconciling both persons' perspectives. It will not do here to sketch conceivable scenarios where there exists agreement that one person in the relationship should decide how both persons' welfare will be promoted. Nor will it do to suggest that both persons agree to some system as to who gets to decide such matters. Agreeing *that* I should defer to someone else's judgments is not the same as agreeing *with* the content of those judgments. And where there is disagreement of the latter kind—which will not be eliminated simply by an agreement of the former kind—there remains scope for resentment, feelings of alienation, and so forth. An agreement by both persons to defer to the advice of a third party will not, for the same reason, automatically bring a reconciliation of perspectives. Yet a certain *kind* of third party does seem to hold the key for the reconciliation we're seeking.

Suppose that a third party knows how each person's welfare is best enhanced in any given situation. Returning to our previous examples, if a move to a retirement home is better for the man's mother, all things considered, then the third party will know this fact. And if the man and his mother are both able to learn this fact from the third party, then by accepting the counsel of the third party they will agree about the best way to proceed. Perhaps it is important for the mother to maintain a certain autonomy in making some decisions about her future in order to avoid life-diminishing feelings of helplessness and to maintain her standing as a bona fide personal agent to whom others can relate interpersonally. If the mother's decision about living arrangements falls within the range of matters where others should give her room to determine her own projects, then our third party will again know this fact.

To avoid irresolvable dilemmas where I promote one person's welfare only at the expense of *another* person's welfare, we will also need to suppose that our world is arranged in such a way that all people's interests coincide. We need not go so far as to say that no person misses out on *any* good thing as a result of someone else achieving something good. Such cases of mutually exclusive advancement of two people's interests clearly exist in our world. For example, I may miss the opportunity to help a neighbor in need because someone else has already provided the required help and begun to benefit from a deeper relationship with that neighbor. Even if it is a good thing that I desire some opportunities that will inevitably fail to materialize (because, e.g., my character becomes shaped in the process so that I am able to participate in deep, loving relationships with others when opportunities *do* materialize), I have still missed out on a relationship with my neighbor that itself would enhance my well-being. So it would be clearly implausible to make an unqualified claim that the world is arranged in such a way that my own welfare could never be promoted at the expense of someone else's welfare.

Still, the Christian idea of heaven supposes that there can be—and indeed is—the kind of coordination of people's interests such that everyone experiences ultimate flourishing. Just how good a person's life needs to be in order for that person to "ultimately flourish" is, I think, a difficult question to try to answer. I do not think the notion of *maximal* flourishing is a coherent notion; there could always be one more person to whom I could relate and thereby experience the positive mental states of connecting in which, I have argued, our well-being consists. Further, the Christian tradition does talk about "rewards" in heaven (which perhaps we should think of as opportunities to connect with others in various contexts). And so, it would seem that there does exist scope in heaven for the lives of the redeemed to go *better* for them than they already do. At the same time, the Christian understanding of heaven precludes the notion that the redeemed will experience any sense of "lack" that produces life-diminishing mental states we associate with frustration, jealousy, and the like. Whatever level of flourishing the redeemed enjoy in heaven, it seems proper to think of it as constituting their "ultimate" flourishing in that their life-enhancing mental experiences (of contentment, joy, and so forth) are in no way compromised by life-diminishing mental states that they desire not to have.[25] Or if the flourishing of the redeemed *is* minimally affected in a negative way by certain mental states—such as disappointment that someone they knew on earth is not among the redeemed in heaven—then we can still maintain that these disappointments will not serve to tempt them to alter their commitment to the benevolent pursuits through which ideal relationships are made possible. The redeemed would have no reason to question their commitment to an omniscient coordinator who continued to ensure that all people had the opportunity to attain ultimate flourishing.

If the world really is coordinated so that all people's ultimate welfare can coincide, then our earlier examples need not lead to irresolvable difficulties. Let us suppose that our third party knows that all people's ultimate welfare can coincide in our world—most straightforwardly, knows this in virtue of having created our world. Indeed, let us go ahead and specify that this third party is God. If the man from our examples comes to see how God has coordinated people's interests$_{(1)}$, he will not need to choose between the welfare of his wife and the welfare of his extended family. Further, if the wife joins her husband in seeking direction from God, then she need not experience feelings of resentment or betrayal from her husband.

Admittedly, it is true that human emotions such as resentment do not always line up with our own reflective judgments on what our feelings *should* be. But it would be a mistake to conclude that we are simply back in the previously discussed situation of agreeing *that* one should defer to a third party's judgments, despite not necessarily agreeing *with* those judgments (or feeling happy about them). The key difference between God and any other third party is that God—on the conception of God as an omniscient being—uncontroversially *will* know where the wife's ultimate best interests lie. Further, on the conception of God as a perfectly loving being, God will be committed to leading all people toward the kind of ultimate flourishing for which Christians affirm they were created.[26] The more the wife learns about God, the more clearly she will come to recognize these facts that stem from God's nature. And if we suppose that her spiritual transformation includes her emotions being integrated with her beliefs and desires in such a way that she attains to the Christian depiction of eternal joy, then she will in no way resent her husband's deferral to God's direction on any matter (including the matter of her family dispute). All this of course could not be said about just *any* third party to whom the husband and wife might turn for direction. The appeal to divine coordination thus seems to provide the only plausible avenue to full and permanent reconciliation of our perspectives on how to promote each other's welfare, or interests$_{(1)}$.

The same type of reconciliation is also available when we turn to the wider question of whether, and how, we should promote each other's projects, or interests$_{(2)}$. From our previous example of the man and his son, the son has his own ideas as to how to further the welfare of people in third world communities. And he has his own views on how he should prioritize the use of resources in furthering their welfare in relation to his own. The father also has views on these matters. Yet if divine coordination ensures that we cannot promote anyone's ultimate flourishing while compromising anyone else's ultimate flourishing, then there is the potential—as both the father and son look to God for guidance—for the father and son to achieve a meeting of the minds as to the role the son can best play in achieving God's plans for the ultimate flourishing of all people. Again, if there is room that the father can and/or should allow the son in prioritizing other people's welfare above his own, then God will know this fact. Further, if there is room that the son can and/or should be allowed to pursue projects, the goals of which include things *other* than people's welfare (such as the preservation of an old tree on the perceived grounds that the tree is intrinsically valuable), then again God will know it. It may even be the case that the son should be allowed room to pursue misguided projects—for instance, because a tree conservation project will further his personal growth in some area, even though he is mistaken in his idea that an impersonal object can be intrinsically good. If so, God again serves as the coordinator through which the father and son can achieve a lasting consensus on the matter as each of them looks to God for guidance.

In our discussion I have assumed, rather than argued, that God can coordinate the world in such a way that no person's ultimate welfare can be promoted at the expense of another person's ultimate welfare. I am not sure what kind of argument might be given for this conclusion, other than to note the unfathomable complexity of detail with which an omniscient and omnipotent God would be able to arrange and govern the world. Further, in appealing to the idea of divine coordination of human welfare, I am not offering a formula that God uses in deciding, for example, when a man should support his son in the son's chosen projects, or how the son should seek to achieve his chosen projects. Certainly, God will maintain the goal of all people's ultimate flourishing. And given the unique combination of gifts and abilities God gives any person, there may be certain tasks and general "callings" that the person will need to pursue in order to best promote his own, and others', well-being. Yet there may also be any number of times when there is no single best option—in terms of the effects on people's well-being—among the projects available to a person. Sometimes this may simply be because the difference in projects has no bearing on well-being, as when I choose whether to paint or to wallpaper the bathroom. At other times personal well-being may be at stake but may be equally well accomplished in more than one way, as when my neighbor and I are equally able to volunteer as the final member of a task force for a neighborhood improvement project. In such cases, an arbitrary decision will need to be made—arbitrary, at least, in the sense that the decision in no way affects anyone's capacity to attain ultimate flourishing. So once again it becomes useful to appeal to a personal decision maker, God, who uniquely has the resources to dispel in the long term any resentment or jealousy on the part of those who submit to his decisions.

To sum up this section, we have sought a way of ensuring that *my* perspective on how to promote another person's welfare will align with *her* perspective on how her interests are best promoted. A mutual commitment to be guided by God in our actions seems the only plausible way for such an alignment to occur—in the long term and with no residual, life-diminishing mental experiences such as resentment.

I have noted that a primary goal of this book is not to provide a tight argument for the truth of Christianity. I do think that the kinds of everyday examples discussed in sections 4.2 and 4.3 serve as cues to the Christian affirmations that we were created by a Trinitarian God and that our well-being hinges on whether our relationships mirror the relationships within the Trinity. But I have assumed—rather than carefully argued for—an orthodox Christian picture of God and of human nature. What I want to note at the end of this current section is that, without an assumption of this sort, we have no hope of realizing what I have been calling "ideal relationships" with others. Inasmuch as our relationships need to approach this ideal in order for our long-term well-being to be secured, then without the kind of divine coordination I have outlined in this section we are faced with serious limitations as to what kind of well-being we can hope to attain in the long term.

We have looked in the past two sections at the general shape of ideal relationships. We might now ask how an ideal relationship is established. A natural initial answer—based on the discussions of the past two sections—would be that an ideal relationship between two people is established when each person seeks to promote the well-being of the other. With various provisos to come later, I shall defend this answer. But first it is worth considering how *any* relationship is established.

## 4.6 Establishing Relationships

Any personal relationship involves a recognition of, and response to, the other person as a personal agent. The conditions for personal agency are a subject I shall explore further in section 5.5. For now, it is the issue of *response* on which I want to focus. The idea of responding to another person within an interpersonal relationship makes sense only if we suppose that we are responding *to* something. Admittedly, there is a minimal sense in which, in seeking to *initiate* a relationship with another person, I am responding to her status as a personal agent. However, the kind of response by which a personal relationship is *established* presupposes that the other person has initiated the steps to a relationship. At least, it presupposes that the person has initiated some new aspect of our relationship by inviting me to respond to her in some new way.

How do we invite others to respond to us within the context of a personal relationship?²⁷ We communicate to them in some way and issue what I will refer to as an "invitational statement." Communication might involve audible utterances or written notes, but it might also involve winks, nods, general body language, and any other of the many ways humans have found to communicate with one another. The invitational statements we issue to others can be, among other things, commands, promises, assertions, or questions that one person puts to another person.

In understanding how an invitation can be imbedded in our communication to others, consider Nicholas Wolterstorff's helpful comments on the normative qualities of speech acts such as promising and commanding. "Speaking consists not in communicating or expressing knowledge (or true belief) but in taking up a certain sort of *normative stance*, as I shall call it. . . . The intended function of promising and commanding is not to inform us of what we don't know but to take on duties *toward* us and to require things *of* us" (1995, 35). Wolterstorff offers the example of a car driver who signals left by flipping the car's left-side blinkers. By flipping the blinkers (which constitutes a speech act, presumably the conveying of an intention), the driver takes on prima facie duties; and those motorists around the driver also find themselves with prima facie duties: namely, to treat the driver "as one who has signaled a left turn" (1995, 83). What for our purposes is most important is the idea that the driver's act of communication is an invitation—or perhaps a demand—that the motorists around her *respond* to her in a certain way.

The invitations that come with our communication to others may be explicit or implicit. For example, an executive might explicitly say to his subordinate, "As your boss, I'm telling you that the reports need to be finished by tomorrow morning." On the other hand, a woman might say to her friend, "You shouldn't make too big of a fuss when your toddler refuses to eat." Here, the woman makes the implicit claim to be knowledgeable enough about childhood development to know that a certain action of her friend would be counterproductive. Similarly, if I promise someone that I will meet him for lunch, I am claiming (implicitly) that I am in a position to ensure that that promise is realized. And if I assert to someone that Jerry had salad for lunch yesterday, I am claiming to be in a position to know and accurately to report what Jerry had for lunch yesterday. In all these cases, I invite someone else to recognize certain features about me and to respond to me in a certain way.

Importantly, invitational statements carry the invitation to respond to *me* as a personal agent—as opposed to responding merely to the message I communicate. Some, though not all, of our communication to others carries such an invitation. To illustrate, consider the example of a newspaper columnist who gives marital advice. It may be the case that the columnist hopes that her readers will read the column, realize that the assertions made in the column make perfect sense, and then proceed to change their habits. It will not matter to the columnist whether the readers even notice who wrote the column. Her only concern is that the statements in her column resonate with her readers. If all this is true of the columnist, then her statements do not constitute an invitation to enter into a personal relationship any more than finding a copy of a poem by an (intentionally) anonymous poet constitutes an invitation by that poet to enter into a personal relationship. For the columnist is inviting her readers to respond to her *statements themselves*; she is not inviting them to respond to *her* as a personal agent.

On the other hand, it may be the case that the columnist insists that her newspaper byline carry the inscription "PhD in psychology with over twenty years' experience as a marriage therapist." Or the columnist may not insist on a byline but instead assume that her readers will remain cognizant of her reputation for offering helpful advice in the past. Here, the columnist desires that her readers follow (or at least take seriously) her advice, at least in part because of her expertise on marriage relationships. Her statements in her column do now constitute invitational statements, as she is inviting her readers to respond to *her* as a personal agent with certain features.

When others invite us to respond to them as personal agents, they not only anticipate *that* we will respond. Their hope is that we will respond in a certain *way* and thereby establish a certain *kind* of relationship with them. In issuing invitational statements to others, a woman may seek a relationship where she is a mentor or a protégé; where she is a peer or a parent; where she expects her advice to be taken with a grain of salt, or seriously considered, or unquestioningly followed. Suppose a woman (Lena) encourages a friend (Frank) to be more relaxed about his young child's eating habits. Perhaps in these conversations with him, she means to convey to him that she has been observing Frank's family dynamics and senses a worrisome, potential problem if he persists in pressuring his child at mealtimes. Her (implicit) claim is to understand Frank's family relationships and to be knowledgeable enough to discern the trajectories of family patterns. And her invitation is for Frank to relate to her as someone who has these kinds of insights and who is deeply concerned for the well-being of Frank's family. However, Frank may understand Lena merely to be making an (implicit) claim to know a bit about common rules of thumb in child development. Consequently, Frank will misunderstand the kind of relationship into which Lena has invited him.

If Frank responds to Lena as one who has only common knowledge and a passing concern for his family, does he thereby establish a personal relationship with Lena? This will depend primarily on whether Lena is willing to accede to a personal relationship with Frank in which he recognizes her general knowledge and concern but not the personal, deeper kind of knowledge and concern she meant to convey that she possesses. Perhaps Lena will go on to state explicitly to Frank that she wishes their relationship to be one in which her role is that of personal confidant and counselor. If Frank is reluctant to relate to her on these terms but still seeks to relate to her as one with general, peer knowledge, then Lena will need to decide whether she is willing to accede to a personal relationship with him on *these* terms.[28] Of course, we can also imagine a case where Frank recognizes Lena as making *more* claims to insight and concern than she intended to make. Suppose that Lena, in offering the advice, meant only to convey—as a means of reminding Frank what she assumed he already knew about child psychology—that she had herself found these general rules of thumb to be helpful. But perhaps Frank understood her to be offering more personal counsel as part of a continuing dialogue about his family life. In such a case, Lena will have to decide whether she is willing to "offer" that part of herself to Frank by relating to him on a deeper level than she had initially intended.

What this discussion points up is that there must be a kind of *meeting of the minds* between two people in terms of the "normative stance" (to use Wolterstorff's phrase) taken up as part of their communication with one another. In our example, Frank's response to Lena will establish a relationship with her only if the normative stance she means to take up in issuing an invitational statement to him corresponds to some degree with his understanding and acceptance of this stance. How close a correspondence is needed? Again, this will be a matter of the terms to which each person is willing to accede in continuing the relationship.

Such decisions are common enough to us. We interact on a daily basis with acquaintances, coworkers, and even close friends who have incomplete or distorted understandings of who we really are and of what kind of relationship we propose to have with them. We realize that, strictly speaking, they are responding to whom they take us (or desire us) to be—rather than to who we really are. Sometimes we are willing to accept a personal relationship with them on these terms, interacting with them in ways that remain possible. At other times their misunderstanding of who we are makes a meaningful relationship impossible. To illustrate: a person may end a friendship by saying, "If you think I would be interested in being your partner in this shady scheme, then you really don't understand who I am or why I wanted to be your friend in the first place." Likewise, a person may break off communication with a coworker by saying, "There can be no meaningful conversation between us as long as you continue wrongly to interpret everything I say to you as an attempt to undermine your position with the company."

Thus far in this section we have sketched the way in which relationships are established. In sum, we invite people (either explicitly or implicitly) to respond to us in a certain way when we communicate to them. Others must then recognize and respond to the attributes we have (explicitly or implicitly) claimed to possess; and this recognition and response must at least roughly match the claims we intended to make. All this is needed for ongoing relationships to be established.

We can respond to, and maintain relationships with, other people for various reasons. Toward seeing this point, as well as certain implications that follow from it, consider our earlier example of the son who informs his father of his intention to drop out of school and use his university fund to launch a project digging wells in third world communities. Let us suppose that the father, who opposes the son's plans, then has a long discussion with the son in which he suggests that his own greater life experiences give him greater wisdom as to how the son can best achieve both personal well-being and his life goals of helping others. In addition to this claim of authority in the sense of *expertise*, the father may also make a claim to authority in the sense of *position*. While the father acknowledges that the son's age is such that the son should not be expected to follow parental directives unquestioningly, the father reminds his son that it is still proper for children to afford parental advice a certain weight. In the end, the son follows his father's advice.

We suppose in this example that the son has responded to the father in roughly the way in which the father invited the son to respond: as one who had a certain amount of wisdom and whose opinions were to be seriously considered. We thus suppose that the son maintains a positive relationship with his father. What we cannot yet discern in our example is the *ultimate goal* the son sought to achieve when he decided to follow the father's advice. Perhaps the son came to agree with the father that his own long-term well-being was more important than he had previously been considering. Or the son might have remained focused on the goal of digging wells, coming to agree with his father's suggestion that a university education could open doors to pursue more effectively this goal. Perhaps the son's overriding consideration was the belief that he still owed his father, as his chief benefactor, this act of deference. Or the simple desire to see his father happy, coupled with the recognition of how much the father cared about the son's decision, might have been enough to sway the son's decision. In the end there may be any number of ultimate goals that could explain a son's decision to respond positively to the authoritative claims of a father in our imagined scenario.

Even so, for our larger discussion we are not simply interested in the goals that can serve to maintain just any working relationship between two people. We are interested in the goals that are compatible with the kind of ideal, loving relationships in which the Christian religion sees our ultimate flourishing as consisting. To preclude the possibility of conflict arising within such a relationship, there will need to be a thorough meeting of the minds in terms of which ultimate goals each person should seek to achieve. As discussed in the previous section, we will need to appeal to divine coordination to achieve such a meeting of minds. For only God can ensure that both persons will accept, without reservation, the projects God allows (or indeed calls) each person to pursue—secure in the knowledge that his own (or any other person's) ultimate flourishing will not be compromised. Without a thorough meeting of the minds on the projects each person should pursue (as well as the room for choice of projects each should allow the other), the potential will always exist for feelings of resentment, frustration, and the like.

Returning to our example of the father and son, the potential for disagreement will involve all sorts of projects, or interests$_{(2)}$, that the father and, most notably in our example, the son may have. But let us set aside issues having to do with whether the son may have other projects he can or should pursue. Let us instead focus on how the son might achieve the single project of establishing an ideal relationship with his father (and vice versa). From the Christian perspective, ideal relationships involve our giving and receiving love in the fullest way possible for us humans, in the way we are most able to mirror the self-giving relationships within the Trinity. On the question of how such relationships are established, the obvious, initial answer continues to be that they are established when each person pursues the goal of furthering the other person's well-being. But given the considerations of this section as to how relationships are established, we face the following question: What if the other person does not invite us to respond to her as one whose welfare we should pursue as an ultimate goal?

Plenty of everyday examples exist in which others seek to relate to us in certain ways and yet do not expect that we will adopt as an ultimate goal the furthering of their well-being. A bank employee may interact with her colleagues, supposing that they will be focused on the goal of meeting their respective job descriptions. An orienteering team may collaborate in reading a map with the shared presumption that each person on the team has the common, ultimate goal of making it to the next control point. Perhaps there is a trivial sense in which, while seeking to establish almost any kind of relationship with others, we are inviting them to adopt a disposition to help us in certain ways under certain conditions (or at least to adopt a disposition not to harm us). But many of our relationships with others really are not of the kind of depth where we expect or invite others to focus their attention on our own well-being as an ultimate end. Further, some of our very *deep* relationships are not characterized by a mutual commitment to further the other person's welfare as an ultimate end. For instance, parents do not expect of their small children that they adopt as an ultimate end the parents' well-being; and a benefactor may explicitly say that he neither needs nor expects anything in return for the assistance he lends someone.

The short response to this point about some of our relationships is that these kinds of relationships simply are not ideal ones. They are not the ones in which we experience the kind of "connecting" with others that makes our ultimate fulfillment as humans possible. There may admittedly be particular aspects within these relationships that mirror the kind of mental experiences associated with connecting within ideal relationships. Collegial cooperation may produce a feeling we associate with both supporting others and being supported by others; and this feeling tone may resemble in some ways the much more life-enhancing feeling of being wholeheartedly committed to someone's well-being while knowing that he or she is whole-heartedly committed to our well-being. Parents of small children may experience the one aspect of being fully committed to another's well-being. But the positive experiences that come with loving small children will be tempered over time if the children never reciprocate in some measure the concern the parents have for them. Admittedly, not all of our eternal relationships will need in every respect to be the symmetrical relationship of peers (as opposed to, e.g., mentor/protégé). And perhaps not all our relationships will need to be equally intimate in terms, say, of verbally sharing the depths of our past mistakes. But if we are to attain ultimate flourishing though the kinds of self-giving relationships that mirror the Trinity, we will need reciprocal relationships in which each person deeply knows the other and is committed to furthering her well-being as an ultimate goal.

Before concluding this section let me address a potential theological objection to my running discussion that other people's well-being is an end toward which we should aim. Some Christians historically have objected to the idea that God should simply guide us as we seek to further *as an ultimate end* the well-being of other people. Rather, the contention has sometimes been that we should act in altruistic or loving ways toward others only for *God's* sakes and not for others' sakes. St. Augustine, for example, after affirming that God created all the good things of this world, cautioned that we "should love none of these things, nor think them desirable for their own sakes" (2007b, chap. 21, 53). Augustine acknowledged that "we are commanded to love one another," but he pressed the question "whether man is to be loved by man for his own sake, or for the sake of something else" (2007a, bk. I, chap. 22, 527). His answer was that, while "God is to be loved for His own sake," every man "is to be loved as a man for God's sake" (2007a, bk. I, chap. 27, 530).

Augustine's conclusion is perhaps understandable given his Platonic background. For Platonists, having a property consists in participating in an ideal form. Thus having the property of goodness consists in participating in ideal goodness—which for Augustine is God. On this understanding of what goodness consists in, it admittedly seems misguided to place intrinsic value on creatures such as humans. But as chapters 1 and 2 should make abundantly clear, I find no good reason to affirm Augustine's Platonic tendencies in spelling out the nature of goodness. Perhaps other Christians will have other reasons for thinking that we should never promote others' well-being as an end and that we should rather promote it only as a means toward fulfilling some aspect of our commitment to God. Though I shall not argue the point here, I find no good reason to affirm such a conclusion. I think the Christian affirmation that God loves us must certainly involve the idea that God places value on our well-being as an end. And it seems very odd to suggest that God would for some reason not wish us to value what he himself values.

To conclude this section, the kind of ideal relationships through which we achieve our ultimate flourishing will involve people sharing a full range of aspects about themselves, inviting the other person to respond to the values, commitments, talents, and shortcomings that make a person who he or she is. And again, only a mutual response of commitment to pursue the other person's well-being will lead to the richest experiences of "connecting" and will provide a safeguard against the otherwise ever-present possibility that feelings of mistrust and resentment may arise.

The following chapter explores further the connection between benevolence and ideal relationships. I begin by discussing the scope for self-interested pursuits, within an ideal relationship marked by benevolence. After responding to objections that benevolence is not sufficient to establish ideal relationships, I shall offer a way of understanding God's invitation to all people to pursue benevolence. This next chapter will also include discussions on the nature of our freedom in choosing to respond to God's invitation to pursue benevolence over self-interest. The chapter will conclude with an argument as to why these two pursuits represent a final dichotomy of fixed dispositions toward which our day-to-day decisions ultimately lead us.

CHAPTER FIVE

# God, the Good, and Our Choices

### 5.1 The Place of Self-Interested Desires

If ideal relationships require that each person seek as a goal the well-being of the other person, need we go so far as to say that this goal should be the *sole* goal each person pursues while interacting with the other? I want to explore this question in this section. But first I want to consider whether it is even plausible to think that a person might ever engage in a relationship without at all seeking as an end her own well-being.

In exploring this last question, we can begin by noting that we commonly pursue multiple goals through the same course of action. Put another way, our actions can be aimed at a certain *intermediate* goal, which is a means to achieving multiple, *ultimate* goals. For instance, I may commit to kicking a football with my son at a certain time every day. I pursue this intermediate project, we suppose in this example, because I have the dual, ultimate projects of furthering his well-being and enjoying for myself a daily dose of fresh air. The former project is one of benevolence, while the latter project is a self-interested goal.

Could my action of kicking a football with my son ever rightly be described as an act in which I have *no* self-interested goal I am trying to accomplish? Suppose one day I meet my son for our daily session even though it is lightly raining and I do not enjoy the activity that day. (I know that my son will still enjoy the activity; boys never seem to mind getting wet.) Would it be right to say in such a case that I genuinely have *no* self-interested goals and that my only ultimate goal is my son's well-being?

Such a description seems to leave out a number of self-interested goals that are surely lurking in the background. While the small discomfort of a light rain might not prevent me from continuing to kick a football with my son, certain other contingencies *would* cause me to discontinue my daily sessions with him. For instance, if my old knee injury started flaring up, then I would probably deem it prudent to stop the activity for a while. Prolonged swelling in my knee accompanied by fairly significant pain is, in my mind, too great a price to pay in order to achieve the marginal increase in my son's well-being that an uninterrupted kicking routine would provide. So in most cases that we tend to associate with benevolence, it surely is the case that our actions are a mixture of attempts to further another person's well-being *and* an attempt to maintain a certain level of well-being for ourselves. To be sure, I think cases do exist where one's sole goal is the well-being of others and not in any way one's own well-being. For example, a soldier may jump on a hand grenade to save the rest of the platoon, even while disbelieving in an afterlife. And when a parent's attention is suddenly redirected toward an infant in danger of rolling off a changing table, I think it plausible that his sole ultimate goal, as he reaches for the infant, is the well-being of the infant. All the same, I think such instances are far less numerous than cases in which we pursue another person's well-being while still seeking to preserve some measure of our own well-being.

Against my suggestion that such instances (of seeking as one's *sole* ultimate goal the well-being of someone else) are few and far between, the critic might object that my line of thought in the previous paragraph ends up reducing the idea of an intentional project to triviality. Consider again the example of my kicking a football. We might suppose that, in addition to the goal of furthering my son's welfare, I do not want to aggravate my old knee injury. Of course, I also do not want to develop a new injury in my other knee. For that matter, I do not want to develop an injury in my hip, my back, my neck, my toe, or anywhere else. And then there are other activities I want to continue in addition to my daily kicking sessions with my son. I want to continue in my job; I want to continue meeting with my book club; I want to continue taking my daughter to her ballet lessons; and so forth. As yet, these activities are not compromised by my daily sessions with my son. But the critic might point out that we can certainly imagine contingencies where these activities could come into conflict with my commitment to our daily sessions. As I kick a ball about the yard, I might daydream about any number of goals I have with which it is at least possible for my activity of kicking a ball to come into conflict. Should we then say, the critic might ask rhetorically, that in kicking a football with my son I attempt to achieve the multifaceted project of furthering his well-being; avoiding injury in either knee (or in any other body part); and continuing my commitments to work, friends, my daughter, and the enormous number of other things to which I want to stay committed? Such a description might be thought unnatural in the extreme, as it prevents us from narrowing the scope of someone's projects in the way we commonly do when we talk about a person pursuing some specific goal.

To recap the discussion of the last couple paragraphs, my suggestion has been that instances of relating to others *solely* with the ultimate goal of their well-being are relatively rare, given that some self-interested considerations seemingly remain in the background as continued goals when we pursue the goal of furthering others' well-being. The critic may object that this idea of "background goals" reduces the idea of an ultimate goal to triviality. On a plausible, narrower understanding of an "ultimate goal," so the critic's line of objection concludes, it is indeed plausible that a person might quite often interact with others, pursuing as a sole, ultimate goal their well-being.

Let me offer a rejoinder now to the critic's objection. I will then move to the question of whether ideal relationships actually call for us to pursue others' well-being as our sole, ultimate goal as we interact with them. I acknowledge with the critic that it strains too far the idea of a goal, or project, to suggest that my goals (as I kick a ball with my son) include the whole taxonomy of self-interested goals that I recognize as potentially coming into conflict with my goal of furthering my son's health and enjoyment by daily kicking a ball with him. However, it still seems plausible to me to suggest that I do have *some* self-interested goals as I kick a ball with him in the rain. For instance, it seems clear to me that I retain the goal of avoiding the recurrence of pain in my injured left knee. For, whenever I kick with my left foot, I am mindful (at some level of consciousness) never to do so with full force. Similarly, a parent who reaches for a crying infant typically remains mindful of certain self-interested goals. True, if a child is perceived to be in imminent danger—such as the danger of falling from a changing table—the parent may retain no self-interested concerns and may with every effort reach for the child. Much more typically, though, as a parent reaches to help or comfort a crying infant, he will remain mindful (again, at some level of consciousness) not to spill his coffee or drop his cell phone. So I continue to doubt just how often a person will act without a self-interested goal of *any* sort making up at least one of her ultimate goals as she interacts with someone else.

At any rate, suppose we grant the critic's assertion that it is possible—either at specific points in time or during prolonged periods—to relate to others with the sole, ultimate goal of furthering their well-being. There remains the question of whether ideal relationships actually call for such a pattern of action. Consistent with the discussion of section 4.5, the question of when I need to pursue others' well-being as an ultimate goal, along with the question of whether this pursuit needs to be my sole, ultimate goal as I interact with them, will be a matter for divine coordination. As we have seen, only in a shared deference to God's directives on such matters can we ensure that feelings of distrust and resentment will not emerge as each person within a relationship comes to know the commitments of the other.

Would God ever require a person to pursue, as she interacts with someone else over time, *only* the other person's well-being as an ultimate goal (to the exclusion of any self-interested, ultimate goals)? Such a scenario strikes me as incredible. First, it seems difficult to imagine how our relationships might *begin* if we did not engage in any self-interested pursuits. Consider the best examples of mature, human relationships on earth. Though they may serve as our closest approximations to the kind of ideal relationships Christians describe as characteristic of the heavenly community, they tend not to start out in that way. A long-term marriage relationship now marked by loving service may have begun from self-interested, physical attractions. A long-standing, loyal friendship may have begun with the discovery of a shared interest in sports or art. It seems difficult to imagine how our relationships could develop in their early stages if the range of our pursuits had to be purely benevolent pursuits. It would arguably not be psychologically possible for humans—at least, without a radical change to our natural psychology—to choose to be committed solely and indefinitely only to the pursuit of someone else's well-being as an *initial step* in establishing a relationship with that person.

Further, even if we confine ourselves to the mature, ideal relationships among the redeemed in heaven, self-interested pursuits surely have their place. If we think of the joint projects that the redeemed will pursue together as they join God in God's ongoing work, it admittedly seems possible that a person might at times pursue a joint project only as an intermediate goal—with the single, ultimate goal of furthering another person's well-being. After all, parents sometimes choose to pursue an activity—such as watching a Disney movie or venturing into a tree fort—solely because they need to find *some* activity to pursue jointly during a scheduled "family time." Though the parent has no desire to navigate a tree fort as an ultimate goal, she may of course still experience joy from seeing her child's enjoyment.[1] Even in adult relationships we sometimes undertake a joint activity that we ourselves would not choose to undertake if left to our own devices; but we undertake the joint activity because we know that others about whom we care find particular joy in the activity. And in the end we enjoy ourselves because we are in good company. Nevertheless, it seems difficult to imagine that one could experience eternal and boundless joy if, while pursuing joint projects, one *never* had as an ultimate end the engagement itself with the project, motivated by one's own attraction to the project.

So it seems implausible to me that we could initially establish relationships with others, and then receive eternal joy from our joint pursuits of projects with them, if God's directives *never* allowed us scope to pursue projects out of a desire to pursue the project itself as an ultimate end.[2] Happily, there is no good reason to think that ideal relationships in fact require us to pursue others' well-being as our sole and continuous ultimate end. Again, I can be committed to my son's well-being as I kick a ball with him, even as I have an additional goal of enjoying fresh air.

Perhaps we might ask whether ideal relationships require that we be *willing* to pursue the other person's well-being whenever this pursuit may conflict with a self-interested pursuit of ours. My answer is "yes"; but I should quickly emphasize that there are safeguards to the natural worry that this answer may raise. The worry is that it seemingly becomes psychologically impossible—or, at least, psychologically unhealthy—to commit to prioritizing others' interests above our own at *all* times and in *all* contexts. Adding to the worry is the Christian claim that God invites us to relate to him as "lord." Whatever else that term means in the context of the various biblical passages where the term is used, I take the term to include the following implication. To relate to God as lord is, roughly, to allow him to make (if he so chooses) all the final decisions as to which actions one will perform. So is there not the worry that God *calls* his followers to relate to him in just the way we have suggested is problematic: namely, by committing always to prioritize his interests over our own and, whenever he so directs, to prioritize other people's interests over our own?[3]

Some Christians historically have tackled this worry by biting the bullet and insisting that we *do* need to be willing to defer our own interests to God's directives, no matter the perceived consequence. Thus some Christians have thought appropriate an affirmative answer to the question Samuel Hopkins famously discussed: "whether men ought or can be willing to be damned, if this be necessary for the glory of God and the greatest general good" (1852, 756). Even if one believes that God never *would* direct us in a way that ultimately compromises our attainment of heaven, the line of thought here is that a commitment to God as lord requires that we at least be willing to do the unthinkable.

My own response to the pending worry is different. I would emphasize that the scenarios we are now considering are indeed unthinkable. I assumed in section 4.5 that God's coordination of all people's welfare precludes the possibility that my pursuit of anyone else's interests might come at the expense of my own ultimate flourishing. If suddenly that model of divine coordination were shattered, then I for one would no longer be able to make sense of the claim that *God* was directing me to prioritize his or others' interests. Put another way, I could not continue to understand God as essentially loving if I believed his will for me, for whatever reason, was to compromise my own ultimate flourishing. Either I would believe myself mistaken about his directives or my model of God's essential nature would collapse. So I think there are natural safeguards—grounded in a proper understanding of God's essential nature—against the worry that a willingness always to prioritize God's interests (and the interests of others, according to God's directives) over our own is psychologically impossible and/or unhealthy.

## 5.2 Can We Desire Relationships?

Thus far in talking about "ideal relationships" I have emphasized that such relationships are established when each person adopts as his or her goal the furthering of the other person's well-being. In the previous section I discussed how self-interested pursuits still have their place within ideal relationships. Notwithstanding this point, I have assumed that self-interested pursuits do serve as the alternative to the benevolent pursuits required for ideal relationships. In section 6.2 I shall go on to argue that our "morally significant decisions," as I shall call them, indeed always amount to a choice between self-interest and benevolence. But for now we are merely concerned with the link between benevolence and ideal relationships. My working thesis is again a simple one: that ideal relationships are characterized by the mutual pursuit of the other person's well-being.

A good many philosophers, though, have wanted to argue that things are not so simple. While acknowledging that altruistic concern for the other person's well-being is *one* important element within positive, lasting relationships, they sometimes argue that *other* motivations can play necessary roles within such relationships.

Robert Adams maintains that the two general motivations of altruism and self-interest do not exhaust the motivations we can and should have within a loving relationship. He states that "noninstrumental relational interest seems to me to be part of anything that would be recognized as a paradigm of *love* of any sort" (1999, 139). In matters of friendship, then, "a good friend values the personal relationship for its own sake" (1999, 144). Adams goes on to describe this aspect of a close relationship in terms of "car[ing] appropriately about the relationship" and having "loyalty . . . to the relationship, as well as to the other person" (1999, 144). But on the surface these seem odd phrases, especially the last one. If I released my parents from their promise of an inheritance so that they could give the money to another relative, I would not understand them if they explained their continued resistance to doing so on the grounds that they felt loyalty not only to me but also to our relationship. I would have thought that the latter was reducible to the former.[4]

I do not wish to deny that there are "reasons for love," as some moral philosophers have emphasized. I would not take issue, for example, with Niko Kolodny's claim that love "partly consists in the belief that some relationship renders it appropriate, and the emotions and motivations of love are causally sustained by this belief" (2003, 146). If I recognize that I am in a particular kind of relationship with someone else, then I may well be concerned to continue that relationship in its current shape. But this point seems less controversial than the suggestion that I might be loyal to, or desire, a relationship *in addition to* my desire to further either my own or the other person's well-being.[5]

Adams goes on to provide a typically thoughtful defense of his general conclusion that benevolence alone will not characterize the best examples of close, human relationships. He contends that it can sometimes actually be a good thing in our close relationships to be motivated by concerns that override our concern for the other person's well-being. With regard to the place of loyalty within a relationship he remarks, "One's loyalty is to the relationship, as well as to the other person, and one is not fully loyal in some relationships unless one is willing to hazard something of the other person's happiness, as well as one's own, for the sake of the relationship. . . . The stability of friendships, and particularly of family relationships, depends on the parties caring about the relationship, and being committed to it, in such a way as to override periodic temptations to believe that it is detrimental" (1999, 144–45). But surely it remains very counterintuitive to think it a good thing ever to "hazard aspects of the other person's happiness" for the sake of our relationship with that person. At least, it is very much at odds with the welfarist conclusions of chapter 2 regarding the nature of noninstrumental value. It may perhaps be wise in certain contexts to sacrifice some aspect of a person's well-being for other aspects of her (or even others') well-being. And perhaps experience will tell us that the kind of great flourishing made possible through long-term relationships often requires us to persevere in these relationships through times when, in the heat of the moment, we (temporarily) find ourselves believing that each party would be better off apart. Yet these considerations can be reconciled with my claim that ideal relationships require us to pursue consistently the well-being of the other person.

For those who suggest that loving relationships can require more than the simple, altruistic pursuit of the other person's well-being, a favored illustration is a relationship where Eros plays a central part. Adams describes paradigm cases of Eros as ones in which "the lover desires or prizes, for its own sake, some relationship with the beloved" (1999, 139). He emphasizes that Eros escapes analysis in terms of a person's goals to further the beloved's well-being and/or his own well-being. "The mistake, in trying to force Eros into a dichotomy of self-interest and altruism, is failure to recognize a desire for relationship for its own sake as a third type of desire that is not just a combination or consequence of desire for one's own good and desire for another person's good. It is indeed this third type of desire that is most characteristic of Eros" (1999, 140). How might one argue that this third type of desire really is present in—indeed characteristic of—relationships marked by Eros?

Adams contends that the desire in question is most readily seen in cases of "tragic or destructive Eros. There are doubtless instances in which a close personal relationship is strongly desired by both of the parties to it although neither of them believes it will be good for either of them" (1999, 139). C. S. Lewis, in his study of Eros, makes a similar point (and with much flair). In arguing that "Eros does not aim at happiness," Lewis offers the following observation.

> Everyone knows that it is useless to try to separate lovers by proving to them that their marriage will be an unhappy one.... For it is the very mark of Eros that when he is in us we had rather share unhappiness with the Beloved than be happy on any other terms. Even if the two lovers are mature and experienced people who know that broken hearts heal in the end and can clearly foresee that, if they once steeled themselves to go through the present agony of parting, they

would almost certainly be happier ten years hence than marriage is at all likely to make them—even then, they would not part.... Even when it becomes clear beyond all evasion that marriage with the Beloved cannot possibly lead to happiness—when it cannot even profess to offer any other life than that of tending an incurable invalid, of hopeless poverty, of exile, or of disgrace—Eros never hesitates to say, "Better this than parting. Better to be miserable with her than happy without her." (1963, 98–99)

While cases of tragic Eros are cited as the clearest examples of how Eros involves a desire "for the relationship for its own sake," this desire is said to be present in all instances of Eros—including, for instance, the best examples of beneficial marriages.

I think cases of tragic Eros do help us see interesting facts about human motivations and decision making. However, these facts seem to involve the phenomenon of weakness of the will. Tragic Eros is best interpreted as a matter of believing that one's best interests lie, all things considered, with one course of action—and yet deciding to pursue an alternative course of action. Typically, weakness of will reveals a lack of prudence, a lamentable readiness to sacrifice one's perceived long-term well-being for the sake of lesser, more immediate enjoyments. For example, flipping through the television channels late one evening, a person may find a B movie playing that he has previously seen. Knowing that he must get up early for work the next morning, he recognizes that, all things considered, he will be better off by going to bed immediately and getting a good night's sleep. Yet the person may well stay up to watch the movie, lamenting this fact both when he finally does go to bed and, especially, when his alarm clock goes off the next morning. If imprudence explains why two lovers stay together while knowing that their long-term better interests lie elsewhere, then the struggle is not between welfare and some desire "for the relationship for its own sake." Rather, the struggle is between short-term well-being and greater, long-term well-being.

The same phenomenon of weakness of the will equally explains examples of imprudent pursuits of short-term relationships with *different* partners. A person might seek a string of different romantic partners, where there is none of the obsessive focus found in the previous examples of tragic Eros. One partner will do as well as another. In cases both of tragic Eros and of a string of short-term romantic pursuits, a person can believe that his long-term best interests lie in pursuing a different course of action. So why would a person in such a case choose to pursue the romantic partner(s) in question? We find a ready answer when we note that, though the person is acting contrary to his perceived *overall* best interests, this does not mean that he is somehow ceasing to act out of his own interests. There is *something* attractive about these pursuits: physical pleasure; familiarity that is comforting; a sense of self-worth from feeling attractive to others; and so forth. Conversely, the decision to change one's romantic pattern comes at certain costs: the struggle to resist one's romantic urges; the feelings of uncertainty that come when one reorients one's goals; and so on.

In short, there are plenty of self-interested desires that can explain why someone might pursue a romantic relationship while believing that one's overall, long-term best interests lie elsewhere. On the further question of why one pursues *these* desires instead of a more reflective desire to attain one's greater overall well-being, we again note the common human phenomenon of imprudent and weak-willed actions. Humans can sustain these patterns of weak-willed actions over a period of years— whether in a case of tragic Eros, a case of serial philandering, or for that matter a case of chronic overeating, overspending, or excessive drinking. Like the other cases, tragic Eros is readily explained in terms of self-interested (though weak-willed) pursuits. We need not posit some further desire for the *relationship*.

### 5.3 Self-Directed Reasons for Benevolence

If we dismiss the idea that a desire "for the relationship" can compete with benevolent desires, we might now explore whether it is possible— at least within ideal relationships—for our benevolent desires to be separated from our self-directed desires. The issue at stake here is whether, *in addition* to a desire that the other person flourish, loving relationships require what we might call a self-involving, or self-regarding, desire concerning *how* the other person's well-being is achieved. This issue gets to the kind of reason one might have for pursuing another person's well-being. Do loving relationships require that each person seek to realize her desire "that the other person flourish"? Or do they instead require that each person pursue the desire "to (herself) help the other person flourish"?

As part of his line of argument against the sufficiency of mere benevolence, Robert Adams contends that, without self-regarding desires, a genuinely *loving* relationship will not be established. He provides the following thought experiment to illustrate how mere benevolence is too general to ground our close relationships. "Suppose that a friend of mine, seized (as he at least supposes) by benevolent impulse, takes it into his head one day to confer a benefit on a number of people. The means he chooses for this purpose is to give each of them twenty dollars. Making his rounds, he comes to me. He pulls a twenty-dollar bill from his pocket and holds it out to me, saying, 'Here, Bob; I'd like to give you this.' Perplexed, I respond, 'Well . . . thank you. But why?' He replies, 'I just wanted to do something nice for you'" (1999, 142). While Adams notes that we may respond in different ways to this situation, one thing is clear: "My friend has not succeeded in doing something nice for me" (1999, 142). Adams divulges that he would naturally ask himself questions such as why the friend did not invite him to lunch—which would have cost no more money. "Does he not care for my company?" Adams would wonder (1999, 142).

As an initial point, I think we need to be careful how we characterize benevolence. Adams depicts benevolence, in contrast to self-involving desires, as "the strictly selfless desire that the other person or persons be benefited" (1999, 140). He remarks that "if all one has is the latter desire, one does not care who benefits them, whereas, if one wants to be of service, one wants to be one of those that do it" (1999, 140). All the same, benevolence cannot be characterized merely as a desire that someone else flourish, without any accompanying desire to help realize that goal. Instead, a desire that another person's life go well for her will carry at least *some* desire to further that end. If I claim a concern that my sick aunt should not have to suffer loneliness but I admit no urge of any kind to visit her myself, you would be right to question the genuineness of my purported benevolent concern. Granted, I may choose to realize other desires—such as my desire to rest comfortably at home—instead of my desire to visit my aunt. Indeed, there may be a number of considerations—for example, I have fallen out with her, and our conversations inevitably end in arguments—that result in an all-things-considered judgment that it would be better for everyone if I did not visit. Also, constraints of opportunity and resources greatly limit what kind of help I could myself offer to all the people in all the countries in our world about whose well-being I care. Still, if I care about anyone's well-being, then I will have at least *some* urge to help ensure that person's well-being. It really does not make sense to say that I genuinely desire someone's flourishing but have no desire whatsoever to play a role myself in helping her life go well for her. If "mere benevolence" is taken to exclude any such self-involving desire, then we are not truly talking about benevolence.

Returning to Adams's example of the monetarily generous friend, the friend does reveal at least some desire to advance my flourishing. After all, he gives me twenty dollars. Admittedly, though, this act does not reveal the deeper kind of commitment to advance my flourishing that I would expect from a close friend. It is true that *one* way for a person to be more deeply committed to someone else is simply to have a stronger, benevolent concern for her well-being. But Adams's point seems to be that a friend's commitment to us should arise in a different way.

While I have already questioned whether it makes sense to say that the commitment should arise from a "desire for the relationship," we can still consider Adams's point that a friend's desire to advance our flourishing should not be a desire that is completely satisfied when we flourish.[6] Rather, it should be satisfied only when the *friend* plays a role in advancing our flourishing. Again, Adams's point against the adequacy of benevolence is that, when we have (mere) benevolent concern for others, "we do not care who benefits them." This attitude, he wants to press, is not indicative of close, loving relationships.

Would our close relationships with loved ones be undermined by the thought that they would be equally happy if they flourished through different relationships that did not involve us, and vice versa? As an initial point of response, I doubt that in many of our closest relationships we can disentangle enough issues to form a clear intuition on the matter. It is exceedingly difficult for me to imagine that my spouse and children could be as well off with another husband and father. And this is not because I consider myself to be a better husband and father, in principle, than any other person could possibly be. Rather, the thought of our shared experiences and emotional attachments prevents me from imagining how a new set of relationships could offset the loss of my sudden absence from their lives. For my part, I certainly cannot imagine a scenario in which I might think myself no worse off for being unable to play any role in the lives of the family I currently have.

Still, I think we can shape certain examples so that they do reveal the kinds of intuitions Adams wants to highlight. When our children marry, their relationships with us of course do, and should, change in many ways. Some changes may be optional. For example, there may be some activities that my child could pursue with her new spouse or continue to pursue with me—such as entering an annual tennis doubles tournament—where her positive relationships with both of us would continue irrespective of her choice of a partner for this event. Likewise, a friend with a ticket to the Super Bowl might choose to take me or to take a mutual friend of ours, with all our friendships continuing without any harm, whatever the choice. On such occasions, I may believe that my daughter and my friend will have an equally good time with someone else. I may even believe that, were they to opt for others and not for me on these occasions, they would still be as committed to my well-being as they ever were. And yet, when they do not choose me, I may still experience some sense of loss. Does not this show, Adams might stress, that we want those close to us to desire more than our well-being? I think the answer is: yes, we do typically desire more than mere benevolence from others whom we love. That is, we want our loved ones' benevolent desires for our well-being to be *self-directed* desires such that our loved ones desire to be the ones who help make our lives go well for us. In the remainder of this section I want to explore what does and does not follow from this point.

In probing the reasons we might want others to view us with more than merely benevolent concern, one reason is that we simply want others to like particular things about us—that is, to be attracted to our specific character traits. This point is not lost on Adams, who notes that "we want others to think well of us" (1999, 143). In discussing the example of the money-giving friend, Adams again remarks that we might well ask ourselves: "Does he not care for my company?" (1999, 142). In reflecting on this point, it is certainly true in various contexts that we hope that people will like us in particular. We hope that others will find us engaging and insightful. We like to think that at least some people find us funny and physically attractive. If we somehow discovered that a friend did not like anything in particular about us, but rather associated with us because he was in general benevolent and had committed to befriending those with whom he happened to cross paths frequently, we might admittedly feel alienated from him.

The desire that others find us uniquely attractive is seemingly a necessary part of human development. A small child, in order to feel that he is special to his parents, may need to think that he has uniquely likable traits that propel his parents to spend time with him. The same may be true for a bride with respect to her husband, and vice versa. Just as clearly, however, there can exist at times for us an unhealthy level of pride, susceptible to injury whenever others do not find us especially worthy of praise. The Christian tradition has had much to say about the vice of pride, which involves the pursuit of a desire to be recognized and feted in ways that resist the role God intends us to play in the created order. More colloquially, we might ask: Who am I that I should feel insulted if someone does not find my jokes particularly funny or my thoughts uniquely inspiring? While there may be a legitimate role in ideal relationships for wanting others to be attracted to us, there are limits (which are all too easy to exceed) to what we should appropriately expect others to feel about us.

Of course, we may genuinely believe—perhaps rightly—that we will miss out on vital experiences if particular people are not attracted to us and do not enjoy spending time with us. This feeling is again consistent in certain contexts with an ideal, loving relationship. For example, if one feels that God has provided particular people with whom we can build unique relationships—such as our children—then of course it is appropriate, when they do not return our feelings of personal affection, to have feelings of loss at the knowledge that we will miss out on life-enhancing experiences that cannot be replicated. At the same time, the appropriate role for such feelings of loss should not be overstated. Given the appropriateness of self-interested pursuits within ideal relationships, as discussed in section 5.1, there will always be scope for different attitudes and different points of view in our relationships. Others may not always return the kind of, and level of, attraction we feel toward them. Yet, as discussed in section 4.5, divine coordination should serve to ensure that no one's ultimate flourishing is in competition with other contingencies like others' flourishing or, we can add here, others' personal preferences.

Again, it is true that I will need *some* people to be attracted to me in certain ways that make our joint pursuits of projects possible and mutually enjoyable.[7] But if I know that I am in a state of ultimate flourishing, which assumes I am connecting with others in ways that make my ultimate flourishing possible, is there scope for me to begrudge a particular person's differing preference as to how much time we should spend together? Perhaps *some* level of disappointment is appropriate if a particular person does not share my interest in a particular kind of relationship. But any disappointment would surely be greatly tempered by the recognition that I (and he) am experiencing what I have called ultimate flourishing. Certainly, there would be no room to begrudge a person his personal preferences or to feel resentment toward him. At least, there would be no room for such things within the heavenly community where everyone is flourishing as Christians describe.

Despite the cautions I have outlined against desiring too strongly that others find us attractive, let me now acknowledge that such desires do play an important role in loving relationships. (And this discussion will lend further support for the conclusion of section 5.1 that self-interested desires have a place within ideal relationships marked by benevolence.) As Adams's example of the monetarily generous friend shows, we hope that those we love will have more than the purely benevolent desire that we flourish. We want them to desire—and to desire quite strongly, in a way that preserves the shape of our relationship—to be the one who helps us flourish. Further, we want them to have this desire because we want our interactions to satisfy some need *they* have. Ideal relationships, after all, involve both the giving and receiving of love. I doubt we could truly feel loved by others if we did not believe that they *needed* us in some way.[8] And in principle giving love to others by working to further their welfare requires of course that we identify some benefit to them that our actions will bring. Further still, the phenomenology of connecting with others involves the feelings that come when there is mutual understanding of the other person. I may have a strong desire that I be the one who satisfies certain needs another person has;

and I might desire that this other person have a reciprocal desire. If so, then as part of our need to be understood by those with whom we relate I will need the other person to understand that I have these desires. These self-interested desires are part of who I am; and the other person needs to know this in order for his benevolent pursuits toward me to result in actual beneficence.

Adams's discussion of benevolence helps point us to these conclusions. What I have wanted to challenge is the idea that these conclusions in any way undermine the simple thesis that all ideal relationships are marked by the benevolent pursuit of the other's well-being. Admittedly, loving relationships may require various feelings of personal attraction and self-interested desires that also motivate one to interact with the other person. In section 6.2 I will provide further reason for thinking that God will ensure that such contingencies are satisfied, so that our participation in ideal relationships will hinge on our choice whether to pursue benevolence or self-interest. Our concern in this chapter (and in the previous one) has been, not with the nature of moral choice, but rather with the connection between benevolent pursuits and ideal relationships (with ideal relationships affording us the experiences of "connecting" that ensure our ultimate flourishing). A main conclusion thus far has been that only the mutual, benevolent pursuit of the other person's well-being will establish lasting, stable relationships where uncertainty and resentment cannot gain a foothold. Accordingly, self-interested motivations must not take undue precedence over the sustained, benevolent commitment of each person to pursue the other person's well-being. Each person's benevolent commitment to the other's well-being must again take precedence among her pursuits to the extent that the other person acknowledges it should take precedence, as informed by the expectations God has for people's pursuits in keeping with his coordination of all people's ultimate flourishing.

Having seen once again the need for divine coordination if ideal relationships are to be established and sustained over time, I want to turn in the next section to consider the broad way that God invites us to pursue benevolence (and thereby move toward the good life of ideal relationships). As part of my discussion, I will offer a context for understanding divine commands, as part of God's invitation to pursue the life that is good for us.

## 5.4 God's Invitation to Pursue the Good

The ethical framework that I have been outlining throughout this book obviously emphasizes the good, as opposed to the right. Assuming the Christian picture of an afterlife, our choices will have eternal significance if they move us either toward or away from the good states of affairs that are constitutive of our ultimate flourishing. Acting rightly or wrongly is, in the end, significant only inasmuch as such actions affect the realization of good or bad states of affairs. I do not want to say that rightness (or wrongness) *is* a matter of acting in a way that affects in some manner (e.g., by means of the acts' consequences) that which is good. Our conclusions from chapter 3 about the meaning of rightness and wrongness—as connected to the cluster of concepts involving blame, punishment, and obligation, and as understood by appreciating the phenomenon of social sanction—pointed elsewhere. However, I think the ultimate *justification* for any system of rules, proscriptions, or commands (including God's commands) will be their effect on the goodness/badness of states of affairs.

When making decisions, people often focus on the perceived rightness/wrongness of some action. As noted in chapter 3, sometimes in articulating their search for "the right" action to take or endorse, they may actually have in mind the "most good," or "best," action. Still, at other times they may focus on the true nature of rightness/wrongness: namely, the proscription by some individual(s) of some action. Their motivation to pursue a perceived right action will include the desire to avoid the unwelcome outcome of social sanction; and they may also have further, motivating desires such as a desire to set a good example to others, a desire to be well thought of, and so forth. If focusing on a proscription—that is, the wrongness of an action—leads one to act in a way that furthers the good, then so much the better. But there is nothing necessary about focusing on rightness and wrongness as a means to achieving the good.

At least, there is no a priori necessity here. It may be the case that, in order to realize certain aspects of a trusting relationship with God where he is acknowledged as lord, we must pursue some actions focused, not on whether these actions will further the good, but instead solely on the fact that God has commanded these actions. More generally, perhaps it is an empirical fact about humans that, without a focus on the cluster of concepts surrounding rightness and wrongness, we often will not be sufficiently motivated to pursue the good.[9] Nevertheless, the conclusion remains from chapter 2 that final value consists only in the positive mental states constitutive of the flourishing of sentient creatures or beings. All other things, including actions performed while one is focused on the rightness or wrongness of those actions, will be of instrumental value.

A similar discussion could be developed about the role of categorical imperatives. Perhaps, for some people, focusing on the idea of what we might call "non-person-relative duties" helps provide motivation to perform actions that further others' well-being as well as one's own. The motivational force of a perceived categorical imperative will be along the lines of the motivation for a perceived right or wrong action, as discussed two paragraphs ago. Since a categorical imperative will be thought to exist independently of the contingency of anyone's proscription, however, the unwanted outcome linked with social sanction will involve a vague association with such sanction—as opposed to the more specific sanction we can identify when we identify a specific person who proscribes some action. (This kind of vague association with social sanction was discussed in sections 3.2 and 3.4 with regard to cases in which one believes that some action is *really*, or "objectively," wrong—even while one cannot identify a specific person who would blame or punish one's action.) If a focus on some perceived objective duty helps motivate one to pursue good ends, then again so much the better. We could then say that a person's focus on categorical imperatives has instrumental value.

Since the motivation to act in accordance with any perceived categorical imperative will be found in some *desire(s)* one has, the distinction between a categorical imperative and a hypothetical imperative becomes relatively unimportant within our broader discussion. Normative pressure that moves us to act will always take the form: *Given* some project one has (or, we might say, given some desire one has for some project to be realized), then in order to realize that project one should act in such and such a way. Thus, when exploring the motivation to act in accordance with some imperative, we will arrive at the form of a hypothetical imperative. This point simply follows from the Humean account of normativity offered in section 3.2.[10]

This point about *motivation* does not of course imply that rules, laws, and commands somehow also come to us, on closer analysis, in the *form* of a hypothetical imperative. Given the emphasis on goodness within the ethical framework I am advancing, it should come as no surprise that I myself understand God's interaction with humankind primarily in terms of God inviting people to participate in the network of relationships within the Trinity. That is, God invites us to relate to him and to others in loving, self-giving ways—often by inviting us to join him in the ongoing projects that Christians understand God to be pursuing in our world (e.g., helping end oppression, ministering to the poor, and so forth).[11] I think it is thus accurate to summarize as follows the situation of humans: If we want to pursue the well-being of others and in the process attain ultimate flourishing for ourselves, then we should follow the directives of God, who both pursues, and has the resources to provide for, the flourishing of all people. All the same, it remains the case that God's directives to us, as recorded in the Christian scriptures, often come in the *form* of unconditional commands. And so it is worth saying a bit about the role that God seemingly intends his commands to play in drawing people into the kinds of relationships for which Christians affirm we were created.

I think divine commands serve three main roles. First, God's commands help us identify good states of affairs and how to attain them (as well as bad states of affairs and how to avoid them). Here divine commands serve much the same role that J. S. Mill ascribed to societal laws: they indicate what is viewed as crucial for people's well-being. To ensure that people's lives are going well for them, we must of course do more than merely refrain from murdering, cheating, exploiting, and demeaning others. But these are a few good starting points. And while God's commands—at least as revealed in the Christian scriptures—do not extend to *every* specific way in which we might promote good states of affairs, they seemingly cover many crucial ways in which we should promote the good, if the good is indeed to obtain. Further, God's commands will be extensive enough that, if we follow them, we will indeed at some point be able to take our place within the heavenly community.

(To suppose otherwise would allow for a—surely incredible—scenario in which a person cannot be finally reconciled to God even though she has done nothing for which God blames her.)

Second, divine commands reveal to us the shape our relationships with God are to take, along with the points at which breaks in the relationship will emerge such that steps will need to be taken to repair the relationship. Partly, this revelation takes the form of God telling us which projects he wants to pursue with us, along with those projects against which he stands. If we fail to keep God's commands—that is, if we do that which God has proscribed—then some cost will have to be absorbed. God will have to forgive the refusal (or, at least, the failure) to relate to him on the terms he has invited people to relate to him. And someone will need to provide a means of reparation if it is needed to restore the relationship.[12] If we *do* meet the terms of the relationship into which God invites us, then there is no basis for reparation or forgiveness (or whatever other components are involved in a restored relationship).[13] This is not to say that by obeying all of God's commands we immediately establish ideal relationships with God and others. Participation in such relationships may require growth (some aspects of which will shortly be discussed) over time. It is just that, if no commands of God are broken, there will be no need of reparation and forgiveness along the way.

Third, God's commands reveal the kind of measures he intends to (or, at least, may) take in leading us toward the goal of our participation in ideal relationships. Following the discussion of the nature of wrongness in section 3.3, in commanding some action God conveys an intention to sanction those who fail to perform it. Granted, God may for some reason choose not to go through with this sanction. But in identifying some action as wrong, God conveys that those who perform that action are subject to blame and punishment from him.

I think it is worth being careful at this point not to overstate the distinction between acts that are bad (in the sense of less than optimally good) and acts that God declares wrong. On the one hand, this distinction is very important for the reasons mentioned above with regard to the first and second roles that divine commands play. Again, divine commands show us what is crucially needed if we are to further the good and if we are to have a positive, unbroken relationship with God and others. And each failure to keep God's commands requires some sort of reparation if our relationship with God is once again to move toward the kind of ideal relationships that are enjoyed by the redeemed in heaven and in which our ultimate flourishing can occur. In terms of the third role of divine commands, though, we perhaps should take care not to overstate the difference between God's intention to sanction wrongdoers and God's intention at all times to draw people into the kind of ideal relationships for which Christians affirm they were created.

Consider two points. First, as noted in section 3.3, the distinction between permissible actions and punishable actions can at times be fuzzy. If my pattern of laziness includes no genuinely *wrong* actions, God may still relate to me—for example, when deciding whether to entrust me with some new responsibility—as one who does not yet undertake his tasks with much seriousness. And this begins to resemble the kind of sanction we associate with punishment. Second, any punishment God administers can, like *non*-punitive measures God might use, plausibly be seen as a means God uses toward the ultimate end of drawing us into positive relationships with him and others. I shall not be able here to defend this conclusion against such objections that God might prioritize other ends—such as the realization of justice or his own glorification—over the well-being of the creatures he has created. But I do think this conclusion can be successfully defended. And if this is correct, then any punishment from God does not *itself* accomplish any ultimate goal God might have. Rather, punishment will always be intended as a means of prompting us to pursue the good. The social sanction associated with a (broken) command thus reveals to us the kind of "negative" prompting that is in store for us as God continues his broader goal of prompting us to turn to him. While this kind of prompting obviously is of a particular kind, we arrive at the same justification for it as we do for any other act of divine prompting.

Thus far I have assumed that, among the actions we perform that will affect whether we attain ideal relationships as fully realized in heaven, only some of them will be commanded by God. One may question, though, whether we should not think of God's commands as extending to *every* action we might perform in pursuing the good. That is, one might understand God to have commanded us to do all we can possibly do in response to his prompting to take up the cause of God and others.[14]

After all, the life to which Jesus called his followers can be readily interpreted as all-encompassing. He endorsed the summation of the Old Testament laws as the dual commands "'Love the Lord your God with all your heart and with all your soul and with all your strength and with all your mind' and 'Love your neighbor as yourself'" (Luke 10:27). And he pressed his followers to "be perfect, as your heavenly father is perfect" (Matt. 5:48). Might we therefore say that the most good a person can do at all times is also what God commands a person to do?

While it is possible to defend such an expansive view of divine commands, this defense will amount to a denial of the category of supererogatory acts. And this seems to me rather implausible. To be sure, it would be a good thing (and within my ability) to prioritize others' interests in such a way that I give 70 percent of my income to charity, subsisting mainly on rice and beans and living in a very small apartment. But unless God specifically calls my family and me to a life of relative poverty (by Western standards), I think most Christians will doubt that God *commands* that I prioritize others' interests in this way. And this seemingly is so even on the assumption that this pattern of behavior would ensure the quickest realization of the set of firm dispositions I need to participate in the ideal, self-giving relationships that mark the redeemed in heaven. In allowing scope for supererogatory acts, I am here following Aquinas. Aquinas affirmed the precept, or command, that all people attain (with God's help, of course) perfection of charity. But he then made the point that "since that which is a matter of precept can be fulfilled variously, one does not break a commandment through not fulfilling it in the best way, but it is enough to fulfil it in any way whatever" (1947, II-II, 184, 3, ad.2).[15] In other words, even if we suppose that God commands, rather than merely commends, that all people come to participate in ideal relationships marked by thoroughly loving, self-giving commitments, we do not have to say that the *most* loving, self-giving act we can perform at any given point in time is required of us by God. That is, God does not *proscribe* every action that is not the best (i.e., most good) action we can possibly perform at a given point in time.

I want to clarify a point in order to avoid a possible theological misunderstanding within our discussion of divine commands. In some Christian theological discussions divine commands are equated largely with the Old Testament laws, juxtaposed to the New Testament teaching about grace. In our own discussion of people's responses to God's commands, though, I mean to include all the directives God might give us—including directives about the need to rely on grace instead of attempting to justify ourselves before God by appealing to our good works. Thus, in my discussion of God's commands, there is no reason to exclude a command that we admit our inability to meet the Old Testament laws and instead ask for God's grace by pleading Christ's work as atonement for our sins.

Let me summarize some of the points of this section. God invites us to participate in relationships with him and others that are marked by benevolent commitment. Following previous discussions, such relationships are good in that, by participating in them, we have the kinds of mental experiences in which our ultimate flourishing consists. There may be for us, at any point in time, some optimal decision or pattern of behavior that involves prioritizing others' interests and that leads us most quickly into the unwavering commitments that mark the ideal relationships within the heavenly community. Yet while God's commands certainly help us identify the way to ideal relationships and help provide motivation to pursue them, these commands seemingly do not typically extend to the optimal (i.e., *most* self-giving) action we could perform at a given time. Still, when we perform actions that not only are in some way (instrumentally) good but *also* are right according to God, we are assured of freedom from divine sanction. Conversely, among those decisions we perform that are comparatively worse (i.e., more bad) than what is optimal, some of them will also be viewed as wrong from God's perspective. In performing actions that are wrong in God's view, we become candidates for blame and punishment by God—though any punishment can plausibly be viewed as one of the various ways in which God prompts people to pursue the good that comes through ideal relationships.

In section 4.6 I submitted that any interpersonal relationship is established as one person responds to the invitation of another person to participate in a relationship of some specified kind. The communication (or "invitational statements" as I have called them) that contains God's invitation to a relationship with us may take various forms. The Christian doctrine of the Holy Spirit includes the idea that God can "speak" to us both directly and through the speech acts of others. The Christian tradition has testified to the possibility of God communicating directly to people through dreams, visions, an inner (or even audible) voice, and the phenomenon of having beliefs and desires that one (correctly) believes have been formed through the working of the Holy Spirit. Indirectly, God can appropriate the speech acts of others—writers of scripture, preachers, fellow Christians, and so forth—to communicate something (which may or may not be identical to what the original speaker intended to convey) to people.[16] The kind of divine speech act within any of these forms of communication *may* be a divine command; but speech acts such as statements, questions, exclamations, and so forth are possible as well. And invitational statements can of course be imbedded within a variety of kinds of speech acts.

It is perhaps worth clarifying a point here about the extent to which God can communicate to all people. Even if we assume that God's full revelation came in the person of Jesus Christ and that the Christian creeds contain—uniquely among religions—truths about God's nature and activity, we need not conclude that those outside the Christian tradition do not have access to *any* communication from God. Indeed, I have argued elsewhere that Christians have solid reason to think that God gives all people communication to which they can respond and thereby form some positive relationship with him that can eventually lead to a full and final reconciliation with God within the heavenly community.[17] The Christian tradition does indeed make claims that unique, and accurate, descriptions of God and God's activity in our world are found within the Christian creeds and scriptures. But this point about the unique claims within the Christian religion need not be denied in making the point, which is more relevant to our overall discussion, that God can communicate in a myriad of ways to those with varying degrees of true beliefs about him.

God's ultimate purpose in communicating to us, I have maintained, is to draw us into ideal relationships through which we can achieve ultimate flourishing. Whether this communication comes in the forms of commands/proscriptions or counsel/prescriptions, God's ultimate purpose remains the same. God's intention is to help us identify the end of pursuing others' well-being. Complementarily, God intends to motivate us to pursue the benevolent ends he helps us identify—both by helping us attain true beliefs about benevolent pursuits (e.g., that God commands them, that they further our own well-being, and so forth) and by fostering desires in us to see others flourish.[18] That God can "inspire" people by fostering, or arousing, their desires is also a core affirmation in the Christian tradition's doctrine of the Holy Spirit. So by helping shape people's beliefs and desires, God leads people to make decisions to prioritize others' interests instead of their own.

Another way of making the point about God's purposes is to say that God—in creating us, interacting with us, and prompting us to form certain beliefs and desires—is attempting to draw us into the ongoing life of the Trinity. Christians affirm that the persons of the Trinity, from eternity, have been engaged in benevolent, self-giving relationships.[19] By entering into relationships with the persons of the Trinity, we join in the interactions they have with one another and with all our fellow creatures who are also interacting with them. This fellowship is the ultimate end God intends for all of us.[20] And on the ethical framework I am outlining, the key to *whether* we participate in this fellowship will be the decisions we make whether to further others' well-being or our own.

God has provided scope for decisions of this kind by giving us two broad inclinations, or kinds of desire. First, as has already been much discussed, God has ensured that we are motivated to seek our own flourishing. Throughout the animal kingdom, we can readily witness the effort, from infancy, to survive and thrive. The forces that impel us, non-reflectively, to flourish, as well as the more reflective pro-attitudes we have toward our own flourishing, serve us well in the matter of surviving in our world. In this way the desires and dispositions that lead us to seek our own flourishing are instrumentally good things. They also provide scope for us to be tempted from following the second kind of broad inclination God has ensured that we have: namely, a desire to see others flourish. Evolutionary biologists may offer accounts of how we came to have these altruistic desires.[21] But the point for Christian ethical discussions will be that God has ensured that we do feel impelled to further the well-being of others.[22] For example, we feel sickened when we see some person or animal being tortured; we feel outraged when we are told of some child being abandoned; we feel joyful at the sight of our family and friends celebrating some recently received good news.

These two pulls—toward self-interest and toward the interests of others—are each keenly felt from a young age. The pull of self-interest is something we can attribute to babies, who begin their lives already seeking to eat when they feel hunger, to avoid pain when it is experienced, and so forth. And when adults recognize that some instance of benevolence will come at some personal cost to themselves, it is hardly a question *whether* they will feel *some* resistance to pursuing the other person's well-being.

In addition to the pull of self-interest, we find ourselves with affection for other people. This affection is of course much stronger for our spouses, our children, our friends, and people to whom we are attracted for various reasons. But as with self-interest, although we can cultivate the pull of benevolence through patterns of behavior, we do not ask to have affection for others. A young child finds himself sad when he sees his parents sad; relaxed when he sees them happy; amused when he sees them amused.

When the pulls toward self-interest and toward benevolence recommend incompatible courses of action, we face a choice. As a general summary point, choice in these situations allows us scope to decide how we finally want to relate to God and others. Again, the relationships among the persons of the Trinity are marked by self-giving commitments to the other persons within the Godhead. This kind of commitment summarizes the commands of God in the Christian scriptures and is needed to establish ideal relationships with others.[23] The call to benevolence over self-interest is a call to participate in the ongoing life of the Trinity, which we do by mirroring in important ways the relationships within the Trinity. What keeps us from benevolent pursuits is of course self-interest: we have some personal projects of our own that (we believe) do not involve, and come at the cost of, pursuing others' well-being. I shall discuss in section 6.2 why all genuinely benevolent pursuits will ultimately include benevolence toward *God* and the pursuit of God's projects. But I have already noted in my discussion of divine coordination that God has the resources to ensure (the possibility of) all people's ultimate flourishing and that any genuinely benevolent action toward someone will not come at the expense of someone else's ultimate flourishing. Given that our pursuit of others' well-being must ultimately involve the pursuit of God's interests, and given the point (also to be defended later) that the pursuit either of others' well-being or of our own exhausts the possibilities for long-term pursuits, then this choice whether to pursue others' well-being or our own really will determine how finally we are related to God.

Of course, the Christian view of self-interest and benevolence is that they do *not* in the end diverge. But God provides scope for choice by making this coincidence less than obvious to us in this life—though the redeemed in heaven will surely have a clear and persevering grasp of this point. Why, though, should God make this coincidence less than fully obvious to us in this life? And why should God ensure that we have *such* strong desires for our own flourishing that we can be tempted to prioritize self-interest over benevolence? Another way of putting these questions is to ask why God did not simply create us with, or at least determine us to have, the fixed desires and beliefs that the redeemed in heaven have. Why is it important that we have the power to determine whether or not we participate in ideal relationships?

## 5.5 Freedom in Choosing the Good

The orthodox Christian position is that nothing about God's nature *necessitates* his creating a world. And given God's decision to create, nothing necessitates his creating in that world humans with the power to help determine whether they relate positively to God and to others for eternity. God could have, say, created a world of butterflies or even a world of creatures with many mental abilities similar to humans but without any power of self-determination. God's relationships with such creatures, as well as the creatures' relationships with one another, could have included any number of elements. But there are certain elements that these relationships could *not* include. Specifically, there is a kind of shared partnership that can occur only when each party in a relationship contributes something, as an ultimate cause, to that relationship.

I noted in section 4.6 that an interpersonal relationship is established when one person responds to the invitational statements (as I called them) of the other person. If either person is the ultimate cause of *both* the invitation and the response, then the kind of partnership I am outlining cannot occur. I shall not defend at length here either the coherence of, or the importance most people place on, the idea of an agent being an ultimate cause of some action. But I do think it rather obvious that, as we seek a better understanding of some person to whom we are relating, one question we often deem important is the question: For what is the person ultimately responsible? I am using the word *responsible* here in the broad sense of "being a causal contributor to" some event that occurs. There is a narrower sense of *responsibility*, much discussed by moral philosophers, as to the conditions for so-called "moral responsibility." The search for responsibility in this narrower sense is the search for the conditions under which a person becomes a candidate for such things as blame and punishment. One condition, upon which most all moral philosophers agree, for this narrower sense of responsibility is indeed the question of whether a person was responsible in some broad sense of being part of the causal explanation for the action or event in question. What is more controversial among moral philosophers is whether the importance of causal contribution in this context is a matter of being an *ultimate* cause.

While space allows only for the briefest remarks on these points, let me at least point to where I think a thorough and adequate defense lies of the coherence and importance of an agent's power to serve as an ultimate cause. The Christian religion affirms that God created the world without being caused to do so. What is thus affirmed is that God can be motivated to act in some way—for instance, be motivated by the desire that others share in the ongoing life of the Trinity—without these motivations causally necessitating God's actions. Christian theists can allow that these motivations served as partial causes of God's action of creating; but I think they must maintain that God—as an irreducible *agent*—also serves as a partial cause of his own actions. The idea of an "agent causing some event" (specifically, the event of the agent's own actions) is perhaps mysterious.[24] But I do not see that it involves anything internally contradictory. If this is correct, then there is some plausibility to the idea that God would create a world where humans also came to have this capacity, as irreducible agents, to serve as ultimate (even if partial) causes of events.

Such an affirmation amounts to more than merely affirming indeterminacy—that is, a lack of causal determination—within human decision-making processes. For such indeterminacy might be spelled out in terms of undetermined *events* within one's brain (or even among one's mental states) causing other events, resulting in some action one performs.²⁵ Such indeterminacy with respect to event-event causation, though, is a phenomenon quite different from *agent*-event causation. Personal agency, as I am describing it, will not admit to any reductionist analysis in terms of events within an agent. There is no more fundamental description of an agent serving as an ultimate cause than to say that the "agent caused some event." Because the mechanics (if that is the right word) of agent-event causation are not observable, they may remain mysterious to us. But again I do not see that the affirmation of agent causation involves any internal contradictions.

The best defense of the *importance* of being an ultimate cause will, I think, appeal to our intuitions about various cases in which we either do or do not hold others to be proper subjects for praise and blame. In investigating the chain of events that led to some welcome (or unwelcome) outcome, one question in which we are interested is the question of whether any personal agents feature in the ultimate (and not merely proximate) causal explanations of the event. To mention just one frequently discussed case, we excuse the thief if we conclude that his action was performed under the irresistible impulse of posthypnotic suggestion. Our attention turns to the hypnotist as the appropriate candidate for blame. If we find that the thief employed the hypnotist—say, as a way of plucking up the courage to steal—then our attention turns back to the thief. While of course it would take a great deal more argument to address possible complications with this and other examples in which we might seek to assess praise and blame, I think that examples of this kind will in the end bear out our deep intuition as to the importance we place on being an ultimate cause of one's own actions.

If people were *not* an ultimate cause of any of their own actions, then we could still have certain kinds of relationships with one another and with God. Moreover, I see no reason to think we could not enjoy various aspects of these relationships. Still, there is a certain kind of relationship that would not be possible. There is a particular feeling that comes when we see ourselves as part of a project to which we contributed, though only partially. We feel a particular kind of connection with another person when we recognize that we are each partial, ultimate contributors to our shared project. To be sure, some of the feelings we can experience in pursuing joint projects with others might remain if we supposed that neither of us were ultimate causes. After all, philosophers who affirm the thesis of determinism can still find certain enjoyments in joint projects: they can experience surprise at the other person's perspective, appreciation of that perspective, and so forth. Still, if the pursuit of joint projects serves as a way of establishing a relationship with the other person, the question is ever before us as our relationship deepens: Who exactly is this other person?

There is an obvious sense in which the beliefs and desires and values of other persons are *theirs* if they possess them. The persons' contributions to joint projects with us of course reveal these things. Yet we can also ask whether their contributions are theirs in the sense that they are *irreducibly theirs* and cannot be attributed to someone or something else that is the sole, ultimate cause of their current values and actions. While we can still appreciate others' contributions (qua contributions), we again sometimes reflectively resist such responses as praising, thanking, blaming, or condemning unless we think others' contributions are *theirs* in the sense that they are ultimate causes of their actions and current values.

In trying to make sense of the world and our place with others in it, we often seek an (causal) explanation for the way things are. When we identify some causal chain, or explanatory story, we can ask the question whether some link in the causal chain is where the "buck stops" (in terms of being an ultimate cause within that causal chain) or whether we should instead look for some preceding cause that helps explain the origins of that causal chain. We again sometimes reserve responses such as praise and blame for ultimate causes. To be sure, it is possible—indeed common—to interact with, and (to borrow a phrase from Peter Strawson) have "reactive attitudes" toward, people whether or not we regard them as ultimate causes. Nevertheless, there remains a way of viewing them as personal agents that depends on identifying them as ultimate causes. It is *they*, as irreducible agents, who have added something to the shape of our world in a way that objects without the power to create—that is, to initiate causal chains—cannot.

The importance of identifying others as partial, ultimate causes becomes acute when we consider how we might view others if we had a full understanding of, and unwavering belief about, God's existence and creative acts. In our current world the complete causal history of the things we observe—trees, tables, people, and so on—is not at all clear to us. We may have no idea, for example, which people or machines assembled the parts of our new computer, or how these parts came to exist in the first place in their current form. And even when we do have beliefs about the causal history of our world—as in the case of the theological determinist who believes God is the sole, ultimate cause of all things—it is surely rare that these beliefs will be held with certainty and will consistently inform all our interactions with people and other objects. The result is that day to day we tend to relate to people and objects with reactive attitudes and without a conscious or clear reflection on their roles as ultimate causes.

But if we think about the Christian picture of an afterlife where we will understand God, others, and ourselves more clearly, we presumably will have a much greater awareness of God's activity in shaping the world (including the creatures in it). If we came to see that God causally necessitates, or is the ultimate cause of, *all* events—including all human thoughts and actions—then what would be our understanding of other people? How would our relationships with them be different than with other objects whose movements God causally necessitates? We might perhaps still experience *some* of the feelings we associate with interpersonal relationships: we could be surprised at others' perspectives, appreciative of their capabilities, amused at their wit, and so forth. But there surely remains a certain kind of appreciation personal agents can have of other personal agents, stemming from a shared knowledge of how each person contributed (as an ultimate cause) to the shape of the relationship and of the projects jointly pursued within that relationship. Correspondingly, there remain certain kinds of feelings we can have (only) as we connect with others who are genuinely co-creators with us.

Admittedly, some of the best examples of loving relationships in this life—such as a husband embracing acts of service to his wife, a parent loving a small child, or a child growing up feeling attached and unswervingly loyal to her parents—can plausibly be construed as motivated by irresistible desires. If these actions are determined, then, when we gain a full understanding of everyone's creative contributions to the network of ideal relationships within the heavenly community, these actions will *not* serve as the basis for the kind of interpersonal, co-creative connections discussed earlier. And this may initially seem too dismissive of the incredibly high value we place on the love of family and close friends, even though their attitudes toward, and commitments to, us may well be something they didn't *choose*, as ultimate causes. In rebutting this possible objection to the significance I have placed on agent causal power, I might point out that a person need not be an ultimate cause of *all* her actions in order to maintain ideal relationships with others. As we noted in section 5.1, attractions (including irresistible ones) can certainly play necessary roles in ideal relationships within the heavenly community, even if they do not play sufficient roles. But this rebuttal would be inadequate. The point remains that I will need to be committed to the idea that there are greatly worthwhile feelings of connecting available only to those agents who are ultimate causes, qua agents, of their interactions with others. And the critic may question the plausibility of this commitment, seizing the point that some of the best examples of loving relationships in this life do not always seem to require the freedom *whether* to interact benevolently with others.

A more adequate response to our critic begins by allowing that, in this life, we perhaps are often most appreciative of parents' unconditional love and of a close friend's unswerving loyalty. But we can press the point that in the heavenly community we will presumably have a much fuller understanding of how others have used their agent power. As we continue in an afterlife to make sense of why the world is as it is, it seems plausible to think that we will appreciate much more others' contributions, as ultimate causes, to the network of relationships God has initiated. In this life we may relate to spouses, children, and close friends largely with reactive attitudes that do not require anything close to a complete knowledge of these individuals' contributions to the shape of relational networks. But again the redeemed in heaven *will* come to have more and more of this knowledge, as they relate to one another for eternity. And in these ever deepening relationships the question is ever before us: *Who is this person to whom I am relating?* On a Christian understanding of the role God plays in creating and directing us, answering this question will surely always begin by exploring how the person has (as an ultimate cause) causally contributed to the relationship that exists between the person and God, who of course initiated our networks of relationships and sustains our part in them as we relate to him as lord. Thus, although in this life the best examples of human, loving relationships may often be sustained without reflection on how others have contributed, as ultimate causes, to the shape of their relationship with God and others, there is reason to think that ever-deepening relationships within the heavenly community *do* require such reflection.[26]

It is perhaps difficult at present to think how our interpersonal interactions might differ, given a greatly increased understanding of the roles, as ultimate causes, played by the people with whom we interact. But consider how a response of *thankfulness* to other humans would seem inappropriate if we believed that God played the role of ultimate cause—that is, of creator—of all the states of affairs we welcome. We might experience a "connection" with others as we reflected on our similar fortunes of being used as instruments as God. But there would be no feelings of "connection" that arise when we believe that both *we* and *they* have contributed to the shape of our relationship. We might be thankful *that* we are in relationships with them—as I would be thankful for other objects, whether sentient or not. But it is not *them* I should want to thank (or in any way relate to as co-creator of our joint projects). Rather, inasmuch as it is appropriate to thank some*one*, I should want to thank only God. In a world where God was the only ultimate cause, our response to anyone's thanks should be: "Don't thank *me*; I'm not the one who decided whether the event you welcome should have come about!"

Likewise, and importantly, in a world where God was the sole ultimate cause, God would be relating *interpersonally* only to himself. There would be no other personal agents in the picture—at least, where we understand personal agency as involving the power to help create and determine, qua agent, the shape of one's relationships and joint projects. In interacting with humans, we would be but one kind of object—albeit an object with a center of consciousness and various intellectual and physical abilities—that God manipulates. I do not use *manipulate* in any pejorative sense; rather, I am pointing out that God could not *but* manipulate us, as I am currently manipulating a computer keyboard. When I look at, and "respond" to, the words on my computer screen at present, I am relating only to myself. There are no other personal agents in the picture. God could of course build *randomness* into his creatures so that, strictly speaking, he is not ultimately causing our actions in the sense of causally necessitating our actions. But the question still remains: What of our identity? To *whom* would God be relating? There seems an important difference between (1) relating to a creature whose actions were partly caused by chance events within that creature; and (2) relating to a creature *who caused*, qua agent, these events. Of course, one might question the intuition that personal agency cannot be reduced to events within a person's brain and/or within one's mental realm; and I do not think there is a non-question-begging way of settling such a question. But if it makes sense to think of God as (irreducibly) a personal agent with causal power, then again there is plausibility to the idea that God would create, and seek relationships with, personal agents with causal power.

Before we move on, it may be worth clarifying how the emphasis I have placed on the need for freedom differs from an emphasis on the need to use that freedom in some particular way. If my own observations are any guide, it is common in Christian circles to argue that, in order to make relationships of *love* with humans possible, God gave us the kind of freedom, or agent causal power, I have discussed. I think the emphasis on love misses the mark for two reasons. First, power of agent causation, as already noted, makes a relationship of a certain, general kind possible. The kind of relationship here is one in which both parties contribute, qua agents, to the shape of that relationship. This point remains, regardless of whether the relationship happens to be characterized by love. So it is more broadly the nature of *personal agency*—not merely any distinctive aspect of those interpersonal relationships more narrowly characterized by love—that requires the divine gift of agent causal power.

Second, I think it implausible to suggest that loving relationships at all times *do* require agent causal power or at least that one's choices and actions be free from determinism. After all, the redeemed in heaven interact with one another in ideal, loving relationships. Yet the Christian tradition has always affirmed that there is no possibility of humans sinning once they are part of the heavenly community. In other words, the range of actions the redeemed in heaven can perform (as ultimate causes) do not include sinful actions. To be sure, there is no reason to think they cannot exercise a certain measure of agent power in making various decisions—such as initiating and creatively helping to shape various projects and pursuits. But, consistent with the impossibility of sinning, they will not possess the power to relate to God and others in ways that are at odds with God's directives toward benevolent service.

I take it that the reason the redeemed in heaven cannot sin is that it is psychologically impossible for them to do so. That is, no goal is attractive enough genuinely to tempt them to renounce their self-giving pursuits.[27] Of course, before it became psychologically impossible for them to reject God's directives, the redeemed would have needed (in order to establish the kind of personal agency I have been discussing) to have exercised their agent power to choose whether, as ultimate causes, to respond positively to God's invitation to a personal relationship. They would have needed to develop freely chosen habits—by acting benevolently in response to God's initiative to do so—that dispose them now to act benevolently without being tempted to do otherwise. And, crucial to the Christian understanding of sanctification, they would have needed to use their freedom to ask God to change their desires in such a way that their desires are now aligned with what God's plans are for them. In this way, God could change their desires without unilaterally determining to do so (which would leave no room for human agents to make ultimately significant decisions about how they relate to God).

Still, the point remains that, within the heavenly community, the redeemed relate to one another in loving ways, without the power to choose whether they will do so. And this is enough to show that the nature of *love* does not require those in loving relationships to possess the kind of freedom I have described in this section. To be sure, participation in ideal, loving relationships for humans does require that they (at *some* point) have exercised causal power as to whether they will relate lovingly to God and to others. But this requirement again stems from the nature of any *interpersonal relationship* between agents of a certain kind, rather than from the nature of *love*.

## 5.6 The Final Dichotomy of Benevolent and Self-Interested Ends

We can think of agent power as I have described it—that is, the ability to serve as an ultimate cause of one's own actions—as a kind of freedom of self-determination. Crucially, what we help determine is how we end up relating to God and others. At the same time, we should be quick to acknowledge the point that of course we do not *completely* determine how we will relate to God and others. Though this seems an obvious point, some of the criticisms of the kind of freedom I have outlined do seemingly focus on the impossibility of completely determining oneself. And so let me make clear that I certainly would not be committed to the idea of self-determination with no qualification.

As Alfred Mele notes in his discussion of our psychological histories, "Many of our principles, values, desires, and beliefs come to us unbidden. Undeniably, our characters and values are in the process of being shaped before we are in any position to chart the course of our lives, to set up for ourselves principles and values with reference to which we may steer" (2001, 147). More than merely as an empirical point, Susan Wolf summarizes the difficulty, in principle, with suggesting that an agent can shape herself: "Either something is behind the agent, making the agent what she is, or nothing is. The idea of an autonomous agent appears to be the idea of a prime mover unmoved whose self can endlessly account for itself and for the behavior that it intentionally exhibits or allows. But this idea seems incoherent or, at any rate, logically impossible" (1990, 14). Galen Strawson's summation is even more succinct: "True self-determination is logically impossible because it requires the actual completion of an infinite regress of choices of principles of choice" (2010, 25).[28]

Drawing from these quotations, one might offer (at least) two broad kinds of objections to the idea of self-determination. First, one might question whether, *at a particular slice in time*, a human might serve as an ultimate cause of his own action. But to deny this possibility would simply be to deny the possibility of agent causal power, as I described it in the previous section. I discussed there how I think a defense of agent causal power might go, so I shall not cover that ground here. The second question one might ask is whether, from our earliest occasions of choosing (as an ultimate cause) how we will relate to God and others, we are making choices in a vacuum, as it were. Obviously, the answer to this second question is "no." Our range of choices is both hugely limited by, and influenced by, a wide variety of factors: the time and place of our birth, our desires from the earliest age, the beliefs we (involuntarily) form when reflecting on ethical dilemmas, our exposure to others' pursuits (which serve as examples as to which pursuits are possible), and so on.

Our discussion of agent causal power can readily accommodate this point. Even while God attempts to move all people toward settled, benevolent dispositions, each person will have a unique way of getting there. Differing combinations of desires, beliefs, emotions, and uncritical habits keep us from the benevolent dispositions we need in order to participate in ideal relationships. Accordingly, the changes in these areas that God will need to effect will differ from person to person. What is crucial, on the account of freedom I am offering, is that, at any point in time, we (qua agents) can be ultimate, determining factors in whether we perform a benevolent action instead of a self-interested action. In the next chapter I will explore the various forms that a choice "whether to pursue self-interest or benevolence" might take. But for the remainder of this section I want to outline why our choices will move us in the long run *either* toward settled, benevolent dispositions *or* toward settled, purely self-interested dispositions.

Just as the redeemed in heaven can have settled dispositions to respond *positively* to God's directives, the majority Christian view historically has been that it is also possible to decisively *reject* God. That is, it is possible for a person's desires and commitments to become settled so that benevolent choices—which are requisite for participation in ideal relationships—are no longer psychologically possible. I shall not explore here the question of what fate—such as ongoing existence in hell or annihilation—awaits a person once his dispositions become genuinely settled so that future participation within the heavenly community is impossible. And I shall not explore the substantive question of whether there is reason to think that many people have in fact acquired such settled dispositions. I simply want to establish the formal possibility of having settled dispositions *against* benevolence, just as the redeemed in heaven have settled dispositions to act benevolently.

In support of the Christian view that there are two broad final destinies for humans, heaven and hell, there is indeed reason to think that our dispositions over time will either become settled in line with the redeemed in heaven or become more and more settled toward the pursuit of self-interested projects at the expense of any benevolent pursuits. As noted in section 4.5, ever deepening relationships are protected from life-diminishing experiences like disappointment and resentment only when there is mutual understanding of a mutual commitment to further the other person's well-being. As God leads us toward ideal relationships marked by such benevolence, he must ensure the elimination of those self-interested desires that compete with the benevolent commitments contained within God's coordinating directives.[29] If we are to have a relationship with God and others based on the truth about who we are and who God is, various truths about ourselves—including truths about how our characters/dispositions came to be as they are and how we contributed, as ultimate causes, to them—will need to be collectively known. In sum, in the process shaping us so that we can take our place within the heavenly community, our self-interested desires that might tempt us from following God's directives must be brought to light and eliminated.

It might be questioned at this point whether truths about ourselves and others must really be *known* (where "knowledge" involves a true belief), as opposed merely to *believed*. That is, why could not God simply have given people (false) beliefs about their own histories and choices, all the while unilaterally determining that all people possess the kinds of settled, benevolent dispositions requisite for ideal relationships?[30] After all, if the conclusions of chapter 2 are correct that life-enhancing mental states are the only things of noninstrumental value, then such false beliefs would be instrumentally good in that they would allow for everyone's experiences of connecting with one another—that is, for everyone's ultimate flourishing. So again the question is why our movement toward settled, benevolent dispositions has to involve *true* beliefs about ourselves and others.

One possible response to this question is that the very nature of God is inconsistent with misleading people—at least, with misleading them for eternity. I think this response is probably correct. But if one is not entirely convinced of it, let me offer another line of response. When we have incorrect information about other people—for example, the ways they have or have not contributed to a project as ultimate causes—there is always the potential for discord as we interact with them in the future. We interact with others against a backdrop of background beliefs about the person's history. In ever deepening relationships the scope of these beliefs obviously becomes extensive. These background beliefs affect our appreciation of the person as well as our expectations of the person as we consider future, joint projects. If our beliefs about others did not coincide with *their* beliefs about themselves, then there exists an ever present danger of feelings such as disappointment (as one realizes that others do not have the character one thought they did) or alienation (as one realizes that one is misunderstood by others).

The critic might rejoin that God could coordinate everyone's false beliefs and pursuits so that this danger would never be realized. However, I think it incredible that even God could coordinate our false beliefs in such a manner. I am at a loss to imagine how we could have false beliefs about others' and our own contributions to the shape of the world—including the shape of our own characters—and still interact in a network of relationships in which we connected with each other, (falsely) thinking we and others were contributors (as creative, ultimate causes) to the projects we continued jointly to pursue. At any rate, what does seem clear is that we all would have a profoundly distorted view of who God is and what God has done in human history.[31]

The critic might yet rejoin that, in such a scenario, it would be God who would absorb the cost of being profoundly misunderstood. And a God of love should be willing to do just that. Yes, our relationships with God would lack a certain kind of integrity in that they would not be based on mutually held, true beliefs about who God is and what God has and has not done in shaping our relationships with him. But of course there is nothing *intrinsically* good about "integrity within a relationship." As we saw in chapter 2, all that has intrinsic value are the positive mental states of sentient beings.

In response to this further rejoinder, I think we should ask ourselves: In a world where we "related" to such a distorted picture of God, what benefits could we actually reap? Suppose God *could* coordinate everyone's false beliefs so as to ensure that we all had positive experiences of connecting with others, (falsely) viewing others as the partial shapers, qua agents, of their own characters and of the projects we pursued with them. Or, in a case I think is at least imaginable, suppose God put all people in Nozick-type experience machines so that they had these positive experiences of connecting with others. Could God really simulate the mental experiences of actually encountering *God* as God really is?

The Christian tradition has always affirmed that our best experiences on earth are but foretastes of the kind of experience that Christian theologians have attempted to describe in terms of the "beatific vision" or of beholding God "face to face." The effects of encountering God in the next life are thought to be such that they—and only they—can provide for a life of ultimate flourishing, which would otherwise be compromised by painful memories, self-destructive patterns of thinking, and so forth. Simulating an encounter with a being who transcends this universe would not be like simulating sense experiences such as feeling a pinprick or even seeming to see a tree. God could presumably simulate the sense experiences we have as we encounter physical objects in our world by manipulating the physical workings of our brains. But simulate an encounter with the one who is not reducible to anything in the physical realm of our universe or even the mental realm of sentient creatures' first-person experiences? The Christian tradition has again relied heavily on suggestive language (such as the beatific vision) in affirming how God's spirit might "witness to our spirit" as part of our experience of eternal joy. Still, a metaphysical encounter with a transcendent being—to which this suggestive language is meant to point—is just that: a metaphysical encounter. And I think it very implausible to suggest that such an encounter could be simulated by a Nozick-type experience machine or by any other action God might take that would not involve our encountering God as God truly is.

Our conclusion at this point is that God, in order to lead us toward ideal relationships that provide for our ultimate flourishing, must press the truth upon us as to the roles we and others (including God) play in shaping these relationships. Those desires or other mental states that could undermine ideal relationships must be removed (or transformed, if that is the better word). For those who embrace the steps needed to attain settled, benevolent dispositions, the end point will always be such settled dispositions. But what of those who resist God's efforts to draw them toward benevolent commitments?

Given the need for unwaveringly benevolent dispositions if ideal relationships are to be established and maintained, God will surely continue to prompt those without these dispositions to perform acts that will help in cultivating these dispositions. This prompting may of course take various forms, as we noted briefly in our earlier discussion (cf. section

5.4) of how God might communicate to people. If a person is pursuing *some* patterns of benevolence, or at least continues to have desires that motivate her to pursue benevolence, then God has avenues to continue prompting the person toward increasing patterns of benevolence. Just as a person can attain settled, benevolent dispositions, though, in principle a person can also attain settled dispositions whereby it becomes psychologically impossible for him to perform genuinely benevolent actions.

One might respond to this last claim by questioning just how plausible it is to think that many people would cease to have *any* desires to perform benevolent actions. My rejoinder begins by noting that most benevolent desires we have in this life are a far cry from the settled dispositions we will need for ideal relationships within the heavenly community. Typically, our benevolent desires need to be developed, or cultivated, on two fronts—if they are to serve as motivations for our continued participation in ideal relationships. First, the *scope* of people toward whom we have benevolent feelings must be *expanded*. It is one thing for us to desire the well-being of our family members and close friends. But Jesus's instructions on love extend to such individuals as those whom we consider natural enemies, those who have persecuted us, those who stand in need of our forgiveness, and those who ask for our forgiveness but who repeat patterns again and again of hurting us.[32] Yes, we may have less difficulty committing ourselves to the well-being of a child of ours. But when we are asked to commit equally to any role God may want us to play in pursuing the well-being of our *enemies*, then we may balk at the idea.

Second, for any individual toward whom we *do* have benevolent feelings, the *depth* of commitment will need to be increased. Committing to a spouse on our wedding day, or to a child on the day of his birth, may come rather easily for us. But ventures into marriage and parenting are long paths of discovery: we discover—perhaps daily—what is actually involved in seeking the well-being of this person before us. To continue to seek the other's well-being requires a growing, a deepening (if that is the best word) commitment in terms of our willingness to absorb the perceived costs of benevolent deferrals to the others' interests.

To summarize the last two paragraphs, we must be willing to commit to *everyone's* well-being and to *whatever* actions these commitments require, if we are to participate in the heavenly community of ideal relationships coordinated by God. As God moves us toward being able to participate in this network of relationships, he must reveal to us more and more of the truth about what our benevolent commitments need to be. When a person gains some new understanding of these matters, she may of course pull back from the benevolent pursuits she was previously committed to. "Yes, I'm willing to serve *this* person; but I will *not* be reconciled to *that* person." "Yes, I'm willing to do *this* for the person; but I'm *not* willing to go *that* far in helping out." With regard to Jesus's recorded interactions with those who followed him in the initial stages of his ministry, we read of exchanges in which Jesus gave new information about what is involved in making him lord of one's life. We read of a rich ruler who testified to keeping all the commandments "since I was a boy" but who balked at Jesus's instruction to "sell everything you have and give to the poor" (Luke 18:18–23). And we read of the response by a flock of Jesus's early disciples to his teachings on the need to be sustained by his own flesh and blood: "This is a hard teaching. Who can accept it?" The narrator of the story then tells that "many of his disciples turned back and no longer followed him" (John 6:30–69).

So, yes, we can plausibly say of many people that there exists some kind of benevolent desire to seek the interests of others—whether God or other humans. But as people learn over time about the *scope* and the *depth* of the benevolent commitments required for them to take their places within the network of perfected relationships in heaven, they may resist their previous patterns of deference to God and/or others. "If *this* is what it means to seek abidingly the good of my spouse, my child, my neighbor, my enemy, my God, then I'm not sure I want to enlist in this work after all." When some fuller truth about the implications of self-giving love are pressed upon us, we may opt to pursue a self-interested desire at the expense of the original, benevolent desire God was seeking to cultivate in a wider, deeper form.

When the original, benevolent desire no longer serves as an avenue by which God can prompt a person to relate to him more fully as lord, then God will presumably move to another desire. Again, God must seek to lead the person in *some* way to cultivate the consistently benevolent desires or dispositions she needs, if she is ever to attain ultimate flourishing. In principle, a person may eventually possess no remaining desires to which God can appeal in seeking to elicit fully contextualized benevolent actions.

Once again, let me be clear about certain questions I am *not* seeking to address here. I am not attempting an exploration of the substantive questions of whether many people remain for periods of time in a state of having neither fully benevolent nor fully self-interested dispositions. I am also not exploring what the Christian view should be as to the specifics of the ultimate fate of those with settled dispositions that are self-interested as opposed to benevolent. What I *have* sought to establish is that the end result of God attempting to draw people into ideal relationships is that people will move toward either settled, benevolent dispositions or settled, self-interested dispositions.

We can conclude as a general point that God will lead us toward the pattern of benevolent pursuits needed for ideal relationships and away from those self-interested pursuits that compromise those benevolent pursuits. At the same time, it would be too simple to conclude that God can lead us toward benevolence only by appealing to our desires to perform benevolent actions. Interestingly, God can lead us toward (long-term) patterns of benevolence by appealing to certain self-interested desires we have. I am thinking here of those self-interested desires the realization of which, we believe, are attained by responding positively to God's invitational statements.[33] Let me elaborate.

In discussing how a personal relationship is established when one person responds to the "invitational statements" of another person, we noted in section 4.6 that this response may be an intermediate goal one has as one attempts to achieve some further, ultimate goal. This ultimate goal may well be a self-interested one. For example, I may chat with a colleague simply because I personally enjoy his company, or because my boss has demanded I do so and I want to keep my job, or because I want to know a piece of information and I believe my colleague will tell me if I ask him. While dispositions to pursue benevolent actions (as ultimate goals) may be the key to participation in ideal relationships, Jesus seemed clearly at times to appeal to people's self-interested goals as (ultimate) reasons for them to turn to God and follow his directives.

Take, for instance, Jesus's recorded teachings from the Sermon on the Mount. Why should I not judge others? Because "in the same way as you judge others, you will be judged, and with the measure you use, it will be measured to you" (Matt. 7:1–2). Why should I consider myself blessed if persecuted by others because of Jesus? Because "great is your reward in heaven" (Matt. 5:11–12). Why should I not give in to things like anger and lust? Because these are paths that can lead to hell (Matt. 7:22, 28–29). If God will ultimately be concerned to draw people into ideal relationships marked by benevolent commitments, then one may question why these appeals are made to the self-interested desire to flourish in the long run.

Of course, I should be quick to point out that Jesus by no means indicated that God would *leave* people, indefinitely, with these motivations. It is just that a self-interested response seems compatible with at least some initial response to God whereby a positive relationship with God is established. As one learns more and more about what God's directives are—that is, learns more about the *type* of relationship into which God is inviting us—then purely self-interested, ultimate goals will become less and less achievable by our responding positively to God's directives. After all, God's directives to us at some point will need to focus on consistently benevolent pursuits, if the main arguments of chapter 4 are correct.

One might wonder why God would appeal to self-interested pursuits at all, even if his directives in time will turn more and more toward matters of benevolence. But when we think of the strength of desire people have for their own flourishing, I think it is of little surprise that God would appeal to self-interested desires as a way of encouraging many people to turn to God. If God's initial communication to people came as a directive to abandon all self-interested pursuits that might come at the expense of benevolence, surely he would elicit few followers. Though we seem to have a natural affinity for others, our natural desires for our own flourishing are arguably much more powerful. (Indeed, it is difficult to imagine how we could survive as individuals or as a species if our self-directed desires were not so powerful.) It is true that our natural affinity for others can *become* exponentially stronger as we interact with them over time. Our affection for, say, spouses and close friends can be powerful enough to elicit deep self-sacrifice without our being seriously tempted to do otherwise. Yet one typically does not begin a relationship with such affection. Rather, one's self-interested desires—to enjoy being with a person who makes us laugh, to whom we are physically attracted, and so forth—often play large roles in the initial states of those relationships that over time become marked by benevolence and, when needed, self-sacrifice.

It is little wonder, then, that God may first emphasize certain benefits that come when we respond positively to him, allowing our affection for him to grow over time before pressing other truths upon us about the need for benevolence. Perhaps in some cases there will be little need to press these truths upon a person, as the enjoyment the person experiences as she focuses on God (and others) may motivate her to keep her focus on God without being prompted to do so. But where the need for benevolence *does* need to be pressed upon us, our history of positive experiences with God will allow us more readily to keep in check any worries about our own flourishing during those times when the call of benevolence seems in some respects costly.

Given the dual, contrasting set of settled dispositions toward which we ultimately will move, the decisions that affect *which* set of settled dispositions we acquire have special significance. I am calling such decisions "morally significant," in contrast to other decisions we might make that do *not* move us toward either set of settled dispositions. Even when our decisions *do* have "moral significance," as I am using that term, people will not always (or even typically) be focused on the kind of eternal consequences I have been outlining. Most of our everyday decisions do not involve reflective deliberation on the contrasting, overarching paths toward resolute self-interest or unwavering commitment to God and others. In the following chapter I want to explore some of the ways in which our everyday decisions affect our final state as creatures committed either to self-interest or to God. I will also in this final chapter offer ways of understanding such decisions as decisions whether to cultivate certain desires with particular feeling tones to them. The feeling tones of our desires, then, become our key indicators of where the path to the good life lies.

CHAPTER SIX

# Feeling Our Way toward the Good

### 6.1 The Positive Feeling Tones of Benevolence

Most of us clearly do perform various benevolent acts in our day-to-day lives. It is worth exploring the motivation we feel in doing so. An obvious, initial point on which to reflect is the fact that we often experience enjoyment when we see another person happy. As discussed in section 4.2, Aristotle and Aquinas both described how another person can become "another self" to me as her happiness becomes my happiness. The positive feeling tones we experience when we see others happy can offset, in terms of motivations for continued action, any contrasting, negative feeling tones that we experience as a result of ensuring their happiness. Indeed, genuine sacrifices for our loved ones can feel altogether inconsequential when we see that our loved ones are safe and well as a result of our actions. "It's a pleasure" can be an honest response to people who thank us for our acts of sacrifice for them.

The enjoyment we receive in seeing others well off merits close analysis. In section 1.4 I reviewed how a desire involves a feeling of being impelled, accompanied by the dichotomous feelings of frustration or release when one believes that the world is or is not as one desires it to be.

Thus being "motivated by benevolence" is, strictly speaking, shorthand for being "motivated by those positive feelings we experience as we consider the other person's flourishing." For both benevolent and self-interested actions, then, one is motivated by one's own positive feelings associated with those actions (or the goals one believes can be achieved through those actions). Put in these terms, it is not immediately clear how benevolence is to be distinguished from self-interest. After all, in each case what motivates one to act are the positive feelings of "release" and the corresponding, negative feelings of "frustration" that constitute a desire. And there is nothing so far that precludes the psychological egoist from suggesting that the moralist's so-called choice between benevolence and self-interest is really just a choice whether to pursue one kind of pleasant feeling over another.

As a first step toward preserving the notion of benevolence, I note that the desire that another person's life go well for her arises when we focus our attention on *her* well-being and not on our own. Some self-interested desires arise as we focus our attention on external objects. For example, to have a desire to visit Paris, I must be aware that the city exists and imagine the possibility of being there. Other self-interested desires arguably do not require us to focus on any external objects, as when a hungry infant desires to continue nursing even though he cannot yet appreciate that there are external objects—such as his mother—distinct from himself. But as regards the desire for someone else's life to go well, we obviously need to be aware that the other person exists and has a welfare. And for benevolent actions to be possible, we need to focus our attention on the other person in at least some minimal sense. More specifically, our conscious focus must be such that certain, distinct feelings arise in connection with this focus on the other person.

I noted that "positive feelings" can characterize both the consideration of our own well-being and our consideration of others' well-being. At the same time, when we reflect further on the respective phenomenology of each set of feelings, I think it becomes clear that differences exist. While the limits of public language make it difficult to characterize this distinction neatly, consider cases in which we have worked to further someone's welfare. Our reflections on our own benevolent actions arouse feelings we associate with being noble, or gallant, or venerable. These feelings seemingly are boosted by the higher-order reflection that the satisfaction we have thus far received from our acts of benevolence is a kind of satisfaction we can embrace and cultivate without reservation. These feeling tones are, when we reflect on the matter, simply different from the feeling tones we experience when we succeed in pursuing our own well-being as an ultimate, intentional end. While public language may again be of limited help in identifying the feeling tones in question, poets and novelists often seek to draw attention to them. They are the feeling tones we imagine Sydney Carton to experience at the end of *A Tale of Two Cities* that lead him to talk about the "far better thing" he is doing. In section 6.3 I shall try to characterize more fully these feeling tones common to acts of benevolence. But for now it is enough to note that we can distinguish these feeling tones from feeling tones that tempt us to pursue acts of greed or cruelty or self-aggrandizement that come at others' expense.

In offering an account of benevolence, we might stress either an "outward" or an "inward" aspect. If stressing the former, we might define benevolence as either the intentional pursuit of another person's well-being and/or the intentional focus of our attention on the other person (qua person who has a welfare). It might be objected here that the mere focus of our attention on another person hardly merits the description of an *act* of benevolence. But if one chooses to consider the well-being of another person—perhaps choosing to turn one's attention *from* considerations of one's own well-being in the process—then it seems right to say that the act of focusing on another person can indeed be an act of benevolence. Further, the previously discussed feeling tones associated with benevolence can arise both when we focus on some *act* of furthering another's well-being (e.g., when I focus on my act of shoveling snow off my elderly neighbor's driveway) and when we focus on the other person herself (e.g., when I think of my neighbor and feel an urge to support her in some way). In section 6.2 I shall offer a fuller analysis of benevolence based on the "outward" aspect of a benevolent *act*.

It is also possible to offer an "inwardly" focused description of benevolence by appealing to the unique feeling tones that occur when we act to further others' well-being or consider another person (qua person who can be helped or harmed). This inward analysis will again be the focus of section 6.3. For now, let me note that this inward focus on benevolence carries a danger of being misleading. For we can easily (and wrongly) suppose that benevolence is marked by the *attempt to further the pleasant feeling tones associated with benevolence*. And this is decidedly not the case. Such a pursuit would clearly be a self-interested pursuit.

We now find ourselves in a position of affirming that particular, pleasant mental experiences associated with benevolence *motivate* one's benevolent actions, while denying that these pleasant mental experiences serve as one's intended *goal* when one goes on to perform benevolent actions. Any paradoxical aspect of this scenario is simply a feature of the general "paradox of Hedonism" discussed in section 1.4. We discussed in that section scenarios such as playing basketball, where one's focus is on making baskets (and not on increasing one's pleasant feelings) even though one's pleasant feelings are what moves, or impels, one to continue playing.

I acknowledge that, if a parent is asked to "give a reason" for some benevolent action she performs toward her child, she may respond by saying, "The reason is: I wanted my child to be happy." As long as we equate a "reason" here with the *actor's intended goal*, then I would in no way quibble with the response. However, the response will not do as a genuine explanatory reason. In terms of giving a full explanation of the parent's benevolent action, we will need to include her mental experiences as she focuses her attention on the child. She has a desire that the child's life go well for him, which involves feeling "impelled" to some degree to further his well-being. The impelling force of a desire I have characterized in terms of the dichotomous feeling tones of release and frustration—associated in this case with the respective beliefs (or imaginings) that the child's life is or is not going well for him. We will need to refer to these details if we are fully to explain the parent's benevolent act (as discussed more fully in section 3.1).

In sum, I affirm that humans are indeed capable of benevolent actions, which I have sought to characterize thus far in terms of the pursuit of another person's well-being. I am simply raising in this section the question of why we would seek to pursue another person's well-being (i.e., what motivates us to do so). My claim is that the answer will have to involve some positive mental experience we associate with our focus on the other person (either on the person herself or on an action that we believe furthers the person's well-being).

When we note these more nuanced ways in which benevolent actions are motivated by one's own positive mental experiences, we avoid the flawed supposition that purely benevolent pursuits provide no benefit to the one who pursues them. Stephen Post, for instance, has argued that "the religious image of the selfless saint is morally problematic because it fails to give an accurate picture of interpersonal relationships and their moral value" (1988, 214). Instead of idealizing "one-way benevolence," Post urges an alternative picture of "reciprocal exchanges of love." Post rightly notes that such exchanges are "sources of joy in themselves." Yet a crucial question is *how* a relationship characterized by joy gets established. I have urged that ideal relationships require each person to pursue the other person's well-being as an ultimate end and that each person's benevolent commitment must not be overridden by any self-interested pursuits, in keeping with divine coordination. I have also contended that ideal relationships established and maintained in this way will provide a person with experiences of "connecting" such that the person achieves ultimate flourishing. So I need not turn from any of my previous conclusions about the role of benevolence in order to say now, with Post, that reciprocal exchanges of love provide joy for those in the relationship.

Why would Post think that one's benevolent pursuit of another's well-being would *not* bring one positive mental experiences like joy in return? Post operates with an understanding of selfless love along the lines of Anders Nygren's depiction of *agape*, which involves being "spontaneous and unmotivated" and "pure and disinterested" (Nygren 1982). The idea of God's love (which the saints are said to mirror in important ways) being "disinterested" is apt to leave a wrong impression for at least two reasons. First, it may suggest that God could not *also* have self-interested goals as he pursues the goal of furthering a person's well-being. Although God would not allow the former goals to compromise the latter goal, we saw in section 5.1 that there is nothing about a firm commitment to the latter goal that necessarily precludes having the former goals. An action—for example, an interaction with someone else—can be performed as a means of achieving multiple goals. Second, the idea of "disinterestedness," if brought into discussions of benevolence, may suggest that one is somehow not attracted in any way to the goal of pursuing another person's well-being. But of course my discussions of the Humean model of motivation have brought out the point that the impelling force of a desire motivates *both* a benevolent action *and* a self-interested action (though again I think there are important phenomenological differences between these respective kinds of motivations). Although a benevolent action is not characterized by the *attempt to further* the positive feeling tone that moves, or impels, one to perform that benevolent action, the positive feeling tone is nonetheless what moves, or impels, us to perform the benevolent action. Accordingly, the benevolent action may satisfy the desire that motivated it, bringing enjoyment to the actor in question. Given that Post's understanding of benevolence is informed by ideas of "disinterested" and "unmotivated" pursuits, it is perhaps understandable that he would position mutually beneficial relationships as an *alternative* to interactions marked by benevolence. But there is no good reason to deny that desires (the satisfaction of which can benefit us greatly) can motivate, and be satisfied by, the genuinely benevolent pursuit of someone else's well-being.

The central line of discussion thus far in this section is really just spelling out the point—with benevolent actions in mind—that we are motivated to perform any action because that action is attractive to us in some way. When we focus our attention on objects, or when we consider possible actions we might take, we may experience a range of positive mental sensations with certain feeling tones to them. As regards benevolence, when we focus our attention on another person (or animal or sentient being) qua person with a welfare, or when we consider a certain action that we believe will achieve the goal of helping the person's life go well for him, we may find ourselves with an accompanying mental experience with positive feeling tones to it. These feeling tones motivate, or impel, us to act benevolently.

For the remainder of this section I want to address two related objections to my current line of discussion. First, it might be claimed that morally significant decisions involve seeing an action *as* some *kind* of action. Thus many moral philosophers emphasize the "universalizable" properties that an action might have—as well as the importance of performing an action because of these properties. Second, it might be claimed that, since I have depicted both benevolent and self-interested actions as motivated by desires, I have no way of making the important distinction between good motives and bad motives.

*i. Universalizability*

R. M. Hare was of course the most persistent and forceful advocate in modern times of the idea that the morally relevant features of a situation are universalizable features. Hare's most straightforward explanation of universalizability is as follows: "If we make different moral judgements about situations which we admit to be identical in their universal descriptive properties, we contradict ourselves" (1981, 21). Thus, when we make a genuinely moral judgment, we are making a judgment about a *kind* of situation. I do not want to focus on the distinction between the moral and the nonmoral. If we take common usage as a guideline, the term *moral* is a very, very nebulous term. I for one do not think there is much profit in trying to sharpen the moral versus nonmoral distinction (which, following some aspect of common usage, one might conceivably do in any number of ways).[1] So let us omit references to the potentially complicating criteria for a decision to be classified as a "moral" one. Let us instead simply focus on whether, in order for a decision to be character-shaping in such a way that it merits a central place in an ethical framework, the decision should be motivated by a consideration of features that are universalizable.

Taking my previous, brief depiction of a benevolent action being motivated by a particular kind of feeling tone when one considers that action (or considers simply the other person), I have made no mention of the features of that action (or person) that one might consider. And indeed I do not think we should insist that (character-shaping acts of) benevolence need involve any particular kind of consideration. It is true that some people may, in deciding whether to promote someone else's well-being in some particular way, identify features of the situation that are universalizable. For example, someone might recognize a neighbor *as* a person in need, might recognize herself *as* someone with resources, might recognize the gift of a meal *as* a gesture of support, and so on. Yet it is implausible to suggest that all attempts at benevolence will involve some recognition of features that could even in principle be put in universal terms. A toddler does not necessarily recognize his older sister's outburst *as* an act of crying or *as* a case of being upset. The toddler may not have previously witnessed any such act of crying and may not have the conceptual framework to identify features that we could describe in universal terms. There *is*, though, a certain feeling tone to the toddler's mental experience as he witnesses his sister's distress; and this feeling motivates the toddler to take a step toward his sister, reaching out to her in an attempt to alter her situation for the better. I see no reason to think why adults could not also have a similar, prereflective response to another person in distress. Adults can, without realizing it, physically lean forward or reach out their hands as an immediate response to another person in distress. Arguably, at least part of an adult's response to seeing someone in distress can occur *before* the adult recognizes the other person *as* someone in distress. At the very least, the example of the toddler shows that an act of benevolence need not necessarily involve any recognition of universalizable features.

Humans have a general desire for the well-being of others. Accordingly, there are (ceteris paribus) feeling tones—which I have characterized in terms of "frustration"—that come when we witness someone we believe in distress. (Feeling tones of "release" of course characterize our mental experiences when we witness others' joy and contentment.) It is perhaps an interesting question how we humans came to have this general desire for the well-being of others. Evolutionary biologists commonly suggest ways we humans might have developed this general desire. But most all of us do have this general desire, along with more particular feelings of affection toward our inner circles of family, friends, and colleagues. If the feelings of affection and concern for others—which I take to be part of a person's desire for others' lives to go well for them—*can* motivate us to seek to further their well-being, is there reason to insist that they *should not* so motivate us as we grow in our relationships with others?

Perhaps it might be argued that the positive mental experiences we associate with affection do not guarantee the *stability* of loving relationships, especially where some kind of self-sacrifice may at times be needed to sustain the relationship. Consider a parent who finds particular things endearing about her young child: the curly blond hair; the chubby arms; the timbre of laughter. Strong feelings of attraction and affection may well make it psychologically impossible *not* to work hard to ensure the child's well-being—at least initially. The problem, it might be argued, is that such attractions do not automatically lead to any kind of long-term commitment to further a child's well-being. The novelty of cute physical features wears off; and responsible parenting may require a parent to perform benevolent actions in spite of having, at that moment, minimal—if any—feelings of attraction to the child. A similar point can be made about two adults who are initially very attracted to each other physically but whose relationship will not be sustained down the road if they have no commitment to serve one another even during moments when they feel no attraction—and perhaps feel downright antipathy—toward one another. Love, as the saying goes, can at times be hard work. Accordingly, would it not be better, so this line of argument concludes, for benevolent actions within a relationship to be motivated by the recognition that there are (universalizable) features of one's situation that provide compelling reasons to perform these benevolent actions?

The first thing to note in response to this line of argument is that the mere recognition of some feature—that is, one's *belief* about some feature—does not itself *motivate* one to act. Recognizing some feature of a situation (and the same goes for other kinds of reflective reasoning, like thinking through the possible long-term effects of one's immediate actions) motivate us only inasmuch as we have certain mental experiences (namely, those associated with a desire) as we focus our attention on these features. True, the feeling tones that come when a mother looks upon the physical traits of her child may differ from the feeling tones she experiences when she reflectively considers some act of hers *as* an act of parental responsibility or *as* an act commanded by God. But the feeling tones, if they motivate her to pursue the child's well-being as an ultimate goal, will constitute positive mental experiences in either case. These motivating mental experiences, like all mental experiences, are subject to change. Accordingly, the motivation provided by our reflection on universal features may wax and wane from one moment to the next (just as the motivation stemming from a gaze at a child or lover's physical traits may wax and wane). Perhaps an empirical point can be made that the motivating feeling tones associated with reasoned reflection—as one sees one's situation *as* a kind of situation—are typically less likely to wax and wane than the feelings associated with a mother's initial gaze at her child's chubby arms or a husband's glance at his new bride's physical features. And if any kind of reasoned reflection helps foster the positive mental experiences that motivate us to further someone else's well-being in the short or long term, then so much the better. But there is nothing *necessary* about the role that reasoned reflection may play as one performs acts of genuine benevolence.

Further, if we insisted that the motivation to further other people's well-being should always involve a recognition of universalizable features that give us reason to further their well-being, we would rule out some of the best examples of loving relationships. One's affection for a long-term romantic partner may stem in large part from idiosyncrasies— the person's penchant for laughing at inopportune times or stubborn commitment to some rule-based ethic—that one finds downright annoying in other people (including other potential romantic partners). In truth, it seems doubtful that many, if any, of our loving relationships could be motivated solely by the consideration of features that can be abstracted from the person who has them. Bernard Williams's well-known allusion to the husband who has "one thought too many" (1981b, 18) is enough to cast doubt on the appropriateness in many of our relationships of higher-order reflections by which we see our interactions with the other person *as* some kind of interaction. In truth, a plausible argument can be made that *none* of our attractions stem from considerations of universalizable features. That is, perhaps it is dubious to suggest that one might have a pro-attitude toward a person because one sees him as instantiating some universalizable feature. Perhaps instead it is more plausible to construe one's pro-attitude toward some universalizable feature as a summary, or abstraction, of one's pro-attitudes toward the particular people who possess that feature.[2]

Having said all this about genuinely benevolent responses not requiring that our motivations stem from any process of reasoning, we should acknowledge the role that reason will inevitably play in ever-deepening relationships. In the section 4.6 discussion of "invitational statements" I noted that personal relationships are initiated when one person communicates to another in such a way that the other is invited to somehow respond to her. A deepening understanding of this invitation requires the use of reason on two general matters.

First, there is the matter of understanding who the person is who has invited me into a relationship. Second, there is the matter of the kind of relationship into which the person has invited me. As discussed in section 4.6, positive relationships require a meeting of minds on such issues.

Otherwise, our relationships are susceptible to misunderstanding, with the result that we must absorb the costs that come when others do not relate to us with a true understanding of who we are. And our relationships are susceptible to feelings such as anxiety (and later resentment), due to our lack of assurance that others will be committed to future projects and priorities as we hope they will be. In short, the use of reason makes it possible for us to achieve the kind of meeting of minds requisite for ideal relationships. It allows us to compile an accurate and ever-broadening understanding of God and of others as we relate to them for eternity.

This role for reason in no way implies that we must see our particular relationships with God and others *as* instances of something. It does not imply that our motivations in responding to God and others should be based on universalizable considerations. Again, such considerations *may* motivate us to respond in positive ways to God and to others; but there is no necessity about this kind of motivation.

*ii. Good and Bad Motives*

A second kind of objection to my early discussions in this chapter is that I have no way of distinguishing good and loving *motives* from bad and selfish motives. After all, I have emphasized that *any* intentional action is motivated by some kind of enjoyable mental experience that comes when we consider that action (or by the unpleasant mental experience that comes when we consider that action *not* being performed). And if, from the arguments of chapter 2, any positive mental experience is non-instrumentally good, then how could there ever be a "bad motive" for any action?

I want to focus on this question of whether I can—or need try to—account for a motivation being noninstrumentally good or bad. But first let us note that I can of course describe motivations as *instrumentally* good or bad. A person may have a positive mental experience that motivates a particular action. This action, as a factual matter, may lead the person to experience unpleasurable mental states—in the short run and/or in the long run. The action may lead others to experience unpleasurable mental states. The action may cultivate further motivations and habits that lead to further actions, with these further actions leading to unpleasurable mental states for the person or for others. These discussions might again arise in an analysis of the *instrumental* value of a particular mental state that serves to motivate some action. We might also engage in a comparative analysis focusing on counterfactual outcomes that would have resulted from a different original motivation. That is, we might say that the person or others "would have been better off" (in the closest alternative world) in terms of experiencing mental states if some original motivation—and the various actions and events that resulted—had not occurred.

But let us focus on the question of whether an actual motivation might be *intrinsically* bad (leading to the conclusion that it can be noninstrumentally bad). My contention will be that it is difficult to imagine any motivating mental state being *wholly* bad. And while I allow that there is some sense in which a motivating mental state could qualify as a "bad" one, it is a different sense from what moral philosophers traditionally have seemingly had in mind when denouncing the bad motivations that can give rise to objectionable actions.

First let me say why it would be difficult to imagine a motivating mental state being wholly bad. If we suppose that motivation consists of a desire(s) that some aspect of the world be a certain way, we can recall our discussion from section 1.4 that desires will typically carry dichotomous feeling tones. I have characterized these feeling tones as, respectively, a feeling of frustration (when our beliefs or imaginings about the world convey a picture at odds with our desire) and a feeling of release (when they convey a picture in concert with our desire). The feeling of release is of course one we would reflectively associate with the advancement of our own flourishing: it is pleasant or satisfying or in some way enjoyable. As such, it is—given the arguments of chapter 2 about the nature of noninstrumental goodness—good.

For a motivating mental state to be (intrinsically) wholly bad, it would need to be devoid of any positive feeling tone associated with the feeling of release. I am not sure such a scenario is possible. We would seemingly have to imagine a case in which a person viewed a particular action, which she went on to perform intentionally, as wholly undesirable. As to why she would perform such an action, the answer would have to be something like: because it was not psychologically possible to do otherwise. Whether or not such a scenario makes sense, it is at least safe to say that overwhelmingly most motivations will involve at least *some* positive feeling of release as one considers, or is, performing an action.

Motivating desires may of course differ as to whether the preponderance of the feeling tones associated with them are positive or negative. Thus, in choosing among broadly attractive options, my mental experiences may contain predominantly positive feeling tones as I shift my focus among the various options I am considering. Conversely, my mental experiences may contain largely negative feeling tones when I am faced with a range of broadly unattractive options from which I must choose. In this way, we might speak of one motivation as *better* than another motivation in that it contains comparatively more positive feeling tones (or less negative feeling tones). But this is hardly the sense in which moral philosophers historically have tended to speak of good or bad motivations. Instead, their (understandable) concern has been to stress that concepts like culpability and blameworthiness are linked, not simply to a person's actions, but also to her dissolute state of mind that in some relevant way preceded her actions.

While I agree that assessments of character must of course involve a person's states of mind and dispositions, I also think that any reference to a "bad desire" is a potentially misleading—if not misguided—way of spelling out concepts like blameworthiness. Desires, again, are nothing more than a combination of pleasurable and unpleasurable feeling tones. Take some state of affairs, such as a child being comforted or a child being disappointed. If we are attracted to either of these states of affairs, this is simply another way of saying that we experience a pleasurable feeling tone as we consider it. Does it make sense to say that a pleasurable feeling tone could be "bad" in any sense?

Again, we could certainly offer an account of how it could be *instrumentally* bad. On the Christian worldview, a desire to see a child disappointed is an instrumentally bad thing, if for no other reason than that it serves to tempt one away from the pursuits that God invites us to pursue with him—thereby closing off avenues of connecting with God. We could also raise questions about why some person has an enjoyable mental experience at the thought of a child being disappointed; and we could explore whether the conditions for culpability—whatever they are—

were met such that the person can rightly be blamed for his current condition.

In terms of the *non*instrumental badness of someone's pleasurable feeling when considering a child's disappointment, we can again make the comparative point that it is not nearly *as* enjoyable a feeling as other feelings. We might also make the point that pleasurable experiences at another's expense, when cultivated, have diminishing returns as far as the extent to which they really are pleasurable. And it may be that, in many cases of schadenfreude and other similar mental experiences, the experience as a whole is itself a life-diminishing experience on account of the negative feeling tones (associated, e.g., with shame at the fact that one has any positive feeling tones at all) within the experience outweighing the positive feeling tones within the experience. Nevertheless, per the discussion of schadenfreude in section 2.6, any genuinely positive (i.e., pleasurable) element within a mental experience is, again by definition, a noninstrumentally good thing.

What, then, of our assessments of people's character? Can we distinguish good and laudable states of mind from bad and loathsome states of mind? I think appeals to instrumental badness and goodness, and to comparative states of value, allow us to make the kinds of character assessments we find it useful to make. Of a person who continually follows self-interested desires at the expense of benevolent desires, we can note all the ways in which this habit or cultivated disposition may cause others extreme harm. We can note how his experiences will have diminishing returns in terms of his own flourishing. We can note all the future, good things that will be precluded—as well as all the future, bad things that will arise. There are thus plenty of angles from which to press the point that the person's character is bad: bad for him and for others. We can again also make comparisons to counterfactual scenarios in which following alternative motivations would have led to much greater flourishing for himself and for others—both in the short term and in the long term. In sum, there are plenty of reasons for us to reach the conclusion that a person's character is decidedly bad. The point I have defended is merely that the intrinsic qualities of a person's motivating desires are not the place to draw the distinction between good and bad character.

## 6.2 "Morally Significant" Decisions

In the previous sections I discussed some of the ways I think we should *not* characterize morally significant decisions. As a quick review, I am using the phrase *morally significant decision* to denote a decision that moves one either toward or away from the life of ultimate flourishing that Christianity affirms is possible for each person. A life of ultimate flourishing, on the analysis I provided in chapter 4, is one in which we have mental experiences of connecting with God and others within ideal relationships. We again establish such ideal relationships through mutual decisions to pursue the other's well-being. In this current section, as well as in the next one, I want to offer further ways of analyzing and understanding this kind of decision.[3]

In advancing the claim that "morally significant decisions" are decisions whether to pursue another's well-being or to pursue one's own well-being, I do not want to suggest that other kinds of decisions are unimportant or dispensable, even to the maintenance of ideal relationships. I do want to draw attention to the specific kind of decision that ultimately determines *whether* we will have the eternal, ideal relationships that Christians describe as existing in heaven. Still, a number of conditions are of course needed for ideal relationships to exist: desires to pursue various joint projects; affections for, and interests in, particular people; positive mental experiences that accompany our interactions with others and that thus provide motivation to continue these interactions; and so forth. Also included among these conditions are certain choices we make, such as the choice to pursue a certain, attractive project and the choice to engage with a particular person because one feels particular affection for that person. The Christian picture of divine providence, though, is that God will ensure that nearly all the conditions for ideal relationships are guaranteed. More specifically, God will ensure that each of us will have sufficient interests in projects and particular other people to preclude ennui and general lack of interest, which of course would undermine our flourishing. Equally, God will ensure that enough *other* people have interests and affections for each of us, allowing for meaningful interactions that lead to all people's ultimate flourishing.

Some of these points were examined in our section 4.5 discussion of divine coordination.[4]

I discussed in section 5.5 the importance of God allowing people to exercise meaningful freedom (i.e., to causally contribute, as agents, to events without being caused to do so). Again, of central importance here will be freedom in responding to God's invitation to relate to him and to others. In preserving this freedom, God will not unilaterally ensure that *all* the conditions for ideal relationships—and thus for people's ultimate flourishing—are met. God will allow us to help determine whether, and how, we will relate to God and others. I now want to distinguish more sharply the decision "whether to further another's well-being or one's own" from other decisions one might make. And I want to say more in defense of the idea that this decision is indeed morally significant in a way that no other decision is.

There are obvious cases in which our individual pursuits of projects do not in any way affect some relationship we have. For instance, my decision to choose tuna over chicken at the deli lunch counter has no effect on my relationship with my wife. Other individual pursuits, though, would clearly undermine our relationships—for example, if I sold the family home on a whim without consulting my wife. To maintain the kind of partnership my wife and I have established within our marriage covenant, I would need to consult her about such decisions. A failure to do so is a failure to consider, and pursue, her interests.[5] Where there exists no failure to pursue someone's interests, then my decision to pursue one favored project over another is not a morally significant one. It leads me neither toward nor away from the kind of ideal relationship described in chapter 4. It is true that my decision, say, to pursue guitar lessons over tennis lessons may affect *which* specific relationships I do or do not develop over time. In pursuing guitar lessons, I may make it more likely that in the future I will pursue projects and form relationships with those people who have developed a musical interest. But my decision itself to pursue one favored project over another, supposing that I am not aware of anyone else's welfare being at stake, neither cultivates nor undermines a disposition to relate to others in benevolent ways.[6]

For the many possible pursuits that are neither obviously immaterial nor obviously detrimental to a relationship, there will need to be a meeting of the minds in terms of which self-interested pursuits each person can pursue without potential harm to the relationship. As discussed in section 4.5, divine coordination will ultimately be needed to achieve this meeting of minds. When the kind of agreement in question is achieved, then the self-interested pursuits one undertakes (such as attending a book club instead of spending the evening with one's spouse) do become immaterial to the relationship. That is, they have no bearing on whether the relationship is an ideal one marked by the benevolent pursuit of the other person's well-being.

Having noted the way in which nonbenevolent pursuits may or may not undermine one's pursuit of another person's well-being, it is worth exploring whether one benevolent pursuit might undermine some *other* benevolent pursuit. Given that we move toward ideal relationships by pursuing others' well-being, what of the possibility that I might fail to pursue one person's well-being by in fact pursuing another person's well-being? Happily, an appeal to divine coordination allows us to say how we can avoid potential difficulties related to *whose* well-being we prioritize. In short, there is no reason to think that God cannot ensure that each person has sufficient people who prioritize that person's well-being and whom that person in return prioritizes—where *sufficient* indicates what is needed for that person to engage in a network of ideal relationships that provide for her ultimate flourishing.

Of course, a happy outcome here supposes that all people in the social network *are* taking their cue, in deciding whose interests they are free to prioritize, from God. What of the danger, though, that a person might prioritize someone else's interests *over God's* interests? We are imagining here that a person is prioritizing someone else's interests over her own interests. It is just that God's interests—and specifically God's coordinating directives that identify the individuals at whom our benevolent actions should be aimed—are not pursued. This scenario is potentially problematic for the ethical framework I am outlining. As we saw in section 4.5, without our pursuit of God's coordinating directives, people's ultimate flourishing cannot be secured. Yet is it possible that a person might make the kind of morally significant decisions I have advocated—namely, choosing to pursue others' well-being instead of her own—and still open the door to the problematic scenario where God's directives are not followed? If so, this presents a serious objection to my thesis that our ultimate flourishing is secured when we consistently pursue others' well-being instead of our own.

In response, I think it can be shown that any pattern of genuinely benevolent actions actually *will* lead one to follow God's directives. If I am genuinely pursuing someone else's well-being, then, ceteris paribus, I will avail myself of the best (known) means of realizing that person's well-being. If I did not avail myself of these best means, we would (again, ceteris paribus) rightly question whether my project really was the benevolent pursuit of the person's well-being. On the Christian understanding of God, a shared pursuit with God of another person's well-being will always be the best way of achieving that person's well-being. God is, after all, more committed to the pursuit of any person's well-being than we are; God knows better than we do what will make any person's life go well for her; and God has enormously greater resources than humans do in working to ensure any person's well-being. We could make these points about God in comparison to *any* person or group. A failure to pursue God's interests, as we pursue someone else's interests, could occur for only two reasons: either we fail to have correct beliefs that, by following God's directives, the person's well-being will be best secured, or we *do* have these correct beliefs, but we succumb to weakness of will.

A failure to hold correct beliefs about God may be something for which a person is culpable or nonculpable.[7] Let us suppose a case in which, for nonculpable reasons, a person does not believe that the pursuit of another person's well-being is best achieved by ensuring that this pursuit is consistent with God's directives. One's choice to pursue another person's well-being instead of one's own will still, we can maintain, constitute a morally significant and instrumentally good decision—even if this pursuit is made in isolation from God's directives. At least, we can maintain this point on the assumption that God will allow only decisions that are within our ultimate control to determine whether we attain the ideal relationships and ultimate flourishing for which we were created. Given the way habits are formed and character development occurs, a choice to pursue someone else's well-being instead of one's own makes one, ceteris paribus, more likely to choose benevolence over self-interest in the future. This is especially true given the Christian thesis that, while there are diminishing returns to what can be gained through selfishly ignoring the plights of others, there are in contrast increasing returns to benevolent patterns of behavior. Even if done in ignorance of the resources represented by God's directives, the decision to pursue someone else's well-being instead of one's own makes one more like the kind of person who naturally pursues the interests of God and others. Once such a person acquires true beliefs about the ongoing work and commitments of God (which could conceivably happen in this life or the next), she will readily, ceteris paribus, include God's directives in her decision-making procedure as she continues her pattern of benevolence. So, in sum, choices of benevolence over self-interest constitute positive, morally significant decisions—even where one is ignorant of the benefits of, and need for, God's coordinating directives in ensuring that one's benevolent efforts are effective. One is still moving toward—not away from—the fixed disposition that allows one to take a place within the heavenly network of ideal relationships.

If a person *does* hold true beliefs that her pursuits of someone else's well-being are best achieved by ensuring that her pursuits align with God's coordinating directives, then a failure to align her pursuits in this way seemingly constitutes a straightforward case of *akrasia*. When we pursue our *own* well-being, we can (all too often) settle for some lesser good because of the cost of pursuing a greater good. Recall here our earlier example of the imprudent person who watches a late movie while recognizing that he has more to gain by turning off the television and getting a full night's sleep. Similarly, we may sometimes pursue *others'* well-being in ways that are weak-willed. A parent may find it too difficult to discipline a child, even while believing that such discipline is the best way to prepare the child for the greater adversities the child will face in the future. A person may hesitate (indefinitely) to confront a friend with a difficult truth, even while believing that the friend needs to be confronted if the friend is to change certain self-destructive tendencies that will eventually lead to long-term problems.

The difficulty in disciplining or confronting others surely often stems, at least partly, from the unpleasantness that inevitably accompanies a confrontation. Suppose now that the motivating desire of a friend, as she resists confronting another friend, is the desire to avoid undergoing the uncomfortable experiences that come when we confront another person. If so, then the friend's concern of course is her *own* well-being. And it seems correct to say that the decision to avoid confronting the friend is in this case not, after all, a decision to pursue another person's well-being instead of one's own. The decision is still a morally significant one; but the decision is a "negative" one in that it moves one *away* from the pattern of behavior that disposes the redeemed in heaven always to pursue the interests of God and others to the extent directed by God.

While a self-directed focus on the unpleasantness of confrontation can amount to a negative, morally significant decision, let us instead suppose that one's resistance to confrontation is motivated by a concern for the *other* person's feelings. We imagine here that one's concern is not one's own discomfort but rather the pain the *friend* will feel if confronted. Keeping with a Humean model of motivation, one is, as before, motivated by various negative feeling tones as one considers confronting the friend. But here we imagine that the negative feeling tones arise when one considers the pain that the friend will experience if forced to face some difficult truth. Of course, perceived greater, long-term aspects of the friend's well-being are sacrificed, given that the person, ex hypothesi, does think that the friend will suffer even greater pain in the long run if the friend does not change his pattern of behavior. But the motivation in pursuing the friend's lesser good remains, we imagine, a benevolent concern for the friend's well-being.

To the extent that one's motivation here in pursuing another person's perceived lesser good is indeed (we are supposing) a benevolent one, then I think we should maintain that it constitutes a positive, morally significant decision. For the decision itself moves one toward the pattern of benevolent prioritizing that marks the relationships within the heavenly community. To be sure, a person's akratic pursuit of someone else's lesser good will reveal various contingencies that are keeping the person from acceding to God's directives and thus from participating in ideal relationships. For instance, we can imagine cases where an intense shyness or fear of upsetting others really is crippling in the sense that these things make it genuinely psychologically impossible to confront the friend. Or we might imagine cases where one becomes emotionally distraught at the idea of having to confront a friend. Owing perhaps to unresolved conflicts in one's past or to painful memories (even if suppressed) about abusive confrontations in one's childhood, the act of now confronting a friend may be a genuine psychological impossibility for someone. In these cases, we imagine that a person is still pursuing the other person's well-being instead of her own; it is just that the pursuit takes the form of pursuing a perceived lesser good because the greater good is psychologically impossible. Still, the person is indeed, as much as lies within her power, choosing to prioritize her friend's well-being over her own. And so in such cases I think we again should describe an akratic pursuit of someone else's lesser good as constituting a positive, morally significant decision.

It is worth here making the general point that the most we can do in *any* circumstance is to pursue another person's well-being as best we understand it and within the range of what is psychologically possible to us. If our (single) project is another person's well-being, then we may not always be able—because of ignorance or other factors that render us unable—to pursue this project in a way that best brings about that person's well-being. But these contingent factors are among those contingencies that will not, so I am maintaining, ultimately determine whether we attain ideal relationships within the heavenly community. On the Christian ethical framework I am outlining, any contingency that might prevent ideal relationships and ultimate flourishing for every person will in time be removed—save one. This one contingency is the free decisions we make whether to pursue others' well-being or our own.

The general thesis I am defending is again that we move toward the settled, benevolent dispositions characterized by those in ideal relationships when we choose to pursue others' well-being instead of our own. A further, potential objection to this thesis arises when we consider that some patterns of benevolence we witness are seemingly *self-destructive*. I am thinking here of the person who continually accedes to the demands of an overbearing friend or manipulative work colleague or spoiled child or abusive spouse. Instead of helping develop positive relationships with others in these cases, one's engagement in such relationships seems primarily to bring disappointment, depression, and an injurious self-image. What is the "moral significance" in such contexts of the benevolent choice to prioritize others' interests over one's own?

The first thing to say is that we must be careful in isolating one's ultimate goals to be sure that the pattern of behavior is indeed one of prioritizing others' well-being over one's own. A so-called martyr's complex can stem from various self-interested desires: to generate compassion from others who see one as a victim; to have others recognize the selfishness of those to whom one is always deferring; to cultivate a self-image as one who is entirely innocent and who owes no reparation to anyone; and so forth. But suppose we stipulate that, as one relates to others in the excessively deferential way we are imagining, self-interested pursuits are excluded as one's ultimate goals.

Excluding self-interested goals does not automatically mean that one's excessively deferential behavior is genuinely benevolent. Suppose, for instance, that a girl grows up identifying with her mother in a home where both of them are intimidated by her controlling father. We can imagine the girl reaching adulthood and then repeating the patterns of behavior she saw modeled by her overly deferential mother. Her motivation to defer to others' interests might be motivated by an amalgam of feelings associated with familiarity, fear, and guilt. Her actions would in this case *not* be an example of a (morally significant) decision whether to pursue others' interests or her own.[8]

Suppose it is possible, though, to sort through the complications of the previous two paragraphs and arrive at a case in which a person truly is performing benevolent actions. And this pattern of behavior comes at a cost to her own well-being, leading to experiences of depression and resentment instead of the positive mental experiences associated with connecting with others within ideal relationships. Her benevolent actions, we are supposing, are actually *hindering* her flourishing. Does such a case undermine the thesis that the choice of benevolence over self-interest moves one *toward* the ideal relationships in which all people's ultimate flourishing lies?

I think this would be the wrong conclusion. Wherever genuinely benevolent choices are made, I think these decisions do help one become the kind of person who can participate in ideal, self-giving relationships fully realized in heaven. It is just that, in our current example, the person's decisions in this life happen to be undermining certain other conditions needed for ideal relationships: freedom from unhealthy emotions such as fear and timidity; freedom to pursue personal projects to which one is attracted; loving care from others who support one's projects; and so forth. The promise from God, Christians understand, is that such contingencies will not ultimately determine whether one takes one's place within the heavenly community (in which a state of ultimate flourishing is secured). God will provide opportunities to explore the desires he has given us, he will heal damaged emotions, and he will ensure that we receive a loving and reciprocal commitment (from himself) more firm and sacrificial than that of which any human is even capable. In such a context it would be impossible to focus *too* much on others' interests. So I acknowledge that, in this earthly life, there can be cases in which a continuous, benevolent focus on others exacerbates the negative impact that unreciprocated concern and unmet needs have on us. But on the assumption that such contingencies do not exist in heaven, there seems no reason to think that we might focus too much on others. And inasmuch as any benevolent act in this earthly life moves us toward the fixed dispositions we need to take our place within the heavenly community, then in this sense any benevolent act in this earthly life can rightly be described as worth pursuing.

Thus far I have discussed morally significant decisions as though they are decisions in which one consciously weighs the contrasting, ultimate ends of furthering someone else's well-being or one's own. We should add at this point that a great many of our decisions do have moral significance even though they do not involve such a conscious focus. Sometimes the decisions we make are "implicit" decisions to further someone else's well-being. And even when such implicit decisions are not made, the decisions we make can at least affect our desires and subsequent decisions whether to further someone else's well-being.

As an example of an implicit decision, a person one day may resolve to treat strangers more kindly, to listen more carefully to those who voice complaints, or to show more generosity to those who ask for help. In making this resolution, a person may be mindful of past instances in which, by his own accounts, he has been too brisk or indifferent or stingy. But the person may not have any specific individuals in mind toward whom he is resolving to act more generously. Perhaps he just wants to be a better person or a more faithful follower of God. His decisions nonetheless amount to implicit decisions to prioritize the interests of Anne, or David, or Marie, or whomever else he then encounters and treats differently as a result of his previous decision to be more generous to others.

Aside from such obvious cases in which a decision to further someone's interests can follow inevitably from a previous decision, a great many other decisions at least influence the shape of our desires and make us either more or less disposed in the future to prioritize others' interests over our own. We can choose to reflect on how others might feel as we interact with them, putting ourselves in their shoes. We can inquire as to how others feel more generally, what their interests are, what opportunities might be available to them, what assistance might be most helpful to them, and so forth.

Much of our character is shaped by the way in which we continually reflect on, and imagine, our place in the world. We humans have an ever-present need to make sense of the world, to interpret and categorize our observations and encounters. Making sense of the world of course involves, crucially, identifying some role(s) that we ourselves play in relationship to other things and other people. This quest to arrive at, and maintain, a fixed and desirable picture of ourselves takes any number of forms, ranging from focused self-analysis to "mindless" daydreaming. We think through past conversations with others, we remember past accomplishments and disappointments, and we do a lot of imagining. We imagine ourselves winning some prize, or being feted at work, or being admired by some attractive person, or winning some argument, or at least being bolder about standing up for ourselves, or being a hero of some kind. We can also imagine ourselves being more patient with family members, or deflecting undue credit, or spending our money on others in need, or giving gentle answers to colleagues, or being an enduring peacemaker.

While our choices to continue these kinds of patterns of thinking may not rise to the level of an implicit decision whether to further someone's well-being, the habits we develop as we cultivate various patterns of thinking nonetheless greatly affect the motivation we may come to feel to further someone else's interests in a particular situation. In this sense much of the imagining we do every day—as we consider our place in the world—is morally significant: it affects our inclination to focus on, and pursue, the well-being of others at those times when we are faced with the decision whether to pursue their well-being. When we continue to focus on our own interests and well-being—whether we imagine ourselves as the hero or as the victim—we naturally develop a greater and greater concern for our own well-being. On the other hand, when we continually focus our attention on the feelings and interests of others, these things naturally become more important to us. So there are a great variety of ways in which our ongoing choices move us toward or away from the set of fixed, benevolent dispositions needed to participate in ideal relationships. These decisions thus have moral significance, even while we may have no one's well-being in mind when we make them.

For any decision we make that does have moral significance, complications may arise in discerning whether this significance is positive or negative—that is, whether the decision moves us toward or away from ideal relationships. Consider a case of so-called "pursuit behavior." Tess, we imagine, is nearing retirement and decides to take a young, new colleague, Teresa, under her wing. Tess constantly gives her advice on what she should say, how she should act, and even what she should wear in the workplace. Tess often inserts herself into conversations Teresa is having with others, justifying (to herself) this practice on the grounds that Teresa must be saved from saying the wrong thing. Tess initiates all the (unwanted) "help" she offers to Teresa; and we can imagine Tess believing that she is sacrificially donating her own time and energies to further Teresa's well-being. Yet we can also suppose that Tess's true, ultimate goals are self-interested ones. For example, Tess might feel threatened by Teresa. Perhaps Tess has had a number of problems with colleagues at work, and Teresa does not seem to have these same kinds of problems that Tess had when she was Teresa's age. This recognition prompts the uncomfortable thought that she, Tess, might be more responsible for her earlier problems than she has been willing to accept. Tess continues to tell herself that she is only trying to save Teresa from the same problems she experienced. But her actions, we imagine, are actually motivated by the desire that Teresa, Tess, and their colleagues all recognize that she (Tess) is in no way worse than Teresa and that she herself would not have had her own problems if she had had a mentor like the one Teresa currently has.

This example is but one of any number of examples we could explore in showing the difficulties in determining whether some action really is a benevolent pursuit or a self-interested one. Very often, of course, a person's motivation will be mixed—even when one recognizes that self-interest and benevolence are incompatible in the instance in question. Recognizing that self-interest prevents me from always prioritizing

God's directives with ease, I may resolve to pursue an act of pure benevolence, trying my best to set aside self-directed concerns. I may then perform an act of service toward my neighbor; and an ultimate goal of my action may genuinely be my neighbor's well-being. Yet, try as I might, there may remain a self-interested goal that my boss (who is a friend of my neighbor) be impressed when he hears of my charity. The phenomenon of mixed motivations of course raises the possibility that a given action may in some respects cultivate benevolent dispositions characteristic of those in ideal relationships, while in other respects weakening such dispositions.

The examples from the past few paragraphs highlight some of the immense complications that arise in assessing whether some decision we make is one of benevolence or self-interest (or both). Whatever the complications, though, on the substantive question of whether some action really is a benevolent or self-interested one, the formal point remains. Decisions are morally significant if they move us either toward or away from the set of fixed dispositions needed for humans to participate in ideal relationships.

I have noted briefly in a few places that an act of benevolence can be analyzed from either an "outward" or an "inward" perspective. An outward perspective involves focusing on the ultimate goals a person seeks to achieve through that action; an inward perspective focuses on the feeling tones of the desire(s) that motivate the act of benevolence. The analysis of benevolence—and of self-interest—in this section has primarily been an outward one. In the next section I shall explore morally significant decisions from an inward perspective, looking at the contrasting feeling tones that motivate, respectively, benevolent and self-interested pursuits. An analysis of motivating feeling tones, it turns out, will be a clearer guide as to whether a given action moves one toward or away from the fixed, benevolent dispositions needed for ideal relationships.

## 6.3 Feeling Tones as Our Indication of the Good

The outward analysis of benevolence has been useful for various reasons. Foremost, it helps us see the implications of our everyday decisions. We may act without conscious awareness that we are actually prioritizing our own well-being over someone else's well-being (or vice versa). And we may make decisions that do not involve any other specific person's well-being. Even so, our decisions and patterns of action may move us either toward or away from the consistently benevolent dispositions needed to participate in ideal relationships within the heavenly community. An outward analysis of benevolence also helps us see that, from a Christian perspective, benevolence and self-interest exhaust the possibilities of settled, final human dispositions.

While this outward analysis helps in identifying common outcomes to which our everyday decisions lead, we saw in the previous section that the ways in which our decisions can lead to these outcomes are extremely varied. Given this wide variety of contexts in which morally significant decisions can occur, is there any way to identify a *commonality* to morally significant decisions *themselves*? An outward analysis of benevolence and self-interest seems to offer little help here. Again, an outward analysis is useful in identifying the dual, common *outcomes* to our everyday, morally significant decisions. But I am asking now about a commonality to the benevolent decisions themselves and to self-interested decisions themselves. In this exploration an "inward" analysis of benevolence and self-interest is much more promising.

When we reflect on the phenomenology of striving to perform benevolent actions, I think we find a unique set of feeling tones that move us to perform benevolent actions, whenever we are motivated to do so. I discussed this point briefly in section 6.1, and I would like now to say a bit more about it.

It is more difficult in some cases than in others to discern the differing feeling tones associated with, respectively, the desire to further someone else's well-being and the desire to further one's own well-being. In cases of close relationships where, as Aristotle put it, we form a kind of "we-self" with another person, the feeling tones of benevolence and self-interestedness are mixed and difficult to separate. When we love a spouse or a child or a close friend, we do want their lives to go well for them. If a situation called for it, we would be willing to sacrifice aspects of our own welfare to ensure that their welfare was enhanced. Along with these desires to see our loved ones happy, we also recognize that our own lives would be greatly impoverished if our relationships with them ceased. Our interactions with them are crucial for our own well-being; and we strongly desire to spend time with them, in the way in which we desire to engage in other (self-interested) activities and pursuits that bring us enjoyment. Again, cases of close relationships are marked heavily by both kinds of desires I am intending to distinguish: desires that impel benevolent actions, and desires associated with self-interested pursuits. Still, this point does not undermine the proposal that the feeling tones associated with, respectively, benevolence and self-interest really are distinct.

Cases in which we can more readily distinguish the contrasting phenomenology of benevolent versus self-interested motivation are those in which we view benevolence as coming at the expense of (aspects of) our own welfare. For instance, we may be mindful that a donation to Oxfam will preclude our purchase of a leisure gadget; and we recognize that we will never experience the positive feedback from knowing how, and to what extent, anyone was genuinely helped by our donation. We may thus approach our decision of whether to donate the money as a straightforward matter whether to look after others or ourselves. Even within close relationships, there will be times when we view the pursuit of others' interests as coming at the expense of our own interests. We may recognize that a family member or friend needs our time when we would rather relax, or needs our participation in a project we do not especially enjoy, or needs an apology when we ourselves are struggling with feelings of being a victim. In cases where we feel the diverging pulls of the desire to help others and the desire to look after our own interests, I think some phenomenological patterns emerge.

While mindful of the limits of public language, let me suggest three ways we might characterize the feeling tones that accompany those cases in which we choose to pursue others' well-being despite feeling the pull to do something different as a way of preserving our own well-being. These three recurring themes to our experiences in such cases can perhaps best be cast in terms of nobleness, second-order approval, and surrender. When we pursue others' well-being at cost to ourselves, there arises a feeling that our action is more noble than if we had chosen instead to pursue our own well-being. This sense of nobleness is, as mentioned earlier, that which we imagine Sydney Carton to experience at the end of *A Tale of Two Cities* and that leads him to talk about the "far better thing" he is doing. Whatever else might be said in some situation both for pursuing others' interests and, alternatively, for pursuing one's own interests, we have a sense that the former option is the more noble one.

We also feel a kind of second-order approval about our benevolent actions that we do not feel about our self-interested ones. Admittedly, we sometimes approve of our own self-interested actions. A timid person may, for example, applaud her recent efforts to "stand up for herself" by demanding rightful credit for a work project or by refusing to give in to the demands of overbearing relatives. But there is, I think, a unique kind of approval that we reserve for benevolent actions. While we approve of a timid person's courageous attempts to stand up for herself, the approval we give of Sydney Carton's actions is not based simply on the fact that he exhibits courage. There is a certain "purity" to his motives that put them, we think, beyond question. Even if we deem some person's (extravagantly) benevolent act as unwise or a bit rash, we still applaud the person's motives. Perhaps the unique kind of approval we bestow on benevolence is best seen in the way communities define and praise certain heroes: whether the soldier who falls on a grenade to save his platoon, or the educator who works with troubled children, or the teenager who cares for a disabled parent. Communities bestow a certain kind of commendation on such people. And this commendation is not identical to that which is bestowed on inventors, entrepreneurs, and artists—who benefit a community and whom a community therefore also has reason to praise. Further, communities confirm the second-order sentiment we have that any personal rewards that happen to come to us from our genuinely benevolent actions can be embraced without the fear of others' disapprobation. In sum, the approval we offer of benevolent actions is unique. And when we find ourselves with the contrasting attractions to a benevolent pursuit and to a different, self-interested pursuit, there is a unique feeling tone (associated with approval) that makes up part of the former attraction and not the latter.

My suggested third way of characterizing the feeling tones associated with desires to perform benevolent actions involves the idea of surrender. When faced with the choice between prioritizing others' interests or our own, we feel, when we choose (or sometimes even consider) the former option, that we are *deferring* to others. There is a sense of "giving in" when we surrender to a cause outside ourselves; and this same sense of giving in is just not present when we resist our benevolent desires to focus instead on our own needs. Even when we conclude that we *should* in fact prioritize our own needs in some instance, we do not feel this sense of submission that, I think, uniquely characterizes the desires to perform benevolent actions. While we do not feel this sense of surrender in cases where the pulls of benevolence and self-interest coincide, we do feel this impulse when the desire to pursue benevolence is accompanied by a countervailing impulse toward self-preservation that recommends an opposing action.

The decision whether to pursue someone else's interests or one's own can thus be recast in terms of a decision whether to embrace and cultivate the feeling tones associated with benevolent desires or with self-interested desires. This of course is not to say that the experiencing of these feeling tones is the *ultimate end* we will seek to achieve. But the feeling tones of a desire are nonetheless what motivate us. And in analyzing benevolent actions from the "inward" perspective of motivations (as opposed to the "outward" perspective of the ultimate goals on which we focus our attention), a choice of benevolence over self-interest will be a matter of which (respective set of) feeling tones we add our efforts to, in willing some action.

Consider how we can use an inward analysis of feeling tones to explain why a decision is morally significant, even while that decision does not admit to a straightforward, outward analysis in terms of pursuing the end of another's well-being over one's own. Suppose that two friends, Stan and Simon, form a "we-self," as Aristotle put it, in the sense that each friend very much desires that the other person's life go well for him. Each friend's own happiness depends in significant measure on his beliefs about whether the other person is happy. We imagine that, as Stan and Simon interact with one another, each person pursues as an ultimate goal the well-being of the other person.

Suppose the relationship is then ruptured. Perhaps Stan becomes offended or disillusioned or simply annoyed with Simon. Stan now turns his attention from the pursuit of Simon's well-being to other matters. What exactly are these other matters? Possibly, these other matters may be Stan's own well-being. That is, Stan may say to himself, "This relationship isn't working for me," and he may consciously focus, as an ultimate goal, on his own well-being, resolving to pursue new activities and relationships through which he will reap greater rewards. In this scenario, it seems obvious that Stan is choosing whether to pursue his own welfare or the welfare of another person. But of course the obviousness is largely due to the fact that our example thus far is a neat and tidy one.

Suppose instead we imagine that Stan, in turning from his pursuit of Simon's well-being, does not consciously reflect on his own well-being as an ultimate goal. He may simply allow his thoughts to wander when Simon attempts to speak to him; or he may continue reading a book instead of picking up the phone when he knows that Simon is trying to phone him. Even if we allow—which we should—that people can fail to be aware of the ultimate goals they are in fact pursuing, Stan arguably may make no inferential calculations (at any level of consciousness) about how his actions toward Simon are affecting his own well-being. I say this point is arguable because it is not entirely implausible to suggest: "Of course Stan is looking after his own welfare; after all, he has some awareness that he will be better off by not taking Simon's unwanted phone call." However, I think it more plausible to allow that Stan may well have no settled beliefs about how his turning away from Simon will affect either his own short-term or long-term well-being. Perhaps he does not enjoy the book he is reading, is fighting the lethargy that is keeping him seated on the couch, and realizes that he needs to get up and do *something* different to make the day more rewarding. Yet he may still glance at his phone's caller identification and resist taking Simon's call, remaining instead on the couch reading his boring book.

If we think of Stan's state of mind (including his beliefs) when deciding not to answer the phone, we again seem to have trouble analyzing his decision in terms of a decision to pursue the ultimate goal of his own well-being over Simon's well-being. But we *can* still offer an inward analysis of the contrasting feeling tones that move him to pick up the phone and, alternatively, to resist doing so. As Stan resists picking up the phone, the feeling tones to which he adds his efforts are ones we might describe as associated with lethargy (like the motivation to continue watching a late-night movie when one knows one ought to go to bed) and stinginess (like the motivation to take some resource for oneself, knowing that others will miss out as a result).[9] This is only an initial stab at describing these motivating feeling tones; but we should not have too much difficulty imagining the kind of feeling tones that in our example motivate Stan to ignore the phone call. By contrast, the feeling tones (which Stan resists) motivating Stan *to* answer the phone are ones we might describe as associated with difficult charity (like the motivation to listen to a troubled friend when one has had a trying day oneself) and self-denial (like the motivation to exercise early in the morning on a day one really wants to sleep in, because one has a long-term goal of good physical health). These latter feeling tones are associated with (an inward analysis of) benevolence, whereas the previously described feeling tones of lethargy and stinginess are associated with self-interested pursuits. To state now the important point: Stan's decision not to answer the phone arguably is not any conscious decision to perform a "self-interested action instead of a benevolent one." Still, he chooses to add his efforts to certain feeling tones, while resisting the pull of contrasting feeling tones. And these feeling tones *do* (at least partly) make up the contrasting sets of feeling tones that motivate us whenever we face choices between benevolence and self-interest. In making his choice to ignore the phone call, Stan is resisting the kinds of desires that characterize the settled motivations of those in ideal relationships; and he is cultivating the kinds of desires that are consistently followed by those who have decisively rejected God's invitation to join the network of relationships that mirror the ones within the Trinity.

I have thus far tried to offer a rough guide to distinguish, phenomenologically, the sets of feeling tones associated with, respectively, benevolence and self-interest. For a given person, there is a straightforward way of pinpointing the specific desires the cultivation of which will lead that person toward or away from the set of fixed dispositions needed to participate in ideal relationships. As a formal point, the desires the person needs to resist are those that might tempt her from acceding to God's directives at all times. Conversely, the desires that need to be cultivated are those that help dispose her to accede at all times to God's directives.

As noted briefly in section 5.6, each person on earth will have a different set of obstacles that at present are preventing a fixed, benevolent commitment to others characteristic of those in ideal relationships. As a result, the same general action may, if performed by different people, have different implications as to whether, and in what way, the action is morally significant. Consider again the example of Stan, who refuses to answer Simon's phone call. It may be for Stan that this action *is* morally significant and that the feeling tones that impel him not to answer the phone are the ones we often associate with vindictiveness or with "hard feelings." Perhaps Stan has a habit of wishing ill on those who have offended him, often imagining them "getting their comeuppance" and taking a kind of pleasure in that thought. These kinds of feeling tones will need to be purged if he is to enter into ideal relationships with others; and his choice whether to answer Simon's phone call has moral significance largely because it is a chance either to cultivate or to resist desires with these kinds of feeling tones.

Steve, we imagine, has also been offended by Simon. He too faces a choice whether to answer the phone when Simon calls. Steve, though, does not struggle with, or even at all feel much of the force of, vindictive feelings. The feeling tones that motivate him to ignore Simon's phone call have more to do with a "superiority complex," or a need to appear powerful. Steve does not particularly desire to hurt Simon by ignoring him; Steve is not really thinking of how his actions will affect Simon. But Steve *is* very cognizant at present that tomorrow he will be relaying to his circle of friends the events of the day before. And Steve relishes being able to tell a story in which he has neither the time nor inclination to be bothered by people of Simon's ilk. Steve enjoys the feelings we associate with self-importance; and he expects to experience those feelings when he recounts the story of how he spurned the advances of Simon. Desires that contain these feeling tones for Steve are of course an obstacle to the set of fixed, benevolent dispositions needed for ideal relationships. Our point here is that these kinds of desires are different from the desires that impede Stan's attainment of fixed, benevolent dispositions.

An act of refusing to take a phone call may in other cases move a person in *some* respects *toward* settled, benevolent dispositions, while moving her in *other* respects *away* from such dispositions. Let us imagine that Sarah has also been offended by Simon and is subsequently faced with a decision as to whether to take his phone call. Suppose Sarah decides to answer the phone, overcoming the kinds of desires that Stan and Steve faced. But suppose also that Sarah's father has advised her to ignore Simon. In this case we can imagine that Sarah is cultivating certain desires that help dispose her toward benevolent actions: a desire that Simon not feel rejected and isolated; perhaps a desire to be the kind of person who does not allow schadenfreude to gain a hold on her; perhaps a desire to strengthen her commitment to God by following God's commands to forgive others. The cultivation of these kinds of desires seems pretty clearly to move Sarah toward a settled, benevolent disposition. Yet it may be that part of her motivation in answering Simon's call is associated with continued anger at what she judges to be the overbearing manner in which her father dispenses unsolicited advice. She has a desire that her father witness the good outcomes that occur when his advice is *not* taken. And this desire, we suppose, is not merely a wish—consistent with healthy relationships—that her father come to appreciate that his actions are causing the daughter to feel alienated from him. Rather, we suppose that the daughter's desire is more in line with an angry wish that the father experience the hurtful feelings of alienation—whether or not such feelings ultimately bring healing to their relationship. This kind of desire of course needs to be eradicated, as it serves to tempt her *from* the kind of benevolent commitments she needs in order to engage in ideal relationships. So in sum, her action of picking up the phone may work toward cultivating *some* dispositions she will need in order to participate in ideal relationships, while working toward cultivating *other* dispositions that, if unchecked, will ultimately make ideal relationships impossible.

In still other cases, a choice whether to answer a phone call will be morally *in*significant. That is, it will move one neither toward nor away from the set of fixed, benevolent dispositions needed for ideal relationships. Sven may be among the pool of individuals offended by Simon and may be debating whether to answer a phone call from him. Sven may also have the kind of self-destructive personality discussed at one point in the previous section: he has an overwhelming fear of standing up to others and making his own wishes known, with the result that he is not able to participate in the kind of "give-and-take" characteristic of collaborative pursuits that provide occasions for our positive experiences of connecting with others. If Sven picks up the phone, unable to resist his fear of offending others, his decision will not amount to cultivating any feeling tones associated with desires to act benevolently. And so the decision will not move him *toward* the settled dispositions of those in ideal, self-giving relationships. (We are again supposing that Sven does not experience either of the contrasting feeling tones associated with desires toward benevolence and toward self-interest; he instead is wrestling with the pull of self-destructive emotions that do not admit to either of these kinds of feeling tones.) Equally, if Sven *resists* picking up the phone he will not be moving *away* from the settled, benevolent dispositions of the redeemed. For he will not be cultivating any self-interested desires that may tempt him away from following God's directives. His reason for resisting picking up the phone, we suppose, is his conscious attempt to try to overcome what he recognizes as a crippling fear of standing up for himself. True, Sven's decision to pick up (resist picking up) the phone will have negative (positive) effects on his own self-image, his ability to express his desires, the value he places on his own needs, and the like. But these matters involve various contingencies that must be in place if a person is to engage in ideal relationships. I have again suggested a Christian framework in which such contingencies will eventually be removed and will not ultimately affect *whether* Sven engages in ideal relationships within the heavenly community. In sum, then, Sven's choice whether to answer the phone, though certainly important in the implications it has for his own ability to flourish in the here and now, does not have the kind of ultimate, moral significance that it had for Stan, Steve, and Sarah.

To cite just one more case of how the moral significance of an action changes as the feeling tones that motivate that action (subtly) change, consider Sally-Ann and Sally-Beth. As with our previous examples, we imagine that each person is deciding whether to answer a phone call from Simon. Additionally, let us suppose that each person really gives no thought to how answering the phone will affect Simon. "He won't really care whether I answer the phone or not," each person tells herself. Still, Sally-Ann and Sally-Beth both have a nagging feeling that they really ought to answer the phone. This general feeling, we imagine, is the result of what J. S. Mill called "customary morality": a pattern of instruction and social sanction to which Sally-Ann and Sally-Beth were both exposed from childhood. This customary morality included propriety in recognizing and responding to forms of communication such as letters and phone calls. If asked why they feel they ought to answer the phone, both Sally-Ann and Sally-Beth will probably say something like "It's just the right thing to do." For each person, there exists a vague feeling—stemming ultimately from a long string of encounters with social sanction from childhood onwards—that an act of ignoring a phone call will be cause for disapproval and sanction (even if no specific, disapproving person can be identified).

What *distinguishes* the two of them, let us now imagine, is that Sally-Ann (but not Sally-Beth) wrestles with a persistent desire to rebel against authority figures—even against those whom Sally-Ann recognizes as having legitimate authority. This desire hinders a consistently benevolent pattern of behavior toward others, particularly toward others who make claim to various authority-making features. And this desire of course affects the overall mental experience she has as she feels the contrasting motivational pulls to answer and to refrain from answering the phone. Sally-Ann again has a vague feeling that, by not answering the phone, she will invite disapproval (even if she cannot identify a specific person who might disapprove). Mixed with this vague feeling is a feeling tone we associate with the desire to resist others' claims to authority. Though she cannot identify anyone specifically who will disapprove if she ignores Simon's phone call, her vague association of this action (of ignoring the call) with social sanction from (unnamed) others is sufficient to incite her persisting desire to resist claims to authority. Her thought process might be something like "If anyone wants to make a big deal of me not answering the phone call, that's just more reason not to do it! What right does anyone have to tell me whom I should talk to!?" Suppose Sally-Ann finally opts to answer the call, overcoming these feelings we associate with defiance. Her decision is morally significant because, in making her decision, one of the desires (among the various desires we might identify that contribute to her mental experience at the given slice in time) that she resists has the potential to prevent her from ultimately attaining settled, benevolent dispositions.

By contrast, we can imagine that Sally-Beth also decides to answer the phone but that her decision is *not* morally significant. Like Sally-Ann, she is motivated to answer the phone by a vague feeling of obligation. But we imagine that the feeling tones that make up Sally-Beth's motivation do not include any feeling tones that could ultimately tempt her from the settled, benevolent dispositions of those in ideal relationships. (Sally-Beth has no problem with proper authority, we are supposing.) Her decision to answer the phone is more along the lines of Donald Davidson's example of the person who realizes that he has forgotten to brush his teeth. Although he is exhausted and judges that there is more reason to remain in bed than to get out of bed to brush his teeth, his "feeling that [he] ought to brush [his] teeth is too strong for [him]" (2001, 30). And he succumbs to this motivating association with the conventionally right.

What this discussion points up is that the moral significance (or lasting impact on ourselves) of our choices is tied to the kinds of feeling tones we resist or add our efforts to. When we cultivate desires with certain kinds of feeling tones, and as these desires come to motivate us more and more, we become more and more like the redeemed in heaven: inclined to follow God's directives without being tempted to do otherwise. I have sought to describe these feeling tones in terms of nobleness, second-order approval, and surrender. Again this description is by no means as complete or fully nuanced as it might be. (I invite help from others.) But I do think we can appeal here to the phenomenology of those times when we feel the impulse to better the position of others, even while perhaps thinking that our own position may in some way be compromised by doing so.

Nagging thoughts may remain that *feeling* tones are just not "weighty" enough to ground the moral significance of our actions. Surely, it might be thought, the consequences of heaven and hell cannot be a matter of what feeling tones we choose to cultivate. But *all* choices, if Hume's model of motivation is basically correct, are a matter of what feeling tones we choose either to cultivate or to resist. It is true that part of God's communication to people, as he seeks to make them fit for heaven, will involve truths that we need to believe. After all, if we want to join God in the work he is doing, and if we want to help others effectively, we need true beliefs about how we can achieve these goals. Further, continued cognitive reflections on the character and work of God may be a prerequisite for vital responses to God that we need to make within a maturing relationship with him. But if we are to have a say, as an ultimate cause, in how we relate to God and others, our choices will be a matter of adding our efforts to certain kinds of desires and not others. Accordingly, much of God's efforts in drawing us to himself will involve sparking certain desires we have.

Far from being a peripheral part of our mental experiences as humans, the kinds of feeling tones God leads us to cultivate arise in a huge variety of activities. When we read articles and news reports about the suffering of others, we feel an urge to reach out in some way and help them. Reading novels and poems can cause us to shift our conscious focus from ourselves to the plights and viewpoints of others (fictional or real), generating new, positive feelings as we do so. Listening to inspiring music or viewing a sublime painting can "soften our hearts" toward others—that is, can diminish the pleasure we feel when we think of an adversary getting his comeuppance, while increasing the pleasure we feel when we consider forgiving an adversary. Witnessing a scene in nature can remind us of the many activities and projects beyond our own creation, stirring our desires to seek out projects that do not center on ourselves. In limitless ways the kinds of desires that can prompt benevolence can be stoked.

## 6.4 Some Theological Connections

In Part II I have offered an ethical framework for understanding the Christian claim that God invites us to participate in the good life. I have not attempted any systematic review of Christian theology. However, in this final section I want to connect, even if very briefly, some of the broader themes that have emerged in Part II with selected Christian doctrines.

Some of the discussions in chapters 5 and 6 have already touched directly on Christian doctrine. Specifically, I have looked at the doctrines of heaven and hell in my discussion of the way in which our morally significant decisions (as I have called them) inevitably lead us toward one of two end points: either settled dispositions to act benevolently or settled dispositions against benevolent pursuits. My discussion of the final dichotomy between benevolence and self-interest straightforwardly allows the theist to say why heaven and hell exhaust the final possibilities for all people.

I have also noted in chapters 5 and 6 the various ways in which God might communicate to people as a way of prompting them to make benevolent choices. Christians take this prompting as part of God's efforts to draw people into the ideal relationships for which they were created. In more theological terms, a doctrine of prevenient grace—at least as articulated by religious figures like John Wesley, who stressed the universal nature of prevenient grace—will understand God as drawing (though not irresistibly) all people to himself, whether or not they yet have beliefs about, for example, the person and work of Jesus Christ. The discussions in this chapter allow us to say how God can do this.

We have seen that a person's choices between benevolence and self-interest can affect the final shape of her relationship with God and with others, even if she is not aware of this consequence. Sometimes God may prompt us by helping us to hold certain beliefs. And indeed, specific beliefs about God are necessary for a person to have an explicit relationship with—that is, to have "explicit faith in"—God.[10] Nevertheless, much of God's prompting will take the form of stirring our desires to act benevolently. In more theologically precise terms, the stirring of our desires will be a form of communication from the Holy Spirit, spurring us to join in the loving works that Jesus Christ is already undertaking in other people's lives. And there are again limitless contexts in which we might experience the kinds of desires associated with benevolence to which we can add our efforts, thereby moving us toward the settled, benevolent dispositions needed to participate in ideal, heavenly relationships.

I offered in section 5.5 reasons why the kinds of interpersonal relationships we humans can have with God would not be possible if God did not allow us freedom to serve as ultimate causes. These reasons, along with the enormous difficulty I think theological determinists face in accounting for all the evils in our world (especially the evil of some persons being separated from God for eternity), would serve as the main philosophical arguments I would offer against the idea that God irresistibly draws (a limited number of) the elect to himself. Still, there is nothing in my emphasis on the role of our benevolent choices that undermines more broadly the Christian doctrine that salvation comes by faith and not by works.[11] The theologian can complement my discussions by maintaining, for example, that God enables us to make the benevolent choices we make and that, as we strive to change our dispositions, God changes our dispositions in ways we never could by ourselves through mere habit. The theologian can also emphasize the earlier point that God invites us into a relationship where he is lord of our lives. Thus, when choosing whether to pursue God's interests or our own, we will all at some point face this choice of whether to defer to God's objective of directing our lives. Given that Christians understand God's directives as including our acknowledgment of our own shortcomings and need to be saved (through the atoning work of Jesus Christ) from the predicaments brought about by these shortcomings, we will all face the choice—when we relate to God as lord—whether to relate to God as savior. In sum, there is nothing within the ethical framework I have offered that precludes the complementary, Christian affirmation that we are "saved by faith."[12]

Doctrines about the nature of God have been debated historically within the Christian tradition—including the question of whether we can *add to* God's flourishing or eternal joy. In characterizing morally significant decisions in terms of decisions whether to promote another's welfare or one's own, I will be committed to the idea that it *is* appropriate to speak in terms of humans acting with the goal of furthering God's welfare.[13] Not all Christians have been comfortable speaking in these terms. For example, after noting that Martin Luther did use the language of Christians "endeavour[ing] to please God" (Luther 1833, 42), Robert Adams comments, "It is not likely that Luther thought that he could increase the (doubtless infinite) sum of God's pleasure.... The motive he commends, therefore, is presumably not a general and abstract desire for the augmentation or maximization of God's pleasure as such, but rather the particular and self-regarding, agent-centered desire *to act* in a way that is pleasing to God" (1999, 141).[14] I am not sure what it would mean for God to have an "infinite sum" of pleasure. But I do want to comment on the view that we cannot add to God's well-being. Frankly, I do not think there is anything compelling to be said for this view. If one allows for the possibility that we might "grieve the Holy Spirit" (Eph. 4:30), and if one thinks of God as joining in the "rejoicing in heaven over one sinner who repents" (Luke 15:7), then I do not see how one might *not* think of us as affecting in some way God's well-being. If, as discussed earlier, we can act apart from God's deterministic control, then we can affect, as ultimate causes, whether some of God's plans for us come to fruition. Perhaps we should view "rejoicing" and "grieving" as anthropocentric and analogous descriptions of what God experiences when his plans (which involve drawing us into eternal relationships that provide for our ultimate flourishing) for the creatures he loves do and do not come to fruition. Nevertheless, if these terms are to be analogical (and not simply equivocal), I do not see how we could deny that one effect of God grieving (or rejoicing) is that God's life in at least *some* way goes worse (or better) for him.

It should be clear from the discussions of Part II how I will understand the nature of sin. Pursuing one's own interests at the expense of others' interests moves one away from the self-giving relationships into which God invites us. While there is not space here to defend the claim that the vices Christians have emphasized historically are all perversions—through the pursuit of self-interest at the expense of others' interests—of some virtue, I think that claim can indeed be defended.

Understanding morally significant choices along the lines I have indicated allows us to see how sinful choices can indeed be freely made. More traditional summations of the nature of sin often do not allow scope for such free choices. That is, these summations often do not provide a clear answer to the formal questions: What exactly do we choose *to do* when we choose to sin? And what is the nature of the alternative, virtuous choice we might have made? The account of the fall in Genesis 3 has often been taken by Christians as the prototypical sin, revealing to us the root of sinful choices humans make. It is common among Christians to hear Adam and Eve's disobedience explained in terms of their lack of *trust*. Certainly, if we link 'trust' with *action*, then Adam and Eve's disobedience exhibited a lack of trust.[15] But the deeper question is the ultimate goals one is seeking to accomplish when one acts in disobedience to God, along with the motivation that leads one to do so.

In addressing these questions, references to pride are commonly favored among Christian theologians historically. Augustine proclaimed that "[sinful] things are done whenever Thou art forsaken, O Fountain of Life, who art the only and true Creator and Ruler of the universe, and by a self-willed pride any one false thing is selected therefrom and loved" (2008, bk. III, §16, 37). Peter Lombard stated that "pride is the root of evil, and the beginning of all sin" (1854, bk. II, dist. xlii, 7). Martin Luther remarked that justification before God is possible only when humility overcomes pride (1961, 5, 105–6). Accordingly, Joseph Butler, in his discussion of resisting temptation, noted that "religion consists in submission and resignation to the Divine Will" (1970, xv, §9). My own ethical framework is in line with the general tenor of these comments, given that a decision whether to prioritize God's will or one's own can be recast as a decision whether to prioritize God's well-being (or interests) or one's own. So much, then, for the question of how we spell out the alternative goals associated with, respectively, choices of virtue and vice.

But we will also need to account for the *motivation* to pursue each of these alternative goals if we are to say how it is that both alternatives are psychologically possible options between which a person might freely choose. The common references by theologians to pride often give the impression that it is one's *beliefs* that somehow motivate both choices of virtue and choices of vice. The choices of Adam and Eve are depicted as prideful because, instead of trusting God for their well-being and security, they came to regard their own opinion (as informed by the serpent) about these matters more highly than God's opinion. Thus John Wesley links pride to "idolatry; it is ascribing to ourselves what is due to God alone" (1984–87, II, sermon 44, II, §7, 179). So the motivational work of pride within Adam and Eve seemingly amounts to a *belief* that, by following their own opinions instead of God's dictates, they will best secure their own well-being. Aside from the lingering question of how beliefs might move us to action (cf. section 3.1), we can ask at this point whether beliefs are something we choose. I have argued elsewhere that, at least in standard cases, belief is involuntary (Kinghorn 2005, chap. 2). And so it becomes untenable to suggest that the nature of moral choice involves a choice *to believe* one thing over another.[16]

Happily, the choice to pursue someone else's well-being over one's own is indeed the kind of choice a person can freely make. (I discussed in sections 5.4 and 5.5 how and why, from a Christian perspective, God has provided us with dual motivations to pursue each end.) It seems untenable to read the account of the Fall in Genesis as Adam and Eve "choosing to believe" the serpent's narrative over the one God had given them, or as "choosing to believe" that they knew better than God how their own welfare could best be secured. But it *is* certainly intelligible to spell out this choice in terms of a decision to pursue God's interests or their own. Or, to analyze the choice from what I have called an "inward perspective," we can make sense of Adam and Eve's dual motivations in terms of the contrasting feeling tones (to which they were free, qua agents, to add their efforts) associated with benevolent pursuits and with self-interested pursuits. This account of the nature of morally significant choices accords well with the Christian emphasis that the sinful choices of Adam and Eve—again as a prototype for all human sin—amounted to a prioritizing of self-autonomy over deference to God.

Further, within the ethical framework I have offered one can readily make sense of how sin entered the world, even while upholding the Christian affirmation that God did not create a world with sin, or moral evil, in it. As noted at various, earlier points, the natural dispositions and reflective pro-attitudes we have toward our own flourishing serve us well in this world. At the same time, these instrumentally good dispositions and attitudes can at times recommend a course of action at odds with an action that (we believe) will promote someone *else's* flourishing. Thus these dispositions and attitudes provide scope for understanding the Christian theologian's dual affirmations of (1) theistic monism (as opposed to a dualistic understanding of good and evil as essential forces) and (2) the phenomenon that all humans (including the first ones) have faced temptation to sin.

Finally, our broader ethical framework allows us to acknowledge, with the Christian scriptures, both the pleasures and the self-destructive aspects of sin. From our discussion in chapter 2, any pleasure *itself* associated with sin is no bad thing. But given that a sinful pleasure arises from the pursuit of a self-interested action at the expense of someone else's interests, the effects of this action move one away from the kinds of self-giving relationships through which we can experience ultimate flourishing. Sin will have diminishing returns in terms of the pleasures it can afford. As one's dispositions become more and more resistant to the pull of benevolence, the opportunities lessen for the kind of mental experience associated with "connecting" that must be part of our overall mental experiences if these overall experiences are to be positive ones. Since benevolent pursuits are necessary if we are to establish ideal relationships with others, and since these ideal relationships are necessary for our long-term flourishing, our depiction of sinful choices as choices of self-interest over benevolence allows us to say why it is that the pleasures of sin cannot last. By contrast, the pleasures associated with connecting with others are ever-increasing, as our network of positive relationships increases and deepens.

From the discussions of this final chapter, the nature of morally significant decisions in the end amounts to the kinds of positive, motivating mental experiences to which we choose to add our efforts. I have again characterized the feeling tones associated with the motivation to act benevolently in terms of nobleness, second-order approval, and surrender. There may of course be other ways of trying to characterize them. But I submit that they are distinct from the kinds of positive feeling tones that motivate us to pursue our own well-being. Discerning which kinds of positive experiences to cultivate requires wisdom; and we must lean on (and instruct) others as we learn together about the kinds of pursuits that have, respectively, ever-diminishing and ever-increasing returns. And we must practice prudence and temperance, not allowing our pursuits of immediate enjoyments to come at the expense of greater, long-term enjoyments. The Christian religion is of course one that points to the possibility of eternal enjoyments beyond our current comprehension. The great paradox of the Christian religion is that these enjoyments are realized when we prioritize others' enjoyments above our own.

NOTES

*Introduction*

1. See, e.g., Baggett and Walls (2011), voted *Christianity Today*'s book of the year in apologetics. Or see the numerous YouTube debates on the subject, spearheaded by William Lane Craig.

2. Foot (2001, esp. chaps. 2–4). Cf. Thompson (1995) on the relationship between "Aristotelian categoricals" and evaluative judgments.

3. Or for "states of affairs" substitute "bearers of value" if one thinks that these are something other than states of affairs. See Zimmerman (2001, 52–64) for this discussion.

4. See Adams (1999); Baggett and Walls (2011). Adams in particular will be a key interlocutor throughout a number of sections in this book. It is largely because I find his work so outstanding that I use him as representative of various viewpoints against which I will argue. Contra Adams, I find it more plausible to conclude that all noninstrumental value is welfarist value; that a semantic analysis of "good" adds further plausibility to a welfarist picture of value; that "mere benevolence" really *is* sufficient for ideal relationships; and once again that the search for objective wrongness is a vain one.

*Chapter One. The Meaning of* Good

1. But see also Paul Ziff, who argues that the dictionary definition (on which Ross partly relies) of *good* in terms of "commendation" is somewhat misguided (1960, 229–32).

2. For the difference between the attributive use of a word and the predicative use of a word—a distinction we need not explore here—see Ross (1930, 65); Geach (1956, 33).

3. I will discuss exceptions later in the chapter.

4. On the subjective nature of this sense of "experience," Thomas Nagel offers the useful analysis that "an organism has conscious mental states if and only if there is something that it is like to *be* that organism—something it is like *for* the organism" (1979b, 166).

5. Cf. John Locke's analysis of the sensations of pleasure and pain: "These like other simple *Ideas* cannot be described, nor their Names defined; the way of knowing them is, as of the simple *Ideas* of the Senses, only by Experience" (1975, bk. II, 20, §1).

6. R. M. Hare goes so far as to remark that "it is perhaps an analytic truth that everybody wants to flourish, because 'I want not to flourish' sounds at least logically odd" (1981, 78). Though not affirming it as an analytic truth, the *Catechism of the Catholic Church* reads: "We all want to live happily; in the whole human race there is no one who does not assent to this proposition, even before it is fully articulated" (pt. III, sec. I, chap. I, art. II, II, §1718).

7. Philippa Foot, in summarizing her own adaptation of the Aristotelian tradition that links the good with *life*, remarks, "The fact that a human action or disposition is good of its kind will be taken to be simply a fact about a given feature of a certain kind of living thing" (2001, 5). In this chapter I am explaining *why* there is a conceptual link between life and our use of the term *good*.

An interesting complication—which I cannot explore—to my discussion here involves the way children first come to experience their own flourishing as in fact *their own*. Those in the field of psychology may advise that newly born children *develop* an understanding of *self* over time. And this opens the door to a small child's developing some appreciation for well-being—interacting with, especially, his mother—before developing any understanding of self-hood. The child would come to experience the phenomenology of "flourishing" before experiencing the phenomenology of "my own flourishing." If this scenario is indeed possible, then I think my discussions in this chapter could be adjusted without any significant loss. It remains safe to say, on my own account, that a person would not be able to appreciate the concept "good" without first having an appreciation of "my experiences of flourishing"—even if "my experiences of flourishing" did not equate with "my experiences of *my own, singular* flourishing."

8. Of course, to gain a conceptual understanding of "good" and "bad" in the first place, I will have needed in some way to reflect on the common phenomenology for my respective experiences of flourishing and failing to flourish.

9. See Kraut (2007, §21) as to why we could not speak of "good" in the sense of "good for" without specifying at least *some* things about the person whose interests are answered to.

10. Cf. Bernard Williams: "On various occasions we want certain outcomes; we usually want to produce those outcomes; we usually want to produce them in a way that expresses our want to produce them. Obviously enough, on those occasions we do not want to be frustrated, for instance by other people. Reflecting on all this, we can see that we have a general disposition to want not to be frustrated, in particular by other people. We have a general want, summarily put, for freedom" (1985, 56).

11. For anyone who herself has these goals, a pro-attitude would of course accompany this evaluation that the seats are good. Cf. Railton (1986, 166): "It would be hard to make much sense of someone who sincerely claimed to have certain ends and yet at the same time insisted that they could not provide him even prima facie grounds for action."

12. As Korsgaard (1983) has pointed out.

13. In section 2.4 I shall discuss this point at more length that it is one's *belief* that one is engaging in some activity that gives rise to our experiences of flourishing.

14. There are various ways to analyze a desire, admittedly only *one* of which would be to explore the phenomenology of a desire. Further, not all desires we may have will have a certain phenomenology to them that we can recognize through introspection at that moment. (Cf. Hume's comment that, in contrast to the recognizable phenomenology of "violent" passions, or desires, there also exist "calm desires and tendencies, which, tho' they be real passions, produce little emotion in the mind, and are more known by their effects than by the immediate feeling or sensation" [1978, II, iii, 3, 417].) But for the purposes of this project, the aspect of a desire with which I will be most interested is its phenomenology. The main danger of restricting a discussion of desires to a discussion of their phenomenology is that it (too easily) opens the door for the critic to argue that desires are not sufficient to explain certain actions of ours—for example, why we tend to act in accordance with our moral judgments. (See the discussion in Smith [1994, 104–11].) As will become clear in chapter 3, however, I will in no way use our narrower, phenomenologically based analysis of desires to argue *against* Humean models that rely on desires to explain our pursuits of what we believe to be good and/or right. Rather, in chapter 3 I shall very much defend a Humean model in explaining the nature of normativity in general.

15. To my mind, the terms *release* and *frustration* best capture these respective phenomena; but there is nothing crucial about these terms. Hume's lan-

guage is that, "when we have the prospect of pain or pleasure from any object, we feel a consequent emotion of aversion or propensity, and are carry'd to avoid or embrace what will give us this uneasines or satisfaction" (Hume 1978, bk. II, pt. iii, §3, p. 414).

16. The reason this is almost always—and not always—the case will be discussed in section 3.2.

17. Again, the ethical framework I myself wish to advance in this book does not depend on there being any important distinction between moral goodness and nonmoral goodness. I am merely giving an account here of what would make an action or event such that it would amount to an overriding consideration or a consideration of special normative weight that so-called nonmoral goods, by comparison, would not have.

18. Cf. Moore's comment on the so-called naturalistic fallacy mentioned earlier: "Even if ['good'] were a natural object, that would not alter the nature of the fallacy nor diminish its importance one whit. . . . Only the name which I have called it would not be so appropriate as I think it is. And I do not care about the name: what I do care about is the fallacy" (1993, §12).

19. Adopting the view that the Good is to be identified with God, Baggett and Walls observe that "the affinities between the Platonic conception of the Good and God himself are so pervasive and striking at so many levels that it is hard to exaggerate" (2011, 95). See pp. 92–95 for the authors' concise overview of why "God" and "the Good" have been equated by various Christian thinkers.

20. Gen. 1:31: "And God saw every thing that he had made, and, behold, it was very good" (KJV).

21. One might further press the point that God's recorded declarations about our world in the earlier parts of Gen. 1 (e.g., verse 10) include descriptions of our world before it contained sentient life. Thus, one might continue, the only one who *could* flourish would have been God; and God's flourishing cannot be increased. In response, I should first note that I find this strong view of God's impassibility quite problematic, as I will discuss later in section 6.4. But leaving that point aside, God's earlier recorded declarations about an as-yet-lifeless world surely do not automatically rule out the interpretation that God was considering the ways in which the world *would* affect the flourishing of future, sentient creatures, answering to their interests.

22. *Expository Dictionary of Bible Words*, ed. Lawrence Richards (Grand Rapids, MI: Zondervan, 1995), 315–16.

23. *Dictionary of Scripture and Ethics*, ed. Joel B. Green (Grand Rapids, MI: Baker Academic, 2011), 332.

24. Sentences as colloquially expressed are, after all, commonly misleading when strictly analyzed. When explaining a broken vase lying on the floor, one

rarely says, "I held the vase between my hands with a pressure insufficient to keep the vase from falling." One instead typically says, "It slipped." The structure of this colloquial statement implies that the vase is something other than a passive object. But of course none of us is tempted to conclude that the vase actively wriggled in any way analogous to an escape artist who "slips" a knot tied around his wrists.

25. Perhaps instead the critic will argue that we are *not* in fact using this same concept "good" when we refer to things to which we assign intrinsic value. That is, perhaps as we grow into adulthood we acquire a new, more mature understanding of the concept "good"—along the lines of "valuable in its own right"—that can be applied to objects, attitudes, practices, and events whether or not they answer to anyone's interests. But, problematically for the critic's proposal here, we still could not grasp and apply this more mature concept without at the same time holding onto (at some level of consciousness) an appreciation of the distinction between flourishing and failing to flourish. Suppose a person somehow lost the capacity to have mental experiences that were phenomenologically distinguishable to her in terms of pleasure and unpleasure. Suppose this person also remembered only a select few of her previous mental experiences, which happened all to have been equally pleasurable. Such a person could not appreciate the idea that some event was desirable (versus undesirable). For she would be able neither to experience at present, nor to recall, the contrasting feeling tones of "frustration" and "release" associated with a desire. Her consideration of any object or event might give rise to various mental states; but they would be mental states among which she would have no preference. In short, she would lack the background a person needs to form the view that something is desirable or valuable. Thus my argument against the idea of a more mature concept of good will be: this more mature concept of good (as meaning "valuable in its own right") *cannot* in fact be conceptually divorced from the idea of answering to someone's interests. To appreciate that anything can be valuable, we have to draw upon our appreciation of the contrasting experiences of flourishing versus failing to flourish (or having our interests answered to versus not answered to).

26. This obvious contingency means that, even if Sidgwick is correct in suggesting that "when beauty is maintained to be objective, it is not commonly meant that it exists as beauty out of relation to any mind whatsoever: but only that there is some standard of beauty valid for all minds" (1981, bk. I, chap. ix, §4), we still do not have an avenue for concluding that objects have qualities that are beautiful in an objective sense.

27. J. S. Mill observed: "Questions of ultimate ends are not amenable to direct proof. Whatever can be proved to be good must be so by being shown to

be a means to something admitted to be good without proof. The medical art is proved to be good by its conducing to health; but how is it possible to prove that health is good? The art of music is good, for the reason, among others, that it produces pleasure; but what proof is it possible to give that pleasure is good?" (1987, chap. I, 275). Cf. Michael Zimmerman's remarks about how we might defend such principles as

> *Pleasure in the good is intrinsically good.
> *Pleasure in the bad is intrinsically bad.
> *Displeasure in the good is intrinsically bad.
> *Displeasure in the bad is intrinsically good.

"Justification for the assignment of these intrinsic values would appear straightforward. (It is hard to *argue* for the truth of the principles. Their justification can only come from an appeal to intuition)" (1980, 35). (While I take Zimmerman's point about the inevitability of appealing to intuitions at some point, it will become clear in the next chapter that I think a good deal more can be said for and against the various principles that Zimmerman outlines here.) Cf. also Roger Crisp: "Intuitions appropriately reflected upon are unavoidable in ethical theory" (2006a, 636). For a brief discussion of what an intuition *is* exactly, see Crisp (2006b, 78–79).

*Chapter Two. The Nature of the Good*

1. For further discussion, see Sumner (1996, 6–7, 16–17).

2. While most moral philosophers have tended to talk in terms of the contrast between pleasure and *pain*, pain is a rather poor candidate as a contrary to pleasure. Bouts with poison ivy and mosquito bites make for experiences very much opposed to pleasure. But maddening itches are not at all naturally described as *pains*. How "pain" came to be the accepted contrast to "pleasure" is unclear to me. Happily, though, as Stuart Rachels observes, "'Pleasure' does have an antonym: *unpleasure*." Rachels also remarks: "If you don't believe this is a word, look it up" (2004, 248).

3. See, e.g., the discussion in Feldman (2004, chaps. 2 and 3).

4. Hedonists like Bentham, J. S. Mill, and Sidgwick all spoke of "happiness."

5. The question of how we might possibly compare states of well-being among different subjects (especially among different *kinds* of subjects, such as nonhuman animals) is a question beyond the scope of this current project. What for our purposes is important is that the range of subjects that are capable of

being harmed or benefited will include, and be limited to, subjects with a mental life.

6. Cf. Kraut's comment, given in defense of his own focus—within his study of the good—on what is good *for* individuals: "One can say that it is bad that people feel pain, and then support that claim by saying that it is bad for them" (2007, 73). For Kraut's further reasons why a focus on what is "good for" is more promising than a focus on what is "good that," see Kraut (2007, §18). Kraut's own ethical framework has important resemblances to my own: an emphasis on welfarism; a priority given to the good over the right; and suggestions for identifying what a good human life consists in. Our accounts differ as well in important ways: his rejection of mental statism; my own specifically Christian answer to substantive questions about human well-being; and my attempt to focus on human motivation for seeking the good. I mentioned this last point in my introduction, commenting that moral philosophers in the Aristotelian tradition (like Kraut) offer a more "teleological" (to give it a name) analysis of the good, while leaving unanswered what seem to me to be crucial questions about why we have pro-attitudes toward the good. Thus the methodology I myself favor in analyzing the good builds on the psychology of how we come to understand the concept "good" (chapter 1) and goes on to focus on the mental states that motivate us to pursue it (chapter 3).

7. See Kraut (2007, §19) for a further discussion of why the good of pleasure is surely noninstrumentally good for us, rather than merely good as a means to some further end we might have.

8. For a discussion of what hedonism *is* exactly, see Feldman (2004, chap. 8).

9. See Sumner (1996, 83–112). See also Crisp (2006b, 103–11).

10. Beyond these two broad considerations, see also Rachels (2000), Smuts (2011), and Bramble (2013) for how the internalist can plausibly respond to various, further objections that have been leveled at internalist accounts of pleasure and unpleasure.

11. Cf. Gosling (1969, 37–40); Griffin (1986, 8); Sumner (1996, 92–93); Sobel (2002, 241).

12. While Feldman (2004) stresses the importance of one's *attitudes* toward one's mental sensations, see also the externalist view of Heathwood, who stresses one's concurrent *desires*: "A sensation S, occurring at time $t$, is a sensory pleasure at $t$ if the subject of S desires, intrinsically and de re, at $t$, of S that it be occurring at $t$" (2007a, 32).

13. As a note to readers, responding to these objections, and in general running through this discussion of internalism versus externalism, will take some time. Those readers not particularly interested in this more detailed debate can

skip to the next section and pick back up with the broader line of argument of the chapter.

14. Similarly, Smuts suggests the following as a way we should view the commonality of pleasures: "Pleasurable experiences are those that feel good" (2011, 254).

15. Heathwood finds Crisp's analysis lacking in that it "doesn't actually explain perhaps the most important thing we want a theory of enjoyment to explain—namely, *what makes* enjoyable feelings enjoyable, or what enjoyment *consists in*.... Crisp's view seems to be that it is just a primitive, inexplicable fact that *these* feelings are the enjoyable feelings. Insofar as we think this fact is a fact that should be explicable, Crisp's theory is unsatisfying" (2007b). In defense of Crisp, and as some of the main lines of argument in chapter 1 might suggest, I would offer the kind of response Smuts offers in defending his own version of internalism (i.e., his "feels good" theory of pleasure): "To 'feel good' is about as close to an experiential primitive as we get" (2011, 254). I for one do not feel the force of Heathwood's complaint that something further needs explaining. Like Heathwood, Bramble (2013) also views the kind of internalism advocated by Crisp and Smuts as unable to explain adequately what makes pleasurable experiences pleasurable. Unlike Heathwood, though, Bramble does not opt for externalism but instead offers a different version of internalism. And here we can note the two internalist theories that can be debated, succinctly defined by Smuts: (1) the "distinctive feeling" view, which claims that "pleasure is a distinct, common aspect of experiences that we call pleasurable" (2011, 255); and (2) following C. D. Broad, the "hedonic tone" view, which claims that "the experience overall has a tone that cannot be cleanly extracted or focused on apart from the experience itself" (2011, 256). I myself find the latter view the more plausible, but I am unsure how we might finally adjudicate this matter decisively. What I *am* convinced of is that *some* phenomenologically based internalist theory of pleasure is correct, in contrast to externalism.

16. Cf. Goldstein: "Our reason for a negative attitude toward pain lies in the intrinsic nature of the experience. It is by feeling the way it does, i.e. awful and bad, that pain justifies our aversion of it. Similarly, our justification for desiring pleasure and calling pleasure 'desirable' and 'good' lies in the intrinsic quality of the experience. It is by being good and meriting our desire that a pleasant experience provides justification for desiring it and commending it as 'good'" (1980, 360); and Bond: "In respect of pain, suffering, misery, anguish, depression (the contraries or opposites of pleasure and of feeling good), . . . just as pleasure and feeling good are *evidently* good, because they are experienced as such (because they are such in their natures), so their opposites are *evidently* bad or evil because they are experienced as such (because they are such in their

natures)" (1983, 127). For a recent discussion of some of the (insurmountable, in my view) problems with denying that we desire things *because* they are pleasurable, not the other way round, see Smuts (2011, §3).

17. See Feldman (2004, esp. chap. 4).

18. Cassell's original reason for making the distinction was to point out that the suffering of patients not only stems from physical maladies but occurs more broadly when "an impending destruction of the person is perceived" (1991, 33)—where personhood is spelled out in biological, familial, emotional, and cultural terms, to name but a few.

19. Cf. Sidgwick on the instrumental role that physical processes play in matters of "Ultimate Good": "It is in their purely physical aspect, as complex processes of corporeal change, that they are means to the maintenance of life: but so long as we confine our attention to their corporeal aspect,—regarding them merely as complex movements of certain particles of organised matter—it seems impossible to attribute to these movements, considered in themselves, either goodness or badness" (1981, III, xiv, §3, 396). Sidgwick's broader conclusion is that we should link Ultimate Good with "Good or Desirable conscious or sentient Life" (1981, III, xiv, §3, 395–96).

20. Granted, Feldman can simply *define* sensory pleasures with reference to attitudinal pleasures. We noted a few paragraphs back that Feldman in fact does this. But we also noted the implausibility of this move. Interestingly—though somewhat puzzlingly—Feldman continues in the paragraph just quoted that "if this goes on much longer, he [i.e., the neuroscientist] will start taking pain in the fact that he has destroyed an important part of his own nervous system." The puzzle is why we would link a large amount of worry with "pain" and a smaller amount of worry with "no pain" (instead of with "lesser pain"). Is not worry—at any degree of intensity—something we identify as a life-diminishing mental experience?

21. While I shall not go on to discuss the further (and interesting) examples Feldman provides—such as the enjoyable life that Stoicus may have lived (2004, 68–71) and the enjoyment the snow shoveler gets from a hot shower (83–85)—I would want to make this same point in thinking through how we might describe these examples.

22. See Feldman (2004, 173–74) for a helpful discussion of the idea of a mental "episode."

23. Cf. Goldstein's discussion of those who may desire an unpleasant experience (e.g., because they view themselves as unworthy of happiness) and subsequently find an unpleasant sensation pleasant: "What people call 'pleasant pain' is a *mixed* experience containing both pleasantness and unpleasantness" (1989, 263).

24. I will discuss further in section 4.1 the idea of a human's "ultimate flourishing," as I shall call it.

25. I again am not committed to saying that pleasure is itself a distinct feeling tone that is common to all instances of pleasurable experiences. (See note 15 from this chapter.) It is enough simply to say that the overall mental experience changes, even though the feeling tones associated with taste sensations do not change.

26. Adams's following example is actually offered as an objection to a certain implication he sees as stemming from the requirement that our experiences always play a part in our enjoyment: namely, that the enjoyment of one's life becomes directly related to the *time* one spends experiencing enjoyable segments of life. Still, his example also serves as a defense of his statement that we enjoy things besides our own experiences.

27. See Rachels (1998) for an accessible discussion of the kinds of examples that most clearly seem to render transitivity of value very implausible. Along with his own examples, Rachels considers some of the key examples provided by Temkin (1994, 361–63) and by Parfit (1984, §148). Tempkin's fuller and most recent examination of these issues is found in Temkin (2012).

28. See Sumner (1996, 113–23). These two reasons by no means form an exhaustive list—though they do seem to me especially important.

29. See Kraut's similar, and more extended, discussion of problems with desire-satisfaction accounts of well-being (2007, §§24–31). For different criticisms of desire-satisfaction accounts of well-being, see also the well-nuanced discussion in Lauinger (2012, chap. 2).

30. Cf. Rachels (2004, §4) on "background pleasures."

31. This line of argument incorporating Haybron's example could also be used against externalist theories of pleasure, as discussed in the last section.

32. Besides the objections outlined in this section against desire-satisfaction theories, which strike me as decisive, we can also note Ben Bradley's argument that "they are paradoxical" (2009, 40). The problem related to paradox occurs in cases in which "a person desires to be badly off or takes pleasure in being badly off" (30). In such cases, on a desire-satisfaction account of well-being, "A person's life goes well if and only if it does not go well" (30). Bradley also raises the problem that desire-satisfaction theories "cannot account for momentary well-being" (40). For an attempted rebuttal to this last charge, see Dorsey (2013).

33. Sumner explains that information becomes relevant to a subject "whenever it would make a difference to a subject's affective response to her life, given her priorities" (1996, 160). Regarding autonomy, see Sumner (1996, 167f.) for

a discussion of what it means for a subject's endorsement to be "truly *hers*," as opposed to socially conditioned.

34. Cf. the externalist tenor of Sumner's remark: "It is not the phenomenal properties of the sensation itself which determine just how much a particular pleasure will contribute to our happiness, but rather the meaning or significance which we attach to it" (1996, 141).

35. Silverstein remarks, "In anthologies of moral philosophy, Nozick's experience machine is often the only argument offered in response to classical hedonism" (2000, 282). Silverstein goes on to cite a number of said anthologies.

36. Cf. Nagel's comment that "what we find desirable in life are certain states, conditions, or types of activity. It is *being* alive, *doing* certain things, having certain experiences, that we consider good" (1993, 63).

37. As another example, consider Midgley's observation: "Avengers do not want the sensation of avenging; they want people's blood" (1995, 117). Examples from the arts also make the point well: "A real actor or musician is not trying to tinker with his own subjective states. He is trying to practice his art" (117).

38. What we desire of course affects *in*directly what occurrences will and will not make our lives go well for us. Desiring a shoulder massage from my spouse, and not desiring a massage from a kidnapper, I will have overall, positive mental experiences from the one but not the other. But if one's well-being is *not* a matter of having one's desires satisfied (cf. section 2.2), the question of whether one's desires are satisfied does not directly settle the question of how a person's life is going for her.

39. Silverstein takes a bit of a different tack in his own defense of hedonism from Nozick's experience machine. Silverstein focuses on the way in which the very desires we have *not* to be hooked up to the machine are actually formed as a way to track our own happiness: "We must not ignore the system that underlies the creation of those desires. Our desire to track reality—like all of our intrinsic desires—is related to happiness in an important way: it owes its existence to happiness. Even though it leads us away from happiness in the case of the experience machine, our desire to track reality points indirectly to happiness.... Happiness itself, therefore, is what fundamentally effects our intuitive fear of the experience machine, and we must not be misled by that fear. The mere existence of our intuitions against the experience machine should not lead us to reject hedonism. Contrary to appearances, those intuitions point—albeit circuitously—to happiness. And as a result, they no longer seem to contradict the claim that happiness is the only thing of intrinsic prudential value" (2000, 296). While this line of argument is interesting, I myself find it a bit more suggestive than air-tight. At any rate, my own line of response can allow that we may desire things far removed from our own happiness.

40. Of course, one might object to mental statism because one has a more general objection to welfarism as an account of noninstrumental value. I defended welfarism in section 2.1.

41. The mental statist therefore has no need to rely on J. S. Mill's appeal to "association" in explaining why any person might strive for things like power or pursue things like music: "In these cases the means have become a part of the end.... What was once desired as an instrument for the attainment of happiness, has come to be desired for its own sake.... The desire of it is not a different thing from the desire of happiness" (1987, chap. 4, 310). We can defend a purely mental-state account of well-being while still acknowledging that people can have ultimate goals other than their own happiness.

42. On the kind of mental statism I am defending, it is not merely that mental states provides a person, as Griffin states, "*greater* utility" than other things. Rather, mental states are the *only* (direct) contributors to one's welfare.

43. As a note to readers, my response to this set of potential objections will take some time. Readers who do not find this set of potential objections worrisome for the mental statist, or who otherwise have little interest in debates about the ways death is and is not bad for us, can skip to the next section and pick back up with the broader line of argument of the chapter.

44. The literature is replete with this pattern. Consider Thomas Nagel's example intended to illustrate the obvious implausibility of the sentiment that what you don't know won't hurt you: "It means that even if a man is betrayed by his friends, ridiculed behind his back, and despised by people who treat him politely to his face, none of it can be counted as a misfortune for him so long as he does not suffer as a result. It means that a man is not injured if his wishes are ignored by the executor of his will, or if, after his death, the belief becomes current that all the literary works on which his fame rests were really written by his brother, who died in Mexico at the age of 28" (1993, 64). It is only obvious that the man in this example is injured if one assumes a desire-satisfaction account of welfare. Consider also George Pitcher's example of "the living Mrs. Blue who is wronged" by the slander of a spiteful neighbor after Mrs. Blue's death (1993, 161). Pitcher is at least upfront in acknowledging his assumption about that which makes a person's life go worse for her: "I shall construe harm, or misfortune, in the following more or less orthodox way: an event or state of affairs is a misfortune for someone (or harms someone) when it is contrary to one or more of his more important desires or interests" (162).

45. If the woman also thinks that, because her goals were not met, her life was not going well for her at these earlier times, then she has simply assumed a desire-satisfaction account of well-being. However, whatever the woman's possible view on this further claim within the field of ethical theory, the arguments in section 2.2 against desire-satisfaction accounts of well-being still stand.

46. Or, more generally, the wishes of someone who will not be in a position to know whether we honor those wishes. See Foot's discussion of Mikluko-Maklay, who was tempted to photograph a sleeping Malayan native, even though the natives held spiritual views against having one's image taken (2001, 47–48).

47. See also Kraut (2007, §56) for a discussion why there is no reason to keep any promise "for the sake of the promise" outside considerations of the goodness and badness (*for* someone) of doing so.

48. Or, if we follow Fred Feldman, "eternally"—which seems to me to come to the same thing, depending on one's philosophy of time. Cf. Feldman's answer to the question when a young girl's death is bad for her: "When we say that her death is bad for her, we are really expressing a complex fact about the relative values of two possible worlds. If these worlds stand in a certain value relation, then (given that they stand in this relation at any time) they stand in that relation not only when [the girl] exists, but at times when she doesn't" (1993, 321).

49. Conversely, a different set of counterfactuals could also be offered in imagining a society where members of that society would regard as a great *blessing* a scenario in which a person is able to live to adulthood and survive two or three good years with his brain functioning well. Because of the number of worse scenarios we might imagine as typical in that society, people would regard the man's life as having gone exceedingly well for him.

50. I will make this point more fully in section 4.1 when assessing Aristotle's account of the good life.

51. For Bradley's arguments against *presentism* (the view that only present objects exist—there are no past or future things) and in favor of *eternalism* (the view that past and future objects exist), see pp. 80–82.

52. Bradley notes that we should not be surprised at the claim that something can be instrumentally bad for us without causing anything intrinsically bad: "But many things are instrumentally good without causing anything intrinsically good, and many things are instrumentally bad without causing anything intrinsically bad. These are goods and evils of *prevention*" (2009, 47–48).

53. Cf. Bradley's own summation of what is at stake: "Suppose the mental state theory says that the only things that can move one's well-being level up or down are intrinsic features of one's own mental states. . . . If mental statism says something more—e.g., that one has a well-being level at a time only if one has mental states at that time—then my story is incompatible with mental statism; but why say the extra thing?" (personal correspondence, fall 2009).

54. As to why these negative properties are not "paradigmatic" negative properties, see pp. 10–18.

55. His positive argument for this conclusion centers on the following example: "Suppose Ishani drops an anvil on Kris's head tomorrow, and consider

two possible futures for Kris. In one future, F1, Kris dies instantly. In the other future, F2, Kris goes into a comatose state, never regains consciousness, and dies in ten years. Insofar as Kris's own well-being is concerned, he should be indifferent between these two futures. He has no self-interested reason to prefer one to the other. I think it is reasonable to conclude from this fact that *Kris is exactly as well off in the comatose state as he would have been had he not existed*" (108).

56. So that, again using Nagel's terms, "there is something that it is like to *be*" that subject, "something it is like *for*" that subject.

57. Bradley's formal articulation of the property of responsiveness is: "Person S is responsive at time $t$ only if there is some world $w$ and some time $t^*$ such that S has a positive or negative well-being level at $<w, t^*>$" (2009, 104).

58. If we were to pursue further, related objections to Bradley's responsiveness condition, we might focus on the odd implication that the first organism X with a mental life would, with pleasant mental states, undergo an *increase* in its well-being. Or we might explore Bradley's appeal to possible worlds and ask whether a great many kinds of organisms—*too* many, to make plausible the appeal to possible worlds as part of a responsiveness condition—might *possibly* have a mental life in some world. If an old shoe cannot have a mental life in any possible world, could the bacteria growing in an old shoe?

59. Of course, if one feels shame at experiencing some pleasure, that feeling will be a part of her overall mental experience at the time. But we are supposing that the mental experience nevertheless continues to be marked by pleasure of some kind.

60. Epicurus surely had the instrumental value of pleasures in mind when he warned: "Every pleasure is a good thing, since it has a nature congenial [to us], but not every one is to be chosen. Just as every pain too is a bad thing, but not every one is such as to be always avoided" (2002, 297).

61. Moore (1993, §56) appealed to the intuitions of "Common Sense" in insisting that base pleasures associated with, for example, bestiality surely undermine the general position of hedonists like Sidgwick.

62. In appealing to our intuitions, Ross claims that we have "a decided conviction" that happiness is good when it is *deserved* (1930, 136); and he states that we "must recognize" it as a good thing when pleasure and pain are apportioned to the virtuous and the vicious, respectively (138).

63. This same point—as well as the broader line of argument I am advancing in this section—could be adapted to deal with cases in which one experiences *un*pleasure while reflectively being *glad* that one is experiencing it. For example, a person might experience grief when a loved one dies, and at the same time be grateful that one's feelings are appropriate to the occasion. See Kraut's example of appropriate sorrow (2007, §39).

64. Such a claim is different from the claim that the desire-satisfaction proponent will make. The desire-satisfaction proponent will not—or, at least, need not—claim that extrinsic considerations affect the intrinsic value of a pleasurable mental state. The proponent need only claim that one's well-being is not linked simply with these pleasurable mental states.

65. Kagan provides this example as a case "where the actual causal history of the object is taken to be relevant to its intrinsic value" (1998, 285).

66. Cf. G. E. Moore's well-known response to the suggestion that J. S. Mill had provided a "proof" for utilitarianism. Mill had stated: "The only proof capable of being given that an object is visible, is that people actually see it. The only proof that a sound is audible, is that people hear it: and so of the other sources of our experience. In like manner, I apprehend, the sole evidence it is possible to produce that anything is desirable is that people do actually desire it" (1987, chap. 4, 307). Moore's response is: "The fact is that 'desirable' does not mean 'able to be desired' as 'visible' means 'able to be seen.' The desirable means simply what *ought* to be desired or *deserves* to be desired; just as the detestable means not what can be but what ought to be detested" (1993, §40). (In fairness to Mill, he plausibly did not actually have a deductive proof in mind. Rather, as Roger Crisp notes, "By appealing to the natural fact of what his readers and all other human beings desire, rather than any self-evident or intuitive proposition, Mill believes that he has provided a philosophically respectable reason for his reader to accept that happiness is desirable" (1997, 76).

67. In addition to this ad hominem argument, Goldstein's own arguments as to why we should affirm the goodness of "pleasures" within malicious pleasures, even while condemning "malicious pleasures" as a whole, are found in Goldstein (2003, esp. 27f).

68. Cf. Goldstein: "Since at least some pleasure is good intrinsically simply because of its pleasurableness, pleasure should always be good intrinsically, whatever the society, and so be an unconditional value" (1989, 273).

69. If one doubts Rachels's supposition that there could be such "generalized euphoria" with genuinely *no* object, consider a person who awakens in a sensory deprivation tank, who has been given a drug producing a euphoric feeling, and whose first thought upon awakening is a reflection on the fact that he feels euphoric.

*Chapter Three. Motivations, the Good, and the Right*

1. Philippa Foot, in explaining a key difference between humans and other animals, notes that a human child "gradually comes to use words not only to get

what it wants but also to speak about what it is going to do; and comes to understand and use the locutions by which choices are debated and actions explained, justified, and recommended. . . . It makes sense to ask what someone *thought* about the pros and cons of a particular choice because we can ask him and be given an answer" (2001, 55). For my broader line of argument in this chapter, I am happy to accommodate these points. I merely resist the suggestion that *beliefs* of any kind—even beliefs about what there is most reason to do—are the kinds of mental states in which human motivation consists.

2. I do not wish to explore possible distinctions between desires and other affective mental states like emotions—and whether these other mental states might serve as a substitute for a desire in explaining one's motivation to perform some action. I myself doubt that we can dispense with the idea of a desire in explaining any intentional action a person might perform. But I shall not argue this point here. I want here only to contrast (noncognitive) desires with (cognitive) beliefs and note Hume's position that it is desires—not beliefs—that provide a way for us to understand motivations.

3. As noted in section 1.4, I acknowledge that there are various ways to analyze a desire, admittedly only *one* of which would be to explore the phenomenology of a desire. And admittedly not all desires have a recognizable phenomenology to them. Yet, as again noted in section 1.4 (see note 14 of chapter 1), the main danger of restricting a discussion of desires to a discussion of their phenomenology is that it (too easily) opens the door for the critic to argue that desires are not sufficient to explain certain actions of ours—for example, why we tend to act in accordance with our moral judgments. (For a discussion of this point, see Smith [1994, 104–11].) However, I shall in no way use a narrower, phenomenologically based analysis of desires in order to argue *against* Humean models that rely on desires to explain our pursuits of what we believe to be good and/or right. Instead, I shall go on in this chapter to defend a Humean model in explaining the nature of normativity in general.

4. I do not mean to suggest that desires *compel* (i.e., *causally necessitate*) one's actions—only that they propel one to act. The nature of human freedom will be the focus of section 5.5.

5. In my judgment discussions of reasons can become unclear because they can all too easily (though improperly) move between "explanatory reasons" and "motivating reasons," as well as between "there being reasons to do something" and "a person's reasons for doing something." Also, I noted in section 2.1 that it seems clear to me that comparisons of *value* do not even adhere to the logical rule of transitivity. Since the impetus for talking about reasons is often a concern that our actions—stemming from what we value—be subject to rational constraints, there seem to me unwarranted assumptions made about how our

values (and resulting actions) can and/or should be subject to rational constraints.

6. See the example of the late-night movie viewer in section 5.2 for one obvious case to which most of us can surely relate.

7. I will explore these conceptual connections much more fully in section 3.3. For present purposes, I only want to offer these briefest remarks about the concepts "right/wrong" and how they differ from the concepts "good/bad."

8. Again it will not be until section 3.3 that I will defend this claim more fully.

9. We could perhaps construct an Aristotelian/Thomist normative framework by adopting a metaphysic that things naturally "tend toward" certain ends. And perhaps this metaphysic could be developed in such a way so as to claim that the normative force we feel moving us to act cannot be reduced to our psychological states. So, e.g., human tendencies to perform intentional actions become explained in a way analogous to the way fire "tends upward" toward its natural place, qua fire. I mention this metaphysic only to set it aside.

10. A point brought out quite well in Russell (2006).

11. See Humberstone (1992) for the history of the phrase "direction of fit" and for ways we might seek to sharpen further our characterization of the contrasting directions of desire and belief.

12. Though of course there can be a great deal to say about the conditions of, and series of events that led to, a person having this psychological phenomenon of feeling impelled to do something. And Foot has a number of insightful things to say about the "power" humans have "to see grounds for acting in one way rather than another" (2001, 56).

13. See Parfit (1997, 100–101) for his overview of the Internalist-Externalist distinction in this context, drawn from Williams (1981a).

14. At least, we do not arrive at them beyond the weaker use of the terms within hypothetical statements: e.g., "If you want this good or better or best outcome $A$, then you 'should/ought' to perform action $X$."

15. E.g., a person might be concerned that she is weak-willed or otherwise often fails to follow through (with actions) on judgments about what is to be done. Once she has then judged that some action is to be done, her reflection on her own judgment might then add to the pro-attitude she has toward that action. For she now sees the action as an opportunity to develop the desired habit of following through on her own judgments.

16. I emphasize *beliefs* as the contrast to desires. A further, interesting discussion—which unfortunately would take us too far afield, for purposes of my current project—involves the question of whether our options in explaining

a person's action should be limited to a discussion of the roles that belief and desire may play. Foot comments that "an action can be explained by all sorts of causes, as for instance (a) habit, (b) a tendency to mimic the actions of others, (c) something significant about the occasion on which one first did what one is now going to do, (d) the fact that it is substitutionally representing some other action, or (e) even something as far out as post-hypnotic suggestion" (2001, 61). Foot's broader concerns involve her discussion of practical rationality and what can constitute a reason for acting in some particular way. My concern is of course the psychological phenomenon of feeling impelled to act. Still, Foot's comments raise interesting questions about the range of ways one might come to experience the psychological force I am linking with normativity.

17. Perhaps the best defense of this thesis is simply to consider a case where a person genuinely could not identify—even in principle, or with a complete understanding of all her mental inner workings—*any* unwelcome (i.e., undesired) outcome associated with a failure to perform some action. In such a case, I do not see how we could understand the person as feeling normative pressure to perform that action. At least, I do not see how we could understand it unless we adopt an anti-Humean model whereby beliefs themselves—e.g., about the "rightness" of some action—can motivate us. But such a model once again inevitably fails to explain why we should be *moved*, or *impelled*, to act.

18. Perhaps we can distinguish here (1) the negative feeling tones associated with a *desire* and (2) the negative feelings associated with an *emotion* (or some other affective state). If this distinction ultimately holds, then I will be primarily interested in the former sense of *negative feeling*, since I want to link motivation with desires. Still, the negative emotions we experience as we imagine some unwelcome outcome can certainly affect the strength of the desire we have to avoid that outcome. And if the affective state of an emotion can both be separated from a desire and serve, like desires, as a motivation for an action, then I again think it possible to adjust the Humean model of motivation without too much trouble.

19. Suppose I regard my current actions as inevitable, or at least irresistible for me. I might perhaps believe I am in my current predicament because of past decisions where I *did* have other, better options. In this sense I might say that I "ought not" to be in my current predicament where I am doing lamentable things. But lament is all I would feel. I would not experience the kind of normative pressure that moves, or impels, us to act in some way.

20. Discussions over whether "ought" implies "can" usually focus on whether it is appropriate to hold someone morally responsible for failing to do some action if he was unable freely (in some sense of "free") to perform that action. The

weaker claim in my current discussion is simply that we cannot feel normative pressure to avoid some outcome unless we believe we might somehow do something to avoid it—whatever our actual capacity to avoid it.

21. Scenarios like this one are the reason I said in section 1.4 that desires "*almost* always" contain feeling tones of release and of frustration. While there is a potential for any motivating desire to contain *both* kinds of feeling tones, certain other conditions need to be met—such as a reflective consideration of the possibilities of one's desired state of affairs either obtaining or not obtaining.

22. One reason Tom *could* not, in principle, have experienced normative pressure up until this point is that, thus far in the example, he is being motivated to continue watching the movie only by the positive aspect of a desire. On my view, the positive feeling tones of a desire are *not* constitutive of normative pressure for us in any context. My argument remains an appeal to the phenomenology of feeling that we *should* or *ought* to do something. As the names *normative force* and *pressure* suggest, I think the phenomenology of normative cases—where we conclude that we should or ought to perform some action—includes the feelings that come with an awareness that the action in question may potentially mean something unpleasant for us. That is, the action in question does not, or at least may not, align only with those things (including our own pleasurable experiences) toward which we have an unambiguously pro-attitude.

23. One might try to press the point that, e.g., in the case of the speeding motorist, we choose to create laws that give police the authority to assign fines for speeding. Thus the scenario where we must choose between speeding and being fined is a scenario ultimately of our own choosing. But the response to this point is again to note that, in deciding to make laws about speeding, we have been forced to choose between such matters as safety and personal freedom. We did not create or ask for a world where personal freedom sometimes comes at the expense of safety for citizens. Nor did we create a world where citizens in general rarely obey guidelines without such deterrents as monetary fines. So again, even though we may make decisions that affect the particulars of *which* unwelcome outcomes we face, the possibility of facing *any* unwelcome outcomes is not something on which any of us have a say.

24. In section 3.3 I will examine in more detail this link between (1) associating an action with social sanction and (2) thinking that action wrong.

25. I do not mean *better* in the sense of being more meritorious or praiseworthy. I am referring only to the way we might make comparisons of value among possible worlds.

26. As another example, the line between prohibiting cigarette smoking and merely frowning upon it (with accompanying disincentives) may in certain contexts be difficult to establish.

27. Sometimes a would-be sanctioner will be explicit that her expectations are that others *try* to do what they *believe* to be right, with no specific action in the sanctioner's mind. For example, a parent may send her child to camp with the instructions to try to remember and follow the behavioral guidelines on the camp's brochure, whatever those guidelines may be. Or a parent may instruct her older, university-age child to navigate moral dilemmas by trying to identify the various obligations he has—again, whatever the obligations turn out to be. Probably more typically, though, a proscription comes in the form of proscribing a specified action. And this is true even when, strictly speaking, the proscriber is actually seeking to elicit something a bit different from her stated proscription—as when a parent commands a child to "never fail to pluck out your eye if it causes you to sin," even while, in the parent's own mind, she merely expects the child to take more modest steps in eliminating some tempting influence. For our discussion it seems easiest just to talk about proscriptions against identifiable actions.

28. I argued in chapter 2 for a welfarist understanding of final value. And indeed I think for most people the things they identify as most valuable (which lead them to identify as "wrong" the actions that threaten those things) will be the flourishing of themselves and others about whom they care. However, I have of course allowed that a person might be mistaken about the nature of noninstrumental value and might place value in, e.g., the preservation of an old tree. What is important in discussing the concepts of right and wrong is how we proscribe actions we view as threatening those things we do greatly value, whatever those things are.

29. Decisions about when an agreed-upon bad action (e.g., marijuana or cigarette smoking) is bad enough to sanction is of course a frequent public discussion. Also, following an earlier point in this section, the line between unmistakable sanction and merely frowning upon a bad action (where the action is permitted but not encouraged) may at times be difficult to draw.

30. And now we have a fuller explanation of the second of our two broad considerations, raised in the previous section, as to why normative force so often feels as though it comes from the "outside," irrespective of how we may personally want things to be. This second consideration, it will be remembered, involves cases where we believe that some action is *wrong* for us to do.

31. For what it is worth to the reader, let me share the source of my anecdotal evidence. For the past decade my wife has worked with families with young children, organizing group education and play times. I myself have attended on average about three of these sessions per week, taking our own children to them. In the course of an average week I thereby have had the chance to interact with perhaps forty to sixty families. Given that Lewis's description

of the *Tao* has interested me for some time, I am always alerted when a child uses a phrase like "That's not fair." When possible, I have tried gently to engage the child on his or her understanding of what "fairness" does and does not entail. While I admit the possibility that perhaps I have not asked the correct questions, it remains true that I have received a widely varied range of responses. And very rarely, frankly, has the response resembled anything close to what a moral or political philosopher would typically offer as a broad characterization of fairness. The natural question might then be to ask why a child would employ the phrase "That's not fair!"—as opposed to other phrases like "I don't like that" or "That's harmful." My guess is that children, taking their cues from their parents' teachings and from their parents' responses to their own appeals, have found the appeal to "fairness" to carry more weight as a pragmatic matter. Children admittedly do often fall back on the explanation "Because it wouldn't be fair," in response to questions about why it is important not to break promises, not to refuse to share toys, and even not to disobey one's parents. However, when pressed further, the true concerns that emerge inevitably seem to be ones of welfare. Thus, to use a couple of examples from children I have engaged: Why is it important to be fair by always keeping your promises? "Because the other person would probably get sad if you didn't." Why should children always be fair and obey their parents? "Because if someone didn't she could get hurt—like when parents tell you not to go in a parking lot where cars could bump you." I acknowledge that it is *possible* that children's common references to "fairness" stem from a vague sense of a "moral law" to which they just cannot offer conceptual clarity. But alternative theses—ones starting with the pragmatic and welfarist considerations I have mentioned in this paragraph—seem from my experience quite capable of explaining the data of children's use of terms like *fairness*. And so my own conclusion is that an exploration of the moral sensibilities of children does not provide any special evidence for C. S. Lewis's conclusion about a universally appreciated moral law over alternative theses focusing on children's desires for their own and for others' well-being.

32. See, e.g., Simmons (1981); Damon (1981); Charlesworth (1992); Lerner (2002).

33. Especially William Damon, Martin Hoffman, and Melvin Lerner. See Kristjánsson (2006, chap. 4).

34. Children unfortunately are sometimes *too* keen to identify such practices, with competitive attitudes sometimes emerging in desires not simply for proportionality but for *more* than others receive.

35. My arguments thus far in this section have largely been that we have no reason to posit the existence of properties of rightness and wrongness that could exist independently of anyone's standpoint. I thus resist the metaethical view

that non-natural facts exist about an action's wrongness or rightness. (I count as a natural fact any person's or being's intention to sanction, including God's.)

36. Thus Mackie's conclusion that our ordinary moral thought and language is steeped in error. See Mackie (1977, chap. 1).

37. See Adams (1973). For Adams's later shift submitting that "contrariness to the commands of a loving God" is best seen as a property that explains the *nature* of wrongness, as a matter of metaphysical necessity, see Adams (1979).

38. Such disagreements sometimes do and sometimes do not carry the further suggestion that we are prepared to take punitive measures against those who take punitive measures against those who perform the action.

39. I concede to not having a knock-down argument—beyond the appeal to simplicity and ontological parsimony—against the suggestion that moral "rightness" and "wrongness" (along with moral "goodness" and "badness") are non-natural properties that supervene on natural properties. A standard argument *against* the naturalistic reductionism I advocate (in which purported moral, non-natural properties are reducible on conceptual analysis to natural properties) is that, if we agreed on all the natural properties of some action, there would be no room left for moral disagreement over whether that action was actually right or wrong. But I see no problem with affirming that our moral disagreements are indeed over such naturalistic questions as whether someone (e.g., God) has proscribed some action or whether some action furthers the overall well-being of some person(s).

40. Richard Kraut is one who also holds that "all justification proceeds by way of good and bad" (2007, 208). See his chap. 4 for interesting discussions in support of the claim that the justification for all claims to moral rightness and wrongness is found in appeals to what is good or bad for someone.

*Chapter Four. Others and the Good*

1. Cf. Aquinas: "God only satisfies and infinitely exceeds man's desires; and, therefore, perfect satiety is found in God alone" (1939, art. 12, 74); and the *Catechism of the Catholic Church*: "The Beatitudes respond to the natural desire for happiness. This desire is of divine origin: God has placed it in the human heart in order to draw man to the One who alone can fulfill it" (pt. III, sec. I, chap. I, art. II, II, §1718).

2. If we don't assume this theistic understanding of human nature, I think the best we can probably do is to trace with Kraut the "development" of actual humans through the course of their lives and then form a rough sketch of what a flourishing human life seems to us to look like (2007, chap. 3). Or perhaps in

our search for what is good for us we might look also to other animal species in seeking insights into, as Midgley puts it, "what we are naturally fit for, capable of, and adapted to" (1995, 169). But of course if God did create this world and has revealed truths about our origins, our nature, and what will ultimately satisfy us, then these facts have enormous implications for how we understand the good life and how it can be attained.

3. On the nature of God's necessity, see Findlay (1948); Swinburne (1993, chaps. 13 and 14); Plantinga (1979, chap. 10).

4. Though see Kraut's discussion for preferring the term *developmentalism* over *perfectionism*, in exploring the good life toward which humans might strive (2007, 36 n. 4).

5. Rousseau, *La nouvelle Héloise*, pt. 5, letter 3, quoted in Passmore (1970, 178).

6. See Plato, *Charmides* 161a8–9; *Euthyphyro* 6d9–e1; *Gorgias* 497d8–e3; 506d2–4; *Protagoras* 332b4–6; *Meno* 87d8–e1. As C. D. C. Reeve comments, "The *aretê* of a knife might include having a sharp blade; the *aretê* of a man might include being intelligent, well-born, just, or courageous. *Aretê* is thus broader than our notion of a moral virtue. . . . It is sometimes more appropriate to render *aretê* as 'excellence.'" Reeve's comment is in Plato (1992, 10 n. 12).

7. Aristotle's concern was to identify an *ideal* life, not simply a graduated scale of well-being on which any person's life could be charted. He did not think that many people could ever achieve the kind of ideal life he went on to describe.

8. The list from Gal. 5:22–23 is: love, joy, peace, patience, kindness, goodness, faithfulness, gentleness, and self-control.

9. See, e.g., Adams (1984) and Hebblethwaite (1992).

10. I use this phrase to denote the kind of well-being attainable for all people in an afterlife, a subject discussed more fully in section 4.5.

11. To be sure, self-discovery may not *always* involve discomfort. The challenging standards God places before us may sometimes actually be a source of joy for those who do not lose sight of the role these standards play in shaping them into the kind of person who can enjoy more and more aspects of God's life-giving nature. The psalmist, for example, speaks frequently of God's laws being "my delight." (See Ps. 119: 16, 24, 47, 70, 77, 143, 174.) Still, it is certainly true that, for many of us, the truths God might help us see about ourselves may not be truths we unequivocally welcome.

12. As I shall discuss further in section 4.5, these life-enhancing experiences will ultimately lead to a state of flourishing that one embraces without reservation (including reservation as to the process through which one attained this state of flourishing).

13. For a theistic ethical framework that offers a desire-satisfaction account of the good life (as opposed to my own mental-statist account), see Carson (2000).

14. It is this consideration that led Sidgwick to offer his externalist definition of pleasure, as discussed previously in section 2.1.

15. We noted in section 2.1 (see note 15 of that chapter) that two internalist theories of pleasure can be distinguished: (1) the "distinctive feeling" view, in which pleasure is seen as a distinct, common aspect of those experiences we call pleasurable; and (2) the "hedonic tone" view, in which the overall tone of the mental experience can be described as pleasurable, but no distinct "pleasant feeling tone" exists that, in combination with other feeling tones, makes up that mental experience. I remarked that I find the latter view—which Crisp endorses—more plausible as an analysis of pleasure. For our present discussion, I think it plausible to think that "connecting" *is* a distinct feeling tone that contributes to one's overall mental experience. However, if, contrary to what I find most plausible, the better analysis of "connecting" is that one's *overall* mental experience can have a general tone to it that we can identify as including the phenomenological element of "connecting," then my discussion in this section can be adjusted accordingly. Still, I will continue to speak of "connecting" as an identifiable feeling tone, among those distinct feeling tones that constitute one's overall mental experience at a given time.

16. How we categorize "feeling tones" at this point can be settled by stipulation; not much, if anything, hangs on the matter. We might say that, within the feeling tone of connecting, there are two elements associated with (1) giving love and (2) receiving love. Or, we might say that these two elements are feeling tones in their own right, combining to form a further, identifiable feeling tone of connecting. (Or, applying the form of the "hedonic tone" view discussed earlier, we might say that an *overall* mental experience can admit to a general tone that is affected by the aspects of a relationship I am describing—even though we cannot identify further, distinct feeling tones within our overall mental experiences as we relate to others.)

17. Or perhaps *foretastes* is the better term.

18. Cf. Mounier: "When communication fails or is corrupted, I suffer an essential loss of myself: every kind of madness is a severance of my relations with others" (1952, 20).

19. See Adams (1999, chap. 1, esp. 13–14 and 28–38, also 93–101).

20. For humans to relate to each other meaningfully in this earthly life, there need to be activities in which they can cooperatively engage and that provide opportunities to enjoy one another and, ideally, to learn more about one another. Plausibly, there will need to be such activities in heaven that serve as

occasions for the redeemed to relate meaningfully to one another. Also, the idea of a resurrected body raises such questions as whether the heavenly community necessarily requires some sort of space to inhabit as people relate to one other. Happily, for our larger discussion we need not attempt a taxonomy of the conditions that must obtain if we are to have the opportunity to relate to other personal agents. All that is needed for our discussion is the point that, once these conditions *do* obtain, then our flourishing will ultimately hinge entirely on the state of our relationships with others.

21. A small child may continually yell, "Watch me dance! Look at my drawing!" The biggest reason adults do not do this is not that their relational needs no longer exist. Rather, adults learn decorum.

22. See Kinghorn (2005, chap. 7, esp. 147–50, 155–57).

23. I of course am using the term *interests* in the sense of a person's well-being, as opposed to the sense in which one is interested in, or desires, some state of affairs.

24. If we imagine our playwright as forgetting the script he has written, then perhaps he can approximate this relational dynamic when he reads through the dialogue of his characters, all the while uncertain of what the characters will say next. But in the end the most we could say here is that the playwright might be relating to the person the playwright *used* to be (at the earlier time in which the dialogue was written). The extent to which the playwright would be approximating a true, interpersonal dynamic would be the extent to which it is correct to describe the playwright as now a distinct personal agent from the agent who earlier wrote the script. Of course, even if we suppose that this "later person" can react to the "earlier person" in a way characteristic of interpersonal relationships, the "earlier person" can do no such reacting and relating. So the point remains that the playwright could not participate in the ongoing, responsive give-and-take of an interpersonal relationship.

25. Consistent with our discussion in section 2.1, one's reflective desires about one's mental states do not *make* these mental states life-enhancing. Rather, one's reflective desires merely serve to indicate that the mental states do have intrinsic qualities that are life-enhancing.

26. At least, most Christians have wanted to affirm that God seeks to lead all people toward this end of ultimate flourishing.

27. I have discussed this question, along with much of the material in this section, more fully in Kinghorn (2005, chap. 3).

28. Such kinds of decisions are not uncommon. A mother may find herself with a teenage son who responds to her instructions as though she were a peer and not a parent. The mother may decide that she is willing to carry on in a less-than-ideal relationship with her live-in son in which he relates to her as a

peer. Alternatively, she may threaten to kick her son out of the house, stating, "You may continue to live here only if you're willing to obey my rules without exception!"

*Chapter Five. God, the Good, and Our Choices*

1. This fact, of course, does not imply that the experience of joy was an ultimate goal the parent was seeking to achieve.
2. Whether our attention is focused on the project itself or, more reflectively, on the personal enjoyment we anticipate experiencing as we pursue the project.
3. In section 6.4 I will consider (though ultimately dismiss) the objection that our response to God is not appropriately catalogued as a choice to prioritize or further God's interests.
4. Perhaps my intuitions are quite welfarist, whereas Adams, as I have noted in various places, allows for the intrinsic value of nonpersonal things.
5. Kolodny does not himself make this more controversial claim, clarifying that "the sense in which, according to my account, we are 'loved for a relationship' is simply that those who love us believe that their attitudes toward us are appropriate in virtue of the relationships that they have to us" (2003, 156).
6. As an example of how a person's desire to do something *can* be satisfied even if he himself is not the one who does it, consider a basketball player whose desire to make the winning basket stems solely from his desire for his team to win the game. When a teammate finds himself with the ball in the dying seconds of the game and makes the winning basket, the original player's desire to make the winning basket is satisfied. Similarly in the case involving benevolence, if a friend's desire to advance my flourishing stems from a desire that my life go well for me in a certain respect, then his desire is satisfied when my life does go well for me in that respect (whatever the causal factors leading to my increased welfare).
7. If divine coordination of people's flourishing needs to involve God's ensuring that there are others who have natural attractions to us, then there seems no problem in God's doing so as needed.
8. "Needed," not in the sense that no one else could, even over time, come to contribute to important aspects of their flourishing in the way we do, but rather in the sense that, given their actual circumstances and the state of their relationships with others (including with us), we contribute to important aspects of their flourishing.

9. Nicholas Wolterstorff describes his motivation for writing *Justice: Rights and Wrongs* as coming from "seeing the faces and hearing the voices of victims." His stated purpose for writing the book is "an attempt to speak up for the wronged of the world" (2008, ix). This general motivation is one I myself applaud and admire. Toward working against the unfortunately common human practice of ignoring or discounting the hurts that others endure, Wolterstorff zeroes in on the idea that "the presence of the other before us places a claim on us, issues to us a call to do justice" (ix). Accordingly, Wolterstorff's strategy in improving the plight of the marginalized involves "doing what I can to undermine those frameworks of conviction that prevent us from acknowledging that the other comes before us bearing a claim on us, and of offering an alternative framework, one that opens us up to such acknowledgement" (ix). In section 3.3 I offered my own argument that "rights" cannot be divorced from some person's or group's proscription—thus seemingly undermining Wolterstorff's description of the normative social bond of rights as involving "the other bearing a *legitimate* claim on me as to how I treat her" (emphasis mine) (4). But as a practical matter, whether our society should—for axiological considerations of how best we can promote people's well-being—maintain the language of, e.g., people's "inalienable rights" is a legitimate question for public discussion.

10. Others who have reached conclusions linking normativity only with hypothetical imperatives include Foot (1978b) (at least in this earlier writing of hers) and Murphy (2002, esp. chap. 7).

11. Cf. Jesus's reading aloud of the passage from Isaiah, about which he remarked, "Today this scripture is fulfilled in your hearing": "The Spirit of the Lord is on me, because he has anointed me to preach good news to the poor. He has sent me to proclaim freedom for the prisoners and recovery of sight for the blind, to release the oppressed, to proclaim the year of the Lord's favor" (Luke 4:17–21). Jesus later directed his followers to continue his work, asking Simon Peter, "Do you love me?" and then charging him, "Feed my sheep" (John 12:15–17).

12. Christian teaching is that humans are incapable of providing this means of reparation for their ruptured relationship with God—as I would, e.g., provide the means of reparation for my son's breaking of a neighbor's window by paying for a replacement. So God must provide these means, which of course Christians affirm God to have done through Christ's atoning work on the cross. For those who have made Christ lord of their lives, Christ takes responsibility for them in such a way that they can plead to God Christ's passion as atonement for their own failures to meet the terms of the relationship into which God invited them. (We might think, by analogy, of how a parent takes responsibility for the naughty actions of a small child. When the child pours juice on

a dinner guest, it is the parent who apologizes and offers to pay for dry cleaning. We think this practice appropriate in virtue of the kind of asymmetrical relationship a parent has to a small child, where the parent accepts responsibility for the child's actions in virtue of accepting the dependent relationship a small child must have toward an adult. Christian teaching is that, when we make Christ lord of our lives, we similarly enter into a role of great dependence upon God. And I think part of the plausibility of the idea that Christians can plead Christ's passion as atonement to God for their own sins can be seen in the appropriateness we afford to a parent's efforts to make amends for the children in their care.)

Though I shall not argue the point at any length, I think any adequate justification of the Atonement (i.e., Why did Jesus have to die? Why could not God have simply forgiven people?) will need to emphasize the way in which the Atonement is needed for *our* sake rather than for God's sake (e.g., rather than to satisfy some requirement God has that justice be administered). Given that an ongoing relationship with God needs to be built on a mutual and correct understanding of its history, it becomes an important point that only in the cross of Christ do we see the full extent of what we do to God and what God has, from creation, been prepared to do to restore the relationships we rupture with him.

13. See Swinburne (1989, 81–89) for a discussion of what may be needed in atoning for wrongs done to another. Swinburne lists four components that can aid in removing guilt—repentance, apology, reparation, and penance—along with the wronged person's act of forgiveness.

14. Martin Luther went so far as to suggest that God commands us to do *more* than we can possibly do "so as to lead us by means of the law to a knowledge of our impotence" to fulfill the law. He notes the analogy to parents who often "have a game with their children by telling them to come to them, or to do this or that, simply for the sake of showing them how unable they are, and compelling them to call for the help of the parents' hand!" (1969, 184). I ignore this complication here. I myself take the point, affirmed by the Christian tradition, that we are unable to obey God's commands without God's assistance. But, as shall become clear in the following section, I reject what seemingly is the broader point Luther, following Augustine, wants to make that we cannot obey God's commands unless God moves us irresistibly to do so.

15. Swinburne makes the point perhaps more clearly, noting that, in this "normal medieval view from Augustine onwards" that Aquinas affirmed, "The distinction was made between 'precepts' (commands which impose obligation) and 'counsels' (advice as to how best to progress towards the sanctity needed for salvation). 'Counsels of perfection,' which were held applicable to many, advised

the poverty, chastity, and obedience of the monastic life. However, there was no obligation on men to pursue salvation with such directness; following a less demanding way with less guarantee of attaining Heaven, at any rate so immediately, would involve no breach of obligation" (1989, 132).

16. For a fuller discussion of how speech acts of others are appropriated, see Wolterstorff (1995).

17. See Kinghorn (2005, chap. 8).

18. The true beliefs *themselves* do not motivate us; desires alone, I have argued, motivate us. By mentioning beliefs I mean here only to draw attention to the fact that new desires can arise in us as we form new beliefs.

19. Cf. Seamands: "As the doctrine of the Trinity developed in the church and theologians searched for language to describe the mutual indwelling and interpenetration of the three persons, they eventually landed on the beautiful Greek term *perichoresis*. Perichoresis conveys a number of ideas: reciprocity, interchange, giving to and receiving from one another, being drawn to one another and contained in the other, interpenetrating one another by drawing life from and pouring life into one another as a fellowship of love" (2005, 142).

20. The Christian tradition has long affirmed that the self-giving love *within* the life of the Trinity disposes (if that is the right term) the persons of the Trinity to move beyond themselves and include others in the ongoing life of the three eternal persons. We might think by analogy of the inclination a married couple often feel to have children who might then be incorporated into the family's ongoing network of relationships. Cf. Moltmann: "The life of God within the Trinity cannot be conceived of as a closed circle—the symbol of perfection and self-sufficiency. A Christian doctrine of the Trinity . . . must conceive the Trinity as the Trinity of the sending and seeking love of God which is open from its very origin. The triune God is the God who is open to man, open to the world and open to time" (1993, 55–56).

21. See Midgley (1995, esp. chap. 6), for discussions of the picture of human nature we end up with, staying within the investigative methodology of evolutionary biologists.

22. Exceptions may of course exist in the form of sociopaths whose social development did not allow them to empathize with the plight of others. And there may be those who, owing to occurrences in the brain, are for these physical reasons kept from identifying with others. I ignore here the further issue of how God might provide for those who in this life are unable to make choices of the kind I am outlining.

23. Cf. again Jesus's summation of the kind of response God tries to elicit from us: "'Love the Lord your God with all your heart and with all your soul and with all your mind.' This is the first and greatest commandment. And the

second is like it: 'Love your neighbor as yourself.' All the Law and the Prophets hang on these two commandments" (Matt. 22:37–40). As to the nature of love—plausibly interpreted as in keeping with my own emphasis on the choice between benevolence and self-interest—cf. Jesus's declaration: "Greater love has no one than this: to lay down one's life for one's friends" (John 15:13).

24. Though, it can be argued, no more mysterious than event causation. See Taylor (1966, esp. part I); and O'Connor (2000, 68–74).

25. See, e.g., Kane (1996).

26. There are strong hints within the Christian scriptures—e.g., Jesus's recorded statement that "at the resurrection people will neither marry nor be given in marriage; they will be like the angels in heaven" (Matt. 22:30)—that our best examples of human relationships on earth are but a shadow of (and therefore different from in significant ways) the heavenly relationships through which we experience ultimate flourishing. Thus I think we must be cautious in certain contexts about drawing too many inferences from these kinds of earthly relationships, even though they admittedly serve as some of our best examples of loving relationships in this life. My specific caution at present involves drawing undue inferences from the fact that, in many of our *current* relationships, our focus may not be on the ways in which others contribute as ultimate causes to the shape of networks of relationships.

27. Examples of psychological impossibilities abound in this life as well: e.g., the psychologically healthy mother whose "choice" whether to sell her beloved child for five dollars is determined. Such an offer does not genuinely tempt her; the action of selling her child for the purpose of gaining five dollars is not within the range of psychologically possible actions for her. As for the redeemed in heaven, the plausibility of supposing they cannot act contrary to God's directives stems largely from the affirmation that they will be experiencing ultimate flourishing (cf. section 4.5). Admittedly, since ultimate flourishing is not the same as maximal flourishing, there may be unmet desires (e.g., a desire that others currently not in heaven *be* in heaven). However, it surely is implausible to think of the redeemed as continuing to have significant, false beliefs such that they somehow fail to recognize that their own and others' flourishing cannot possibly be achieved by acting outside God's directives. In sum, the redeemed will have no reason to act outside God's directives.

28. Strawson (2010, 25). One's "principles of choice" in any instance are one's "preferences, values, pro-attitudes, ideals, whatever—in the light of which one chooses how to be" (25).

29. God can again leave us free, as ultimate causes, to help determine whether such self-interested desires will be eliminated. He can do this by (1) creating a world in which we naturally develop habits and dispositions as a

result of our actions to which we contributed as agents, and (2) by changing our desires supernaturally upon our requests, as agents, for him to do so.

30. For that matter, one might ask why God could not simply create humans, put them in Nozick-type experience machines, and cause them to have all the beliefs and other mental states needed for experiences of connecting with others, thus ensuring their ultimate flourishing.

31. After all, if our experiences of connecting with others as creative, ultimate causes were based on false beliefs that other humans were in fact exercising creative power as ultimate causes, we would have innumerable false beliefs about God. We would think of God—who in reality would be the ultimate cause of all things—as having done much less than he had actually done.

32. See Jesus's parable of the Good Samaritan (Luke 10:25–37), as well as his statement in Matt. 5:44 to "love your enemies"; his instruction to "pray for those who persecute you" (Matt. 5:44); his injunction to his disciples to pray: "Forgive us our debts, as we forgive our debtors" (Matt. 6:12); and the passage, "Then Peter came to Jesus and asked, 'Lord, how many times shall I forgive my brother or sister who sins against me? Up to seven times?' Jesus answered, 'I tell you, not seven times, but seventy times seven'" (Matt 18:21–22).

33. Strictly speaking, what we must believe is that a positive response to God's invitational statements constitutes at least as likely a way to realize our desires as does any other means of realizing the desires.

*Chapter Six. Feeling Our Way toward the Good*

1. In section 1.5 I reasoned that the distinction between "moral" and "nonmoral" *goodness* is fuzzy and inevitably drawn with some arbitrariness. Some of my reasoning there also applies to my discussion here about how we might distinguish moral decisions from nonmoral decisions.

2. Cf. Adams on this point: "We see something beautiful, and we react to it, valuing that particular thing. For this reason it would commonly be much less accurate to say that one likes this or that that one presently perceives or experiences or thinks about or knows, *as* an instance of something more general that one likes, than to say that liking this particular thing *is* an instance of one's liking the more general thing. Alternatively, we might say that one's liking the more general thing is simply a generalization over one's liking the particular things, or perhaps a disposition to like the particular things" (1999, 166).

3. I recognize that the substantive discussions in Part II about attaining the good life have been very individualistic in nature. That is, I have focused on how relationships are formed between two individuals; and I have focused on

the kind of patterned decisions each individual will need to make in order to establish an ideal relationship. There is a rich history of emphasis within the Christian tradition on our need *collectively* to seek God, to learn about God, to enjoy God, and to enjoy one another. While the scope of this book lies in analyzing the dynamics of decisions available to a single person at some slice in time, I do not want to suggest that the good life God makes available to us is anything but a wider *community* of interdependent relationships. See MacIntyre (1999, esp. chap. 9) for a discussion of the inevitably communal aspects to our flourishing as humans.

4. These points should ease the concern Kraut raises that "we should be wary of all monisms: all philosophical doctrines that deny the multiplicity of the world and of values" (2007, 21). He contends that seeking quantitative goals—such as "the largest number of friends or the greatest amount of power, or wealth, or prizes, or satisfaction, or virtue"—has the potential to "deform rather than enhance our lives" (20). Kraut's concern seems to be one of *displacement*: the worry that the attempt to maximize any one element of a good life will inevitably come at the expense of the needed cultivation of other elements of a good life. But given the leeway I have argued God would give us to pursue self-interested projects, and given a picture of God as more broadly ensuring that "nonrelational" contingencies needed for our ultimate flourishing will be met, I think the concerns Kraut understandably raises recede. In the context of the provisions of heaven, the more and the deeper our relationships, the better. This goal cannot be overpursued by us.

5. It may not, of course, *merely* be a failure to pursue her interests. In failing to consult my wife, I may also be working against one of my own interests: namely, my own interest in maintaining a healthy marriage. But the point remains that I would be failing to pursue, or even consider, her own projects and goals.

6. I leave aside the question of whether I might, through previous choices for which I am responsible, be responsible for being in the position in which I am unaware that my actions are somehow affecting someone else's well-being.

7. For a discussion of the conditions under which a belief about God might be culpable versus nonculpable, see Kinghorn (2005, chap. 6).

8. To anticipate the discussion of the following section—where I shall explore the differing feeling tones associated with, respectively, benevolent and self-interested motivations—she will not be adding her efforts to the feeling tones that motivate genuinely benevolent actions.

9. By saying that Stan "adds his efforts to" these feeling tones, I mean to indicate that, while feeling tones serve as partial causes for his action, Stan himself (qua agent) serves as a partial cause.

10. For a discussion of "explicit faith" versus "implicit faith," see Kinghorn (2005, 170–77).

11. For discussions of how the charge of "works righteousness" is sometimes built upon faulty assumptions, see Brümmer (1992, 84–89) and Kinghorn (2005, 181–83).

12. For a discussion of what exactly it means to put one's "faith in" God, see Kinghorn (2005, chap. 3).

13. Strictly speaking, to make this decision we need only *believe* that we can further God's welfare (as opposed to actually being able to further God's welfare). But I pass over this distinction here.

14. Adams's interpretation of Luther seems plausible enough. The context of Luther's discussion here is his commentary on Gal. 1:10, where St. Paul asks rhetorically (with expected "no" answers) if he is "trying to win the approval of human beings" and "trying to please people."

15. Swinburne defines *trust* as follows: "To trust someone is to act on the assumption that he will do for you what he knows that you want or need, where the evidence gives some reason for supposing that he may not, and there are bad consequences if the assumption proves false" (2005, 144).

16. At the same time, from the starting point of the morally significant choices that I am formally describing, we might then construct an account of how culpable self-deception can occur such that one is "blinded" to the truth about the connection between obedience to God and one's own flourishing. For a discussion of self-deception and spiritual blindness, see Kinghorn (2007).

## WORKS CITED

Adams, Robert M. 1973. "A Modified Divine Command Theory of Ethical Wrongness." In *Religion and Morality*, ed. Gene Outka and John Reeder, 318–47. Garden City, NY: Anchor Press.

———. 1979. "Divine Command Metaethics Modified Again." *Journal of Religious Ethics* 7 (1): 66–79.

———. 1984. "Saints." *Journal of Philosophy* 81 (7): 392–401.

———. 1999. *Finite and Infinite Goods*. New York: Oxford University Press, 1999.

Aquinas, Thomas. 1939. "The Apostles' Creed." In *The Catechetical Instructions of St. Thomas Aquinas*, trans. Joseph B. Collins. New York: J. F. Wagner.

———. 1947. *Summa theologica*. Trans. Fathers of the English Dominican Province. New York: Benziger Brothers.

Aristotle. 1999. *Nicomachean Ethics*. 2nd ed. Trans. Terence Irwin. Indianapolis, IN: Hackett.

Augustine of Hippo. 2007a. *On Christian Doctrine*. Ed. Philip Schaff. Trans. J. F. Shaw. Nicene and Post-Nicene Fathers, ser. 1, vol. 2. New York: Cosimo.

———. 2007b. *On the Morals of the Catholic Church*. Ed. Philip Schaff. Trans. Richard Strothert. Nicene and Post-Nicene Fathers, ser. 1, vol. 4. New York: Cosimo.

———. 2008. *Confessions*. Trans. Edward B. Pusey. Rockville, MD: Arc Manor.

Baggett, David, and Jerry Walls. 2011. *Good God*. New York: Oxford University Press.

Bentham, Jeremy. 1996. *An Introduction to the Principles of Morals and Legislation*. Oxford: Oxford University Press.

Bond, E. J. 1983. *Reason and Value*. Cambridge: Cambridge University Press.

Bradley, Ben. 2009. *Well-Being and Death*. New York: Oxford University Press.

Bramble, Ben. 2013. "The Distinctive Feeling Theory of Pleasure." *Philosophical Studies* 162 (2): 201–17.

Brandt, Richard. 1998. *A Theory of the Good and the Right*. Amherst, NY: Prometheus Books.

Broad, C. D. 1930. *Five Types of Ethical Theory*. London: Kegan Paul, Trench, Trubner.

Brümmer, Vincent. 1992. *Speaking of a Personal God*. Cambridge: Cambridge University Press.

Butler, Joseph. 1970. *Fifteen Sermons Preached at the Rolls Chapel*. Ed. T. A. Roberts. London: SPCK.

Carr, David. 2002. "Moral Education and the Perils of Developmentalism." *Journal of Moral Education* 31 (1): 5–19.

Carson, Thomas. 2000. *Value and the Good Life*. Notre Dame, IN: University of Notre Dame Press.

Cassell, Eric. 1991. *The Nature of Suffering and the Goals of Medicine*. New York: Oxford University Press.

Charlesworth, William. 1992. "The Child's Development of the Sense of Justice: Moral Development, Resources, and Emotions." In *The Sense of Justice*, ed. Roger Masters and Margaret Gruter, 256–77. Newbury Park, CA: Sage Publications.

Crisp, Roger. 1997. *Mill on Utilitarianism*. London: Routledge.

———. 2006a. "Hedonism Reconsidered." *Philosophy and Phenomenological Research* 73 (3): 619–45.

———. 2006b. *Reasons and the Good*. Oxford: Clarendon Press.

Damon, William. 1981. "The Development of Justice and Self-Interest during Childhood." In *The Justice Motive in Social Behavior*, ed. Melvin Lerner and Sally Lerner, 57–72. New York: Plenum Press.

Dancy, Jonathan. 2004. "Enticing Reasons." In *Reason and Value: Themes from the Moral Philosophy of Joseph Raz*, ed. R. Jay Wallace, Philip Pettit, Samuel Scheffler, and Michael Smith, 91–118. Oxford: Clarendon Press.

Davidson, Donald. 2001. "How Is Weakness of the Will Possible?" In *Essays on Actions and Events*, 2nd ed., 21–42. New York: Oxford University Press.

Dorsey, Dale. 2013. "Desire-Satisfaction and Welfare as Temporal." *Ethical Theory and Moral Practice* 16 (1): 151–71.

Epicurus. 2002. "Letter to Menoeceus." In *Classics of Western Philosophy*, 6th ed., ed. Steven Cahn. Indianapolis, IN: Hackett.

Feinberg, Joel. 1993. "Harm to Others." In *The Metaphysics of Death*, ed. John M. Fischer, 169–90. Stanford, CA: Stanford University Press, 1993.

Feldman, Fred. 1993. "Some Puzzles about the Evil of Death." In *The Metaphysics of Death*, ed. John M. Fischer, 305–26. Stanford, CA: Stanford University Press.

———. 2004. *Pleasure and the Good Life*. Oxford: Clarendon Press.
Findlay, J. N. 1948. "Can God's Existence Be Disproved?" *Mind* 57 (226): 176–83.
Foot, Philippa. 1978a. "Are Moral Considerations Overriding?" In *Virtues and Vices*, 181–88. Oxford: Clarendon Press.
———. 1978b. "Morality as a System of Hypothetical Imperatives." In *Virtues and Vices*, 157–73. Oxford: Clarendon Press.
———. 2001. *Natural Goodness*. Oxford: Clarendon Press.
Frege, Gottlob. 1997. "On *Sinn* and *Bedeutung*." In *The Frege Reader*, ed. Michael Beaney, trans. Max Black, 151–71. Oxford: Blackwell.
Geach, Peter. 1956. "Good and Evil." *Analysis* 17 (2): 33–42.
Goldstein, Irwin. 1980. "Why People Prefer Pleasure to Pain." *Philosophy* 55 (July): 349–62.
———. 1989. "Pleasure and Pain: Unconditional, Intrinsic Values." *Philosophy and Phenomenological Research* 50 (December): 255–76.
———. 2003. "Malicious Pleasure Evaluated: Is Pleasure an Unconditional Good?" *Pacific Philosophical Quarterly* 84 (1): 24–31.
Gosling, J. C. B. 1969. *Pleasure and Desire: The Case for Hedonism Reviewed*. Oxford: Clarendon Press.
Griffin, James. 1986. *Well-Being: Its Meaning, Measurement and Moral Importance*. Oxford: Clarendon Press.
———. 1996. *Value Judgement: Improving Our Ethical Beliefs*. Oxford: Clarendon Press.
Hare, R. M. 1963. *Freedom and Reason*. Oxford: Clarendon Press.
———. 1981. *Moral Thinking: Its Levels, Method and Point*. Oxford: Clarendon Press.
———. 1991. *The Language of Morals*. New York: Oxford University Press.
———. 1997. *Sorting Out Ethics*. Oxford: Clarendon Press.
Harman, Gilbert. 1977. *The Nature of Morality*. New York: Oxford University Press.
Haybron, Daniel. 2008. *The Pursuit of Unhappiness*. New York: Oxford University Press.
Heathwood, Chris. 2007a. "The Reduction of Sensory Pleasure to Desire." *Philosophical Studies* 133 (1): 23–44.
———. 2007b. "Review of Roger Crisp, *Reasons and the Good*." *Notre Dame Philosophical Reviews*, July 9. http://ndpr.nd.edu/news/23026-reasons-and-the-good.
Hebblethwaite, Brian. 1992. "The Varieties of Goodness." In *Ethics, Religion, and the Good Society*, ed. Joseph Runzo, 3–16. Louisville, KY: Westminster John Knox Press.

Hopkins, Samuel. 1852. "Letter to Dr. Ryland." In *The Works of Samuel Hopkins*, vol. 2. Boston: Doctrinal Tract and Book Society.

Humberstone, I. L. 1992. "Direction of Fit." *Mind* 101 (401): 59–83.

Hume, David. 1978. *A Treatise of Human Nature*. 2nd ed. Ed. L. A. Selby-Bigge and P. H. Nidditch. Oxford: Clarendon Press.

Hurka, Thomas. 1993. *Perfectionism*. New York: Oxford University Press.

Johansson, Jens. 2013. "The Timing Problem." In *The Oxford Handbook of Philosophy of Death*, ed. Ben Bradley, Fred Feldman, and Jens Johansson, 255–73. New York: Oxford University Press.

Kagan, Shelly. 1998. "Rethinking Intrinsic Value." *Journal of Ethics* 2 (4): 277–97.

Kane, Robert. 1996. *The Significance of Free Will*. New York: Oxford University Press.

Kant, Immanuel. 2004. *Groundwork of the Metaphysic of Morals*. Trans. H. J. Paton. London: Routledge.

Kinghorn, Kevin. 2005. *The Decision of Faith: Can Christian Beliefs Be Freely Chosen?* London: T and T Clark.

———. 2007. "Spiritual Blindness, Self-Deception and Morally Culpable Nonbelief." *Heythrop Journal* 48 (4): 527–45.

Kolodny, Niko. 2003. "Love as Valuing a Relationship." *Philosophical Review* 112 (2): 135–89.

Korsgaard, Christine. 1983. "Two Distinctions in Goodness." *Philosophical Review* 92 (2): 169–95.

Kraut, Richard. 2007. *What Is Good and Why*. Cambridge, MA: Harvard University Press.

Kristjánsson, Kristján. 2006. *Justice and Desert-Based Emotions*. Aldershot: Ashgate.

Lauinger, William. 2012. *Well-Being and Theism: Linking Ethics to God*. London: Continuum.

Layman, C. Stephen. 1991. *The Shape of the Good*. Notre Dame, IN: University of Notre Dame Press.

Lerner, Melvin. 2002. "Pursuing the Justice Motive." In *The Justice Motive in Everyday Life*, ed. Michael Ross and Dale T. Miller, 10–40. Cambridge: Cambridge University Press.

Lewis, C. S. 1963. *The Four Loves*. London: Fontana Books.

———. 2001a. *The Abolition of Man*. New York: HarperCollins.

———. 2001b. *Mere Christianity*. Rev. ed. New York: HarperSanFrancisco.

Locke, John. 1975. *An Essay Concerning Human Understanding*. Oxford: Clarendon Press.

Lombard, Peter. 1854. *Sentences*. Ed. J. P. Migne. Patrologiae Cursus Completus 192. Paris: Garnier frères.

Luper, Steven. 2007. "Mortal Harm." *Philosophical Quarterly* 57 (227): 239–51.

Luther, Martin. 1833. *A Commentary on Saint Paul's Epistle to the Galatians*. London: B. Blake.

———. 1961. *Lectures on Romans*. Ed. and trans. Wilhelm Pauck. Library of Christian Classics 15. London: SCM Press.

———. 1969. "The Bondage of the Will." In *Luther and Erasmus: Free Will and Salvation*, ed. and trans. E. Gordon Rupp and Philip S. Watson, 101–34. London: SCM Press.

MacIntyre, Alasdair. 1998. *A Short History of Ethics*. 2nd ed. New York: Routledge.

———. 1999. *Dependent Rational Animals*. La Salle, IL: Open Court.

Mackie, J. L. 1977. *Ethics: Inventing Right and Wrong*. London: Penguin Books.

Mele, Alfred. 2001. *Autonomous Agents: From Self-Control to Autonomy*. New York: Oxford University Press.

Midgley, Mary. 1995. *Beast and Man*. Rev. ed. London: Routledge.

Mill, James. 1869. *Analysis of the Phenomena of the Human Mind*. 2nd ed. London: Longmans, Green, Reader and Dyer.

Mill, John Stuart. 1987. *Utilitarianism*. Ed. Alan Ryan. London: Penguin Books.

Moltmann, Jürgen. 1993. *The Church in the Power of the Spirit*. Trans. Margaret Kohl. Minneapolis, MN: Fortress Press.

Moore, G. E. 1993. *Principia Ethica*. Rev. ed. Cambridge: Cambridge University Press.

Mounier, Emmanuel. 1952. *Personalism*. Trans. Philip Mairet. London: Routledge and Kegan Paul.

Murphy, Mark C. 2002. *An Essay on Divine Authority*. Ithaca, NY: Cornell University Press.

Nagel, Thomas. 1979a. "The Fragmentation of Value." In *Mortal Questions*, 128–41. Cambridge: Cambridge University Press.

———. 1979b. "What Is It Like to Be a Bat?" In *Mortal Questions*, 165–80. Cambridge: Cambridge University Press.

———. 1993. "Death." In *The Metaphysics of Death*, ed. J. M. Fischer, 59–70. Stanford, CA: Stanford University Press.

Nozick, Robert. 1974. *Anarchy, State, and Utopia*. New York: Basic Books.

Nygren, Anders. 1982. *Agape and Eros*. Rev. ed. Trans. Philip S. Watson. London: SPCK.

O'Connor, Timothy. 2000. *Persons and Causes*. New York: Oxford University Press.

Parfit, Derek. 1984. *Reasons and Persons*. Oxford: Clarendon Press.

———. 1997. "Reasons and Motivation." *Aristotelian Society Supplementary Volume* 7 (1): 99–130.

Passmore, John. 1970. *The Perfectibility of Man*. New York: Scribner's.

Phillips, D. Z. 1977. "In Search of the Moral 'Must': Mrs. Foot's Fugitive Thought." *Philosophical Quarterly* 27 (107): 140–57.

Pitcher, George. 1993. "The Misfortunes of the Dead." In *The Metaphysics of Death*, ed. J. M. Fischer, 157–68. Stanford, CA: Stanford University Press.

Plantinga, Alvin. 1979. *The Nature of Necessity*. New York: Oxford University Press.

Plato. 1871. *Gorgias*. In *The Dialogues of Plato*, vol. 3, trans. B. Jowett. New York: Jefferson Press.

———. 1992. *Republic*. Trans. G. M. A. Grube. Rev. C. D. C. Reeve. Indianapolis: Hackett.

———. *Charmides*. Many editions and translations. Cited by Stephanus pagination.

———. *Euthyphyro*. Many editions and translations. Cited by Stephanus pagination.

———. *Meno*. Many editions and translations. Cited by Stephanus pagination.

———. *Protagoras*. Many editions and translations. Cited by Stephanus pagination.

Platts, Mark. 1979. *Ways of Meaning*. London: Routledge and Kegan Paul.

Post, Stephen G. 1988. "The Inadequacy of Selflessness: God's Suffering and the Theory of Love." *Journal of the American Academy of Religion* 56 (2): 213–28.

Rachels, Stuart. 1998. "Counterexamples to the Transitivity of Better Than." *Australasian Journal of Philosophy* 76 (1): 71–83.

———. 2000. "Is Unpleasantness Intrinsic to Unpleasant Experiences?" *Philosophical Studies* 99 (2): 187–210.

———. 2004. "Six Theses about Pleasure." *Philosophical Perspectives* 18 (1): 247–67.

Railton, Peter. 1986. "Moral Realism." *Philosophical Review* 95 (2): 163–207.

———. 2003. "Facts and Values." In *Facts, Values, and Norms*, 43–68. Cambridge: Cambridge University Press.

Rawls, John. 1999. *A Theory of Justice*. Rev. ed. Cambridge, MA: Harvard University Press.

Ross, W. D. 1930. *The Right and the Good*. Oxford: Clarendon Press.

Russell, Paul. 2006. "Practical Reason and Motivational Scepticism." In *Moralische Motivation: Kant und die Alternativen*, ed. Heiner F. Klemme, Manfred Kuehn, and D. Schönecker, 287–98. Hamburg: Felix Meiner.

Schopenhauer, Arthur. 1915. *The Basis of Morality*. Trans. A. B. Bullock. New York: Macmillan.

Seamands, Stephen. 2005. *Ministry in the Image of God: The Trinitarian Shape of Christian Service*. Downers Grove, IL: InterVarsity Press.

Sidgwick, Henry. 1981. *The Methods of Ethics*. 7th ed. Indianapolis, IN: Hackett.

Silverstein, Matthew. 2000. "In Defense of Happiness." *Social Theory and Practice* 26 (2): 279–300.

Simmons, Carolyn. 1981. "Theoretical Issues in the Development of Social Justice." In *The Justice Motive in Social Behavior*, ed. Melvin Lerner and Sally Lerner, 41–55. New York: Plenum Press.

Smith, Michael. 1994. *The Moral Problem*. Oxford: Blackwell.

Smuts, Aaron. 2011. "The Feels Good Theory of Pleasure." *Philosophical Studies* 155 (2): 241–65.

Sobel, David. 2002. "Varieties of Hedonism." *Journal of Social Philosophy* 33 (2): 240–56.

Strawson, Galen. 2010. *Freedom and Belief*. Rev. ed. Oxford: Oxford University Press.

Sumner, L. W. 1996. *Welfare, Happiness and Ethics*. Oxford: Clarendon Press.

Swinburne, Richard. 1989. *Responsibility and Atonement*. Oxford: Clarendon Press.

———. 1993. *The Coherence of Theism*. Rev. ed. Oxford: Clarendon Press.

———. 2005. *Faith and Reason*. 2nd ed. Oxford: Clarendon Press.

Taylor, Richard. 1966. *Action and Purpose*. Englewood Cliffs, NJ: Prentice Hall.

Temkin, Larry. 1994. "Weighing Goods: Some Questions and Comments." *Philosophy and Public Affairs* 23 (4): 350–80.

———. 2012. *Rethinking the Good*. New York: Oxford University Press.

Thompson, Michael. 1995. "The Representation of Life." In *Virtues and Reasons*, ed. Rosalind Hursthouse, Gavin Lawrence, and Warren Quinn, 247–96. New York: Oxford University Press.

Unger, Peter. 1990. *Identity, Consciousness and Value*. New York: Oxford University Press.

Wesley, John. 1984–87. *The Works of John Wesley*. Vols. 1–4. Ed. A. C. Outler. Nashville, TN: Abingdon Press.

Williams, Bernard. 1981a. "Internal and External Reasons." In *Moral Luck*, 101–13. Cambridge: Cambridge University Press.

———. 1981b. "Persons, Character and Morality." In *Moral Luck*, 1–19. Cambridge: Cambridge University Press.

———. 1985. *Ethics and the Limits of Philosophy*. Cambridge, MA: Harvard University Press.

———. 1993. *Morality: An Introduction to Ethics.* Cambridge: Cambridge University Press.
Wolf, Susan. 1982. "Moral Saints." *Journal of Philosophy* 79 (8): 419–39.
———. 1990. *Freedom within Reason.* New York: Oxford University Press.
Wolterstorff, Nicholas. 1995. *Divine Discourse.* Cambridge: Cambridge University Press.
———. 2008. *Justice: Rights and Wrongs.* Princeton, NJ: Princeton University Press.
Ziff, Paul. 1960. *Semantic Analysis.* Ithaca, NY: Cornell University Press.
Zimmerman, Michael. 1980. "On the Intrinsic Value of States of Pleasure." *Philosophy and Phenomenological Research* 41 (1/2): 26–45.
———. 2001. *The Nature of Intrinsic Value.* Lanham, MD: Rowman and Littlefield.

# INDEX

Adams, Robert
adding to God's flourishing, 297
benevolence as insufficient to
  ground relationships, 223–28
enjoyment of objects, 27, 72–73
the good as excellence, 49, 183
intrinsic value of objects, 53–56
loyalty to relationships, 218–20
meaning of *wrongness*, 158
objective wrongness defended,
  149–50, 158, 161–62
respecting personal autonomy,
  192–93
semantic analysis of *good*, 47–50
universalizable features, 332n2
Aquinas, Thomas
metaphysical assumptions, 3,
  318n9
satiety in God alone, 323n1
supererogation, 234, 329n15
"we-self" description, 179
Aristotle
base pleasures, 105–7
the good not a single Idea, 11–12
instrumental goodness, 18
perfectionist account of good life,
  170–71, 324n7
"we-self" description, 179
Augustine, 168, 210–11, 298,
  329n14, 329n15
autonomy, 81–82, 172, 175, 193–94,
  199, 300, 311n33

Baggett, David
God as the ultimate Good, 46, 48,
  305n19
objective wrongness defended,
  151–52, 155, 162–63
semantic analysis limits, 47–48,
  150–51
benevolence
definition of, 212, 223–24, 327n6
implicit decisions of, 280–82
key to ideal relationships, 181, 211,
  218, 228
problem of excessive, 278–80
Bentham, Jeremy, 63, 75, 84, 177–78
Bond, E. J., 309n16
Bradley, Ben, 99–105, 311n32,
  314nn52–53, 315nn57–58

343

Brandt, Richard, 76
Broad, C. D., 108, 309n15
Butler, Joseph, 28–30, 299

Carr, David, 154
Cassell, Eric, 66, 310n18
"connecting"
    as necessary for flourishing, 179–86
    phenomenology of, 177–79, 181, 325nn15–16
    as sufficient for flourishing, 186–89
Crisp, Roger
    determinable-determinate distinction, 64, 178
    internalist accounts of pleasure, 64, 309n15, 325n15
    Mill's "proof" of utilitarianism, 316n66
    role of moral intuitions, 306n27
customary morality, 136, 146–47, 292–94

Dancy, Jonathan, 125
Davidson, Donald, 294
desires
    vs. beliefs, 122–23
    desiring experiences vs. objects, 27–30, 83–89
    dual aspects of "frustration" and "release," 31, 304nn14–15, 320n21
    as uniquely motivating, 115–16, 118–19, 120–23, 317n2, 318n9, 318n16, 319nn17–18
dying wishes, 93–94

Epicurus, 315n60

feeling tones, 14–15, 63–64, 309n15, 325nn15–16
Feinberg, Joel, 85, 90–91
Feldman, Fred
    attitudinal pleasures, 65–66, 69, 308n12
    badness of death, 314n48
    critique of internalist pleasures, 66–67, 310nn20–21
flourishing
    as more primitive than *good*, 14–18, 41–43, 303n7, 306n25
    ultimate flourishing, 200–201, 210–11, 331n27
Foot, Philippa
    Humean motivation as unnecessary, 3, 122–23, 318n16
    mental statism critiqued, 68–69
freedom
    dual pulls of self-interest and benevolence, 237–38
    possible without God creating evil, 300
    of the redeemed in heaven, 246–47
    as an ultimate cause
    —coherence of notion, 240–41, 248, 331n24, 331n29
    —as condition of interpersonal relationships, 241–46, 331n26, 332n31
fuzzy-edged concepts
    moral vs. nonmoral, 31–38, 155–56, 264
    punishable vs. permissible, 142–43, 233, 320n26, 321n29

God
    as coordinator of welfare, 197–202, 208–9

divine communication to us,
    235–37, 295–96
divine deception, 250–52, 332n30
divine hiddenness, 188–89, 257
    as the Good, 46, 48, 305n19
    as having a welfare, 297–98
    as necessarily loving, 169, 201,
        217–18, 237, 326n26,
        330nn19–20
    role of divine commands, 231–35
    as source of life, 168–69, 172,
        182–84
Goldstein, Irwin, 111–12, 309n16,
    310n23, 316nn67–68
goodness
    meaning of *good*
    —derivative and deviant uses of
        term, 21–23
    —etymology of term, 12–13
    —as primitive concept, 16, 38–39
    nature of good
    —formal vs. substantive accounts,
        57–58, 168–69, 176
    —as a non-natural property,
        46–48, 305n21, 323n39
Griffin, James
    critique of mental statism, 84–87
    critique of perfectionism, 172, 174
    meaning of *good*, 21

Hare, R. M.
    flourishing as naturally good, 303n6
    moral statements as prescriptions,
        157
    overridingness of moral judgments,
        33
    universalizable features of moral
        beliefs, 32, 264
Harman, Gilbert, 145

Haybron, Daniel, 78
Heathwood, Chris, 71–72, 308n12,
    309n15
heaven, 188, 199–200, 217, 227,
    246–47, 294–95
Hebblethwaite, Brian, 173
hell, 249, 253–55, 295
Hopkins, Samuel, 217
Hume, David
    phenomenology of desire,
        304nn14–15
    priority of desire over reason,
        115–16
Hurka, Thomas, 171, 176

imperatives, 230–31
intuitions
    God as the Good, 46, 48
    inevitability of relying on them, 55,
        306n27
    welfarist appeals, 59–63, 306n27
"invitational statements," 204–5,
    235–36

Johansson, Jens, 95
justice, sense of, 152–55, 321n31

Kagan, Shelly, 109–10, 316n65
Kant, Immanuel, 32, 115
Kolodny, Nico, 121–22, 219, 327n5
Kraut, Richard
    concern over value monism, 333n4
    developmentalism, 323n2, 324n4
    non-sentient welfare, 61–62
    pleasure as good, 308n7
    priority of good over right,
        314n47, 323n40
    welfarist conception of good,
        304n9, 308n6

Kristjánsson, Krisján, 153–54

Layman, C. Stephen, 169
Lewis, C. S.
  objective wrongness, 151–53
  tragic Eros, 220–21
Locke, John, 303n5
Lombard, Peter, 298
Luper, Steven, 103
Luther, Martin, 297, 299, 329n14

MacIntyre, Alasdair, 12–14, 150
Mackie, J. L.
  error theory, 159–60, 323n36
  meaning of *good*, 19–21, 24–25
Mele, Alfred, 248
mental experiences, 14–15, 26, 310n22
mental statism
  arguments for, 61–63, 84–86
  defined, 61, 73, 86, 88–89
  mental states establishing vs. affecting a well-being, 101–5, 314n53, 314n55, 315nn57–58
  welfarist critiques of
  —from base pleasures, 68, 105–7, 315n61
  —from desire-satisfaction assumptions, 85, 90–91, 313nn44–45
Midgley, Mary, 312n37, 323n2
Mill, James, 15
Mill, J. S.
  customary morality, 136, 146–47, 313n41
  meaning of *right/wrong*, 141
  "proof" of utilitarianism, 306n27, 316n66
Moltmann, Jürgen, 330n20
Moore, G. E.
  base pleasures, 106–7

"good" as unanalyzable concept, 38–39
naturalism defined, 39
open question argument stated, 39, 43–44
moral
  vs. etiquette and taste, 33–38
  statements, 156–58
  as universalizable, 32–33, 264–67, 332n2
Mounier, Emmanuel, 325n18

Nagel, Thomas
  critique of mental statism, 94–95, 312n36, 313n44
  phenomenology of mental life, 62, 303n4
  valuing achievements, 50–51
naturalism
  conceptual version, 42–43
  defined, 30, 322n35
  vs. reductionism, 39, 305n18
  synthetic version, 40–42
normativity
  as coming from outside, 126, 133–38, 320n23, 321n30
  felt as pressure, 119–20
  rooted in desires, 126–30, 319n17
Nozick, Robert, 83
Nygren, Anders, 262

ownership. *See* rights

"paradox of Hedonism," 27–28
Parfit, Derek, 124
paternalism, 81, 190–93
phenomenology
  of benevolence, 285–87
  of "connecting," 177–79, 181, 325nn15–16

of desire, 30–31, 304nn14–15
of mental life, 62, 303n4
of pleasure, 15, 63–64, 177, 303n5, 309nn14–16, 311n25
Phillips, D. Z., 35–36
physical pain, 66, 186–88, 310nn18–19
Pitcher, George, 313n44
Plato
good life, 170, 324n6
reason over desires, 114
ontology of the Good, 46–49, 183, 211, 305n19
Platts, Mark, 121
pleasure
internalist vs. externalist definitions, 63–72, 308n12, 309nn14–16, 310nn19–21, 310n23, 311n25
as necessarily good, 15–16, 62, 303n6, 308n6, 315n60, 316n68
without objects, 111–12, 316n69
as primitive concept, 14–16, 64–65, 303n5, 309n15
unpleasure as antonym, 307n2
Post, Stephen, 262

Rachels, Stuart
pleasures without objects, 111–12
transitivity of value, 74
Railton, Peter, 77, 304n11
Rawls, John, 76–77
reasons, 120–21, 124, 317n5, 318n12
relationships
conditions for interpersonal, 191–92, 203–7, 241–47, 326n24, 326n28
ideal
—anticipating them, 181
—conditions for, 210–11, 215, 218, 239, 244–45, 332n3
—self-interested pursuits within, 216–18, 227–28, 250, 255–57, 273–74, 325n20
—threats to, 196–98, 209
loyalty to, 218–20
rights
keeping the language of, 328n9
reductionist account of, 139–48
*See also* wrongness
Ross, W. D.
meaning of *good*, 11–13, 52
non-welfarist value, 107, 111, 315n62

salvation by faith, 234–35, 296–97, 328n12
Schopenhauer, Arthur, 107
Seamands, Stephen, 330n19
Sidgwick, Henry
internalist vs. externalist definitions of pleasure, 63, 177
objective beauty, 306n26
"paradox of Hedonism," 27–28
physical pain, 310n19
Silverstein, Matthew, 312n35, 312n39
sin, 298–301
Smuts, Aaron, 71–72, 309nn14–16
social sanction, 117–19, 135–37, 140–42, 146, 149–50, 161–62
Socrates, 114, 170
Strawson, Galen, 248, 331n28
Sumner, L. W.
authenticity needed for welfare, 79–82, 175, 311n33
critique of desire-satisfaction accounts of welfare, 75, 78

Sumner, L. W. (*cont.*)
  formal accounts of welfare, 57, 168
  internalist vs. externalist definitions of pleasure, 63, 66, 70–71, 79, 312n34
  welfare affected by later events, 92–93
  welfarism defended, 59–61
supererogation, 119, 234, 329n15
Swinburne, Richard
  atonement components, 329n13
  obligations, 144
  —supererogation, 329n15
  —trust defined, 334n15

*Tao*. *See* justice, sense of
tragic Eros, 220–22
Trinity, 1, 7, 169, 176–77, 237–38, 330nn19–20

Unger, Peter, 85–86
universalizability, 32–33, 264–68, 332n2

value
  comparative, 74, 95–99, 314nn48–49
  intrinsic value affected by extrinsic properties, 109–10
  transitivity of, 74

Walls, Jerry. *See* Baggett, David

weakness of will, 117, 221–22, 275–77
welfarism
  argument for, 59–61
  critiques
  —that non-welfarist objects and states have value, 46–47, 62–63, 83–89, 107–8, 305n21, 312nn36–37, 315n62
  —that we think of objects and states as having value, 49–55, 69
"we-self," 179
Wesley, John, 296, 299
Williams, Bernard, 171, 267, 304n10
Wolf, Susan, 173, 248
wrongness
  cluster of associated concepts, 118, 139–41
  derivative use as "not-to-be-doneness," 146–48
  as intent to sanction, 142–47
  as less fundamental than goodness, 142, 160–63, 229–31, 323n40
  naturalist call for ontological parsimony, 145, 151, 155, 322n35, 323n39
  relation to good/bad, 117–19, 139–40
  objective, 149–55, 161–62, 321n31

Ziff, Paul, 20–21, 24–25
Zimmerman, Michael, 306n27

# Kevin Kinghorn

is professor of philosophy and religion at Asbury Theological Seminary. He is author of *The Decision of Faith: Can Christian Beliefs Be Freely Chosen?*

CPSIA information can be obtained
at www.ICGtesting.com
Printed in the USA
FFOW04n0251220316
22523FF